First-Time
Asia

A ROUGH GUIDE SPECIAL

P9-DCC-193

Credits

Editorial: Richard Lim, Jo Mead
Series editor: Mark Ellingham
Production: Link Hall, Julia Bovis, Michelle Draycott
Design and layout: Henry Iles
Maps: Maxine Repath, Ed Wright and the Map Studio, Romsey, Hants
Proofreading: David Price

Acknowledgments

Special thanks to David Leffman for the section on China, Chris Humphrey for help with the Philippines and South Korea, and Narrell Leffman and Kate Davis for additional research.

Thanks also to Jerry Swaffield, Annette C Kunigagon, Erwin and Hui Chin Bernhardt, Didi Muncaster-Wright and Peter O'Sullivan.

At Rough Guides, many thanks to Richard for meticulous editing; to Link for enthusiastic layout; and to Ed, Maxine and the Map Studio for patiently dealing with the maps.

Thanks to all the following people for their anecdotes about travelling in Asia: Juliet Acock, Shannon Brady, Sasha Busbridge, Daniel Gooding, Chris Humphrey, Gerry Jameson, Debbie King, Karen Lefere, Mark Lewis, Laura Littwin, Jo Mead, Nicki McCormick, Vicky Nicholas, Neil Poulter, Andrea Szyper, Chris Taylor, Jonathan Tucker, Ross Velton and Bob Williams.

This second edition published February 2001 by
  Rough Guides Ltd, 62–70 Shorts Gardens, London, WC2H 9AB.
  375 Hudson Street, New York 10014
  Internet: mail@roughguides.co.uk

Previous edition 1998

Distributed by the Penguin Group:
  Penguin Books Ltd, 27 Wrights Lane, London W8 5TZ
  Penguin Putnam, Inc. 375 Hudson Street, NY 10014, USA
  Penguin Books Australia Ltd, 487 Maroondah Highway, PO Box 257, Ringwood, Victoria 3134, Australia
  Penguin Books Canada Ltd, 10 Alcorn Avenue, Toronto, Ontario, Canada M4V 1E4
  Penguin Books (NZ) Ltd, 182–190 Wairau Road, Auckland 10, New Zealand

Printed by Omnia Books Ltd, Glasgow

© Lesley Reader, Lucy Ridout 2001

No part of this book may be reproduced in any form without permission from the publisher except for the quotation of brief passages in reviews.

400pp – includes index

A catalogue record for this book is available from the British Library.

ISBN 1-85828-574-7

The publishers and authors have done their best to ensure the accuracy and currency of all the information in *First-Time Asia*; however, they can accept no responsibility for any loss, injury, or inconvenience sustained by any traveller as a result of information or advice contained in the guide.

First-Time
Asia

A ROUGH GUIDE SPECIAL

Written by
Lucy Ridout and Lesley Reader

with illustrations by
Jerry Swaffield

ROUGH
GUIDES

THE ROUGH GUIDES

Travel Guides • Phrasebooks • Music and Reference Guides

 We set out to do something different when the first Rough Guide was published in 1982. Mark Ellingham, just out of university, was travelling in Greece. He brought along the popular guides of the day, but found they were all lacking in some way. They were either strong on ruins and museums but went on for pages without mentioning a beach or taverna. Or they were so conscious of the need to save money that they lost sight of Greece's cultural and historical significance. Also, none of the books told him anything about Greece's contemporary life – its politics, its culture, its people, and how they lived.

So with no job in prospect, Mark decided to write his own guidebook, one which aimed to provide practical information that was second to none, detailing the best beaches and the hottest clubs and restaurants, while also giving hard-hitting accounts of every sight, both famous and obscure, and providing up-to-the-minute information on contemporary culture. It was a guide that encouraged independent travellers to find the best of Greece, and was a great success, getting shortlisted for the Thomas Cook travel guide award, and encouraging Mark, along with three friends, to expand the series.

The Rough Guide list grew rapidly and the letters flooded in, indicating a much broader readership than had been anticipated, but one which uniformly appreciated the Rough Guide mix of practical detail and humour, irreverence and enthusiasm. Things haven't changed. The same four friends who began the series are still the caretakers of the Rough Guide mission today: to provide the most reliable, up-to-date and entertaining information to independent-minded travellers of all ages, on all budgets.

We now publish more than 150 titles and have offices in London and New York. The travel guides are written and researched by a dedicated team of more than 100 authors, based in Britain, Europe, the USA and Australia. We have also created a unique series of phrasebooks to accompany the travel series, along with an acclaimed series of music guides, and a best-selling pocket guide to the Internet and World Wide Web. We also publish comprehensive travel information on our Web site: Ⓦ *www.roughguides.com*

The Authors

Lesley Reader has lived and worked in Bhutan and Thailand and travelled extensively throughout Asia. She is co-author of Rough Guides to Bali and Lombok, and to Indonesia. She has also contributed to the Rough Guides to China and Southeast Asia, and to *Women Travel*, an anthology of travel tales from a woman's perspective.

Lucy Ridout has spent much of the last decade in Asia. She lived in Japan for three years, teaching English to high-school children and working as an editor on a monthly listings magazine. Since then she has travelled widely in India and Southeast Asia, both for pleasure and as a researcher and author for several guidebooks. She is co-author of the Rough Guides to Thailand, Bangkok, and Bali and Lombok, and has also contributed to books on England, Europe and Southeast Asia.

Help us update

We've gone to a lot of effort to ensure that *First-Time Asia* is accurate and up to date. However, things do change and if you feel we've got it wrong or left something out we'd like to know. In addition, we'd love to hear your Asian travel anecdotes and tips for possible inclusion in the next edition. We'll credit all contributions and send a copy of the next edition (or any other Rough Guide, if you prefer) for those we include. Please mark letters "First-Time Asia Update" and send to:
Rough Guides, 62–70 Shorts Gardens, London WC2H 9AH
or Rough Guides, 375 Hudson St, 9th floor, New York NY 10014.

Or send email to ✉ *mail@roughguides.co.uk*

First-Time Asia online

Updates to the information in this book can be found at ⓦ *www.roughguides.com/ftasia* .

Contents

Basics

List of maps

Colour maps (at back of book)
    Asia: Political
    SE Asia
    NE Asia
    India
    Asia: Physical

Introduction

E very year, millions of visitors set off on their own Asian adventure. Some want to see for themselves a few of the world's greatest monuments – to stroll along the Great Wall of China or stand beside India's Taj Mahal. Others are drawn by the scenery – the soaring Himalayas and the chance of viewing Everest at close quarters; the kaleidoscopic coral reefs of Southeast Asia, where you'll find yourself swimming amongst sharks, manta rays and turtles; the steamy jungles of Malaysia and Indonesia, with the prospect of spotting orang-utans, elephants, even tigers. Few people would say no to a week or two on the dazzling white-sand beaches of the Philippines or pass up the chance to watch the sunrise over the Khyber Pass.

But perhaps the greatest draw is the sheer vitality of daily life in Asia, much of it played out on the streets. You can watch Thai boxing in Bangkok and trance dances in Bali; learn yoga in Varanasi and drink rice whisky in Vientiane; eat dim sum in Shanghai and satay sticks in Penang; buy silver in Hanoi and bargain for mangosteens in Manila.

Nearly all these things are affordable even for low-budget travellers, because most of Asia is enticingly inexpensive. Western money goes much further here than it does in Africa or South America. Not surprisingly, this has put Asia firmly at the heart of the backpackers' trail, and many cities and islands already boast a lively travellers' scene, attracting young adventurers from all over the world. Few travellers leave Asia without experiencing at least one of its fabled hot spots: the beaches of Goa, for example; the guesthouses of Kathmandu; or one of Thailand's notorious fullmoon parties.

However, Asian travel can also be a shocking and sobering experience. Few people forget their first sight of a shanty-town slum or their first encounter with an amputee begging for small coins. Many first-timers are distressed by the dirt, the squalor, and the lingering smell of garbage and drains in some Asian cities. They get unnerved by the ever-present crowds and stressed out by never being able to mingle unnoticed among them. And then there's the oppressive heat to cope with, not to mention the unfamiliar food and often unfathomable local customs. There's no such thing as a hassle-free trip and, on reflection, few travellers would want that. It's often the dramas and surprises that make the best experiences, and we all learn by our mistakes.

Preparing for the big adventure

We've both made plenty of mistakes and faux pas during our fifteen years of travels in Asia, and this book is a distillation of what we've learnt. *First-Time Asia* is full of the advice we give to friends heading out to Asia for the first time, and it's the book we both could have done with before setting off on our own first trips. Since then we've returned again and again, backpacking across India, China and Southeast Asia; living and working in the Himalayas, Thailand and Japan; and researching and writing guidebooks to Indonesia, Thailand and Tibet. And we still choose to go back to Asia for our holidays, attracted by the chaos and drama of daily lives that still seem extraordinary to us; by the food, the landscapes and the climate; by the generosity and

FIRST IMPRESSIONS

I flew into Bangkok from Calcutta. I remember the light, diffuse and glowing, and the smells – exhaust fumes, jasmine, and garlic edged with chilli. I checked into *Charlie's Guest House*, sat downstairs and ordered fried chicken and chillis with rice. It was late afternoon and tuk tuks screamed past on the street. And just like that, in a revelatory moment, I was in love with Southeast Asia.

Chris Taylor

friendship of the people; and by the sheer buzz we get from hanging out in cultures that are so different from our own.

This book is intended to prepare you for your big adventure, whether it's a fortnight in Malaysia or twelve months across the continent. It is not a guidebook: it's a book to read before you go, a planning handbook to help you make decisions about what type of trip you'd like to make. And, because we can't pretend to have explored every single corner of Asia ourselves, we've also included tips, advice and funny stories from lots of other travellers.

The first questions you'll need to address are which parts of Asia to visit and, much more difficult, which places to leave out, so the opening section of the book, Where To Go, looks at your options. We focus on the nineteen most accessible and most visited countries of Asia, giving you an opinionated taste of what these destinations hold in store for first-timers. Each country profile includes a roundup of the major highlights and tourist activities as well as a selection of personal recommendations and lesser-known gems. The most remote parts of the continent, north and west of Pakistan, rarely feature on first-timers' itineraries, so we haven't included them in this book. Burma (Myanmar) is also omitted in the hope that travellers will uphold the boycott on tourism requested by Aung San Suu Kyi, the democratically elected leader of the country.

The middle section of *First-Time Asia*, The Big Adventure, deals with the nuts and bolts. This is where you'll find chapters on how to choose the right ticket and which guidebooks and Web sites to consult, plus advice on how long you can afford to stay away and what gear to pack. The second half of this section looks at life on the road in Asia, advising you on how to stay safe and healthy while you're away, grounding you in local cultural dos and don'ts, and giving you an idea of what to expect in terms of hotels and bus services. And finally, the Basics section at the back of the book is stuffed full of useful addresses, Web sites and phone numbers for further information on everything from Taiwanese visas and backpackers' homepages to mosquito-net suppliers and conservation projects. Updates to these and other details in the book can be found online at ⓦ *www.roughguides.com/ftasia*

Even after you've digested *First Time Asia*, we can't guarantee that you'll avoid every problem on the road, but hopefully you'll at least feel well prepared – and excited. When you come back from your trip, be sure to send in your own anecdotes for inclusion in the next edition. We can promise you'll have plenty of great stories to tell.

First-Time Asia

Where to go

Bangladesh

Capital: Dhaka
Population: 130 million
Language: Bangla
Currency: Taka (Tk)
Religion: Eighty percent Muslim, twelve percent Hindu; there are also Buddhists and Christians

Climate: Tropical, with the monsoon from July to October
Best time to go: October to February, which avoids the monsoon and the humid build-up in the months before
Minimum daily budget: $15/£10

With its reputation as a nation of overpopulation, poverty, political instability and devastating floods (the alluvial plains which comprise ninety percent of the country's area are less than 10m above sea level), Bangladesh is not on many Asian itineraries. However, the country contains extensive rivers and lush forests to explore, as well as the longest beach in the world and excellent wildlife. Bangladesh also has some fine archeological sites, including Buddhist, Hindu and Muslim monuments, remnants of empires which flourished until the seventeenth century when the Raj – British colonial rule – was established. Some grand public buildings and *rajbaris*, palaces built by rich Hindu landowners, are the remaining evidence of the Raj era. All of this adds up to a fascinating destination which the more adventurous may wish to consider.

As tourists are still rather rare here, visitors should expect even more attention than usual – especially out of Dhaka – and to be asked for money; the rural people are extremely poor. Bangladesh is mostly Muslim, and both men and women should dress exceptionally modestly. Women should cover arms and legs, even ankles, and a *salwaar kameez*, the baggy trousers and long tunic worn by local women, is a good investment, as is a scarf for the head. Men should stay covered up also, avoiding shorts and vests. Be aware that travel can be extremely slow because of frequent ferry crossings on both road and rail routes.

Main attractions

● **Dhaka**. Almost everyone passes through the Bangladeshi capital at some point. A seething melting pot of over ten million people, it's an incredible city with a fascinating juxtaposition of the old and the startlingly new. Among the more recent constructions, Jatyo Sangsad, the National Assembly building designed by American architect Louis Kahn, and the National Martyrs' Memorial, commemorating those who died in the independence struggle, are the most imposing. The most famous ancient monuments include the Mogul Lalbagh Fort, the grand nineteenth-century Nawab's Palace and the Rose Garden, a dignified palace from the Raj era. Also here is Chowk Bazaar, a maze of twisting alleyways little changed since the nineteenth century. The city abounds in striking, attractive mosques, the most interesting

Average daily temperatures (maximum and minimum°C) and monthly rainfall (mm)

Dhaka	Jan	Feb	Mar	Apr	May	June	July	Aug	Sept	Oct	Nov	Dec
max °C	25	28	33	35	34	32	31	31	31	31	29	26
min °C	12	13	16	23	25	26	26	26	26	24	18	13
rainfall mm	18	31	58	103	194	321	437	305	254	169	28	2

of which are the Sitara Masjid, dating from the eighteenth century, and Sat Gumbad, the seven-domed mosque perched high on the river bank.

● **Cox's Bazaar**. Bangladesh's best-known tourist destination and only seaside resort is an excellent spot for relaxation, with plenty of accommodation and restaurants. Cox's Bazaar is within a few kilometres of the stunning Inani Beach, widely claimed to be the longest beach in the world. Also within easy reach are other equally attractive beaches and some quiet, offshore islands including St Martin's, Bangladesh's only coral island.

● **River travel**. This affords a great opportunity to see all of Bangladeshi life as you sail past. The most useful and popular way to do this is the Rocket service from Dhaka to Khulna, on which vintage paddle steamers make the thirty-hour trip.

● The **Sunderbans**. This tidal forest covers a massive area, stretching along the coastline for nearly 300km. The mangrove forest floor is dissected by rivers, their channels constantly changing as the tides ebb and flow. The area is inhabited by a variety of wildlife; it's the last reserve of the Royal Bengal tiger in Bangladesh (the 350 animals thought to live here constitute a tenth of the world's remaining population), and also home to crocodiles, monkeys, gibbons, turtles, deer, wild boar, lizards and the Ganges river dolphin. The best method of transport is by boat.

● **Sylhet**. Set among rolling hillsides, this tea-growing area consists of lush forests and terraced estates. The centre of the district, the town of Srimangal, is an excellent place to arrange a visit to a tea estate to see the processing of the leaves. Several tribal peoples, including the Khasi, Pangou and Manipur, live in the area, and it's possible to visit their villages. The region is also known for its basketware, including furniture, small household goods and bags.

● **Paharpur**. Dating from the eighth century, the remains of the largest Buddhist monastery south of the Himalayas contain a huge quadrangle, each side of which is over 250m long; the space is enclosed by a three-metre-thick wall containing nearly two hundred monks' cells. In the centre of the courtyard are the remains of a mighty temple, decorated with thousands of terracotta plaques.

Also recommended

● The **Chittagong Hill Tracts**. Atypical of Bangladesh, the hill tracts, whose steep jungle-covered peaks rise to 800m, are inhabited by more than a dozen tribal groups, all of whom are Buddhists of Tibeto-Burmese descent. Unfortunately, most of the area is off limits to tourists with the exception of the towns of Kaptai and Rangamati. The latter, set on a peninsula overlooking the man-made Kaptai Lake, was a favoured hill station of the British; today it's an

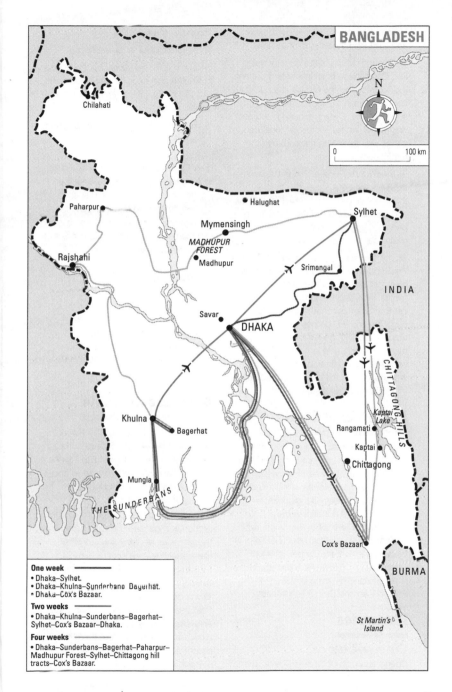

BANGLADESH

Chilahati

Paharpur
Rajshahi

Halughat

Mymensingh
MADHUPUR FOREST
Madhupur

Sylhet

INDIA

Srimangal

Savar

DHAKA

Khulna
Bagerhat

Kaptai Lake
Rangamati
Kaptai
Chittagong

CHITTAGONG HILLS

Mungla

THE SUNDERBANS

Cox's Bazaar

BURMA

St Martin's Island

0   100 km

One week
• Dhaka–Sylhet.
• Dhaka–Khulna–Sunderbans–Bagerhat.
• Dhaka–Cox's Bazaar.

Two weeks
• Dhaka–Khulna–Sunderbans–Bagerhat–
Sylhet–Cox's Bazaar–Dhaka.

Four weeks
• Dhaka–Sunderbans–Bagerhat–Paharpur–
Madhupur Forest–Sylhet–Chittagong hill
tracts–Cox's Bazaar.

excellent centre for swimming, boating and exploring the islands of the lake.

● **Cycling.** Much of the country being flat, Bangladesh is an interesting option for cyclists, and the bicycle is as ubiquitous here as in the rest of the Indian subcontinent. Cycling around is a great way of getting really close to local people as well as seeing the country at a restful pace.

● **Madhupur Forest.** One of the country's few stretches of deciduous forest, this is home to primates, civets and birds, and contains villages of the Mandi tribespeople, originally a nomadic Christian/animist group from eastern India.

● The **Bagerhat area.** To the north of the Sunderbans, Bagerhat is awash with historical Hindu and Muslim monuments, including the famous fifteenth-century Shait Gumbad mosque (its name means "60 domes", though it actually has 77), one of the country's most imposing. The largest surviving brick mosque in Bangladesh, it stands impressively on the bank of a vast pool in an attractive rural setting.

Routes in and out

Zia International Airport in Dhaka has good worldwide connections. There are overland routes between Haridaspur to the northeast of Calcutta in India and Benapole in western Bangladesh; between Dawki in India's Assam province and Tarnabil in the Sylhet region of Bangladesh; and between Haldibari in India (convenient for Darjeeling) and Chilahati in northwest Bangladesh. There is no overland crossing between Bangladesh and Burma to the east.

Itineraries

One week

Spend a couple of days in Dhaka, then do one of the following:

● Explore Sylhet for a few days.

● Take the Rocket service from Dhaka to Khulna and explore the Sunderbans and the historical monuments of the Bagerhat area.

● Visit Cox's Bazaar and the surrounding area.

Two weeks

● After three days in Dhaka, take the Rocket service to Khulna and spend another three or so days exploring the Sunderbans and the Bagerhat area. You can then use internal flights to visit Sylhet and Cox's Bazaar.

One month

● A month is ideal for visiting most of the main attractions – Dhaka, the Sunderbans, the Bagerhat area, Paharpur, Madhupur Forest, Sylhet (which you have time to explore by bike), the Chittagong hill tracts and Cox's Bazaar.

Bangladesh online

Bangladesh – Home of the Royal Bengal Tiger Ⓦ*www.betelco.com/bd/* Covers all the main tourist sites, with plenty of photos and information about Bangla, the national language.

Virtual Bangladesh
Ⓦ*www.virtualbangladesh.com* A comprehensive, general site about the country, with a great many links to other Bangladesh related sites.

Painting Images of Bangladeshi Artists
Ⓦ*lynx.dac.neu.edu/j/jiqbal/painter.html* Features the life histories of Bangladeshi artists and plenty of examples of their work – it's a reminder that there is so much more to Bangladesh than catastrophe and poverty.

Bhutan

Capital: Thimphu	**Best time to go**: Autumn (Oct &
Population: 700,000	Nov) and spring (Feb to mid-April)
Language: Dzongkha	**Minimum daily budget**: All-
Currency: Ngultrum	inclusive tours – the only way to visit
Religion: Mahayana Buddhism	the country – cost at least
Climate: Monsoonal	$200/£130 per person per day

With Tibet to the north, Sikkim and Nepal to the west and the far northeastern states of India to the east, the Himalayan Kingdom of Bhutan is geographically remote and maintains an air of mystery and exclusivity – only around five thousand tourists a year are allowed to visit, all on organized tours.

Bhutan's allure is in its distinctive culture, which has remained largely isolated from Western influence; most of the people are subsistence farmers leading a devoutly Buddhist life in villages with distinctive architecture. The huge, ancient, *dzongs* – each a combination of fortress, monastery and administrative centre – are a feature of every major valley, and the landscape is dotted with evocative temples and *chortens*, akin to Nepalese stupas. National costume is worn everywhere, and Bhutan's intricate hand-woven textiles, their designs passed on from mother to daughter, are gaining renown across the world.

Travel in Bhutan, though time-consuming, is indubitably picturesque. Most visitors spend just a few days in the west of the country, exploring the valleys of Paro, Thimphu and Punakha. Across in central Bhutan, however, Trongsa and Bumthang are drawing more and more visitors, while the eastern towns of Trashigang and Trashi Yangtse are equally fascinating, but only feature on the itineraries of those with the time (and money) to make the long trip across the country worthwhile (it's three days by road from Thimphu to Trashigang).

Main attractions

● **Thimphu**. The town is one of the smallest and most relaxed capitals in Asia, with plenty for visitors to see, including Trashi Chhoe Dzong, centre of government in the kingdom and a massive, imposing presence in the Thimphu valley; several impressive temples; and the Memorial Chorten, dedicated to the memory of the third king of Bhutan. There's also a weekly market and the remarkable takin, a creature unique to Bhutan, with a massive head and looking like a cross between a gnu and a cow. It's most easily seen at the enclosure above the *Motithang Hotel* on the hill above town.

● The valley of **Paro**. Broad and flat-bottomed, the valley contains the vast Paro Dzong near the airport, as well as Bhutan's National Museum, housed in the Ta Dzong – Paro Dzong's own watchtower, standing guard way up on

Average daily temperatures (maximum and minimum°C) and monthly rainfall (mm)

	Jan	Feb	Mar	Apr	May	June	July	Aug	Sept	Oct	Nov	Dec
Thimphu												
max °C	17	14	19	23	23	26	25	24	24	22	19	17
min °C	-1	-3	5	7	11	14	17	17	15	9	0	-2
rainfall mm	40	20	10	30	10	95	105	130	55	0	0	0

the hillside. At the valley's northern end, the ruined Drukyel Dzong is a popular excursion and there are numerous temples, large and small, grand and humble, dotted around. For centuries the ubiquitous image of Bhutan was the temple of Takshang, or Tiger's Nest, built impossibly high up into a sheer cliff on the side of the valley. Sadly it recently burned down and is currently being rebuilt, but the two-hour climb up the valley side is still a terrific hike, if only to look across at the temple site and marvel that anything could ever have been built there in the first place.

● **Punakha.** Lower and warmer than Thimphu, the traditional winter capital of Bhutan has a *dzong* sitting impressively at the confluence of two differently coloured rivers, with the hills rising all around. The *dzong* was badly damaged by fire several years ago, and the rebuilt version is a quite remarkable demonstration of the sheer brilliance and vibrancy of Bhutan's traditional woodcarving, sculpture and temple painting. Each spring a festival, the unique Punakha Dromche, celebrates a famous victory of the Bhutanese over their ancient enemies, the Tibetans.

● **Trongsa Dzong.** The largest *dzong*, it's also one of the most dramatically situated, visible from many miles away before the road twists and turns among the folds of the hillside and eventually reaches Trongsa itself. The watchtower above the *dzong* offers brilliant views of

the area, and the tiny hotels and restaurants of the town, mostly run by Tibetan refugees who have lived in Bhutan for decades, provide a relaxed welcome.

● **Bumthang valley.** For many visitors to Bhutan, the Bumthang valley, right In the centre of the country, turns out to be their favourite spot. The local *dzong*, Jakar, is perched dramatically on a spur overlooking the valley, and there are innumerable temples along the broad valley bottom, the most famous being Kurjey and Jambey. Possible excursions from Bumthang include the weaving workshops of the Chumi valley to the west, and a trip to the beautiful, high-altitude village of Ura, with its impressive new temple.

● **Mongar, Trashigang** and **Trashi Yangtse.** Accommodation in these eastern towns is sparse and the distances you need to travel to get to them can be tiring, but towering hills, rivers thundering through the valley bottoms, lovely temples, fabulous weaving produced on simple looms in people's houses, and the ancient Chorten Kora await those who make the trip.

● **Tsechu.** Every temple celebrates these annual festivals, commemorating the arrival of the Tibetan Guru Rimpoche in the eighth century and the victory of the Buddhism that he brought over evil spirits. Held in spring and autumn, the *tsechu* feature colourful masked dances and often the unfurling of a massive religious hanging, the *thongdrel*; sometimes there's also a scary and dramatic fire blessing, which can involve the populace running through an archway of blazing straw.

● **Trekking**. Bhutan is sparsely populated, the countryside attractive and uncluttered; consequently, trekkers have a wide choice of routes, from the moderately difficult five-day Druk Path between the Paro and Thimphu valleys through to the 24-day Lunana Snowman Trek. On the latter, from Paro to Wangdiphodrang, east of Punakha, trekkers make their arduous way across 4500-metre-high passes via the remote village of Laya, where the people have distinctive language, costume and customs.

Also recommended

● The valley of **Phobjikha**. High up in the centre of the country, this is the winter home of rare black-necked cranes, who fly there every year from Siberia. The venerated monastery, Gangtey Gompa, is also located here, gloriously situated on a spur overlooking the valley.

● **Local alcoholic brews**. Most Bhutanese people love to drink, and there are a huge variety of brews on offer, including several varieties of beer brewed by village women from locally farmed grain, and, for the bravest souls, the highly potent, distilled *ara*.

● **Bhutanese food**. It isn't the most inspiring cuisine in the world, but all visitors should try the unique, delicious red rice, *aima datsi* (chilli curry, as combustible as it sounds) and *suja* (butter tea).

● **Archery** – Bhutan's national sport. The tiny targets are set apparently impossible distances away from the archers, many of whom still use traditional bamboo bows. Try to catch part

of a contest – the entire thing often lasts for days – and enjoy the yelling, singing, dancing and the attempts to deflect the opposition arrows by dodging in front of the target while the arrow is on its way.

Routes in and out

Most visitors fly into and out of Paro on Druk Air, the national airline (indeed the only airline permitted to land in Bhutan). An alternative is to enter by road, at Phuntsholing on the southern border, from where it's a six-hour drive to Thimphu. At Samdrup Jongkhar, in the far east of the country, it's possible to exit Bhutan by road for the Indian state of Assam, though it's not permitted to enter Bhutan this way. The border between Bhutan and Tibet is closed.

Itineraries

Remember that if you're intending to trek, you must allow time to acclimatize at altitude both before you set off and as you climb higher; failure to do so can be very dangerous (see p.306).

One week

● Spend a couple of days each in Paro, Thimphu and Punakha.

● After a couple of days in Paro, take the Druk Path trek across the mountains between Paro and Thimphu, and then spend a couple of days exploring Thimphu.

Two weeks

Combine either of the one-week trips above with either of the following:

● a short trek.

● a visit to central Bhutan, exploring both Trongsa and the Bumthang valley, and returning the same way.

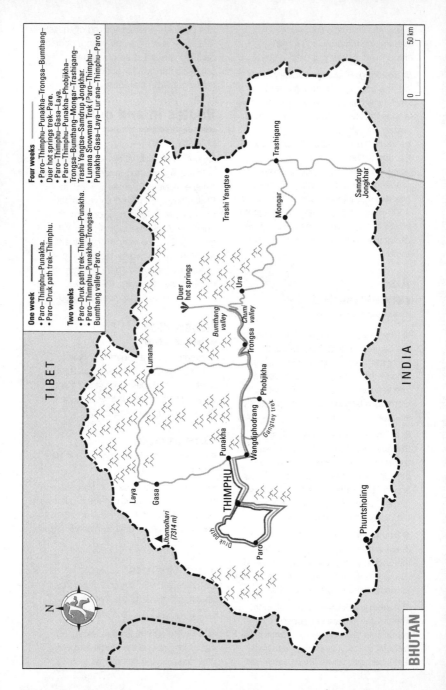

One week
• Paro–Thimphu–Punakha.
• Paro–Druk path trek–Thimphu.

Two weeks
• Paro–Druk path trek–Thimphu–Punakha.
• Paro–Thimphu–Punakha–Trongsa–
Bumthang valley–Paro.

Four weeks
• Paro–Thimphu–Punakha–Trongsa–Bumthang–
Duer hot springs trek–Paro.
• Paro–Thimphu–Gasa–Laya.
• Paro–Thimphu–Punakha–Phobjikha–
Trongsa–Bumthang–Mongar–Trashigang–
Trashi Yangtse–Samdrup Jongkhar.
• Lunana Snowman Trek (Paro–Thimphu–
Punakha–Gasa–Laya–Lurana–Thimphu–Paro).

TIBET

INDIA

BHUTAN

N

0   50 km

Four weeks

● Combine leisurely sightseeing, spending a couple of days each in Paro, Thimphu, Punakha, Trongsa and Bumthang, with a short trek, perhaps to the Duer Hot Springs (eight days from Bumthang).

● Make brief visits to Paro and Thimphu, taking short hikes to acclimatize, and then do the fourteen-day Gasa and Laya trek to these isolated villages in the north.

● Arriving in Paro, head across the country to Trashigang, via Thimphu, Punakha, Phobjikha, the three-day Gangtey trek, Trongsa, Bumthang, and Mongar. Explore the Trashigang area, including a day-trip to Trashi Yangtse, and then it's a one-day drive to exit the country through Samdrup Jongkhar into Assam. There's plenty of time for local exploration and side-trips on this itinerary.

● Do the Lunana Snowman Trek – you'll need four weeks to finish it – or one of the other long treks on offer.

Bhutan online

Bhutan: Last Place on the Roof of the World ⓦ*www.bootan.com*
Colourful and informative general site including plenty of pictures and some in-depth articles on subjects such as traditional architecture, indigenous healing and the yeti. There are also excellent links.

The Bhutanese Refugees
ⓦ*www.amherst.edu/~amshrest/bhutan/menu.html*
All is not perfect in this apparent paradise: since the 1980s over 100,000 Bhutanese people of Nepalese origin, many of whose families have been in Bhutan for generations, have left the country and become refugees in camps in Nepal. This site explains why – and also links to the official Bhutanese government version of what's going on.

Kuensel ⓦ*www.kuensel.com.bt/*
The weekly Bhutanese English-language newspaper gives a fascinating insight into the country.

Thinley Namgyel's Home Page
ⓦ*members.tripod.com/thinley/thinley.html*
One of the few Bhutanese to have studied abroad, in Canada, Thinley Namgyel, now back home, offers a brilliant insight into his country, with some excellent photos and lots of links.

Shangri-La Homepage
ⓦ*aleph0.clarku.edu/~rajs/Shangri_La.html*
Covering the entire Himalayas from Afghanistan through Pakistan, India, Bhutan, Nepal and Tibet to the north of Myanmar, this wide-ranging site has fascinating links and well illustrates its view that Shangri-La is not just a fictional place located amid the world's highest mountains, but is also a state of mind.

Brunei

Capital: Bandar Seri Begawan	**Religion**: Islam
Population: 285,000	**Climate**: Tropical
Language: Malay	**Best time to go**: February–August
Currency: Brunei dollar (B$)	**Minimum daily budget**: $35/£25

Occupying a tiny sliver of land on the northwest coast of Borneo, the Sultanate of Brunei is one of the least popular tourist destinations in Asia. This is mainly due to its size – there just aren't many attractions in the 5765 square kilometres – though it's also an expensive country to visit, with one of the highest standards of living in the region. The country's wealth comes from oil, which was first discovered here in 1903 and generates so much income that all Bruneians enjoy free healthcare and education, and subsidized cars and houses. The Sultan of Brunei, who rules the country, is widely acknowledged as the richest non-American in the world.

Despite Brunei's dearth of tourist attractions, you may find yourself in transit here, as Royal Brunei Airlines often has good deals on its long-haul flights, some of which have connections that leave you with half a day or more to play with. Alternatively, if you're exploring the east Malaysian states of Sarawak and Sabah, which lie either side of Brunei, you can easily stop in Brunei en route between the two.

Brunei's main sights are all in and around the capital, Bandar Seri Begawan (often simply called "Bandar"). Accommodation will be your biggest expense if you stay here – rooms are much costlier than in neighbouring Malaysia or even Singapore, so bring an HI card and consider heading straight for the city's only youth hostel. As Brunei is a strict Muslim country, the sale and consumption of alcohol is banned and there's not much to do after nightfall; you should dress modestly (see p.209).

Main attractions

● The **Omar Ali Saifuddien Mosque**. The focal point of the Brunei capital, this opulent mosque is constructed from the finest Italian marble, with a dome made from Venetian glass that reflects dramatically in the surrounding lagoon. Non-Muslims are allowed inside the mosque except during prayer times, and you can sometimes persuade the caretakers to let you ride the lift to the top of the minaret, which gives good views over the water villages below.

● **Kampung Ayer**. Despite the country's enormous wealth, half the population of Bandar Seri Begawan still live in traditional stilt houses built over the city's three rivers, in the sprawling labyrinth of wooden homes and walkways known as Kampung Ayer. An intriguing and photogenic sight, these "water villages" are best explored by water taxi.

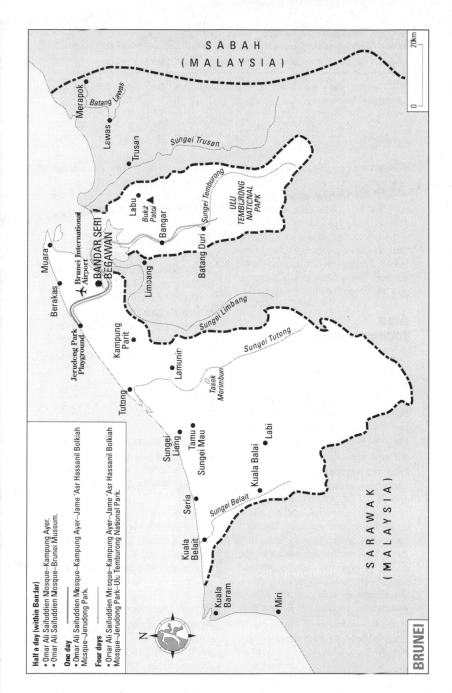

SABAH
(MALAYSIA)

20km

Merapok
Batang
Lawas
Lawas
Trusan
Sungei Trusan

ULU
TEMBURONG
NATIONAL PARK

Labu
Bukit
Patai ▲
Bangar
Sungei Temburong
Batang Duri

Muara
Berakas
Brunei International
Airport
BANDAR SERI
BEGAWAN
Limbang
Sungei Limbang

Jerudong Park
Playground
Kampung
Parit
Lamunin
Tasek
Merimbun
Sungei Tutong

Tutong

Sungei
Liang
Tamu
Sungei Mau
Labi
Kuala Balai

Seria
Sungei Belait

Kuala
Belait

Kuala
Baram
Miri

SARAWAK
(MALAYSIA)

N

Half a day (within Bandar)
• Omar Ali Saifuddien Mosque–Kampung Ayer.
• Omar Ali Saifuddien Mosque–Brunei Museum.

One day
• Omar Ali Saifuddien Mosque–Kampung Ayer–Jame 'Asr Hassanil Bolkiah
Mosque–Jerudong Park.

Four days
• Omar Ali Saifuddien Mosque–Kampung Ayer–Jame 'Asr Hassanil Bolkiah
Mosque–Jerudong Park–Ulu Temburong National Park.

BRUNEI

Average daily temperatures (maximum and minimum°C) and monthly rainfall (mm)

	Jan	Feb	Mar	Apr	May	June	July	Aug	Sept	Oct	Nov	Dec
Bandar Seri Begawan												
max °C	30	30	31	32	33	32	32	32	32	32	31	31
min °C	23	23	23	24	24	24	24	24	23	23	23	23
rainfall mm	133	63	71	124	218	311	277	256	314	334	296	241

● **Jerudong Park Playground**. It may seem strange to travel halfway round the world and end up frittering away your time at a theme park, but the big draw at Jerudong, 25km from Bandar, is the fact that all rides in this huge hi-tech adventure park are paid for by the Sultan. So you can ride as many roller-coasters and spaceship simulators as you like without spending a cent.

Also recommended

● **Jame 'Asr Hassanil Bolkiah Mosque**. Spend a contemplative hour or two in the elegantly manicured gardens of Bandar's enormous mosque, considered by some to be even more impressive than the Omar Ali Saifuddien Mosque.

● **Ulu Temburong National Park**. This protected swath of rainforest south of Bandar is crisscrossed by decent trails, and has a treetop-level walkway and observation towers for watching the resident proboscis monkeys. On the way here from Bandar, you get to travel through the mangrove swamps on the famous "flying coffin" speedboats (so called because of their speed and shape, not their safety record), and can visit an Iban longhouse in Batang Duri.

● The **Brunei Museum**. This is the place to bone up on the story behind modern Brunei's economic success and learn about the country's lucrative rela-

tionship with oil. There's also a gallery of Islamic art, displaying exquisitely designed antique Korans from all over the Muslim world.

Routes in and out

Most travellers fly in and out of Brunei's international airport in Bandar Seri Begawan. Nearly all international bus and ferry routes go via Bandar, from where there are boats to and from Lawas and Pulau Labuan in Sabah, and to and from Limbang in Sarawak; buses also connect Bandar and the Sarawak town of Miri.

Itineraries

Half a day
● From the airport, stop first at the Omar Ali Saifuddien Mosque, then either take a water-taxi tour of Kampung Ayer or head out to the Brunei Museum.

One day
● Visit both Bandar's big mosques, explore Kampung Ayer, and spend the late afternoon or evening making the most of the free fairground rides at Jerudong Park Playground.

Four days
● Spend a day and a night doing the main sights of Bandar, before heading south for a couple of nights in Ulu Temburong National Park.

Brunei Online

Borneo Bulletin

www.brunet.bn/news/bb Find out what's happening in the Sultanate from this online version of the English-language daily.

Royal Brunei

www.bruneiair.com/brunei/brunei.html The tourist-information page of the Royal Brunei Airlines site covers the major sights, with photos as well as details of visa requirements and duty-free allowances.

Tourism in Brunei Darussalam

www.brunet.bn/homepage/tourism/tourhome.htm Not a riveting site, but this is the best there is. You'll find a reasonable introduction to the country, along with some tourist-oriented information.

Cambodia

Capital: Phnom Penh
Population: 12 million
Language: Khmer
Currency: Riel (r)

Main religion: Theravada Buddhism
Climate: Tropical
Best time to go: November–March
Minimum daily budget: $10/£7

Cambodia is attracting a burgeoning number of tourists, most of whom are drawn by the prospect of seeing the utterly compelling thousand-year-old temple ruins at Angkor. This city was the epicentre of the ancient Khmer kingdom, a Hindu-Buddhist empire that for almost 500 years stretched right across Southeast Asia, from Vietnam in the east to China in the north and Burma in the west. These days it is a World Heritage site, and Cambodia's indisputable top attraction. The most visited of Cambodia's other sights are those associated with the horrors inflicted by the murderous Khmer Rouge regime, who tried to force communism on their compatriots between 1975 and 1979 and in so doing drove the country back to the Stone Age. But if you wander further afield you'll also find hilltribe villages, trekking opportunities, Mekong river trips and beaches.

Twenty-first century Cambodia has still not recovered from the devastations of the 1970s and is one of the poorest countries in the world. Public transport is excruciatingly slow and uncomfortable, and outside the main tourist centres there is only very basic tourist accommodation. However, there are plenty of cheap guesthouses in Siem Reap, the town closest to Angkor, and in the capital, Phnom Penh, and tourists generally get a good reception from the amazingly resilient Khmer people. However, you'll

probably need a Khmer phrasebook to help you communicate with them outside the main tourist centres.

Until recently, Cambodia was off the map for all but the bravest travellers, as most people were put off by the reports of continued Khmer Rouge guerrilla activity, bandits, kidnappings and gunpoint muggings. Though many of the guerrilla areas have been returned to the control of the Cambodian army, you should in any case consult newspapers, government travel offices and travellers' newsgroups on the Internet (see p.368) so you can avoid any potentially volatile regions. Many travellers choose to fly in and out of Siem Reap so as to bypass this problem altogether. Gun crime continues to be a major problem in the capital, so do not wander around Phnom Penh alone after dark. Out in the sticks, landmines left over from the Vietnam War and the Khmer Rouge era continue to pose a major threat to local people, particularly in the provinces along the Thai border. The main tourist areas are clear of mines, but you should never venture off well-used tracks.

Main attractions

● **Angkor**. The magnificent ruined Hindu–Buddhist temples and palaces of

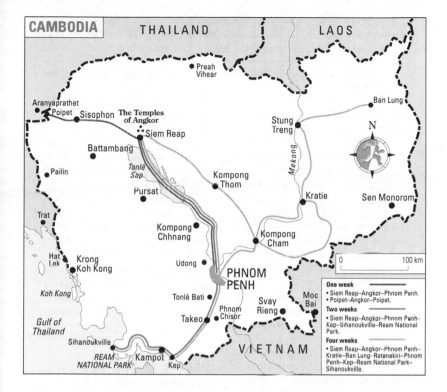

One week
• Siem Reap–Angkor–Phnom Penh.
• Poipet–Angkor–Poipet.

Two weeks
• Siem Reap–Angkor–Phnom Penh–
Kep–Sihanoukville–Ream National
Park.

Four weeks
• Siem Reap–Angkor–Phnom Penh–
Kratie–Ban Lung–Ratanakiri–Phnom
Penh–Kep–Ream National Park–
Sihanoukville.

this ancient Khmer city, built between the ninth and fourteenth centuries, are one of Asia's top five sights – every bit as spectacular and important as better-known lost cities such as Machu Picchu in Peru. Now shrouded in jungle, the crumbling walls, intricate carvings and colossal sculpted faces of Angkor's hundred-plus temples take several days to explore.

● **Phnom Penh**. Cambodia's war-ravaged riverside capital is a crazy, eye-popping place to explore, with plenty of markets, temples, French colonial residences, bars, restaurants and museums, and a small but thriving travellers' scene. The main sights are the elegant single-storey buildings of the Royal Palace, which was built in the early-

twentieth century to a traditional design, the glittering Silver Pagoda, whose floor is paved in over 5000 solid-silver tiles, and the National Museum, which has lots of Angkor-related exhibits.

● The **Tuol Sleng S-21** museum. When Pol Pot's Khmer Rouge seized power in 1975, they turned a Phnom Penh secondary school into Security Prison 21. Over the next four years, an estimated twenty thousand teachers, students, monks and doctors suspected of anti-revolutionary behaviour were brought here, often with their wives and children. They were subjected to horrific tortures, and then killed. The prison has been preserved as the very moving Tuol Sleng S-21 museum, and its thousands of black-and-white mug shots of ordinary

Average daily temperatures (maximum and minimum°C) and monthly rainfall (mm)

	Jan	Feb	Mar	Apr	May	June	July	Aug	Sept	Oct	Nov	Dec
Phnom Penh												
max °C	31	32	34	35	34	33	32	32	31	30	30	30
min °C	21	22	23	24	24	24	24	25	25	24	23	22
rainfall mm	7	10	40	77	134	155	171	160	224	257	127	45

Cambodians who were tortured here will stay with you for a long, long time.

● **Choeung Ek.** A continuation of the misery seen at S-21, Choeung Ek, sometimes referred to as "the killing fields", is where the torture victims were brought to be shot, 15km southwest of Phnom Penh. The focus of the memorial here is the 8985 skulls piled high inside a huge glass stupa.

● The remote province of **Ratanakiri**. This region, 600km northeast of Phnom Penh, is way out in the sticks, but attracts a growing stream of tourists because of its population of hill tribes and its volcanic scenery. Most people base themselves in the provincial capital, Ban Lung, and everyone takes a tour out to nearby Yeak Laom Lake, to swim in the clear turquoise waters of this forest-encircled volcanic crater.

Also recommended

● **Kep.** This tiny palm-shaded fishing village is a lovely little spot where local people cook up fantastic seafood and offer boat tours to the pretty white-sand beaches and reefs of nearby islands.

● **Kratie.** Pint-sized Kratie is another little gem of a town, set beside the Mekong River and full of colonial houses and traditional wooden Khmer homes. There's not much to do here except soak up the atmosphere and perhaps make a couple of day-trips into the surrounding countryside.

● **Ream National Park.** The best way to enjoy this park is to enlist the help of the rangers, who can arrange informal boat trips to nearby fishing islands and guided walks through the forest.

● **Sihanoukville.** Cambodia's beaches can't compare with those of neighbouring Thailand, but the country's main resort of Sihanoukville is an appealing place, with four decent beaches, plenty of accommodation, and a lively nightlife.

Routes in and out

Most people arrive in Cambodia on a flight from Bangkok, from where there are regular planes to and from Phnom Penh and Siem Reap. You can also get flights from other Southeast Asian capitals to Phnom Penh, but there are no direct long-haul flights. As transport in Cambodia is slow and uncomfortable, and as there are still some bandit-prone regions, you may want to consider flying in and out of Siem Reap instead, especially if you're only in Cambodia for a few days.

Overland travel in and out of Cambodia has only recently become safe enough to recommend – and you should still ask other travellers locally before starting the journey. From Thailand there are two entry points: at Poipet, due east of Bangkok, which is seven hours on a horribly potholed road from Siem Reap; and at Krong Koh Kong, near Trat on Thailand's east coast, from where you can travel to Sihanoukville and Phnom Penh. There's a border crossing in and out of Vietnam at Moc Bai, to the southeast of Phnom Penh, but currently no legal exit into Laos, though some travellers do arrange transport up the Mekong into Laos from Stung Treng.

Itineraries

One week

● If your budget allows, buy an open-jaw ticket that takes you into Siem Reap and out of Phnom Penh. Base yourself at Siem Reap for four days, and spend your time exploring the ruins of nearby Angkor. Then take the boat down to Phnom Penh and spend your last few days in and around the capital, before flying out.

● Arriving overland from Thailand, enter via the Poipet border and restrict yourself to Angkor, as the road from Poipet to Siem Reap is abysmal and will take a whole day to cover, in each direction.

Two weeks

● Spend at least four days in Siem Reap/Angkor, then three in Phnom Penh, before continuing south to Kep and then on to Sihanoukville, with perhaps a couple of days in Ream National Park.

Four weeks

● Spend at least four days in Siem Reap/Angkor, then three in Phnom

Penh, before striking out to the north-east, with a day or two in Kratie and then several days in Ban Lung, from where you can explore parts of Ratanakiri province. Return to Phnom Penh for the start of the southern leg, which takes you down to Kep, then on to Ream National Park and Sihanoukville.

Cambodia online

Andy Brouwer's Cambodian Tales Ⓦ*www.btinternet.com/~andy.brouwer/* This exceptionally well-informed home-page is regularly updated with news and travel features about Cambodia and also includes accounts of the author's trips there.

Cambodia Information Center Ⓦ*www.cambodia.org* This site includes basic tourist information and a chat forum, plus links to other Cambodia-related sites.

Cambodia-Web Ⓦ*www.cambodia-web. net* Bills itself as the online yellow pages for Cambodia, and has reasonable sections on travel, culture and business.

Links a'la Laary Ⓦ*www.ala-laary.com/ linksea/* Quality links to Cambodian sites, including lots of interesting travellers' homepages and travelogues, plus online newspapers, government organizations and travel companies. A good starting point.

Phnom Penh Post Ⓦ*www.newspapers. com.kh/PhnomPenhPost* The online version of Cambodia's English-language newspaper can be a useful place to check up on the local security situation.

China

Capital: Beijing
Population: Over 1.2 billion
Languages: Mandarin, plus scores of regional languages and dialects
Currency: Yuan (¥)
Main religions: Buddhism, Confucianism, Daoism and Islam
Climate: Tropical in the south; mixed elsewhere, including temperate (central), desert (northwest) and Himalayan (far west); northern and western winters very cold, southern and northwestern summers very hot
Best time to go: April–June and September–November for most of the country
Minimum daily budget: $25/£16

As the most populous country on earth, with 3000 years of recorded history and borders encompassing everything from the Himalayan plateau to tropical beaches, China exerts a huge pull on anyone planning a trip to Asia. The country's scale and complexity, however, can make planning a trip a little daunting. Short visits are best confined to obvious highlights, such as Beijing, Xi'an's Terracotta Army, or the river and hill scenery around Guilin. But with more time, take advantage of the comprehensive (though often uncomfortable) transport network and explore, for example, eastern China's lush landscapes and historic towns, or the country's remoter reaches which – ethnically at least – are not even truly "Chinese".

Wherever you go, take time to try China's classic regional cooking: Northern (featuring hotpots, Peking duck and even lavish Imperial cuisine, which once graced the tables of China's emperors), Eastern (seafood and river-fish delicacies), Sichuan (pungent, spicy dishes using lots of chillies) and Cantonese (little snacks known as *dim sum*, and main courses using just about any ingredient imaginable – as long as it's fresh).

Right now is an exciting time to visit, as the country is changing at breakneck speed, throwing off years of Maoist stagnation with an explosive lust for modernization under a regime that's, in economic terms at least, relatively liberal. Modern skylines are appearing as whole cities are rebuilt; roads and rail lines are spreading everywhere; and the free market is earning people wages which just a generation ago would have been unthinkable. The downsides are rising inflation, leading to poverty for those unable to take part in the boom, ingrained corruption, and runaway pollution.

As its infrastructure improves, so China is becoming more accessible to foreigners than it has ever been. Though communication problems can complicate independent travel, you'll usually encounter English-speaking students in the cities who might act as guides in order to improve their language skills, and it's not impossible to learn survival Mandarin even on a brief trip. More exhausting is a complex bureaucracy which can make even getting a hotel room an achievement; the intensive, unabashed public scrutiny of foreigners; and the stress of trying to see too much in too short a time. If you plan to explore

Average daily temperatures (maximum and minimum°C) and monthly rainfall (mm)

	Jan	Feb	Mar	Apr	May	June	July	Aug	Sept	Oct	Nov	Dec
Beijing												
max °C	1	4	11	21	27	31	31	30	26	20	9	3
min °C	-10	-8	-1	7	13	18	21	20	14	6	-2	-8
rainfall mm	4	5	8	17	35	78	243	141	58	16	11	3
Chongqing												
max °C	9	13	18	23	27	29	34	35	28	22	16	13
min °C	5	7	11	16	19	22	24	25	22	10	12	8
rainfall mm	15	20	38	99	142	180	142	122	150	112	48	20
Hong Kong												
max °C	18	17	19	24	28	29	31	31	29	27	23	20
min °C	13	13	16	19	23	26	26	26	25	23	18	15
rainfall mm	33	46	74	137	292	394	381	367	257	114	43	31
Lhasa												
max °C	7	9	12	16	19	24	23	22	21	17	13	9
min °C	-10	-7	-2	1	5	9	9	9	7	1	-5	-9
rainfall mm	0	13	8	5	25	64	122	89	66	13	3	0
Ürümqi												
max °C	-11	-8	-1	16	22	26	28	27	21	10	-1	-8
min °C	-22	-19	-11	2	8	12	14	13	8	-1	-11	-13
rainfall mm	15	8	13	38	28	38	18	25	15	43	41	10

widely, avoid doing so on a rock-bottom budget: when travelling long distances in China, it's worth spending a little bit more on flying or for a comfortable sleeper carriage, so that you'll be refreshed and able to enjoy yourself once you arrive.

Main attractions

● **Beijing**. With its skyscrapers, high-ways, and relatively wealthy population, the capital encapsulates the best of modern China. The past survives in some splendid imperial icons, including the elegant palaces and vast stone courtyards of the Forbidden City, which alone require days to explore in depth. Downtown, look for the ever-dwindling number of *hutong*s, the narrow alleyways which make up much of old Beijing, and there's also China's foremost restaurants and nightlife to take advantage of – everything from teahouse theatres and acrobatic shows to punk-rock gigs. Within easy reach of the capital you'll also find several sections of the Great Wall, along with the imperial Summer Palace's spacious and unpolluted parklands, and the stone guardians and chambers of the Ming Tombs, where thirteen Ming-dynasty emperors were laid to rest.

Xi'an. Made rich by the old Silk Road trade, Xi'an was one of China's former capitals. Its most famous sight is the

CHINA

△ Holy mountains
▪▪▪ Great Wall

RUSSIA

KAZAKHSTAN

MONGOLIA

ALMATY
BISHKEK ●
KIRGYZISTAN
Kashgar ●
● Ürümqi
● Turpan

TAKLAMAKAN DESERT
● Dunhuang

Disputed
borders
Golmud ●
Qinghai Hu
Xining ●

Yangzi River   Yellow River

TIBET

● DELHI

NEPAL
Shigatse ● Lhasa ●
Everest ● Gyantse
▲ THIMPHU
KATHMANDU
BHUTAN
Emei Shan
Xichang ●
Lijiang ●

INDIA

BANGLADESH
Dali ●
Kunming ●

Jinghong ●

BURMA

LAO

VIENTIANE ●

THAILAND

One week
• Beijing–Great Wall & Ming Tombs.
• Guilin–Yangshuo.
• Hong Kong.

Two weeks
• Beijing–Xi'an–Luoyang–Shaolin Si–Beijing.
• Chengdu–Lhasa.
• Chongqing–Three Gorges–Yichang–Wuhan–Huang Shan–Hangzhou–Suzhou–Shanghai.
• Guilin–Longsheng/Sanjiang–Zhaoxing–Kaili.

Four weeks
• Xi'an–Qinghai lake–Dunhuang–Turpan–Taklamakan desert–Kashgar.
• Kunming–Dali–Lijiang–Xichang–Emei Shan–Chengdu–Chongqing–Three Gorges.
• Hong Kong–Guangzhou–Shantou–Xiamen–Shanghai–Nanjing–Qingdao–Beijing.
• Hong Kong–Guangzhou–Changsha–Kaifeng–Beijing.

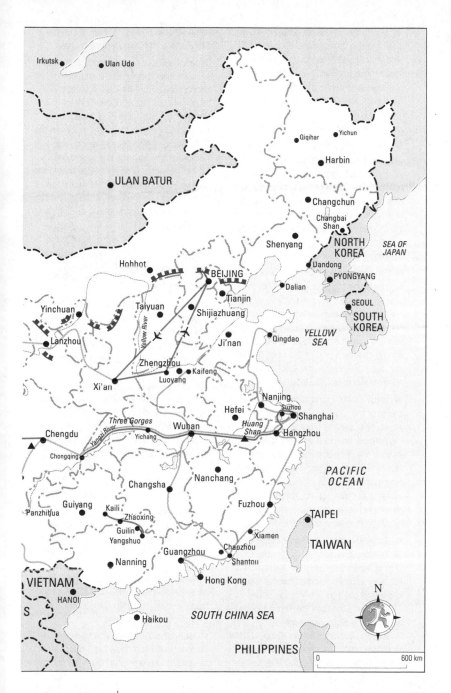

Terracotta Army, life-sized figurines guarding the tomb of the country's first emperor, Qin Shi Huang, but there's much more to Xi'an, including its ancient city walls and a pair of 1300-year-old Tang pagodas. To avoid the hordes of tourists, foreign and domestic, that come here, visit during the winter.

● The **Li river**. Looking exactly like a Chinese scroll painting, a procession of tall, wonderfully weathered limestone peaks flanks 85km of the Li river in south-western Guangxi province. Base yourself at either the package-tour city of Guilin or the more mellow village of Yangshuo, then cruise around or rent a bicycle and pedal off through the countryside.

● **Shanghai**. A former colonial concession near the mouth of the Yangzi river, Shanghai sports pockets of impressive European Art Deco architecture along its riverfront esplanade. Though the city has few sights as such, its sheer upbeat energy makes it one of the best places in the country to get the feel for China's current economic revolution.

● **Hong Kong**. Hong Kong's cityscape is one of the modern wonders of the world, best seen at night while crossing the harbour on the Star Ferry. It's easy to escape the phenomenal crowds that seethe around the glitzy downtown shopping malls and office blocks, and spend a day or two poking around the less developed outer islands, or visiting the former Portuguese enclave of Macau.

● **Three Gorges**. The latter stage of the 6400-kilometre-long Yangzi – called Chang Jiang, the Long River, in Chinese – flows eastwards across central China, and is still used as a transport artery. Catch a ferry through the Three Gorges, between the Sichuanese city of Chongqing and Yichang in Hubei, a 250-kilometre stretch packed with ancient towns, turbulent shoals and spectacular cliff scenery, all under threat of submersion from a massive damming project.

Tibet. The "roof of the world" is a place of red-robed monks and austere monastery complexes set against the awe-inspiring peaks of the Tibetan Plateau. It's also labouring under heavy-handed Chinese military rule, but even the Dalai Lama, exiled in India, encourages people to visit and see the region first-hand. Take your time and, after seeing the mighty Potala Palace – Tibet's foremost tourist sight – in the capital Lhasa, get out to less-touristed monasteries at Shigatse and Gyantse.

Also recommended

● **Guangxi** and **Guizhou**. The rural regions of these provinces are among China's poorest, but it's worth exploring the minority communities dotted throughout the fabulously terraced mountains here. In northern Guangxi, the Dong village of Zhaoxing has five antique wooden watchtowers and similarly old covered bridges, while Miao settlements around the town of Kaili in Guizhou host riotous festivals through the year, featuring bull fights, dancing, dragon-boat races, and youngsters wearing fantastic arrays of silver jewellery and embroidered jackets.

● **Kashgar**. An oasis town in China's northwestern deserts, Kashgar is populated by Muslim, Turkic-speaking Uigur people. Its appeal is in its very remoteness from the rest of China – and its Sunday Bazaar, an Arabian-Nights-style affair which draws 100,000 people to trade in everything from livestock and carpets to plastic buckets.

● **Hangzhou**. Once a vital trade centre on the 1800-kilometre-long Grand Canal in eastern China, Hangzhou is set on the famed beauty spot of Xi Hu, or West Lake, ringed by pagodas and wooded, hilly parkland, its surface dotted with fishing boats. It's also worth making the haul 60km north to Suzhou, another canal city with a host of traditional Chinese gardens.

● **Changbai Shan Nature Reserve**. Set right up on China's frontier with North Korea, Changbai Shan is hard to reach even when the road opens in summer, but the rewards are the stunning blue Tian Chi – "Heaven's Lake" – and the faint chance you may spot Siberian tigers. More likely, you'll get to sample some of the rare fungi and medicinal herbs which locals harvest here and serve up in restaurants; Changbai Shan's ginseng is considered the best in China.

● **Yunnan** and **Sichuan**. China's most varied region, these two provinces stretch from Tibet to the steamy tropical forests of Xishuangbanna, and also share borders with Laos, Vietnam and Burma. Top spots are Sichuan's holy mountain, Emei Shan, where you can sleep and eat in the dozen or more Buddhist temples; the Yunnanese town of Dali, with its ethnic Bai population and vivid mountain and lake scenery; and Lijiang, a delightful maze of cobbled lanes and wooden houses, home to the Tibetan-descended Naxi people.

● **Chaozhou**. A self-consciously traditional town in southern Guangdong province, Chaozhou has nineteenth-century streets and even older architecture, including its city walls and beautiful Kaiyuan Temple, which make it a pleasure to explore. Foodies will also need to try out Chaozhou's restaurants, famed for their bitter, refreshing *gongfu* tea and fruit-flavoured sauces.

Routes in and out

China's international airports are in Beijing, Kunming (capital of Yunnan), Guangzhou (capital of Guangdong), Shanghai and Hong Kong. In addition, Guilin has an airport served by flights from major Chinese cities and from Seoul (South Korea) and Fukuoka (Japan).

You can enter and depart China overland through several designated border crossings. You'll pass into Mongolia if you take the Trans-Siberian Express to or from Russia, and there's another train between the Ürümqi in northwestern China and Almaty in Kazakhstan. There are also roads from northwestern China into Pakistan and Kyrgyzstan, and from Tibet into Nepal, though regional politics can make using these routes problematic for foreigners. Far easier are the crossings from Vietnam and Laos into China's southwestern provinces of Yunnan and Guangxi, from where there's regular transport to the respective provincial capitals.

Itineraries

One week

● Spend the first couple of days in and around Beijing's Forbidden City and nearby parks, plus the city's extraordinary, circular Temple of Heaven. Throw in separate day-trips to the Great Wall, the delightful Summer Palace, and the Imperial Ming Tombs, and you've still a couple of days to explore Beijing's backstreets and shopping precincts.

● Stay two days in Guilin, enough time to cover the half-dozen small limestone peaks, parks and caves around town; then spend another day cruising down to Yangshuo through the spectacular Li-river scenery, and two more exploring daily life in the villages surrounding Yangshuo.

● Spend a week in Hong Kong, varying your trip by alternately throwing yourself into the busiest, most crowded districts – Central, Wanchai, and Kowloon – and taking day-long breathers on Lantau's small beaches and wooded hills; at Macau; admiring the temple statues and hill views from the Ten Thousand Buddha Monastery at Shatin; and the Qing-dynasty walled village of Kat Hing Wai.

Two weeks

◉ Spend the first week in Beijing, then take a trip around Xian's historic sites – including the Terracotta Army, pagodas, and Neolithic remains at Banpo; this will easily fill two days. The energetic could add an extra day and climb northerly Hua Shan; otherwise, spend a couple of days on an eastward circuit to take in the giant Buddhist cave carvings at Luoyang, and the famous kung-fu temple, Shaolin Si.

◉ Catch an internal flight to the charismatic Sichuanese gateway city of Chengdu, famed for its culture and fiery cuisine. After a couple of days there, head to Lhasa for a week's stay, enough to get around the Potala and leave you a day or two to get out to less-visited sights.

◉ Get an internal flight to Chongqing, and spend your first three days cruising through the Three Gorges, then take a bus from Yichang to the historic river city of Wuhan. From here, fly east to Huang Shan, and spend three days hiking around the picturesque heights. Take the train and spend a day in Hangzhou, another in Suzhou, and finish off the trip exploring Shanghai.

◉ After a couple of days in Guilin, head north to spend two days in hill villages around Longsheng or Sanjiang, then spend four days visiting first the Dong hamlet of Zhaoxing, followed by Kaili, getting over the mountains by bus. You can spend five days thoroughly exploring different Miao villages surrounding Kaili, catching at least one market day.

Four weeks

◉ Explore the 3000-kilometre-long train and bus route from Xi'an to Kashgar, much of which follows the ancient Silk Road between China and Central Asia. On the way, you can take in remote sections of the Great Wall, the bird-watching centre of Qinghai lake, astonishing eighth-century Buddhist cave art at Dunhuang, the pleasant oasis town of Turpan, the scorching sands of the Taklamakan desert, and finally, Kashgar itself.

◉ Do a circuit of southwestern China, starting in the Yunnanese provincial capital of Kunming, then heading northwest to Dali and Lijiang to hike through the dramatic Tiger Leaping Gorge. From here it's cross-country on local buses to the Space Centre at Xichang in southern Sichuan, then up to Emei Shan and the aptly named Big Buddha. Soak up the unique atmosphere of the Sichuanese capital Chengdu, before exiting the region via Chongqing and the Three Gorges.

◉ Take a slow trawl through China's heartland, travelling from Hong Kong to Beijing by bus or train. Having crossed from Hong Kong to the chaotic city of Guangzhou, you could either follow the east coast, stopping off in the old colonial towns of Shantou and Xiamen, before heading up to Shanghai and the historic cities of Nanjing and Qingdao; or travel straight north via Changsha (near Mao Zedong's home village), Wuhan, and the pleasantly undeveloped town of Kaifeng.

China online

China.com ⓦ *www.china.com*
Business, travel, culture, history, main

news stories and regular coverage of fairly offbeat destinations. A good browse.

Chinaenvironment Ⓦ*www.chinaenvironment.com* Gives an insight into how the Chinese see – and market – the natural world. Heavy on flowery prose about the beauties of selected nature reserves, plus a suggested eco-tour route around the country – but don't expect anything rugged.

China e-travel Ⓦ*www.chinaetravel.com* Online travel agent with links to hotels, airlines, and tour agents in China, plus thumbnail sketches of the main sights, province by province. It's nothing eye-opening, but gives a good idea of your options.

India

Capital: Delhi	temperate (central), desert
Population: over one billion	(northwest) and Himalayan (far
Language: Hindi, plus fourteen	north)
other main languages	**Best time to go**: October–March
Currency: Rupee (Rs)	(except in the southeast);
Main religions: Hinduism, Islam,	April–September (for trekking in the
Buddhism and Sikhism	Himalayas, and for the southeast)
Climate: Tropical in south India;	**Minimum daily budget**: $10/£7
mixed in the north, including	

For many travellers, India epitomizes the Asia experience. It brims over with bizarre rituals and extraordinary characters; it holds a wealth of temples, ruined cities and dramatic landscapes; and for tourists everything is bargain priced. However, it is also more crowded, more hassly and seems to have a lot more visible poverty than many other Asian countries.

With seven major faiths and over fifteen regional languages, India is impossible to pigeonhole. Much of the subcontinent's cultural history was shaped by the Moguls, an Islamic dynasty who ruled from the sixteenth to the eighteenth century, building majestic forts and exquisite palaces all over the country, many of them now impressively restored. One hundred years later, India came under the sway of the British Empire; known as the Raj, the colonial government built an extensive railway network, introduced a Westernized education system and promoted English as the official state language. Modern-day India is now the world's largest secular democracy, where the Hindu majority is vociferously, and occasionally violently, matched by powerful Muslim and Sikh factions, not to mention countless other religious and political groups.

A journey from the north of India to the south can seem like a trip across a dozen different countries. More than almost any other destination in Asia, India is a place to return to again and again and not somewhere that rewards a whistle-stop tour. And, because distances are phenomenal and public transport notoriously tardy, it also makes sense to confine yourself to smallish areas – aim to see something in depth and you'll have a far better experience than skittering through countless airports, stations and roads.

Many travellers make a beeline for the beaches of Goa and Kovalam, but others head for spiritual centres like Rishikesh and Dharamsala (for more on this, see p.132), for the palaces and desert landscape of Rajasthan, or for the hiking trails and hill stations in the Himalayas.

First-time visitors to India usually worry most about poor sanitation and the prospect of getting sick, but so long as you're sensible and follow the advice outlined in Chapter Eleven, you shouldn't find health is much more of an issue here than anywhere else in Asia. One of the great pleasures of travelling in India is the signifi-

Average daily temperatures (maximum and minimum°C) and monthly rainfall (mm)

	Jan	Feb	Mar	Apr	May	June	July	Aug	Sept	Oct	Nov	Dec
Delhi												
max °C	21	24	30	36	41	40	35	34	34	35	29	23
min °C	7	9	14	20	26	28	27	26	24	18	11	8
rainfall mm	25	22	17	7	8	65	211	173	150	31	1	5
Darjeeling												
max °C	8	9	14	17	18	18	19	18	18	16	12	9
min °C	2	2	6	9	12	13	14	14	13	10	6	3
rainfall mm	13	28	43	104	216	589	798	638	447	130	23	8
Mumbai												
max °C	28	28	30	32	33	32	29	29	29	32	32	31
min °C	19	19	22	24	27	26	25	24	24	24	23	21
rainfall mm	3	3	3	0	18	485	617	340	264	63	13	3
Chennai												
max °C	29	31	33	35	38	38	36	35	34	32	29	29
min °C	19	20	22	26	28	27	26	26	25	24	22	21
rainfall mm	36	10	8	15	25	48	91	117	119	305	356	140

cant number of well-educated local people who speak beautifully eloquent English and are often keen to engage tourists in conversation.

Main attractions

● **Delhi**. Like many chaotic Asian capitals, Delhi can scare the life out of a first-timer, but if you approach the city with patience and a sense of humour, you'll find enough to keep you upbeat for several days. The main sights of the Old City include the Mogul palaces inside the Red Fort; the colossal mosque, Jami Masjid; and the endlessly fascinating bazaars. New Delhi is characterized by sweeping thoroughfares and colonial grandeur, and is also where you'll find the open-air Crafts Museum, whose stunning display of rural crafts

and replicated traditional homes will really whet your appetite for the rest of the country. Further south, you can't miss the ultra-modern Baha'i Temple, which is often favourably compared to the Sydney Opera House. The clubs, pubs and nightclubs of Delhi are also great places to see young, modern and affluent India at play.

● The **Taj Mahal**. The world's most famous monument to love features on almost every first-timer's Indian itinerary. Built by the seventeenth-century Mogul emperor Shah Jahan to enshrine the body of his favourite wife, the vast mausoleum stands on the banks of the Yamuna River in the city of Agra, just a couple of hours' train ride from Delhi. It's worth staying in a hotel that's close by the Taj, so you can visit it at sunrise and/or in the moonlight, when the play of light on marble is especially memorable, and the site is less crowded. Not

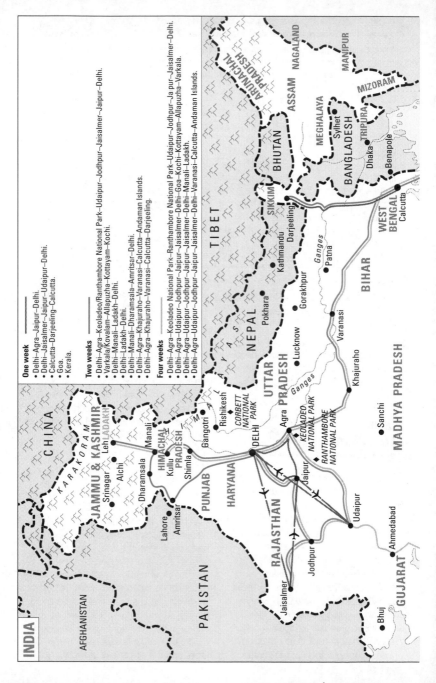

One week
- Delhi–Agra–Jaipur–Delhi.
- Delhi–Jaisalmer–Jaipur–Udaipur–Delhi.
- Calcutta–Darjeeling–Calcutta.
- Goa.
- Kerala.

Two weeks
- Delhi–Agra–Keoladeo/Ranthambore National Park–Udaipur–Jodhpur–Jaisalmer–Jaipur–Delhi.
- Varkala/Kovalam–Allapuzha–Kottayam–Kochi.
- Delhi–Manali–Ladakh–Delhi.
- Delhi–Ladakh–Delhi.
- Delhi–Manali–Dharamsala–Amritsar–Delhi.
- Delhi–Agra–Khajuraho–Varanasi–Calcutta–Andaman Islands.
- Delhi–Agra–Khajuraho–Varanasi–Calcutta–Darjeeling.

Four weeks
- Delhi–Agra–Keoladeo National Park–Ranthambore National Park–Udaipur–Jodhpur–Jaipur–Jaisalmer–Delhi.
- Delhi–Agra–Udaipur–Jodhpur–Jaipur–Jaisalmer–Delhi–Manali–Ladakh.
- Delhi–Agra–Udaipur–Jodhpur–Jaipur–Jaisalmer–Delhi–Manali–Ladakh.
- Delhi–Agra–Udaipur–Jodhpur–Jaipur–Jaisalmer–Delhi–Varanasi–Calcutta–Andaman Islands.

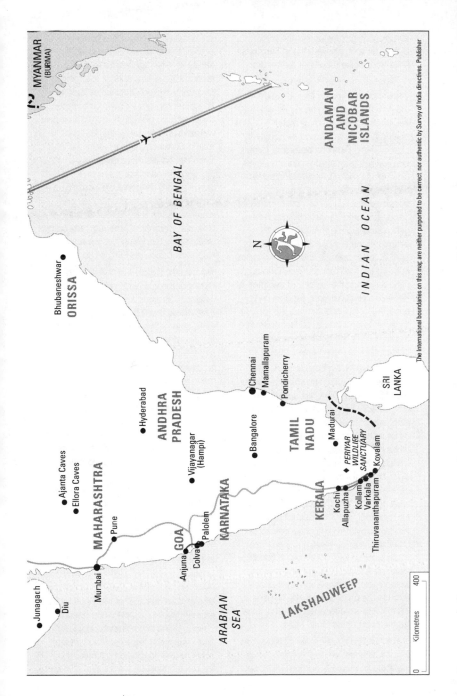

surprisingly, Agra is one of the worst places for touts, hawkers and hassle, so have your polite rebuffs at the ready.

● **Rajasthan**. India's desert state is deservedly the most popular region in the country, with its glorious forts at Jaipur and Jodhpur, magnificent maharajahs' palaces, and flamboyantly clad citizens. Graceful waterside temples, exquisite mansions, and the lovely City Palace make lakeside Udaipur a definite must-see, and the remote desert town of Jaisalmer, built entirely of honey-coloured sandstone, is another gem – and a departure point for overnight camel safaris. When you've tired of forts, palaces and camels, strike out into the state's two most famous national parks: the lakes and swamps of Keoladeo National Park support huge breeding colonies of cranes, storks, flamingoes and ibis, while Ranthambore National Park is one of the easiest places in India to see a wild tiger.

● **Goa**. Once a famous stop on the hippy trail, and now renowned the world over for its beachfront raves, the state of Goa actually comprises a 100-kilometre-long strip of beaches, each with its own distinct character. The beaches with the biggest party scenes are Vagator, Chapora and Anjuna – the latter in particular attracts thousands of European clubbers over Christmas and New Year. If techno music and Day-Glo-painted palm trees are not your thing, either stick to the more mainstream package resorts of Calangute, Colva, Baga and Benaulim, or venture out to less-developed Agonda or Palolem. And don't forget to do some inland exploring, preferably by bicycle, through the palm groves, rice fields and Portuguese-style facades that characterize the heart of the Goan state.

● **Kerala**. The southern tip of India has a quite different feel to the north, and the state of Kerala is particularly appeal-ing because it seems less crazy and intense than the rest of the country. Kerala is most famous for its beach resort at Kovalam, and for the more low-key travellers' enclave at Varkala. The other big draw down here is the chance to go boating through the inland waterways near Allapuzha, but the tourist boat rides are uninspired and overlong, so it's more rewarding to travel through the narrower rivers by local ferry bus. Kerala's delightful old port city of Kochi is full of historic churches and warehouses built by European and Chinese merchants, and regularly stages traditional, elaborately costumed Kathakali dance performances.

● **Ladakh**. Cradled by the soaring peaks of the Himalaya and Karakoram ranges, Ladakh is a fascinating high-altitude outpost of Tibetan culture and religion. One of the furthest flung parts of the country, this arid, stark, mountainous region, dotted with tiny pockets of fertility, offers some of the best trekking in India, from easy two-day strolls to treks of several weeks across the exceptionally remote and spellbindingly beautiful Zanskar region. The other highlights are the temples; Alchi, Tikse and Hemis are the best known, the last of these especially famed for its masked dances at festival time. The popular two- or three-day road journey from the lively hill town of Manali to Ladakh's main town, Leh, is one of the great Asian road trips, with high-altitude passes and stunning scenery (for more, see p.263).

● **Dharamsala**. Through the high profile of one resident, the Dalai Lama, and as a result of the Chinese occupation of Tibet, Dharamsala, the seat of the Tibetan government in exile, is now world famous. Thanks to the large Tibetan population and influence in the area, this is a great place to take meditation courses, shop for Tibetan trinkets, see Tibetan folk opera and even, if you get lucky, shake hands with the Dalai Lama himself. It is also a good place to arrange local treks into the Dhauladhar range.

Also recommended

● **Varanasi**. Watch the sun rise and set over the sacred River Ganges, where pilgrims immerse themselves in the waters and cremate their dead on the banks.

● **Darjeeling**. Famous for tea, its diminutive railway and stunning vistas of Kanchenjunga, the third-highest mountain in the world, this cool and charming hill station is a good spot to arrange treks: from some trails you get to see four of the five highest mountains in the world.

● **Amritsar**. At the heart of the holy city of the Sikhs stands the sumptuous sixteenth-century Golden Temple, encircled by a sacred lake and constantly thronged by pilgrims in their finest ceremonial dress. You can easily spend half a day absorbing the ritual goings-on of the temple: arrive here at sunrise for the most awesome effect of gilt on water, then walk slowly through the long white marble colonnades that frame the lake; cross the causeway to enter the Golden Temple itself; and finally join the pilgrims for the free meal of chapatti and dhal, dished out to all visitors twice a day.

● **Calcutta**. This famously warm-hearted and literary city has dozens of bookshops and a reputation for intellectual liveliness, which makes it a stimulating yet laid-back place to hang out.

● The **Khajuraho temples**. The 25 Hindu and Jain temples here date back to the tenth century and are built of sandstone, with almost every facade carved into exuberantly erotic sculptures and friezes, depicting in graphic and

beautiful detail a whole encyclopedia of Kamasutra-like entanglements.

● Snorkelling and diving in the **Andaman Islands**. This rarely visited archipelago of two hundred picture-perfect islands lies 100km off India's east coast. Tourism is only embryonic here, and although more islands are opening up every year, it's worth bringing a tent to make the most of your stay.

● The seventeen-kilometre trek to the **Gangotri Glacier**. The sacred frozen source of the River Ganges is spectacularly positioned amid spiky snow-clad peaks at 5000m above sea level, but is fairly easily reached along this pilgrims' route.

● **Playing an extra in an Indian film**. India's film industry, known as Bollywood, is based in Mumbai and produces twice as many movies as Hollywood each year. Non-Indians are invariably needed to pad out the cast, so hang out at the city's Salvation Army Red Shield Hostel, where many movie hopefuls are recruited.

Routes in and out

There are international airports in Delhi, Mumbai (formerly Bombay), Chennai (Madras), Calcutta and Ahmedabad, plus plenty of international charter flights to Goa's Dabolim Airport and to Thiruvananthapuram in Kerala. You can also enter and depart India overland at the border crossings with Pakistan, Nepal and Bangladesh. However, you cannot cross to and from Sri Lanka by ferry, which is currently only accessible by air.

Itineraries

One week
● Spend your first couple of days exploring Delhi, then visit Agra and the Taj Mahal for two nights, before continu-

ing to the Rajasthani city of Jaipur for days five and six. Catch a train back to Delhi for your last night.

● Squeeze in a rapid circuit of Rajasthan (you'll need to fly between every town), spending the first night in Delhi, then heading out to Jaisalmer for two days. Next stop is a day and a night in Jaipur, then on to Udaipur for a couple of days before returning to Delhi.

● Divide your time between Calcutta and Darjeeling, flying in and out of Calcutta, and spending three or four days exploring Darjeeling, its tea plantations and hilly surrounds.

● Base yourself on the beach in Goa or Kerala, making a couple of day-trips inland for a bit of variety.

Two weeks

● Spend two or three nights in Delhi, then head down to Agra and the Taj Mahal for a day and a night. From here, strike out west into Rajasthan for a rewarding tour of the best forts, palaces and towns (perhaps stopping for a couple of days' hiking and wildlife-spotting in either Keoladeo or Ranthambore national parks). Spend two days in Udaipur, a night in Jodhpur, three or four days in Jaisalmer and then a night in Jaipur before returning to Delhi.

● Concentrate on the southern state of Kerala – begin with a week on the beach at Varkala or Kovalam, then head north up the coast to Allapuzha. From here, take an early morning boat trip to Kottayam and spend the night there. Round off your fortnight in Kochi, renting a bicycle to explore the historic old city and its old traditional neighbourhoods.

● Explore a small stretch of the Himalayan foothills. Spend two or three days visiting the sights of Delhi. Then head north to Manali, basing yourself here for four or five days in order to do

some day-walks or longer hikes through the majestic Kullu Valley. From Manali, you can either head north or west for the rest of your fortnight. Travelling north takes you into Ladakh, along the famous Manali–Leh Highway, where you can spend the week exploring the mountains and trails of the region. The westerly route focuses on Dharamsala, where there's plenty to occupy you for four days, after which you should stop off for a night at Amritsar in order to admire the Golden Temple, before taking the train back to Delhi.

● Spend the whole fortnight in Ladakh, flying from Delhi to Leh in one direction and tackling the Manali–Leh Highway in the other.

● Spend your first couple of days exploring Delhi, then visit Agra and the Taj Mahal for a night. Next stop should be a day and a night at Khajuraho. Divide the rest of your fortnight between Varanasi, Calcutta and the Andaman Islands. Alternatively, substitute Darjeeling for the Andaman Islands, giving yourself time for a two- or three-day trek while there.

Four weeks

● Spend three or four days in Delhi, then head down to Agra and on into Rajasathan. Spend at least a fortnight enjoying all the highlights of Rajasthan, including hiking and wildlife-spotting in Keoladeo and Ranthambore national parks, plus decent stints in Udaipur, Jodhpur and Jaipur. Aim to spend at least five days in Jaisalmer.

From Delhi, do a decent fortnight's tour of Rajasthan. Back in Delhi, spend the next fortnight doing one of the following:

● Chill out on the beach in Goa for a week, then spend a week touring Kerala.

● Head up into the hills, spending a

week in the Kullu Valley and another week in Ladakh. Or use the whole fortnight to explore Ladakh.

● Divide your fortnight between Varanasi, Calcutta and the Andaman Islands.

India online

Call of the Wild
W*www.allindia.com/wild* All about India's wildlife reserves, with links to detailed Web sites on the country's twelve most important national parks.

Goa Unplugged W*www.goaunplugged.com* Handy all-round introduction to the region, with reviews of beaches, latest news, travellers' tips, a look at the nightlife and even some local recipes.

Indiamart W*www.travel.indiamart.com* Huge site with lots of stuff on destinations and culture, including an excellent roundup of trekking possibilities across the country.

123 India W*www.123india.com* Scores of links to all manner of India-related sites, including those covering the arts, culture and news, as well as introductions to every region and major city in the country and listings of upcoming festivals.

The Times of India W*www.timesofindia.com* Daily news and the best features from the highly respected English-language daily.

Indonesia

Capital: Jakarta	Buddhist, Hindu and Christian minorities
Population: 200 million	**Climate**: Tropical throughout, with nominal wet and dry seasons
Language: Bahasa Indonesia is the national language, with an estimated five hundred or more local languages and dialects	**Best time to go**: during the dry season (May–Oct for most of the country, but Nov–April in northern Sumatra and central and northern Maluku)
Currency: Rupiah (Rp)	
Religion: Predominantly Muslim, though animism is indigenous and widespread; there are also	**Minimum daily budget**: $10/£7

For scale and variety, Indonesia, the world's largest archipelago, is pretty much unbeatable. The fabulously varied scenery (from equatorial rainforest and volcanoes to idyllic white-sand beaches and desert terrain), the equally diverse flora and fauna, and the generally friendly and welcoming people make Indonesia one of Asia's most rewarding destinations. Given the country's sheer enormity, though, you must be selective – with too little time and too much travel your trip could turn into a miserable, stressful race between islands looking at the clock and cursing all the way.

There's an immensely rich melange of peoples, religions and cultures across the archipelago, and their ancient monuments are some of the most dramatic sights of Indonesia. Within this one country it's possible to encounter Westernized city dwellers with mobile phones and plush apartments, as well as hunters armed with bows and arrows, clad in penis gourds and feathered headdresses. Each ethnic group has its own artistic heritage, and their textiles, music, arts, crafts and dance add a rich cultural dimension to most visits to the islands.

Perhaps predictably, the tensions and problems of melding such diversity into one nation have resulted in violence and unrest. In recent years there have been civil disturbances, some lasting a couple of days, others long-running, in Maluku, Lombok, Aceh and Bali. However, it is important not to overstate the risks of a visit. Given the vastness of the country, difficulties in one region often barely impact upon another a few hundred kilometres away. Before you travel, it's vital to get up-to-date information on the situation by keeping track of the international news and checking the Web sites on p.367. It's also worth noting that travel through Muslim areas (this doesn't include Bali) during Ramadan, the traditional month of fasting, can be hard going as local people don't eat, drink or smoke during daylight hours.

Main attractions

● **Bali**. With its alluring mix of beaches, volcanoes, temples, stunning scenery and artistic and cultural wealth, the island has

Average daily temperatures (maximum and minimum°C) and monthly rainfall (mm)

	Jan	Feb	Mar	Apr	May	June	July	Aug	Sept	Oct	Nov	Dec
Jakarta (Java)												
max °C	29	29	30	31	31	31	31	31	31	31	30	29
min °C	23	23	23	24	24	23	23	23	23	23	23	23
rainfall mm	300	300	211	147	114	97	64	43	66	112	142	203
Makassar (Sulawesi)												
max °C	29	29	29	30	31	30	30	31	31	31	30	29
min °C	23	24	23	23	23	22	21	21	21	22	23	23
rainfall mm	686	536	424	150	89	74	36	10	15	43	178	610
Padang (Sumatra)												
max °C	31	31	31	31	31	31	31	31	30	30	30	30
min °C	23	23	23	24	24	23	23	23	23	23	23	23
rainfall mm	351	259	307	363	315	307	277	348	152	495	518	480

long been the jewel in the Indonesian tourism crown. Bali is the enclave of a unique and colourful form of Hinduism, and Besakih, Tanah Lot and Ulu Watu are the three most impressive of its thousands of temples. The annual festivals celebrated at all these shrines are a colourful and vibrant celebration of the devout traditional lifestyle that has drawn tourists to the island for decades. Most visitors also go to the southern beach resorts that have developed around Kuta, a heady hedonistic mix of hotels, shops, restaurants and nightlife, but there are plenty of quieter resorts around the coast, and a few secluded spots remain for total relaxation. Those interested in art, crafts, music and dance usually head for Ubud, a cool, laid-back town with galleries, studios, performances and classes galore and plenty of local walks among the rice-terraces to engage the more energetic. The still-smoking Gunung Batur, in the volcanic centre of the island, is a popular climb, usually done in the pitch dark so as to arrive at the top in time to admire the glowing sunrise.

● **Gunung Bromo** The obligatory sunrise views of this mountain in east Java, with the peak and its equally stunning neighbours rising from an almost otherworldly sea of sand, are simply spellbinding. There are also plenty of walks to enjoy in this cool, attractive region.

● **Borobodur** Java's number-one tourist attraction, this colossal, multi-tiered temple is the world's largest Buddhist stupa. Over a thousand years old, the temple, though now ruined, is still surprisingly evocative, with over three thousand reliefs detailing scenes from everyday life and the path followed by the soul to enlightenment, along with ancient tales illustrating the journey.

● **Lake Toba** In northern Sumatra, this is Southeast Asia's largest freshwater lake. Its central island, Samosir, is the heartland of the Toba Batak people and offers great scenery, trekking and relaxation, with the option of visiting megalithic stone complexes, local villages and hot springs.

● **Orang-utans** The animals at the orang-utan rehabilitation centre at Bukit Lawang in Sumatra are arguably the most famous example of Indonesia's wildlife.

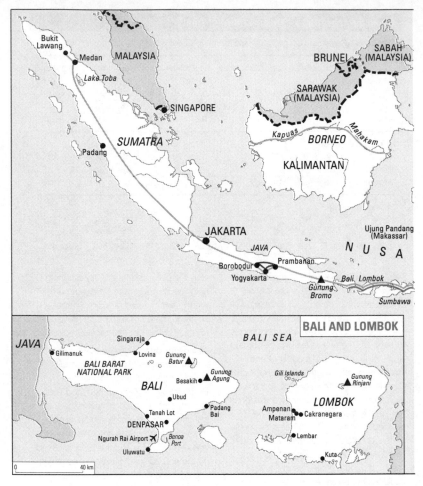

The centre aims to reintroduce into the wild orang-utans that have been rescued from captivity; visitors here are welcome to watch the twice-daily feeding sessions.

● **Komodo dragons**. An apparent throwback to the age of dinosaurs, these creatures, actually the world's largest lizards, live on Komodo in Nusa Tenggara, the chain of islands stretching between Bali and Irian Jaya. The largest ever recorded was more than 3m long and weighed in at 150kg, though most

of the dragons aren't quite so enormous.

● **Tanah Toraja**. This region of Sulawesi is home to the Torajan people, who have a wealth of traditional architecture and ceremonies, most famously funerals. Also on offer are plenty of opportunities for trekking in the scenic highlands.

● **Yogyakarta**. The city is the heartland of Javanese arts; exhibitions of art and batik, and performances of music, drama, puppetry and dance abound, with cours-es available for visitors. The Kraton, the

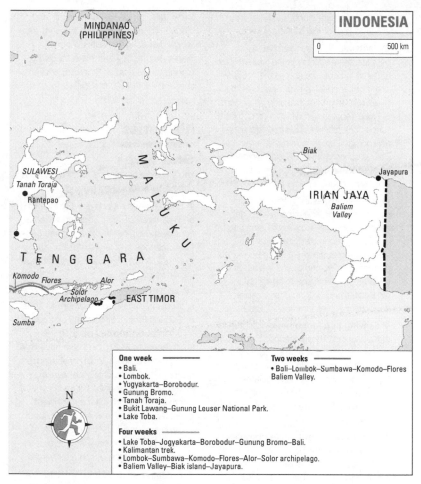

INDONESIA

| 0 | 500 km |

MINDANAO
(PHILIPPINES)

Biak

SULAWESI
Tanah Toraja

Rantepao

Jayapura

IRIAN JAYA
Baliem
Valley

M A L U K U

T E N G G A R A

Komodo Flores
Alor
Solor
Archipelago
EAST TIMOR

Sumba

N

One week
• Bali.
• Lombok.
• Yogyakarta–Borobodur.
• Gunung Bromo.
• Tanah Toraja.
• Bukit Lawang–Gunung Leuser National Park.
• Lake Toba.

Two weeks
• Bali–Lombok–Sumbawa–Komodo–Flores
Baliem Valley.

Four weeks
• Lake Toba–Jogyakarta–Borobodur–Gunung Bromo–Bali.
• Kalimantan trek.
• Lombok–Sumbawa–Komodo–Flores–Alor–Solor archipelago.
• Baliem Valley–Biak island–Jayapura.

old walled city, is well preserved for architecture buffs, and Yogyakarta is ideally placed for excursions into the surrounding countryside and – if it hasn't blown its lid recently – treks up Gunung Merapi, Indonesia's most volatile volcano.

Also recommended

● **Nusa Tenggara**. The most westerly of

these islands, Lombok, is developing a significant tourist industry to cope with the Bali overspill. Its highlights include Gunung Rinjani, Indonesia's second highest mountain, with a huge crater lake; the tiny Gili Islands off its northwest coast; and the unspoilt south-coast beaches, accessible from Kuta on Bali. The further east you go, the less tourist infrastructure there is, so the more time you'll need; highlights here include Sumba's unspoilt beaches and traditional *ikat* weaving,

Komodo's dragons and the three-coloured lake of Keli Mutu on Flores.

● **Festivals**. With such a diversity of peoples, there's plenty in the festivals calendar to look out for across the country. The most accessible events include the Nyale festival on Lombok and other parts of Nusa Tenggara, in which tens of thousands flock to the coasts in search of an aphrodisiac seaworm; temple festivals in Bali, featuring gorgeously clad worshippers; and Sumba's pasola, a ritualized war carried out on horseback.

● The **Baliem valley** in Irian Jaya. It's time-consuming and expensive to get here, and to really explore the area you'll need to trek long distances and often sleep extremely rough. But the scenery is dramatic and splendid, and the tribes of the area are managing to retain an age-old lifestyle and culture, often despite considerable pressure from outsiders.

● **Staying in a longhouse** in the interior of Kalimantan. The indigenous Dyak peoples here have retained their traditional beliefs and ways of life to varying degrees. Their communal longhouse dwellings – long wooden structures raised on stilts – have survived and are being restored, and many welcome visitors.

● The **Prambanan temple complex**. The Hindu temples here, accessed from Yogyakarta in Java, are soaring, intricately carved structures dating from the ninth century AD. Visits at dawn and dusk are especially atmospheric.

● **Underwater exploration**. The highlight of many visits, Indonesia's marine life is startling in its diversity. Current centres for diving are Bali, the Gili islands off Lombok, and Sulawesi.

Routes in and out

Indonesia boasts a huge choice of international airports, the busiest of which are in Jakarta, Denpasar (on Bali) and Medan. There are fast and frequent passenger ferries from Malaysia and Singapore, mostly arriving in the Riau islands to the east of Sumatra; and an overland route from Malaysia into Kalimantan at Entikong.

Itineraries

One week

You'll need to explore a small area, preferably arriving and leaving by air.

● Enjoy a couple of days on the beach on Bali, three days in Ubud and then a couple of days either exploring the central volcanoes and lakes of Batur and Bedugul, or the Bali Barat National Park in the west.

● Head to Lombok – it's possible to fit in a couple of days in the southern foothills of Gunung Rinjani at Tetebatu or Sapit, followed by a couple of days on the south coast at Kuta; you'll also have time to explore the nearby traditional villages or craft villages slightly further away. Finally, spend a couple of days on one of the three Gili islands off the northwest coast. Alternatively, a week is just about enough time to climb to the summit of Gunung Rinjani and have a couple of days relaxing on the beach afterwards.

● In central Java, take in the cultural highlights of Yogyakarta, with excursions to the Borobodur and Prambanan temple complexes.

● Head to Gunung Bromo – a week allows time to get to and from the area, see the sunrise and enjoy several local hikes.

● Basing yourself in Rantepao, the main town in Tanah Toraja, make excursions out to the main villages, and climb to the top of Gunung Sesean, the region's highest peak (2382m).

Combine a trip to the Orang-Utan Rehabilitation Centre in Bukit Lawang with some short treks in nearby Gunung Leuser National Park. For a longer hike, try the trek from Bukit Lawang to Ketambe, lasting five to seven days.

Chill out on Samosir island in the middle of Lake Toba for a few days, cycle around the coast to visit tiny Batak villages, and spend a couple more days trekking across the island.

Two weeks

Combine two of the one-week options, saving time by flying where possible or choosing areas to visit that are reasonably close to each other, eg
Lake Toba and Bukit Lawang, central and east Java, east Java and Bali, or Bali and Lombok.

Island-hop between Bali and Flores, taking in Komodo and Lake Keli Mutu.

Explore the Baliem Valley in Irian Jaya; you'll have time to do one decent trek if you fly out to a remotish village and hike back to Wamena, the main town.

Four weeks

Starting in Lake Toba, head south through Sumatra, then take in all of the Java highlights and end with some R&R on a Bali beach.

Trek across Kalimantan, from Pontianak to Samarinda, via the Kapuas and Mahakam rivers.

Wander, by bus and ferry, through Nusa Tenggara, taking in the main Lombok sights and then heading through Sumbawa, Komodo, Flores and on eastwards.

Trek through the Baliem Valley – a month is ample, and you can combine this with a few days at Irian Jaya's other,

more accessible sights: Biak island (boasting waterfalls, beaches, Japanese WWII caves and coral reefs), and Jayapura (Lake Sentani, Hamadi beach and the surrounding hills).

Indonesia online

Inside Indonesia ⓦ*www.insideindonesia. org* The online version of this topical, hard-hitting magazine, published quarterly in Australia and detailing politics, government shortcomings and human rights and social issues across the country.

Access Bali Online
ⓦ*www.baliwww.com/bali* Offering loads of links to tourist information, magazines, services and hotels, this site includes a tour finder and room finder, and the latest tourism news. An excellent first stop for anyone thinking of visiting the island.

Discover Indonesia
ⓦ*www.serve.com/aberges/* Attractive site concentrating on Sumatra, Java, Bali and Lombok, and also covering aspects of the arts, such as batik and wayang kulit (shadow puppetry). Good links too.

Orangutan Foundation International
ⓦ*www.orangutan.org* This international organization is involved in the preservation of orang-utans and supports the work at Camp Leakey, a rehabilitation centre in Kalimantan. Their Web site is an excellent starting point for information on this remarkable creature.

INDObeads ⓦ*www.indonesian-sources. com/indobeads.htm* A listing of hundreds of useful, interesting and just plain weird facts about Indonesia, many of interest to potential visitors.

Japan

Capital: Tokyo	**Best time to go**: March–May, and
Population: 126 million	Sept–Nov, with cherry blossom time
Language: Japanese	(April) and maple leaf season (Nov)
Currency: Yen (¥)	the most rewarding
Main religion: Shintoism and	**Minimum daily budget**:
Mahayana Buddhism	$60/£35
Climate: Temperate	

Lying east off continental Asia, across the Sea of Japan from Russia, China and Korea, the Japanese archipelago comprises over six thousand volcanic islands, though the bulk of the population lives on the main island of Honshu, which is linked by bridges and tunnels to the other three main islands of Hokkaido, Kyushu and Shikoku.

Many Westerners imagine this isolated island nation to be a cold-hearted country of futuristic machinery and an obsessive work ethic, but beneath the hi-tech veneer, Japan is still a very traditional society, with an absorbingly ancient culture to investigate, from Zen temples to fire festivals, and tea ceremonies to sumo wrestling matches. Some of the most arresting sights are the majestic Buddhist temples and the contrastingly kitsch Shinto shrines; the latter in particular are still an important focus of daily life, with devotees coming here to pray for everything from a new baby to respectable exam results.

As the archipelago stretches over 3000km from north to south, running from the chilly end of the temperate zone to tropical Okinawa in the south, there are varied and plentiful hiking opportunities – in Honshu's Japan Alps; in the mountains, gorges and lakes of the northern island of Hokkaido; and in the national parks on the southern island of Kyushu.

Foreign tourists are rare outside the main cultural centres, but are generally welcomed warmly. Language is a problem for visitors to Japan, but foreigners usually find they can make themselves understood without too much difficulty and there are an increasing number of signs in Roman script. Public transport is fast, efficient and extensive (this is after all, the home of the Bullet Train).

Despite all its attractions, very few independent travellers make it to Japan, for the simple reason that they can't afford it. The cost of living is so high that one of the best ways to experience the country is to get an English-teaching job here for a few months (see Chapter Four for advice on this). Otherwise, buy a train pass, bring a tent and don't hang out in too many coffee shops or pinball parlours.

Main attractions

● **Kyoto**. This historic former capital city should be at the top of every visitor's list. It has scores of breathtaking

Mean Temperatures (°C) and Rainfall (mm)

Average daily temperatures (maximum and minimum°C) and monthly rainfall (mm)

	Jan	Feb	Mar	Apr	May	June	July	Aug	Sept	Oct	Nov	Dec
Tokyo												
max °C	10	10	13	18	23	25	29	31	27	21	17	12
min °C	1	1	4	10	15	18	22	24	20	14	8	3
rainfall mm	110	155	228	254	244	305	254	203	279	228	162	96
Sapporo												
max °C	2	2	6	13	18	21	24	26	22	17	11	5
min °C	-10	-10	-7	-1	3	10	16	18	12	6	-1	-6
rainfall mm	25	43	61	84	102	160	188	155	160	147	56	38
Nagasaki												
max °C	9	10	14	19	23	26	29	31	27	22	17	12
min °C	2	2	5	10	14	18	23	23	20	14	9	4
rainfall mm	71	84	125	185	170	312	257	175	249	114	94	81

Buddhist temples, some of the country's finest Zen gardens, and lovely neighbourhoods of wooden homes and traditional tea houses. Don't miss the 1001 gilded statues of Buddha at Sanjusanngen-do temple, or Ginkakuji's Temple of the Silver Pavilion, or the inspirational Ryoan-ji rock garden. The modern face of Kyoto is energetic and youthful, with good bars, clubs and restaurants, and there are invigorating hill walks within day-tripping distance.

● **Nara** A popular side-trip from Kyoto, and also a former capital, Nara is dotted with venerable temples and shrines, in particular the historic Todai-ji temple, housing a fifteen-metre-high bronze Buddha. Though it has nothing like the energy of Kyoto, the modern city is compact, easy to navigate and noticeably greener than most other big towns.

● **Tokyo** Japan's modern-day capital lacks the refined aesthetic of Kyoto, or the tranquillity of Nara, but comes up trumps with its contemporary icons, like the forest of ultra-sleek sci-fi skyscrapers that dominates the Shinjuku district, the ever-changing gadgets exhibited in the Sony Building and the hyper-trendy street fashions and boutiques of Harajuku. Historic highlights include the country's most venerated Shinto shrine, Meiji-jingu, and the impressive Senso-ji temple, while the early-morning Tsukiji fish market makes for a lively contrast with the shopping malls of super-chic Ginza.

● **Hiroshima** Many visitors to Japan make a pilgrimage to Hiroshima's excellent Peace Memorial Museum here, a balanced commemoration of the dropping of the atomic bomb here on August 6, 1945, and its horrific repercussions. The regenerated city has a breezy, upbeat atmosphere and is a pleasure to explore. Just a twenty-minute ferry ride away is the little island of Miyajima, site of one of Japan's most ooonically located Shinto shrines.

● **Mount Fuji** Although the walk to the top of Japan's iconic snow-capped peak takes a gruelling six hours, thousands of people make it up to the 3776-metre summit every summer. Unfortunately, the tracks are always heaving with hikers, the mountainside

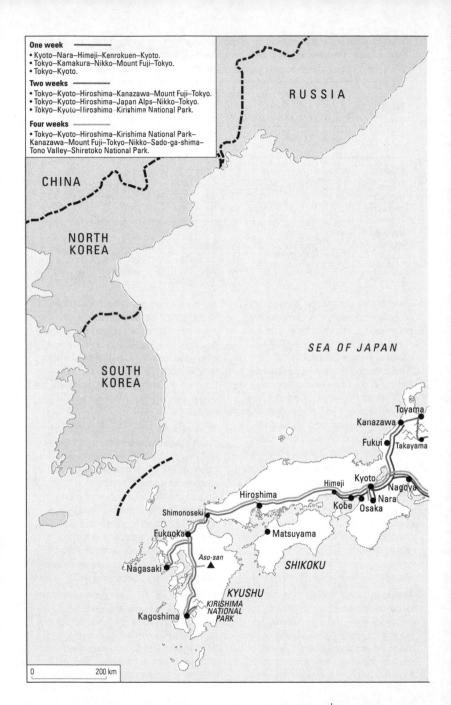

One week
• Kyoto–Nara–Himeji–Kenrokuen–Kyoto.
• Tokyo–Kamakura–Nikko–Mount Fuji–Tokyo.
• Tokyo–Kyoto.

Two weeks
• Tokyo–Kyoto–Hiroshima–Kanazawa–Mount Fuji–Tokyo.
• Tokyo–Kyoto–Hiroshima–Japan Alps–Nikko–Tokyo.
• Tokyo–Kyoto–Hiroshima–Kirishima National Park.

Four weeks
• Tokyo–Kyoto–Hiroshima–Kirishima National Park–
Kanazawa–Mount Fuji–Tokyo–Nikko–Sado-ga-shima–
Tono Valley–Shiretoko National Park.

RUSSIA

CHINA

NORTH
KOREA

SOUTH
KOREA

SEA OF JAPAN

Toyama
Kanazawa
Fukui Takayama
Kyoto Nagoya
Himeji Nara
Hiroshima Kobe Osaka
Shimonoseki
Fukuoka Matsuyama
Aso-san SHIKOKU
Nagasaki
KYUSHU
KIRISHIMA
NATIONAL
Kagoshima PARK

0   200 km

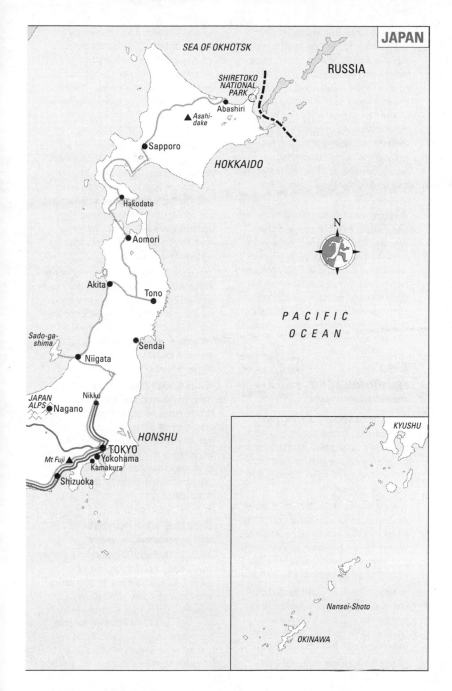

is strewn with unattractive volcanic debris and, due to persistent haze, the views are rarely spectacular. A better way to appreciate Fuji-san is to climb nearby Mount Tenjo, which you can do in just 45 minutes, giving you the chance to admire Mount Fuji from a more interesting perspective. Or, more leisurely still, take a slow train ride through the surrounding Hakone region, an area of lakes and hot springs which also offers fine views of the sacred peak.

● **Himeji castle**. With its five-tiered roofs, elegant proportions and chilly interiors, imposing Himeji castle looks much as it would have done when it housed the local lord and his samurai in the seventeenth century. Take the free guided tour to discover the castle's secret defences – like floors that were designed to creak and a labyrinthine network of corridors.

Also recommended

● The **Tono valley**. For a glimpse of traditional life in rural Japan, hire a bike for a day's cycling here, visiting some of the restored eighteenth-century farmhouses and stopping in at one of the local folk museums.

● **Kenrokuen**, in the city of Kanazawa. Japanese gardens have inspired designers all over the world, and Kenrokuen, the country's top garden, is a classic composition of ponds, pine trees, contemplative vistas and graceful teahouses.

● **Nikko**. Set in a huge forested park of mountains, lakes and waterfalls, this complex of elaborately carved and gaudily painted shrines and temples looks especially fantastical in the snow.

Hiking in **Kirishima National Park**. The southern island of Kyushu boasts the most dramatic volcanic scenery in the country, nowhere more so than in Kirishima National Park, which has 23 peaks within its boundaries. There are plenty of bracing mountain trails here, plus waterfalls, an impressive gorge and an outdoor hot spring.

● **Hokkaido**. The northernmost of Japan's four main islands is also its wildest and least populated. The volcanic landscape is dotted with lakes and forests, which makes it perfect hiking country: Shiretoko National Park is especially rewarding, with five lakes linked by forest paths, plus natural hot springs and challenging trails.

● A night in a **ryokan**. These traditional inns are like a genuine step backwards in time; the rooms have *tatami* mat floors, sumptuous futons, sliding paper doors and views onto traditional Japanese gardens. Everyone pads around in their socks, and you can often ask to have dinner served on low tables in your room.

● The **Kodo drum festival**, on Sado-ga-shima Island. The world music and dance event held over three days every summer makes the perfect excuse to visit this remote island, home to the famous drumming troupe, whose muscular performances at their colossal *taiko* drums are a spectacle that's well worth catching.

Routes in and out

Japan's international airports are in the Tokyo and Osaka areas, the latter convenient for Kyoto. You can also arrive and depart by sea, with regular boats from Pusan in South Korea to Fukuoka (Kyushu) and Shimonoseki (Honshu); from Shanghai in China to Kobe and Osaka; from Taiwan to Okinawa (Japan's southernmost island); and from

Vladivostok (the terminus of the Trans-Siberian rail line in Russia) to Niigata and Fushiki, near Toyama (both on Honshu).

Itineraries

One week

● Stay the whole week in Kyoto, perhaps making day trips to Nara, Himeji and Kenrokuen.

● After three days in Tokyo, make a day-trip to the huge Buddha at Kamakura, and spend the next couple of days in Nikko or around Mount Fuji.

● Spend three days in Tokyo and four in Kyoto.

Two weeks

● After three days in Tokyo, head west for a decent five- or six-day stint in Kyoto before continuing to Hiroshima for a night or two. You can then do one of the following:

● On the way back to Tokyo, stop for a night or two at Mount Fuji, Kanazawa, the Japan Alps or Nikko.

● Continue west from Hiroshima to the southern island of Kyushu for three days' walking in Kirishima National Park.

Four weeks

● Combine the two-week loop, from Tokyo to Kyushu, with a northeasterly zigzag to Nikko, Sado-ga-shima and the

Tono valley, before heading up to Shiretoko National Park in Hokkaido.

Japan online

The Japan Times
Ⓦ*www.japantimes.co.jp* The online version of Japan's main English-language daily is the best place to catch up on latest events in the archipelago.
Kansai Time Out Ⓦ*www.kto.co.jp* The Web site for this lively monthly English-language listings magazine has lots of articles on contemporary and cultural Japan, plus events calendars and restaurant reviews.
Randy Johnson's Japan Page
Ⓦ*www.easo.com/~randyj/japan.htm* Extensive homepage with an especially good section on getaways in rural Japan, complete with descriptions, accommodation ideas and directions. Also interesting stuff on sushi and art, plus decent links.
Schauwecker's Guide to Japan
Ⓦ*www.japan-guide.com* Comprehensive site with over two hundred links to pages on food, culture, tourism, religion, living in Japan, plus a lot more. Well worth checking out.
Teaching English in Japan
Ⓦ*www.wizweb.com/~susan/japan* Useful resource that covers many aspects of teaching in Japan, from finding a job to living in the country. Aimed at Americans, but applies equally to other nationalities.

Laos

Capital: Vientiane	**Main religion:** Theravada Buddhism
Population: 5 million	**Climate:** Tropical
Language: Lao	**Best time to go:** November–March
Currency: Kip (K)	**Minimum daily budget:** $10/£7

Laos is the most traditional corner of Southeast Asia, much less well known to the outside world than neighbouring Thailand and Vietnam. Though ruled by France as part of its Indochinese empire for the first half of the twentieth century, and then fatefully embroiled in the American–Vietnam War of the 1960s and 70s, Laos faded from view between 1975 and 1989 when a revolutionary communist government took over, forbidding contact with the outside world and imposing dogmatic political and economic reforms. Great hardship ensued and, despite recent liberalization, Laos continues to be much poorer and less developed than other Southeast Asian nations.

For visitors however, the old-fashioned lifestyles and traditional rural ways of the Lao people hold great appeal, not least because tourism is still in its infancy. There are few tourist facilities outside the two main cities of Vientiane and Louang Phabang, and with no beaches and few historical gems to write home about, it's not everyone's idea of a great holiday destination. But those who do make it here rave about the dramatic river landscapes, the easy-going, unhurried pace of daily life, and the chance to experience a culture that's still relatively unchanged by the tourist industry. If you do venture out into the sticks,

you'll need to learn some Lao phrases, but you can get by in English in the main towns.

Because it has borders with Thailand, Vietnam and China, Laos works well as part of a leisurely overland trip. Indeed, journeys in Laos generally have to be leisurely, because public transport is frustratingly slow. Travelling in Laos is hard, not least because of the buttock-crunchingly potholed roads; worse still, bandits render some roads too dangerous for tourists to use. Many visitors stick to the rivers – a more scenic, though not always more comfortable, way of getting between towns. Unfortunately, the domestic airlines are not the answer either, as they have a poor safety record on many routes, and run to an erratic schedule.

At the time of writing, the political situation in Laos was unfortunately becoming volatile once again, with anti-government groups of ethnic Hmong tribespeople setting a series of bombs in Vientiane, and crimes against tourists increasing. Before deciding to visit Laos, check the current security situation with government travel advisories and travellers' newsgroups on the Internet (see p.368). Many areas of Laos were very heavily bombed during the Vietnam War and, away from the main tourist areas, there is a real danger of stepping on unexploded ordnance and land mines. Always stick to well-trodden paths, and pay attention to warning signs.

Main attractions

● **Louang Phabang.** The former Lao capital is the most elegant and attractive city in the country, an almost village-like place whose riverbanks and cobblestoned lanes are lined with the graceful gilded spires of dozens of Buddhist temples. Other highlights include the Royal Palace Museum, which was home to the Lao royal family right up until their exile in 1975; the markets; and the view of the city from the north bank of the Mekong river. The city is stacked full of guesthouses, and there are waterfalls and caves within day-tripping distance.

● The **slow boat down the Mekong** from Houayxai to Louang Phabang. Despite the obvious drawbacks – the trip takes two days and the boats are

LAOS

0   200 km

CHINA

Phongsali

Mengla

MYANMAR (BURMA)

Muang Sing

Boten

VIETNAM

Oudomxai

HANOI

Louang Namtha

Nong Khiaw

Xam Nua

Houayxai

Chiang Khong

Pakbeng

Mekong

Viang Thong

Gulf of Tonkin

Xainyabouli

Louang Phabang

Phonsavan

Plain of Jars

Mekong

Vang Viang

Vinh

Kaew Nua Pass

VIENTIANE

Lak Xao

Nong Khai

Udon Thani

Nakhon Phanom

Thakhek

Mahaxai

Mekong

Xepon

Lao Bao Pass

Hué

Mukdahan

Savannakhet

THAILAND

Salavan

Ubon Ratchathani

Pakxe

Chong Mek

Wat Phou

Attapu

Mekong

Don Kong

CAMBODIA

One week
- Louang Phabang–Vang Viang–Vientiane.
- Houayxai–Louang Phabang.
- Pakxe–Wat Phou–Si Phan Don–Pakxe.
- Pakxe–Wat Phou–Attapu–Pakxe.

Two weeks
- Houayxai–Muang Sing–Louang Phabang–Vang Viang–Vientiane.

Four weeks
- Houayxai–Muang Sing–Louang Phabang–Vang Viang Vientiane–Thakhek–Savannakhet–Pakxe Wat Phou–Attapu–Si Phan Don.

Mean Temperatures (°C) and Rainfall (mm)

Average daily temperatures (maximum and minimum°C) and monthly rainfall (mm)

	Jan	Feb	Mar	Apr	May	June	July	Aug	Sept	Oct	Nov	Dec
Vientiane												
max °C	28	30	33	34	32	32	31	31	31	31	29	28
min °C	14	17	19	23	23	24	24	24	24	21	18	16
rainfall mm	5	15	38	99	267	302	267	292	302	109	15	3
Louang Phabang												
max °C	28	32	34	36	35	34	32	32	33	32	29	27
min °C	13	14	17	21	23	23	23	23	23	21	18	15
rainfall mm	15	18	31	109	163	155	231	300	165	79	31	13

designed to carry cargo, not passengers – this continues to be one of the most popular journeys in Laos, chiefly because of the fine river scenery and glimpses of traditional rural Southeast Asian life, and because Houayxai is a designated border crossing point with Thailand.

● **Vientiane**. The Lao capital is surprisingly gentle, and though lacking sights gives a pleasant introduction to the country. Make the most of its eateries, as the city serves the best food in the country – its bakeries, fruit-juice bars, Lao, Thai and Indian restaurants are a world away from those in other parts of Laos.

● **The ruins of Wat Phou**. This seventh-century temple, built by the ancient Khmers in similar style to their temples at Angkor in Cambodia, sits in a gloriously lush river valley near Pakxe, surrounded by forested mountain peaks. It's an atmospheric place, with many of the sculptures and walls half-buried, but also plenty of intact Hindu and Buddhist carvings.

● **Muang Sing**. This remote northwest town is mainly of interest for its population of hill tribespeople, who trade at the now rather overtouristed morning market. You can arrange informal treks out

to hill-tribe villages from here, but many travellers come to Muang Sing for the opium, which is grown and smoked by local tribespeople.

● The **Plain of Jars**. Drawing its name from the hundreds of mysterious two-thousand-year-old stone funerary urns that lie scattered across the uplands of Xieng Khuang, the Plain of Jars is best appreciated from the air. Flying in from Vientiane gives you a gripping view of the plain's dramatic karst scenery and some of the most scarred landscape in Laos – the result of relentless bombing, mostly by the Americans, in the 1964–73 war. Ground-level tours across the plain leave from nearby Phonsavan, but the history of the jars is more interesting than the urns themselves, so it's not worth making a special effort to get here.

Also recommended

● The sleepy little riverside town of **Vang Viang**. Set in a spectacular landscape of limestone karst, this is a friendly place with decent guesthouses, interesting caves nearby and the chance to soak up the scenery while floating downriver in a huge inner tube.

- The tiny island of **Don Kong**, one of the Si Phan Don islands in the far southern stretch of the Mekong River. As there are only two settlements on the island and hardly any traffic, renting a bicycle is the best way to absorb traditional village life here, which has remained almost unchanged for hundreds of years.

- **Attapu**. Spend a night or two in this remote "garden city", where coconut palms and banana trees shade spacious wooden houses with capacious balconies, high on stilts. The journey there, along the scenic Xe Kong River, is a gem too.

- Sweating out all your toxins and other impurities with a **herbal sauna and traditional massage** at the Buddhist monastery of Wat Sok Pa Louang in Vientiane. In between sessions, you can sip restorative teas brewed from carambola, tamarind, eucalyptus and citrus leaves.

Routes in and out

Most international flights arrive in Vientiane, via Bangkok, though it's also possible to fly to Louang Phabang from the northern Thai city of Chiang Mai. Many travellers arrive overland from Thailand, most commonly at the Nong Khai/Vientiane crossing. There are four other land crossings from Thailand, two from Vietnam, and one from China, but pay close attention to visa requirements, which differ at every entry point.

Itineraries

One week

- Buy an open-jaw plane ticket that takes you into Louang Phabang and out of Vientiane. Or fly into Louang Phabang and cross back into Thailand by road at Vientiane. Spend three days in Louang Phabang, before heading south to the capital, stopping for a couple of nights en route in Vang Viang.

- Coming from Thailand, cross the border at Chiang Khong and take the two-day boat from Houayxai down to Louang Phabang. Spend the rest of your stay based in this historic city, before flying out.

- Cross the border from Thailand via Chong Mek to the southern Lao town of Pakxe, where you should stay long enough to explore the nearby ruins of Wat Phou before venturing either south down to Si Phan Don, or east to Attapu. Return to Thailand via Pakxe.

Two weeks

- Beginning at Houayxai, make a clockwise loop around the northwest, travelling by river and road via Muang Sing, where you should spend a couple of days, before moving on to Louang Phabang for four days. Head south for a couple of nights in Vang Viang and then on to Vientiane.

Four weeks

- Starting at Houayxai, do a clockwise loop around the northwest, travelling by river and road via Muang Sing, where you should spend a couple of days, before moving on to Louang Phabang for a few days. Head south for a couple of nights in Vang Viang and then on to Vientiane for two or three days. From the capital, continue travelling south, breaking your journey first in Thakhek for a side trip to the atmospheric Mahaxai caves, then in the attractive southern city of Savannakhet. Continue down to Pakxe and Wat Phou, then to Attapu and on to Si Phan Don, before exiting Laos at the Thai border near Pakxe, or at the Vietnamese border east of Savannakhet.

Laos online

Internet Travel Guide Ⓦ*www. pmgeiser.ch/laos/*A general introduction to the country, plus pages on sights, visas, forthcoming events and transport options.

Rocco Photography Ⓦ*www. roccophotography.com* Inspiring pictures of people and places in Laos.

The Vientiane Times Ⓦ*www. vientianetimes.com* The digital version of Laos's only English-language newspaper features headline stories as well as interesting links.

Visit Laos Ⓦ*visit-laos.com* Recommended general Laos travel site, with handy planning advice, a roundup of destination highlights, travelogues and links.

Malaysia

Capital: Kuala Lumpur
Population: 22 million
Language: Malay
Currency: Ringgit (RM), aka Malaysian dollar (M$)
Main religion: Islam, with significant Buddhist, Hindu and Christian minorities
Climate: Tropical
Best time to go: March–July (December–February for peninsular west coast)
Minimum daily budget: US$15/£10

The history of Malaysia is dominated by a succession of Portuguese, Dutch and British colonists, which means that the country's major sights tend to be rather low-key and quaintly European. Instead, the real interest comes from contemporary Malaysia's remarkably heterogeneous population, half of whom are Malays (whose culture originated in Indonesian Sumatra), a third ethnic Chinese, a tenth Indians (from the subcontinent) and seven percent indigenous tribal people. This dynamic mix gives great energy to the daily stuff of everyday life in Malaysia, with huge variety in everything from food to festivals, places of worship to dress.

An ideal destination for first-time overlanders, Peninsular Malaysia has good transport connections with neighbouring Thailand, Singapore and Sumatra, and a well-developed tourist infrastructure. English is widely spoken, local transport is efficient, and the standard of living is among the highest in Southeast Asia. The peninsula's coast is graced with some of the most idyllic white-sand beaches in the region and plenty of rewarding offshore reefs, and chunks of inland jungle are accessible to hikers via well-maintained national park trails and animal hides.

Six hundred kilometres east across the South China Sea from the peninsula, the East Malaysian states of Sarawak and Sabah offer a more adventurous – and more expensive – experience. They share the huge, thickly forested island of Borneo with Indonesia's Kalimantan province and the tiny sultanate of Brunei, and are only accessible from Peninsular Malaysia by plane. Once there, travel into the interior is mainly by river, particularly if you want to visit the longhouses – traditional communal homes – of the tribal peoples, which usually stand in a remote jungle clearing beside the riverbank. Staying in a longhouse is a highlight of trips to East Malaysia, as are jungle hikes. Most travellers to Sabah attempt a climb up the fearsomely high Gunung Kinabalu.

Main attractions

● The **beaches**. Peninsular Malaysia's beaches compare well with those found in southern Thailand. The biggest, most developed resorts are on the beautiful islands of Pulau Langkawi and Pulau Tioman, but backpackers generally prefer

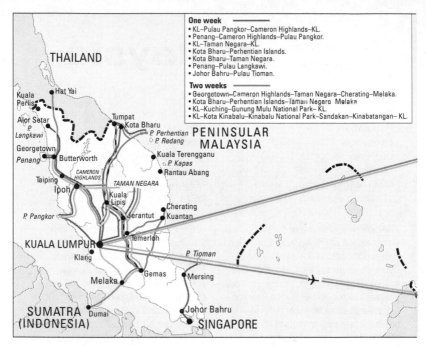

One week ━━━━━
• KL–Pulau Pangkor–Cameron Highlands–KL.
• Penang–Cameron Highlands–Pulau Pangkor.
• KL–Taman Negara–KL.
• Kota Bharu–Perhentian Islands.
• Kota Bharu–Taman Negara.
• Penang–Pulau Langkawi.
• Johor Bahru–Pulau Tioman.

Two weeks ━━━━━
• Georgetown–Cameron Highlands–Taman Negara–Cherating–Melaka.
• Kota Bharu–Perhentian Islands–Taman Negara–Melaka.
• KL–Kuching–Gunung Mulu National Park–KL.
• KL–Kota Kinabalu–Kinabalu National Park–Sandakan–Kinabatangan–KL.

the cheaper, more chilled-out Perhentian Islands, which are also great for snorkelling; the bay at Cherating, where you stay in village-style huts on stilts; and the tiny Pulau Kapas. Your best bet for a beach break from the capital is Pulau Pangkor, a six-hour journey from KL.

● **Taman Negara National Park.** The peninsula's biggest and most popular national park offers something for most outdoor enthusiasts. There's a spectacular canopy walkway through the tree tops, and plenty of day-hikes on well-marked trails. You could spend a night in a hide trying to spot elephants and leopards, or opt to do the guided nine-day trek through the park to the summit of 2187-metre-high Gunung Tahan, the peninsula's highest peak.

● The **Cameron Highlands.** Tea plantations, colonial residences and, above all, the chance to cool down draw

scores of travellers to the hill station here. The rolling green fields are dotted with farms and country cottages, and there are plenty of gentle walking trails through this rather quaint pastoral idyll.

● **Kuala Lumpur.** There's nothing particularly appealing about the humid, crowded, polluted Malaysian capital, Kuala Lumpur, though you'll probably find yourself passing through at some point. The variety of architectural styles is intriguing – from traditional Chinese temples through to the extraordinary Anglo-Indian Railway Station and the ultra-ambitious 88-storey Petronas Towers, currently the tallest building in the world. At the Forest Institute of Malaysia, on the outskirts of the city, you can stroll through the tree tops on a Taman-Negara-style walkway that gives you elevated views of the skyscrapered skyline.

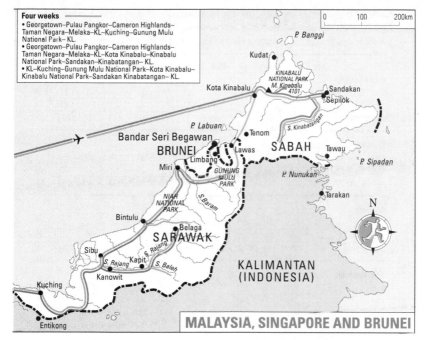

Four weeks
• Georgetown–Pulau Pangkor–Cameron Highlands–
Taman Negara–Melaka–KL–Kuching–Gunung Mulu
National Park– KL.
• Georgetown–Pulau Pangkor–Cameron Highlands–
Taman Negara–Melaka–KL–Kota Kinabalu–Kinabalu
National Park–Sandakan–Kinabatangan– KL.
• KL–Kuching–Gunung Mulu National Park–Kota Kinabalu–
Kinabalu National Park–Sandakan Kinabatangan– KL.

0   100   200km

P. Banggi

Kudat

KINABALU
NATIONAL PARK
M. Kinabalu
4101

Kota Kinabalu

Sandakan
Sepilok

P. Labuan

Tenom

S. Kinabatangan

Bandar Seri Begawan

BRUNEI

Lawas

SABAH

Tawau

Miri

Limbang

GUNUNG
MULU
PARK

P. Nunukan

P. Sipadan

NIAH
NATIONAL
PARK

S. Baram

Tarakan

Bintulu

Belaga

SARAWAK

KALIMANTAN
(INDONESIA)

Sibu

S. Rajang

Kapit

S. Rajang

S. Baleh

Kanowit

N

Kuching

Entikong

MALAYSIA, SINGAPORE AND BRUNEI

● **Georgetown**. Despite being
Malaysia's second largest city, this former British trading post on the island of
Penang still exudes great historic charm.
The elegant old European-style churches, forts and warehouses contrast
appealingly with the atmospheric traditional shuttered shophouses of the local
Chinese merchants.

● **Sarawak**. Sarawak's most outstanding attractions are its river systems and
the chance to travel by longboat along
these jungle waterways, staying in tribal
longhouses along the way. Gunung
Mulu National Park conserves a dramatic landscape of limestone pinnacles and
the largest limestone cave system in the
world, with heaps of hiking and climbing
potential. The state capital, Kuching, is
an appealing old waterside colonial outpost, home to a classy ethnographic
museum.

● **Sabah**. At 4101m, Gunung Kinabalu,
in Kinabalu National Park, is Sabah's
biggest draw; its summit is accessible to
any reasonably fit hiker willing to undertake the day-and-a-half's climb up.
Sabah's other highlights are the Sepilok
Orang-Utan Rehabilitation Centre, where
you can watch the baby orang-utans
learning to swing and swagger, and the
forests around the Kinabatangan river,
famous for their proboscis monkeys.

Also
recommended

● Riding the **jungle railway**. If you have
plenty of time, it's worth travelling the
entire length of this fourteen-hour route,
which starts in Gemas, near Melaka,
and meanders through the mountainous
landscapes of the peninsula's scenic
jungle interior all the way up to Kota

Mean Temperatures (°C) and Rainfall (mm)

Average daily temperatures (maximum and minimum°C) and monthly rainfall (mm)

	Jan	Feb	Mar	Apr	May	June	July	Aug	Sept	Oct	Nov	Dec
Kuala Lumpur												
max °C	32	33	33	33	33	32	32	32	32	32	31	31
min °C	22	22	23	23	23	23	23	23	23	23	23	23
rainfall mm	159	154	223	276	182	119	120	133	173	258	263	223
Mersing												
max °C	28	29	30	31	32	31	31	31	31	31	29	28
min °C	23	23	23	23	23	23	22	22	22	23	23	23
rainfall mm	319	153	141	120	149	145	170	173	177	207	359	635
Kuching												
max °C	30	30	31	32	33	33	32	33	32	32	31	31
min °C	23	23	23	23	23	23	23	23	23	23	23	23
rainfall mm	683	522	339	286	253	199	199	211	271	326	343	465
Kota Kinabalu												
max °C	30	30	31	32	32	31	31	31	31	31	31	31
min °C	23	23	23	24	24	24	24	24	23	23	23	23
rainfall mm	133	63	71	124	218	311	277	256	314	334	296	241

Bharu. But most people break the journey at Jerantut, which is three hours from Gemas and convenient for Taman Negara National Park.

● **Melaka**. This cosmopolitan old port town wears its history on its sleeve, with self-consciously prettified churches and town squares from its days under Portuguese and then Dutch colonial rule. More interesting, for Western visitors at least, are the 300-year-old ancestral homes and temples of the Peranakan, the name given to the descendants of the Chinese merchants who settled here and married local Malay women. The finest Peranakan homes were lavishly furnished with the most exquisite artefacts from China, Europe and Malaysia; some are still inhabited by family members and open for the public to visit. Peranakan culture continues to thrive on the peninsula, and Melaka is a great place to sample

Peranakan cuisine, known for its distinctive blending of sour sauces and coconut milk.

● **Turtle-watching at Rantau Abang**. Every year, from May through to September, a few giant four-hundred-kilogram leatherback turtles lumber ashore here, the beach where they themselves were born, to lay their eggs. Leatherbacks are an endangered species now, so the whole event is supervised by national park rangers, but it's such a fine sight that local guesthouse managers wake up tourists in the middle of the night as soon as a turtle's been spotted in the area.

● **Kota Bharu**. Located close to the Thai border, this small town is renowned for its cultural traditions and makes an interesting place to watch shadow-puppet plays and traditional sports like top-spinning. The town's night market is one of the best in the country, serving everything from freshly barbecued chicken in coconut sauce to fried purple rice and sugar-cane juice.

Routes in and out

Malaysia's main international airport is near Kuala Lumpur, but some travellers fly in or out of Singapore, which is a short bus ride from the southern Malaysian city of Johor Bahru. Penang airport runs planes to and from Thailand and Indonesia. Peninsular Malaysia has several land border crossings with Thailand, with buses and trains connecting the cities and tourist spots of the two countries. There are good boat connections between west-coast Peninsular Malaysia and the Indonesian island of Sumatra. Most people fly to Sabah and Sarawak from KL or Singapore, but you can also cross overland from Brunei and Indonesian Kalimantan.

Itineraries

One week
● Stay just one night in Kuala Lumpur, then head out to Pulau Pangkor for three or four days on the beach before returning to the capital by way of a night or two in the Cameron Highlands.

● Spend one or two nights in Penang, then a couple of days in the Cameron Highlands before chilling out for the rest of your trip on the beaches of Pulau Pangkor.

● Aim to spend most of your week in Taman Negara National Park, using KL only for the first and last night.

● Arriving overland from Thailand, spend a night or two in Kota Bharu before either going out to the Perhentian Islands or heading south, perhaps via the Jungle Railway, to Taman Negara National Park.

● Stay the whole week on the beach. On the west coast, Pulau Langkawi is handy for anyone arriving in Malaysia via Penang, while Pulau Pangkor is feasibly close to Kuala Lumpur. On the east coast, the Perhentian Islands are close to Kota Bharu and the Thai border, while Pulau Tioman is near Johor Bahru and Singapore.

Two weeks
● Arriving from Thailand and overlanding through Malaysia to Sumatra, you could begin on the west coast with three days in Georgetown, then head up into the Cameron Highlands for two or three days. Spend the next four days in Taman Negara National Park before crossing over to the east coast and passing the next three or four days on the beach at Cherating. Make your final stop Melaka, from where boats run to Dumai in Sumatra.

● The alternative route from Thailand to Sumatra (or vice versa) follows more of an east-coast itinerary, stopping at Kota Bharu for a couple of nights before going out to the Perhentian Islands for the next three or four days. Then head south, perhaps via the Jungle Railway, for four or five days in Taman Negara National Park and across to Melaka for boats to Dumai.

● After two nights in Kuala Lumpur, fly to Kuching for a day or two. Spend the next few days exploring the rivers and staying in a longhouse, before rounding off with a good four- or five-day session in Gunung Mulu National Park.

● Spend two nights in Kuala Lumpur, then fly to Kota Kinabalu, the capital of Sabah, for a couple of days. Use the next four or five days to explore Kinabalu National Park before striking east to Sandakan. Stay here for at least two nights, visiting the nearby Orang-Utan Centre and organizing your next two days at one of the forest lodges in Kinabatangan. Fly back to KL.

Four weeks

● Begin on the Peninsular west coast with three days in Georgetown, followed by a nice long session on the beaches of Pulau Pangkor. Spend a few days in the Cameron Highlands, then do a good stint in Taman Negara National Park, leaving via the Jungle Railway and spending a couple of days in Melaka and then another two or three in KL. From the capital, fly out to Sarawak or Sabah, and spend the next fourteen days exploring, as per the two-week itineraries above.

● Do a serious tour of East Malaysian Borneo, exploring Sarawak for the first fortnight, then continuing overland via Brunei into Sabah for the second half of the trip.

Malaysia online

Fascinating Malaysia Ⓦ*www. fascinatingmalaysia.com* Recent tourism and travel news, an interesting emphasis on eco-travel, plus standard introductions to the country and its culture.

Interknowledge: Malaysia Ⓦ*www.interknowledge.com/malaysia* The official site of the New York Malaysian tourist board offers an in-depth look at lots of interesting aspects of the country, including life in a long-house, the Malaysian cultural mix, and overnighting in Taman Negara. Recommended.

The Star Ⓦ*www.thestar.com.my* Find out what's happening in Malaysia with this online version of one of Malaysia's English-language dailies.

Nepal

Capital: Kathmandu	**Best time to go**: Autumn (Oct &
Population: 24 million	Nov) and spring (Feb to mid-April)
Language: Nepali, with a few	**Minimum daily budget**: $10/£7,
dozen other languages and dialects	though organized treks and
Currency: Rupee (Rs)	adventure sports add significantly to
Religion: Hindu and Buddhist	the cost
Climate: Monsoonal	

Sandwiched between the enormous land masses of Tibet and India, Nepal is a relatively small country, but what it lacks in size it more than makes up for in dramatic scenery and the vast range of experiences on offer. Nepal contains a huge stretch of the Himalayas, the highest mountain range in the world, as well as dozens of equally dramatic peaks. Trekking is the main draw, but other attractions include Kathmandu, whose very name conjures up images of mountains and mysticism; the wildlife reserves of the lowland jungles in the south; Buddhist and Hindu temples and festivals; and white-water rafting. Many visitors also come in pursuit of bodily calm and spiritual truth, and Nepal has plenty of practitioners of massage, Ayurvedic and Tibetan medicine and astrology, plus courses in meditation and yoga.

Though ever-expanding tourism provides an important source of foreign exchange, Nepal remains one of the poorest countries in the world, facing not just a population explosion but also enormous environmental degradation. Tourism has added to the problems, especially the deforestation of much-tramped treks; visitors should therefore do what they can to avoid further damage to the fragile mountain eco-system.

Main attractions

● **Kathmandu**. Nepal's bustling, sprawling capital city is noisy, traffic-clogged and appallingly polluted, but also vibrant, excellent for shopping and eating and a great place to arrange trips out into the wilderness. Durbar Square, in the heart of the city, is the location of innumerable temples and ancient monuments, most notably the Old Royal Palace and the Kumari Chowk; the latter is the home of Nepal's own living goddess, the Kumari, a prepubescent girl worshipped as the living incarnation of the Hindu goddess Durga. The other obligatory sight, on a hill west of the centre, is the huge Buddhist stupa at Swayambunath, from where the stylized eyes of the Buddha gaze out in all directions upon the world. There are great views over the city from here, and the site draws an endless stream of pilgrims – one act of worship here is said to carry 13 billion times more merit than elsewhere.

● The **Kathmandu valley**. Some of the best-preserved historic buildings and

NEPAL

HIMALAYA

ANNAPURNA
CONSERVATION
AREA

Annapurna
(8091m) ▲

BARDIA
NATIONAL
PARK

Kali Gandaki

Pokhara

Kali Gandaki

Lumbini

I N D I A

One week
- Kathmandu–Kathmandu valley–Dhulikhel/Nagarkot.
- Kathmandu–Pokhara.
- Kathmandu–Chitwan.

Two weeks
- Kathmandu–Helambu trek–Trisuli river rafting–Chitwan National Park.
- Kathmandu–Langtang trek.
- Kathmandu–Pokhara trek.

Four weeks
- Kathmandu–Pokhara–Annapurna circuit.
- Kathmandu–Everest trek.
- Kathmandu–Langtang trek–Pokhara–Trisuli river rafting–Chitwan–Lumbini.

temples in the area are found in the ancient city of Bhaktapur, which has its own Durbar Square, featuring the five-storey Nyatapola pagoda. Patan, just south of Kathmandu, is the valley's most Buddhist city, with a calmer, less frantic feel than elsewhere; there's yet another Durbar Square here, with a fine Royal Palace dating from the seventeenth century and a number of temples. A trip out

to the valley rim at Shivapuri or Jamacho is rewarded with some fine views of the Himalayas. Easily accessible from Kathmandu, although strictly speaking outside the valley itself, are Nagarkot and Dhulikel, both great excursions for even better mountain views, and excellent bases for treks.

● **Pokhara** One of the most popular destinations in Nepal, the town is excel-

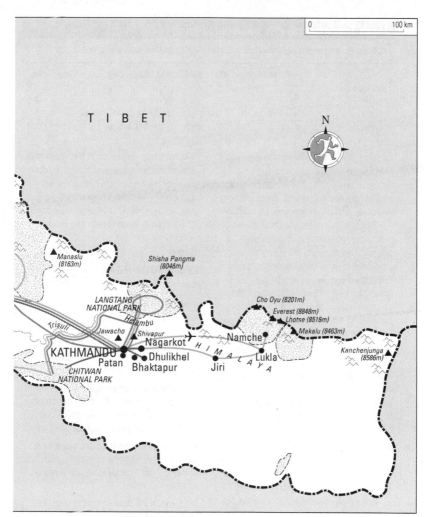

lent for simply relaxing amid great scenery and in plenty of comfort; the views of the unforgettable Machhapuchhre (or "fish-tail peak"), the Annapurna mountain and Manaslu ranges are stunning. There are also plenty of local excursions, including hikes to the mountain viewpoint of Sarangkot or up to the World Peace Pagoda, on a ridge overlooking pretty Phewa lake.

● **Trekking.** Nepal has an enormous variety of treks on offer, varying in length and difficulty; some have comfortable accommodation all along the way, while others require you to be totally self-reliant. It's worth researching the options, especially if you want to get away from the most popular routes. The three-week Annapurna circuit involves climbing up to a heady 5380m, passing

Mean Temperatures (°C) and Rainfall (mm)

Average daily temperatures (maximum and minimum°C) and monthly rainfall (mm)

	Jan	Feb	Mar	Apr	May	June	July	Aug	Sept	Oct	Nov	Dec
Kathmandu												
max °C	18	19	25	28	30	29	29	28	28	27	23	19
min °C	2	4	7	12	16	19	20	20	19	13	7	3
rainfall mm	15	41	23	58	122	246	373	345	155	38	8	3

through gloriously diverse scenery; you'll need to be reasonably fit to tackle it, though there's plenty of accommodation and eating places serving Western food en route, and other trekkers for company. The ten-day Jomosom trek is also highly commercialized, though this doesn't detract from the many small, ethnically diverse villages along the route. **Everest treks**, which get you close to the world's tallest peak, are very strenuous, the cold and high altitude being serious concerns; you'll need to allow three or four weeks to do one of these, unless you fly into or out of Lukla, partway along the route. Those with less time or inclination may want to consider the three- to five-day Royal Trek from Pokhara, or spending seven to twelve days on the Langtang trek closer to Kathmandu.

● **Chitwan National Park**. On the plains in the far south of the country, the park is the jungle home of the famed Bengal tiger and the Indian rhinoceros, as well as plenty of deer and wild oxen, a couple of species of crocodile and over 450 bird species – among other creatures. Elephant rides, jeep tours, canoe trips and walks are all available, though Chitwan's fame and accessibility mean that it can be hard to escape the crowds.

● **White-water rafting** and **kayaking**. Nepal's picturesque rivers offer both beginners and the more advanced plenty of opportunities to try these activities.

Two- or three-day trips on the Trisuli river west of Kathmandu, and three- or four-day excursions out of Pokhara or the upper Kali Gandaki are among the most popular. Agents who arrange trips can be found in both Kathmandu and Pokhara.

Also recommended

● **Mountain flights**. On these excursions, which leave daily from Kathmandu between May and September, you pass just 25km from Everest and get to eyeball a couple of dozen of the world's highest peaks.

● The **Bardia National Park**. In the west of the country, the park doesn't have as many rhinos as Chitwan, but offers a greater chance of spotting tigers.

● **Courses in meditation, yoga or Nepali**. The Kathmandu valley, and to a lesser extent Pokhara, are ideal places to enrol yourself.

● **Lumbini**. A place of pilgrimage for devotees from across the globe, the spot where Buddha was born in 543 BC has ancient archeological monuments as well as modern Tibetan and Theravadan monasteries.

● **Festivals**. Nepalese festivals are exuberant, colourful events. The calendar is dotted with celebrations, perhaps the most colourful and accessible being the Indra Jatra festival, an eight-day confection of music, dance and drama held in

August/September in Kathmandu, when the living goddess, the Kumari, is towed in a chariot through the city.

● **Mountain-biking**. Organized tours, geared to any level of fitness and ability, provide all equipment and accommodation – and a lift if you get tired. Kathmandu and Pokhara are the main centres to arrange trips.

Routes in and out

Kathmandu's international airport is served by several major carriers. There are a handful of overland routes from India, arriving into Sonauli (convenient if you're starting from Delhi), Birganj (convenient from Calcutta and Patna) and Kakarbhitta (convenient from Darjeeling). The crossing from Tibet is between Zhangmu and Kodari; however, only tour groups are allowed into Tibet via this route (though independent travellers can leave Tibet this way) – check the situation at the time you want to travel.

Itineraries

If you're planning to trek at high altitude, remember to allow time to acclimatize both before and during your trek (see p.306).

One week
● Explore Kathmandu and the Kathmandu valley, with excursions to Nagarkot or Dhulikel.

● Spend about two or three days in Kathmandu and the Kathmandu valley, then use the rest of the time to visit either Pokhara or Chitwan National Park, or to do a short rafting trip or trek.

Two weeks
● Get around Kathmandu and the Kathmandu valley, then try a short rafting trip and a short trek. If you don't hang about, you could even fit in a couple of days at Royal Chitwan National Park.

● Explore Kathmandu and then go on the Langthang trek.

● Visit Kathmandu and Pokhara, then undertake a short trek out of Pokhara.

Four weeks
With this length of stay, the options really open up, the essential choice being between alloting all your time to one of the longer treks or spending shorter amounts of time on trekking, rafting, sightseeing and perhaps meditation or yoga.

● Spend three or days each in Kathmandu and Pokhara, then do a long trek, such as the Annapurna circuit.

● Undertake the Jiri Walk-In to Everest, which takes just under four weeks; you'll have time for a day in Kathmandu at the start and end of the trek.

● Spend about a week acclimatizing in Kathmandu and taking short hikes around the valley, then tackle the Everest trek, flying in to Lukla.

● After a few days in Kathmandu and the Kathmandu valley, do the Langtang trek (ten to twelve days) and then head to Pokhara for a few more days. Take a rafting trip down the Trisuli, continue with a visit to the Royal Chitwan National Park and finish up in Lumbini.

Nepal online

Kathmandu Environmental Education Project Ⓦ*www.keepnepal.org* Excellent site for tourist information, with brilliant links to other environmental organizations and plenty of good ideas about how to visit Nepal without doing more harm than good.

International Porter Protection Group
Ⓦ*www.ippg.net* Recently organized
group campaigning for a safe and fair
deal for porters who work in the trekking
business. Their thought-provoking Web
site has plenty of sad examples of what
can go wrong for the people who carry
the loads.

Information About Mount Everest
Ⓦ*www.mteverest.com* Though basic to
look at, this site has dozens of excellent
links to anything you'll ever want to
know about the highest mountain in the
world and the human fascination with it.

Annapurna Circuit by David Metsky
Ⓦ*www.cs.dartmouth.edu/whites/nepal/*
Detailed account of the author's trek
around the Annapurna Circuit, with
scores of excellent pictures.

**Dharmapala Centre – School of
Thangkha Painting**
Ⓦ*www.bremen.de/info/nepal/* Visitors to
Kathmandu enjoy Tibetan art and artefacts but are frustrated by its complexity
and inaccessibility. This English/German
site is a revelation, beautifully illustrating
and explaining over two hundred
Tibetan *thangkha*s – religious paintings
on cloth – and giving details of how to
locate the Dharmapala Centre and its
workshops in Kathmandu.

Pakistan

Capital: Islamabad

Population: 131 million

Language: Urdu is the official language, though largely used as a second language alongside other native tongues, including Punjabi, Sindhi, Pashto and Baluchi

Currency: Pakistani Rupee (Rs)

Religion: Most of the population are Muslim, with small Christian, Hindu, Sikh and Parsee minorities

Climate: There are three climatic zones: dry (which covers most of the country), humid subtropical (from Lahore to Peshawar) and highland (the climate of the northern mountains).

Best time to go: The south is best from November to March, when it is cooler; the north is best from April to October (main trekking season June–Sept), which avoids the harshest winter snows

Minimum daily budget: $10/£7

Relatively few tourists make it to Pakistan, but those that do generally describe it as either being like Nepal without the crowds or like India without the hassles. The country has many attractions, including spectacular mountain and desert landscapes, plus ancient ruins and fabulous mosques, the legacy of prehistoric civilizations and successive Persian, Arab, Mogul and Sikh empires. Travellers generally head for the north, either using the Karakoram Highway and its offshoots, or visiting Peshawar, the Khyber Pass and Chitral. Hiking and trekking are the most popular activities and there are plenty of short walks as well as longer expeditions to suit all levels of fitness and aspiration.

Although the tourist industry in Pakistan is embryonic, there's a fair choice of hotels, especially in towns and cities, but electricity and water supplies can be unreliable. Trains and buses are generally slow, and can be uncomfortable. English is spoken by most educated Pakistanis, and foreigners who respect the local culture are warmly welcomed as honoured guests. Women should dress appropriately for a Muslim country, in long loose clothes. During Ramadan, the Islamic month of fasting, eating, drinking and smoking is banned during daylight hours; many restaurants are closed, offices work shorter hours and tempers can get rather frayed.

Some parts of Pakistan are dangerous, most notably the tribal areas of the Northwest Frontier province and Baluchistan, plus rural areas of Punjab. For many years rural Sind and even Karachi were considered unsafe, although the situation is very variable. Travellers planning to visit Pakistan should check the current situation with their own government advisory body before they go (see p.365) and, once in the country, with local tourist offices and/or the police.

Main attractions

● **Islamabad** and **Rawalpindi**. Built in the 1960s, Islamabad, Pakistan's carefully planned capital, is laid out on a grid design, without the chaos (and the character) usually associated with Asian cities. Its Faisal Masjid, one of the largest mosques in the world, is worth a visit, as are the nearby Margalla hills, which offer opportunities for strolls and longer treks. Just 15km away, the traditional city of Rawalpindi has both chaos and character aplenty and is expanding fast. Rajah Bazaar, the commercial heart of its old market area, is a maze of tiny alleyways lined with shops and work-

shops of every type. Although the two cities have little to detain visitors for long, they do make a convenient gateway to Pakistan if you're visiting the north.

● **Northern Pakistan.** The meeting point of the Himalaya, Karakoram and Hindu Kush mountain ranges, the region offers some of the best trekking in the world, ranging from gentle day-long strolls to extremely strenuous affairs lasting several weeks and involving glac-

One week
• Lahore–Peshawar–Darra–Khyber Pass.
• Islamabad–Gilgit.
• Islamabad–Skardu.

Two weeks
• Islamabad–Gilgit–Chitral–Peshawar.

Four weeks
• Lahore–Uch Sharif–Cholistan desert–Moenjo Daro–Peshawar–Chitral–Gilgit–Islamabad/Rawalpindi.
• Baltoro glacier trek.
• Gilgit–Hunza/Nagar–Peshawar–Lahore.

The accession of Jammu and Kashmir to Pakistan or India remains to be decided.

PAKISTAN

Mean Temperatures (°C) and Rainfall (mm)

Average daily temperatures (maximum and minimum°C) and monthly rainfall (mm)

	Jan	Feb	Mar	Apr	May	June	July	Aug	Sept	Oct	Nov	Dec
Islamabad												
max °C	16	19	24	31	37	40	36	34	34	32	28	20
min °C	2	6	10	15	21	25	25	24	21	15	9	3
rainfall mm	64	64	81	42	23	55	233	258	85	21	12	23

iers, fast-flowing rivers and passes 5500m up. Trekking centres are Shigar near Skardu, Gilgit, Chitral and, further afield, the Hunza, Nagar and nearby valleys. As the trekking infrastructure is much less developed than in Nepal, the need for self-sufficiency is far greater, though the organized treks now offered by some companies are a viable alternative to going it totally alone.

● **Peshawar**. Though it's long had a reputation as a frontier town, Peshawar these days is a thriving, expanding city. The buzz and excitement of the bazaars of the Old City remain, though, offering days of exotic sights, smells and sounds in the twisting alleyways and ancient markets. A popular excursion from Peshawar is 40km south to the village of Darra Adam Khel (usually just called Darra), centre of arms manufacture and trading in the region. Here, gunsmiths' shops line the road, and you'll inevitably be invited to test-fire home-made imitation Kalashnikovs built with only the most basic of equipment.

● The **Khyber Pass**. In Western minds, the pass still has almost mystical status, symbolizing a time when travellers were real adventurers. Travel there by road or steam train from Peshawar, and gaze down into Afghanistan through the barren, desolate hills.

● **Lahore**. The most worthwhile of Pakistan's cities, Lahore has numerous fine examples of Mogul architecture, most famously the Badshahi mosque,

Lahore Fort, Shalimar Gardens and Jahangir's tomb. A walk through the atmospheric alleyways of the Old City takes in mosques, bazaars and markets, while the Lahore Museum is a treasure trove of items from throughout Pakistan's history.

● The **Karakoram Highway**, linking Islamabad with Kashgar in China (see p.24) via the Khunjerab Pass. To travel along this 1300-kilometre-long road is to experience some of the most spellbinding scenery in the world, as the highway weaves between towering mountains, over high passes, beside thundering rivers and along apparently impenetrable valleys. With a visa for China and a double-entry Pakistan visa, you could travel the full length of the highway and spend a few days sightseeing in Kashgar to recover.

● **Moenjo Daro**. The Indus Valley civilization, at its peak four thousand years ago, was centred here; a great deal remains of the original city, much of it brilliantly preserved and well restored.

Also recommended

● The tombs at **Uch Sharif**. These are some of the most beautiful – albeit partially ruined – tombs in the country. Fabulously decorated with ancient tile mosaics that gleam in the sun, the tombs, the oldest of which is thought to

date from the tenth century, are lasting memorials to the prominent figures of Sufi Islam who are buried here.

● A **camel safari**. Venturing into the Cholistan Desert – Pakistan's largest – this way, you'll visit desert forts built along the ancient trading route across the sands, most famously the eighteenth-century Fort Derawar.

● Watching a **polo match**. Some authorities claim the game was invented in the north of the country, and matches in Pakistan are far more enthusiastic and raucous than in the West. There are plenty of polo grounds across the country, among them the world's highest, 3775m up on the Shandur Pass; it's the venue for the annual highlight, the grudge match between Chitral and Gilgit, played out in July.

● **Flying between Gilgit and Islamabad**. On this route, the plane flies between rather than above the peaks, so you get fantastic views — especially as the pilots are only allowed to fly in fine weather.

● **Taking the road between Gilgit and Chitral**. The two- to three-day journey, crossing the Shandur Pass, is one of the roughest but most impressive in the country, with awesome mountain scenery. The most flexible way to do it is by hiring a jeep, and there are some great spots along the way to camp rough.

Routes in and out

Karachi, Islamabad, Lahore and Peshawar have international airports with worldwide connections. Overland routes link Pakistan with China (via the Karakoram Highway), India (the only crossing is between Wagah on the Pakistani side and Attari on the Indian side) and Iran (the only official crossing is at Taftan, more than 600km west of Quetta). There is only one international passenger-ferry service, which runs weekly between Dubai and Karachi.

Itineraries

Remember that if you are planning a trek at altitude, you need to allow time to acclimatize both before you set off and as you climb higher; failure to do so can be very dangerous (see p.306).

One week
● Explore Lahore for a couple of days and then head north to Peshawar and the Khyber Pass.

● Arriving in Islamabad, hop straight onto a plane for Gilgit or Skardu and the mountains, where you can set off on some trekking.

Two weeks
● Fly from Islamabad to Gilgit and take a short trek, then travel by road across to Chitral, where you can do another short trek. Finally, fly to Peshawar for a couple of days' stay.

Four weeks
● Do a longer trek (for example the Baltoro glacier trek starting in Shigar) or a couple of shorter ones from Gilgit or Skardu; it should be possible to fit in some sightseeing plus a few days in Peshawar and Lahore.

● Instead of trekking, spend a few days seeing Lahore, then head to Uch Sharif for a couple more days. Allow a week to arrange and take a camel trek or jeep safari to the Cholistan Desert. Then spend a couple of days each in Moenjo Daro and Peshawar, a few more in Chitral for the mountain views, head up to Gilgit for more mountain views, and finally take the scenic flight to Islamabad to do some sightseeing in Rawalpindi.

Pakistan online

Robert Matzinger's Cycling the Karakoram Highway
www.kr.tuwien.ac.at/~matzi/travel/kkh/kkh.html Excellent pictures, and a detailed account (in German), of the two-month cycling trip that took Robert and partner from the Punjab to Kashgar.

Dawn – the Internet Edition
dawn.com/herald
The Internet edition of Pakistan's most popular monthly English-language magazine is sparsely illustrated, but has digestible, insightful articles on the news and current preoccupations in Pakistan.

Saher – the Monthly E-zine
www.saher.com Colourful and fun, this Pakistani e-zine covers news, showbiz, fashion, business and science, and also reviews local books, music and restaurants, all in easy-to-read style.

Pakistan Travel Web
www.travel.web.pk Enticing pictures, practical information, lots of background information and a couple of good travel ogues make the site well worth a visit for an overall view of what Pakistan has to offer the visitor.

Philippines

Capital: Manila **Population**: 79 million **Language**: Tagalog **Currency**: Peso (P) **Main religion**: Roman Catholic **Climate**: Tropical	**Best time to go**: November–April for the western half of the archipelago, but avoid the eastern islands between November and January **Minimum daily budget**: $15/£10

The Philippines is an outdoors destination, with world-class – and good-value – diving off many of its 7107 islands, as well as plenty of white-sand beaches and hundreds of hiking trails across its lush volcanic terrain. Because of its Spanish colonial history, which lasted over 300 years, its subsequent half-century as an American colony, and its Catholic heritage, there are fewer indigenous cultural sights here than in Indonesia or Thailand, but this is more than compensated for by the exuberant, easy-going Filipino attitude to life, once summed up as "that rare blend of Asian grace and Latin fire". The Filipinos hold great fiestas – their calendar is packed with religious occasions that are celebrated with pageants, fancy-dress parades, music and dancing in the streets, the inevitable beauty-queen contest, and plenty of beer and spit-roasted pork; foreigners are warmly welcomed at these events and offered characteristic Filipino hospitality. Two of the most theatrical national festivals are Mardi Gras in January, and Holy Week in March or April, both of which are well worth altering your itinerary for.

In spite of its obvious attractions, the Philippines is still a relatively unusual backpackers' destination, in part because accommodation and travel are about thirty percent more expensive than in Thailand, but also because you can't get to the archipelago overland. For many travellers, this comparatively low-key tourist development is a big plus, and a welcome relief from some of the more clichéd Southeast Asian havens. Conveniently for the traveller, English is widely spoken and the transport system is generally easy to fathom, though you'll be spending a lot of time on boats unless you budget for a few fast but pricey internal flights.

The last few years have seen an alarming number of kidnappings on the mainly Muslim southern island of Mindanao, so check with your government's travel advisories and travellers' Web sites (both listed in Basics) before going to this part of the country.

Main attractions

● The **beaches**. Filipino beaches are some of the finest in Asia, and with almost 60,000 km of coastline, there's plenty to choose from. You'll find the very best in the chain of islands known as the Visayas, which stretches from the southern tip of Luzon all the way down to Mindanao, includes the major islands of Samar,

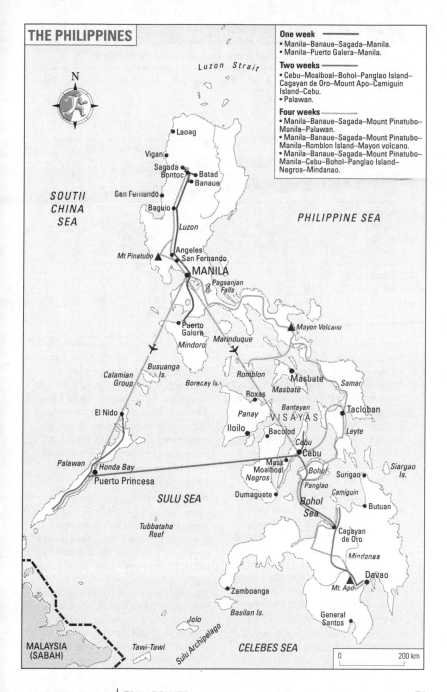

THE PHILIPPINES

One week ————
• Manila–Banaue–Sagada–Manila.
• Manila–Puerto Galera–Manila.

Two weeks ————
• Cebu–Moalboal–Bohol–Panglao Island–
Cagayan de Oro–Mount Apo–Camiguin
Island–Cebu.
• Palawan.

Four weeks ————
• Manila–Banaue–Sagada–Mount Pinatubo–
Manila–Palawan.
• Manila–Banaue–Sagada–Mount Pinatubo–
Manila–Romblon Island–Mayon volcano.
• Manila–Banaue–Sagada–Mount Pinatubo–
Manila–Cebu–Bohol–Panglao Island–
Negros–Mindanao.

N

Luzon Strait

Laoag

Vigan

Sagada
Bontoc   Batad
         Banaue
San Fernando

Baguio

**SOUTH
CHINA
SEA**

Luzon

PHILIPPINE SEA

Mt Pinatubo   Angeles
              San Fernando
          MANILA
              Pagsanjan
              Falls

Puerto
Galera
Mindoro   *Marinduque*

Mayon Volcano

Busuanga
Is.
Calamian
Group   *Boracay Is.*   *Romblon*
                                        Masbate   *Samar*
                            Masbate

                   Roxas
El Nido   *Bantayan*   **Tacloban**
              Panay   VISAYAS
          Iloilo   *Leyte*
                    Bacolod
Palawan   *Cebu*
         Honda Bay   Cebu
      Puerto Princesa   Mask   *Bohol*
                             Moalboal   Surigao   *Siargao
         SULU SEA   *Negros* Panglao   Is.*
                             Dumaguete   Camiguin
                                    Bohol   Butuan
                                    Sea
       *Tubbataha
       Reef*
                                      Cagayan
                                      de Oro
                                       Mindanao

                                         Mt. Apo   **Davao**
         Zamboanga
                    Basilan Is.   General
                                       Santos
              Jolo
**MALAYSIA
(SABAH)**   *Tawi-Tawi*   *Sulu Archipelago*   *CELEBES SEA*

0   200 km

Average daily temperatures (maximum and minimum°C) and monthly rainfall (mm)

Manila	Jan	Feb	Mar	Apr	May	June	July	Aug	Sept	Oct	Nov	Dec
max °C	30	31	33	34	34	33	31	31	31	31	31	30
min °C	21	21	22	23	24	24	24	24	24	23	22	21
rainfall mm	23	13	18	33	130	254	432	422	356	193	145	66
Iloilo												
max °C	29	31	31	33	33	32	31	31	31	31	31	30
min °C	23	23	23	24	25	24	24	24	24	24	24	23
rainfall mm	64	46	33	43	158	264	447	386	315	269	211	119
Surigao												
max °C	28	29	29	31	31	31	31	31	31	31	29	28
min °C	23	23	23	23	24	24	24	24	24	24	24	23
rainfall mm	544	376	506	254	158	125	178	130	168	272	427	620
Zamboanga												
max °C	31	31	32	31	31	31	31	31	31	31	31	32
min °C	23	23	23	23	24	24	23	24	23	23	23	23
rainfall mm	64	46	33	43	158	264	447	386	315	269	211	119

Leyte, Bohol, Cebu, Negros and Panay, as well as hundreds of alluring pint-sized islets in between. The most famous island in the whole set is tiny Boracay, a beautiful but pricey resort island. Quieter, equally lovely Visayan islands include Romblon, Bantayan, Panay, Bohol and Panglao, all of which offer the perfect combination of luxuriously soft sand, a decent choice of beachfront accommodation, and laid-back fishing villages.

● **Diving**. With all that fabulously clear tropical water around, it's not surprising that the Philippines is one of Asia's pre-mier diving destinations. You'll find some of the richest reefs off Boracay, Palawan and Mindoro, but there are also spectac-ular underwater walls, drop-offs and coral arches at Moalboal on Cebu, and ham-merhead sharks and manta rays near Panglao and Cabilao islands, off Bohol.

● **Manila**. Cursed with traffic and pollu-tion that make Bangkok seem like a pic-nic, Manila is one of those capitals that just has to be endured between flights or ferry connections. You can cheer yourself up, though, with a visit to the Chinese cemetery – it's literally a ghost town, with streets and two-storey houses for the departed, many of them furnished with kitchens, bathrooms, electricity and air-conditioning. Otherwise, Manila is best for shopping and drinking, with colossal malls in every neighbourhood, and a trendy nightlife scene in Malate.

● **Banaue**. This little town in northern Luzon occupies a stunning landscape of mountains, steep-sided valleys, and breathtakingly beautiful amphitheatres of sculpted rice terraces. First cut from the hillsides 2000 years ago by Ifugao tribes-people, whose descendants still live in the area, the terraces are so spectacular that they've been given World Heritage status. To make the most of the scenery, follow the popular walking trail from Banaue to the traditional village of Batad. The bus journey up to Banaue is a scenic highlight in itself, as it takes you along the Halsema Highway, one of the most awesome roads in Southeast Asia.

● Shooting the rapids at **Pagsanjan Falls**. The scenery along this stretch of the Bombongan River is impressively dramatic, and it's a genuine thrill to race the fourteen rapids as you squeeze between the jungle-clad canyon walls. If you get a sense of déjà vu, it's because the final scenes of *Apocalypse Now* were filmed here. This is an immensely popular daytrip from Manila, but you can avoid the crowds by staying nearby and doing an early-morning boat ride before the coaches pitch up. Be wary though, as the touts here are the most aggressive and underhand in the country.

● The **Good Friday crucifixions**. Held every year near San Fernando in Pampanga province on Luzon, these are real crucifixions of real people. Under the rapt gaze of hundreds of spectators, a dozen or so pious penitents flagellate themselves before being nailed onto crosses, believing that this earthly suffering will ease their eventual passage into heaven. Although the penitents are taken off the crosses after only a few seconds, it's a disturbing spectacle with plenty of genuine blood – and an act of piety that is not endorsed by the Catholic Church.

Also recommended

● **Palawan**. Graced with peaceful shores, thickly forested crags and a gorgeous rugged natural beauty, the large, remote island of Palawan is probably the single most rewarding destination in the Philippines. It's got everything: snow-white beaches at El Nido, Taytay, Port Barton, Sabang and Roxas, unrivalled diving at El Nido and Tubbataha Reef

Marine Park, hiking trails through the jungle, intact tribal culture, and a noticeable lack of tourists. And there's also the famous eight-kilometre boat ride through the spooky, bat-infested caves of the Underground River in Saint Paul's Subterranean Cave.

● **Sagada**. This charming hill village in northern Luzon is the home of the Igorot tribe, who are famous for their hanging coffins – suspended high in caves out of the reach of wild animals – as well as for their weavings. There are plenty of hiking possibilities around here too, and a distinctly bohemian ambience to the village, all of which make it a really nice place to hang out for a few days.

● Climbing **Mount Apo**. This is no mean feat: at 2954m, volcanic Mount Apo, on Mindanao, is the country's highest peak, and a big draw for trekkers and climbers. It takes four or five days to climb to the top and back, which gives you plenty of time to appreciate the wealth of flora and fauna, including primeval trees, carnivorous pitcher plants, the endangered Philippine Eagle, geysers, waterfalls, hot springs, and a lake. And the view from the top is every bit as magnificent as you'd expect.

● **Camiguin Island**, off northern Mindanao. Famous for its exceptionally sweet and succulent *lanzone* (lychee) fruits (and the raucous Lanzone festival that's celebrated every October by islanders parading through the streets dressed only in lychee leaves), this little gem of an island offers heaps of variety, including sugar-fine beaches, seven volcanoes, hot springs and waterfalls.

Routes in and out

Most people fly into the Philippines and land in Manila, though some Southeast Asian airlines also run international flights to and from Cebu. There are a few international ferry routes from Sabah (East Malaysia), Kalimantan (Indonesia) and Sulawesi (Indonesia) to Mindanao in the southern Philippines, but these are considered unsafe due to frequent pirate attacks in local waters.

Itineraries

One week

● From Manila, travel north into the Cordillera Mountains to explore the rice terraces around Banaue for three days. Continue on for a couple of days in Sagada, before returning to the capital.

● Choose one island to spend the whole week on, perhaps learning to dive while there. One of the easiest and cheapest to get to from Manila is the popular travellers' resort of Puerto Galera on the neighbouring island of Mindoro.

Two weeks

● Fly in to Cebu, the capital of the Visayan islands, which puts you in a perfect position for a fortnight's island-hopping. If you're here for the diving, head to Moalboal, just three hours away. Otherwise, cross over to Bohol and on to Panglao island for a few days. Ride the ferry down to Cagayan de Oro on Mindanao, and then travel south to Mount Apo for five days of challenging climbing. If you're short of time, return to Cebu by plane from Davao. If not, take a bus back to North Mindanao, from where you could strike out to Camiguin Island, before catching a ferry back to Cebu from Cagayan de Oro.

● Do an in-depth tour of Palawan, investigating the myriad beaches and hiking trails as well as the underground river.

Four weeks

From Manila, travel north into the Cordillera Mountains to explore the rice terraces around Banaue for three days. Continue on for a couple of days in Sagada, before returning to the capital by way of Mount Pinatubo, which can be climbed in two days, with a night under canvas on the way up. Then do one or more of the following:

● Spend a week or two on Palawan and its satellite islands.

● Chill out for several days on tiny Romblon Island, then go east across to Mayon volcano, allowing four days to arrange a guide and then get to the summit and back.

● Fly down to Cebu to explore the Visayan islands, the sugar-cane plantations of Negros, and Mindanao.

Philippines online

Across the Philippine Islands with a Travel Nut Ⓦ*www.philippines.com.ph* Detailed, wide-ranging site run by an energetic Filipino. Includes travelogues, slide shows, travel info and a travellers' forum for trading tales.

Bundok Philippines Ⓦ*www.geocities.com/Yosemite/3712* Site specializing in hiking opportunities in the Philippines, featuring hikers' travelogues, slide shows and some maps.

Tanikalang Ginto Ⓦ*www.filipinolinks.com* Links to scores of interesting Philippines-related sites, including travel, airport info, unusual destinations, books and hotels.

The Philippine Diver Ⓦ*www.diver.com.ph* Online version of this glossy quarterly comes up trumps with hundreds of divers' reports on the archipelago's best dives. Also has links to dive centres and courses.

The Philippine Star Ⓦ*www.philstar.com* The national daily newspaper has the day's headline stories plus a stack of archived ones.

Singapore

Population: 2.7 million
Language: Mandarin, Malay, Tamil and English are the official languages; various Chinese dialects also spoken
Currency: Singapore dollar (S$)
Religion: Buddhism, Islam, Hinduism, Sikhism, Christianity

Climate: Tropical
Best time to go: Singapore is extremely hot and humid all year; November–January is slightly cooler, but also has the highest rainfall
Minimum daily budget: US$35/£20

Though some monuments and buildings from its British colonial days remain, Singapore is more a showcase for gleaming modern architecture than a memorial to times past; the speed and ruthlessness of development on the tiny island are quite breathtaking. Most visitors to Southeast Asia pass through here at some point, it being the region's transport hub. While many love the orderly efficiency of the place after a few weeks in wilder parts, others miss the feel of "real" Asia among the high-rises, shopping centres, seamless transport systems and booming economy.

It's easy to mock the authoritarian regulations that have accompanied Singapore's development – don't bring in any chewing gum, don't jaywalk and always flush the toilet after use – but Singapore is the Asia that most Asian nations aspire to, a well-ordered and safe environment both day and night for residents and foreigners alike. It isn't cheap, though, and anyone on a tight budget should try to stay as short a time as possible. Fortunately, the island is compact enough that you can explore the highlights – downtown Singapore, the zoo and Sentosa – in just a few days, eating great meals every few hours along the way;

Singapore has a well-deserved reputation as a foodie mecca, which owes much to the different cuisines of the rich ethnic mix on the tiny island, with Chinese in the majority and sizeable minorities of Malays and Indians.

Main Attractions

● **Chinatown**, the **Arab Quarter** and **Little India**. Towered over by the new Singapore skyline, these remaining ethnic enclaves are relatively untouched by modern development. Some of their tiny, terraced shophouses are still in operation – the shop operates from the front downstairs rooms, while the inhabitants live behind and above. Not surprisingly, traditional places of worship remain most evocative of times past. The Sri Mariamman Hindu temple, with its exuberant carvings; the graceful domes and dignified interior of the Sultan Mosque; and the Thian Hock Keng Chinese temple are especially atmospheric and picturesque.

● The **zoo**. A shining example of the best of such places: most of the bigger animals are kept in huge enclosures, separated from visitors by deep moats.

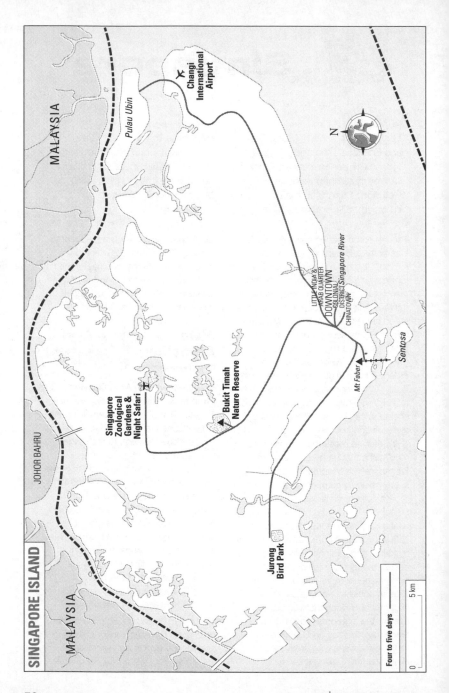

SINGAPORE ISLAND

MALAYSIA

JOHOR BAHRU

MALAYSIA

Pulau Ubin

Changi
International
Airport

N

Singapore
Zoological Gardens &
Night Safari

Bukit Timah
Nature Reserve

LITTLE INDIA &
ARAB QUARTER

DOWNTOWN

COLONIAL
DISTRICT Singapore River

CHINATOWN

Mt Faber

Sentosa

Jurong
Bird Park

Four to five days

0   5 km

Average daily temperatures (maximum and minimum°C) and monthly rainfall (mm)

	Jan	Feb	Mar	Apr	May	June	July	Aug	Sept	Oct	Nov	Dec
Singapore												
max °C	31	32	32	32	32	32	31	31	31	31	31	30
min °C	21	22	23	23	23	23	22	22	22	22	22	22
rainfall mm	146	155	182	223	228	151	170	163	200	199	255	258

Also on offer is a brilliant Night Safari for viewing nocturnal animals.

● **Food**. Head for the food courts, lined with numerous stalls selling their own specialities; you put your meal together from whichever stalls take your fancy. The surroundings at these places may be pretty uninspiring, but the range of Asian cuisines on offer is amazing, from Malay satay to Indian biriyanis via Thai tom-yam soup. Those missing more familiar tastes will be pleased to find that Singapore also offers everything from Italian and French to Mexican, and American coffee-bar chains have hit the city big time.

● **Raffles Hotel**. The luxurious atmosphere of this colonial-era institution is still much in evidence, and a visit is considered a must for tourists, though much of the site has been turned into a shopping arcade. You can even have a Singapore Sling at the very bar where the cocktail was created – though it'll cost you more than a night in one of the city's budget guesthouses.

● **Shopping** – Singapore's number-one hobby. The island's shopping malls are certainly on a grand scale, and boast aggressive air-conditioning – useful if the heat gets too much. If you're on a wider trip through Asia, though, you'll usually find better prices elsewhere.

● **Sentosa**. This offshore-island amusement park has plenty of rides, exhibitions and museums. Underwater World, where a moving walkway carries you through a transparent underwater tunnel with

sharks and other sea creatures swimming around outside, is hard to beat, as are the views of the city's skyscrapers you get as you ride the cable car here.

● **Jurong Bird Park**. In the west of the main island, the park contains over six hundred species of bird, including, remarkably, Antarctic penguins. There's also a gigantic walk-in aviary so visitors can stroll among the birds.

Also recommended

● **Festivals**. The island is at its colourful best during such events. Chinese celebrations include New Year and the Dragon Boat Festival, the latter when a flotilla of colourful rowing boats adorned with a dragon's head and tail take part in a furious, exuberant race; Hindu Indians mark Deepavali, commemorating the victory of light over dark, with prayers in the temples; and Malays mark the ending of the Muslim fasting month of Ramadan with huge feasting on the night of Hari Raya Puasa.

● **A cruise on the Singapore river**. Go on one of these to see the city from a different angle. A huge choice of boats is available – luxury catamarans, traditional bumboats and dinner cruises.

● **Bukit Timah Hill**. Singapore's highest peak (at a mere 162.5m) is home to the island's last pocket of primary rainforest.

Look out for macaques, butterflies and flying lemurs.

● **Pulau Ubin**. Just 7km long and 2km wide, this tiny island tucked into the waters between Singapore and Malaysia gives a glimpse into a rural Singapore long gone elsewhere, with Malay stilt houses and little tracks.

Routes in and out

Singapore's Changi airport is one of the busiest in Asia and is served by all major international carriers. As well as long-haul flights, there are excellent links to all parts of Asia.

A causeway connects Singapore with the Malaysian city of Johor Bahru, and there are direct buses to destinations throughout Malaysia and on to Hat Yai and Bangkok in Thailand; trains also link Singapore with destinations in Malaysia. There are ferries to Tioman Island and Kampung Pengerang in Malaysia, and to the islands of Batam and Bintan in the Riau Archipelago of Indonesia, from where there are connections to Sumatra.

Itineraries

Four to five days

● Spend a couple of days exploring the Colonial District and the ethnic enclaves of Chinatown, Little India and Arab Street.

Then take in the natural world at the zoo, Jurong Bird Park and Bukit Timah Nature Reserve, and spend a day at either Sentosa or Pulau Ubin. You can try out a different cuisine each evening, and don't forget to go back to the zoo for the Night Safari.

Singapore online

Makansutra Ⓦ*www.makansutra.com* Leaving no doubt that Singapore is foodie heaven, this monthly magazine features articles, reviews and listings about every aspect of eating in Singapore – there's also an excellent discussion forum where you can ask specific advice on where to eat.

The Straits Times Interactive Ⓦ*straitstimes.asia1.com.sg* The online version of Singapore's English-language newspaper is a good introduction to Singapore, its news and its view of the rest of the world.

Raffles Hotel Ⓦ*www.raffleshotel.com* Take a peep at the suites, visit the restaurants, learn how to make a Singapore Sling and gasp when you see the prices!

Singapore Changi Airport Ⓦ*www.changi.airport.com.sg* Not only is the airport one of the best in the world, but its Web site is a superb introduction to Changi itself and to the efficiency and organization that pervades Singapore life.

# South Korea

Capital: Seoul	**Climate**: Temperate
Population: 47 million	**Best time to go**:
Language: Korean	September–November; also
Currency: Won (W)	April–June
Main religions: Mahayana	**Minimum daily budget**:
Buddhism and Christianity	$30/£20

Overshadowed as a tourist destination by neighbouring China and Japan, South Korea features on backpackers' itineraries more as a place to find work than as somewhere to explore for its own sake. English-teaching jobs are fairly easy to land in Seoul and Pusan (check the adverts in the local English-language newspapers), and the cost of living is less prohibitive than in Japan, though still a lot higher than nearly everywhere else in Asia. Being so close to China and Japan, South Korea also works well as part of a journey between the two, and there are useful ferry services in both directions.

The same is not true of its immediate neighbour, North Korea, with whom virtually all contact – including transport links – has been banned since 1950, when civil war erupted between the communist, Soviet-backed North and the US-backed South. Though overt hostilities ended in 1953, no peace agreement has yet been signed, so the two countries are still theoretically at war. Indeed the ceasefire line between them – the Demilitarized Zone (DMZ) – is a major tourist attraction. Encouragingly, the new millennium has seen unprecedented dialogue between the two governments and it seems likely that rail links between the two countries

will soon be re-established, which would eventually open up the North to visitors (entry is currently restricted to a few hundred Westerners a year), making South Korea accessible by rail all the way from Europe.

The dominant force in contemporary Korean culture is Confucianism; more of a philosophy than a religion, it originated in China 2500 years ago and is essentially a moral code of family duty and social obligations. The most widespread religion in South Korea is Mahayana Buddhism, and you will find traditional Buddhist temples all over the country, in the heart of the city as well as hidden away on remote mountain sides.

For tourists, South Korea's greatest attractions are the thousands of hiking trails through the forests of its mountainous national parks. Around seventy percent of the country is mountainous, and the autumn colours on the trees that carpet the mountains are at their most spectacular in late October; springtime brings a similarly impressive display of cherry blossom, followed soon after by azaleas. Try to avoid major sights, national parks and hiking trails at weekends, when you'll be competing for space with thousands of city dwellers. Public transport within South Korea is fast and efficient, and the country is so compact that

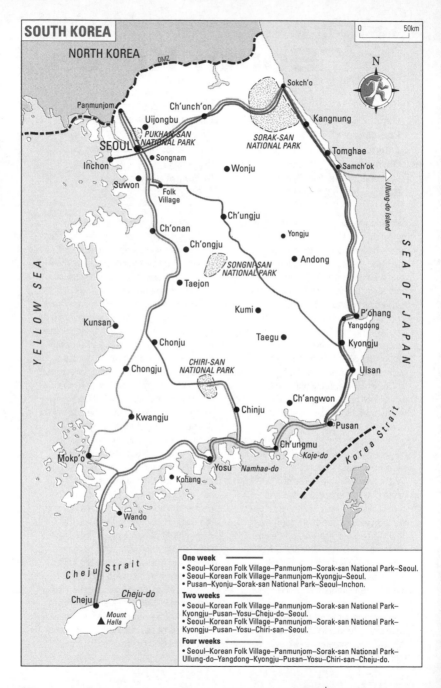

SOUTH KOREA

NORTH KOREA

0   50km

N

DMZ

Sokch'o

Panmunjom

Ch'unch'on

Kangnung

Uijongbu

PUKHAN-SAN
NATIONAL PARK

SORAK-SAN
NATIONAL PARK

Tomghae

SEOUL

Songnam

Samch'ok

Inchon

Wonju

Suwon

Folk
Village

Ullung-do Island

Ch'ungju

Ch'onan

Yongju

Ch'ongju

S E A   O F   J A P A N

Andong

Y E L L O W   S E A

SONGNI-SAN
NATIONAL PARK

Taejon

Kumi

P'ohang

Kunsan

Yangdong

Taegu

Kyongju

Chonju

Ulsan

CHIRI-SAN
NATIONAL PARK

Chongju

Ch'angwon

Korea Strait

Kwangju

Chinju

Pusan

Ch'ungmu

Koje-do

Mokp'o

Yosu

Namhae-do

Kohung

Wando

C h e j u   S t r a i t

Cheju

Cheju-do

Mount
Halla

One week ━━━━━━
• Seoul–Korean Folk Village–Panmunjom–Sorak-san National Park–Seoul.
• Seoul–Korean Folk Village–Panmunjom–Kyongju–Seoul.
• Pusan–Kyonju–Sorak-san National Park–Seoul–Inchon.

Two weeks ━━━━━━
• Seoul–Korean Folk Village–Panmunjom–Sorak-san National Park–
Kyongju–Pusan–Yosu–Cheju-do–Seoul.
• Seoul–Korean Folk Village–Panmunjom–Sorak-san National Park–
Kyongju–Pusan–Yosu–Chiri-san–Seoul.

Four weeks ━━━━━━
• Seoul–Korean Folk Village–Panmunjom–Sorak-san National Park–
Ullung-do–Yangdong–Kyongju–Pusan–Yosu–Chiri-san–Cheju-do.

Mean Temperatures (°C) and Rainfall (mm)

Average daily temperatures (maximum and minimum°C) and monthly rainfall (mm)

	Jan	Feb	Mar	Apr	May	June	July	Aug	Sept	Oct	Nov	Dec
Seoul												
max °C	0	3	8	17	22	27	29	31	26	19	11	3
min °C	-9	-7	-2	5	11	16	21	22	15	7	0	-7
rainfall mm	31	20	38	76	81	130	376	267	119	41	46	25
Pusan												
max °C	6	7	12	17	21	24	27	29	26	21	15	9
min °C	-2	-1	3	8	13	17	22	23	I8	12	6	1
rainfall mm	43	36	69	140	132	201	295	130	173	74	41	31

you can cross from coast to coast in half a day.

Main attractions

● **Kyongju**. Korea's ancient capital, Kyongju, is the country's big must-see, and rates as one of the ten most important ancient cultural cities in the world. In amongst the shops, restaurants, hotels and markets of the modern-day city you'll find abundant relics of its two-thousand-year history, including colossal fifth-century tombs and burial mounds, a seventh-century stone observatory, and the royal pleasure gardens of Anapji, which were designed in 674 AD. Other quarters of Kyongju are rich with elegant pagodas and historic wooden Buddhist temples, and numerous pleasant hiking trails take you up on to the slopes of the sacred mountain, Nam-San, which dominates the south of the city.

● Hiking in the **national parks**. South Korea is full of exhilarating national parks, all of which are crisscrossed by clearly marked walking trails and liberally dotted with good camping spots (and the occasional mountain hut). The cream of the crop is Sorak-san, and in

particular Inner Sorak, an exceptionally tranquil stretch of forested peaks, rivers, waterfalls and temples – and some established rock climbs too. Also well worth seeking out are Chiri-san, which boasts a 65-kilometre-long ridge trail and lots of historic temples; the popular and fairly gentle trails of Songni-san; and Pukhan-san, which is on the edge of Seoul and good for easy day-hikes from the city.

● **Seoul**. South Korea's modern-day capital has a reasonable number of sights to keep you entertained for a few days. Most interesting are the five imposing royal palaces, some of which date back to the fifteenth century. Inside the Changdokkung Palace you'll find one of South Korea's loveliest gardens, the Piwon, a beautifully landscaped haven of ponds and pavilions. In the modern part of town, check out the Kimchi Museum, dedicated to the fiery pickled cabbage that is South Korea's national dish.

● **Panmunjom**. On the 38th parallel, the 1953 ceasefire line between North and South Korea – a four-kilometre-wide strip of land spiked with guardposts – is still in force today, and the village of Panmunjom, which stands on the DMZ just 56km north of Seoul, is a popular day-trip from the capital. In reality, the most interesting thing about the view of North Korea is that – surprise, surprise – the landscape looks just like South Korea. Nonetheless the place attracts busloads of tourists, all of whom are required to dress smartly (no jeans, T-shirts or leggings) and, if male, to have a respectable haircut!

● The **Korean Folk Village**. It may sound like a coach-tour nightmare, but the Korean Folk Village is well worth a day-trip from Seoul, especially if you've not got time to explore the rest of the country. A reconstruction of a typical nineteenth-century village, it's complete with Buddhist temple, Confucian school, pottery and weaving workshops, blacksmiths, and traditional farmhouses. The people you see in the village do actually live and work here, even if they might look like actors dolled up in traditional outfits.

● **Cheju-do**. This southern island has also maintained traditions that have long disappeared from the mainland and is now a popular tourist destination as well as a favourite with local honeymooners. Highlights here include mysterious Easter Island-like statues, hikes to the summit of Mount Halla (South Korea's highest volcano), and a seven-kilometre-long lava-tube cave. The climate down here is warmer and wetter than in the rest of the country, but don't come specifically for the beaches, as you'll find them crowded and disappointingly scruffy.

Also recommended

● The three-hour **boat ride from Pusan to Yosu**. This is one of the prettiest journeys in the country, with fine views of the crenellated coastline and myriad islets. It's so scenic round here

that the whole area has been conserved as Hallyo Waterway National Park.

● The island of **Ullung-do**. Rugged, remote and starkly beautiful, this tiny volcanic outcrop has hardly any roads and is best explored on foot. It takes two days to walk right round the island, giving you ample opportunity to enjoy the temples, forested ridges, waterfalls and famous 2000-year-old juniper tree.

● The fifteenth-century village of **Yangdong**. Prettily set beside a river and beneath a wooded hill, Yangdong is of such historic importance that villagers are forbidden to modify or knock down their antique wooden houses, many of which are magnificent structures, with sweeping roofs, beautifully carved beams and capacious verandahs.

● Bargain-hunting at **Tongdaemun Market** in Seoul. Rising to 34 storeys at its highest point, and covering several square kilometres, Tongdaemun Market is quite possibly the largest in the world. It's probably best not to come with a list of must-buys – it could take you all week to locate the right parts of this labyrinthine rabbit warren – but there's no shortage of goods sold in the pile-'em-high, sell-'em-cheap shops and stalls here, from traditional Korean medicines to army surplus, from carpets to weedkiller.

● **Staying in a yogwan**. If you're on a budget, make a beeline for these ubiquitous traditional guesthouses: they're cheap, family-run, and usually have lots of character. You sleep on a futon on the floor – a special treat in winter when the underfloor heating system kicks in and acts like a huge electric blanket.

Routes in and out

Currently, nearly all international flights arrive at Seoul's Kimpo Airport, but a replacement international airport, due to be ready in 2002, is under construction at Inchon, 28km west of the capital. There are also flights from Japan into Pusan and Cheju-do airports.

South Korea has good international ferry connections with Japan and China. Ferries to and from Japan run between Shimonoseki and Pusan, and between Fukuoka and Pusan, and there's a handy combination rail and hydrofoil ticket from Osaka all the way through to Seoul, via Fukuoka and Pusan. Ferries to China all arrive at and depart from Inchon (near Seoul), running regularly to Tianjin (near Beijing), Qingdao and Weihai (both in Shandong), Dalian and Dandong (both in Liaoning), and Shanghai.

There has been no legal border crossing between South and North Korea since the Korean War; this may change, however, if relations continue to thaw.

Itineraries

One week

● Spend two or three days in and around Seoul, perhaps making day-trips to the Korean Folk Village and Panmunjom. Spend the rest of your week either in Sorak-san National Park, or in the historic city of Kyongju.

● If transiting between Japan and China, take the ferry to Pusan, then continue to Kyongju for two nights. Travel north to Sorak-san National Park for two or three days' hiking, before stopping off in Seoul for a night or two en route to Inchon and ferries to China.

Two weeks

● Spend three or four days in and around Seoul, making day-trips to the Korean Folk Village and Panmunjom. Then head off into the hills for three days' hiking in Sorak-san National Park

before travelling south to Kyongju for a couple of nights in the ancient capital. Continue to nearby Pusan from where you can make the picturesque ferry journey to Yosu. Either round off your fortnight with a few days on Cheju-do, or make an attempt at Chiri-san's four-day ridge trail.

Four weeks

● Spend three or four days in and around Seoul, making day-trips to the Korean Folk Village and Panmunjom. Then head off into the hills for three days' hiking in Sorak-san National Park. Take a boat out to tiny Ullung-do and spend two or three days exploring the island on foot before returning to the mainland for an overnight visit to Yangdong village and then three days in Kyongju. Continue to nearby Pusan from where you can make the picturesque ferry journey to Yosu. Next, make an attempt at Chiri-san's four-day ridge trail, after which you'll appreciate a good few days on Cheju-do.

South Korea online

Korea Insights Ⓦ*korea.insights.co.kr* Huge, varied site with masses of interesting features on Korean history, culture and sights, plus a lively Webzine about contemporary life. Recommended.
Korean Times Ⓦ*www.koreatimes.co.kr* Keep abreast of what's happening in North–South relations as well as all the rest of the news with this online version of South Korea's English-language daily.
National Parks Ⓦ*www.npa.or.kr* Check out prizewinning photos of Korea's most scenic national parks and book a campsite or mountain lodge.
South Korea Yellow Pages Ⓦ*www.yellowpages.co.kr* Carries a handy section on expat life in Korea, and hosts a useful bulletin board for job-seekers.

Sri Lanka

Capital: Colombo
Population: 19 million
Language: Sinhala, Tamil and English are official languages
Currency: Rupee (Rs)
Religion: Buddhists are in the majority, with Hindu, Christian and Muslim minorities
Climate: Tropical, with two distinct monsoons
Best time to go: Nov–April for the south and west coasts; Jan–April for the hills; May–Sept for the east coast
Minimum daily budget: $15/£10

A small country, Sri Lanka nonetheless offers an enormous variety of quintessentially Asian experiences. The island is dotted with ruins from ancient Buddhist empires, including serene, gigantic Buddha figures, as well as dagobas, white-painted domed shrines ranging from just a few metres tall to immense, imposing structures; variations of these are found in India, Thailand, China and other Asian countries. Other architectural features worth keeping an eye out for are buildings dating from the Portuguese, Dutch and British colonial periods, which lasted from the first European arrival in 1505 through to Independence in 1948.

Sri Lanka also boasts glorious landscapes, with lovely beaches, cool rolling hills, mountains and huge tracts of rainforest, excellent for spotting wildlife. Many bird species like it here, too, spending the winter on Sri Lanka's southern coasts before returning to temperate zones.

Outside Colombo, the only city, the island has a rural feel, making it more manageable than chaotic India to the north. However, Sri Lanka is plagued by a violent religious and ethnic conflict, a civil war between the Tamil minority and the Sinhalese majority that has been raging

since the mid-1980s. The disputed territories, which essentially comprise the whole of north and east Sri Lanka, are too dangerous to visit; while a good number of travellers do come, they confine themselves to the south and the west. Check with embassies, newspapers and travellers' newsgroups on the Internet before making up your own mind (see Basics, p.345).

Main attractions

● **Colombo**. Though this is where everyone arrives, the fear of terrorist bombings means most visitors don't linger long in the capital. However, the National Museum and the Dutch Period Museum are worth a look, while the Raja Maha Vihara, 13km from the city centre, is the most visited Buddhist temple on the island, built on a site that Buddha himself is said to have visited.

● **Hikkaduwa**. Some people find this resort just too developed for their tastes, but its four-kilometre stretch of beach does offer a huge range of accommodation, and it's the most popular place on the island for snorkelling, diving, surfing, shopping and just hanging out. However, recent reports suggest the coral here has mostly died; ask around among other travellers if underwater life is your main reason for planning a visit. The coastline to the south, between Hikkaduwa and Galle, is glorious, with broad, sweeping bays offering plenty of choices for lazing on the beach, though be warned that the undertow can be extremely dangerous.

● **Anuradhapura.** The island's capital from the fourth century BC until the ninth century AD, Sri Lanka's holiest town has much of historical interest, including tombs of ancient rulers, artificial lakes almost two thousand years old, and plenty of dagobas. One of these is said to contain the right collarbone of Buddha himself, while another, the Ruwanwelisiya dagoba, is over 50m tall and surrounded by life-sized carved elephants. However, the town is best

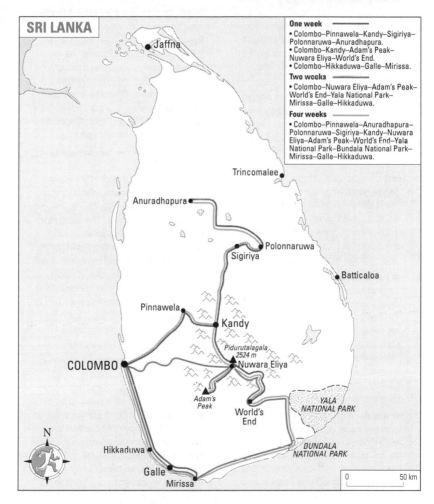

SRI LANKA

One week
• Colombo–Pinnawela–Kandy–Sigiriya–Polonnaruwa–Anuradhapura.
• Colombo–Kandy–Adam's Peak–Nuwara Eliya–World's End.
• Colombo–Hikkaduwa–Galle–Mirissa.

Two weeks
• Colombo–Nuwara Eliya–Adam's Peak–World's End–Yala National Park–Mirissa–Galle–Hikkaduwa.

Four weeks
• Colombo–Pinnawela–Anuradhapura–Polonnaruwa–Sigiriya–Kandy–Nuwara Eliya–Adam's Peak–World's End–Yala National Park–Bundala National Park–Mirissa–Galle–Hikkaduwa.

Mean Temperatures (°C) and Rainfall (mm)

Average daily temperatures (maximum and minimum°C) and monthly rainfall (mm)

	Jan	Feb	Mar	Apr	May	June	July	Aug	Sept	Oct	Nov	Dec
Colombo												
max °C	30	31	31	31	31	29	29	29	29	29	29	29
min °C	22	22	23	24	26	25	25	25	25	24	23	22
rainfall mm	89	69	147	231	371	224	135	109	160	348	315	147

known for the Sri Maha Bodhi tree, which draws pilgrims from throughout the Buddhist world; the tree is believed to have grown from a cutting – brought to the island well over two thousand years ago – taken from the original bo tree in India under which Buddha attained enlightenment.

● **Polonnaruwa**. Set beside a huge artificial lake, Polonnaruwa was the medieval capital of the island, after the decline of Anuradhapura. The town is the site of numerous well-preserved chambers, palaces and temples spread over a huge area, many still boasting fine carvings and friezes. Best known are sublime Buddhist images, the Gal Vihara, carved by an unknown artist out of a towering granite rock face; there are three figures, shown standing, seated and reclining respectively.

● **Pinnawela Elephant Orphanage**. Elephants are a pervasive Sri Lankan image, whether painted or sculpted; the live variety is accessible here, where orphaned, abandoned or injured infant elephants are reared and trained. Pinnawela affords a great chance to see them at close quarters, including at bathing and feeding time, when they guzzle down vast quantities of milk.

● **Kandy**. Set beside a lake in the hills and reachable by a scenic train ride from Colombo, Sri Lanka's cultural capital is not just an ideal place to hang out and cool down – there's plenty to see here, too, including one of the most

venerated temples in Sri Lanka, the Dalada Maligawa or Temple of the Tooth. It's so named because it holds what's believed to be a tooth of the Buddha, rescued from his funeral pyre. Wars have been fought over the relic, though, at 5cm long, it was thought by the British more likely to belong to a tiger. The annual Perahera procession, held here in July or August, honours the sacred tooth; it's the most elaborate spectacle on the island, featuring dancers, drummers and fabulously costumed elephants.

● **Sigiriya**. Built on top of a massive 200-metre-high granite monolith, this fifth-century fortress stands sentinel over the surrounding plains. The stronghold was created by the murderous King Kassapa who, after killing his father to grab the throne, feared retribution from the rightful heir, his brother. Kassapa laid out pretty water gardens on top and at the base, and about halfway up, a sheltered overhang in the rock face contains well-preserved fresco paintings.

● **Nuwara Eliya**. The highest town on the island, this old British hill station is surrounded by tea estates and vegetable gardens. Still containing many relics of the past, it's a place to appreciate the juxtaposition of old colonial trappings and a modern Sri Lankan town. The most enticing excursion is the two-hour climb up nearby Mount Pidurutalagala, Sri Lanka's highest mountain at 2524m; you'll need to check locally however, as the mountain can be closed to visitors for security reasons.

Also recommended

● **Sunrise over World's End**. The highest plateau in Sri Lanka has a viewpoint over a one-thousand-metre drop, from where you can admire the clouds several hundred metres below.

● **Adam's Peak** (2224m). The mountain is a place of pilgrimage for Muslims, Hindus and Buddhists, who believe that the metre-long foot-like imprint in a rock on the peak belongs to Adam, Shiva and the Buddha respectively. However, the less devout can also make the four-hour ascent to see the sunrise and marvel at the Shadow of the Peak, best seen under the clearer skies of January to April, when the silhouette of the mountain is distinctly visible on the countryside below.

● **Galle**. Enclosed inside the ramparts of the old Dutch Fort, this port town retains much of its colonial ambience. It is possible to walk all the way around the ramparts for great views across the town and out to sea, especially lovely at sunset.

● **Mirissa**. A peaceful, tiny beach on the south coast, it has just a couple of guesthouses on its palm-fringed shore.

● **Cricket**. Sri Lankans are mad about the game, and there's often a foreign side on tour. Go to a match and experience the wild atmosphere and loud, exuberant crowd.

● The **flamingos** of Bundala National Park. The park is Sri Lanka's best area for bird-watching at any time of year, with thousands of flamingos crowding its lagoons and wetlands from January to April.

● **Yala National Park**. Although its elephants are the main draw, you'll probably see more tourist jeeps in Sri Lanka's most popular park. You've also a chance of spotting leopards here, as well as more numerous deer, sloth bears, crocodiles, wild boar, jackals and around 130 species of bird, including the impressive hornbill.

Routes in and out

Although Sri Lanka is separated from India only by the narrow Palk Strait, there is no ferry route between the two countries; arrival and departure are through the international airport at Colombo.

Itineraries

One week
● After spending a night in Colombo, hire a car and driver, and head to Kandy for two days, calling in at Pinnawella on the way. Then get out to Sigiriya, Polonnaruwa and Anuradhapura for a day each before returning to Colombo.

● Spend your first day in Colombo, then two days in Kandy and another two days getting to and climbing Adam's Peak. End your trip in Nuwara Eliya, taking a day excursion to World's End and Horton Plains, before returning to Colombo.

● From Colombo, head out to Hikkaduwa, Galle and Mirissa, spending one or two days in each place.

Two weeks
● Overnight in Colombo, then spend three days getting to and exploring Nuwara Eliya. From there, take an excursion to Adam's Peak and then move on to World's End and Horton Plains. Allot another two days to Yala

National Park and a day in Mirissa. Finally, stay a couple of days in Hikkaduwa, getting there via Galle, before heading back to Colombo.

One month

● A month in Sri Lanka is enough to cover all the sights at your leisure. Starting in Colombo, a plausible route is to head first for Pinnawela, then continue north to Anuradhapura, Polonnaruwa and Sigiriya, before relaxing for a few days in Kandy. Then continue south to Nuwara Eliya, Adam's Peak and World's End. Head down to the coast at Yala National Park, before returning west to Colombo via Bundala National Park, Mirissa and Hikkaduwa.

Sri Lanka online

Explore Sri Lanka Ⓦ*www.explore-srilanka.com* Travel site providing a thorough, attractive and easy-to-read introduction for visitors.

WWW Virtual Library – Sri Lanka Ⓦ*www.lankapage.com/wlib/* Excellent general site with a monster number of links to sites on Sri Lankan tourism, culture and religion, as well as up-to-the-minute news.

Infolanka Ⓦ*www.infolanka.com* General umbrella site with links to articles and other sites on every aspect of Sri Lankan life, including religion, politics, travel, sport, cooking. Check out their Discover travel Webzine, which has some good articles.

Elephants of Sri Lanka Ⓦ*www.ozemail.com.au/~cannont* Site maintained by Teresa Cannon and Peter Davis, who've studied the elephants for several years and produced a book about them. Besides good links, the site includes many fine pictures of elephants, in real life and in art, and a description of the Kandy Perahera procession.

Ari Withanage's Welcome to Sri Lanka Ⓦ*members.tripod.com/Withanage/* A Sri Lankan living in London, where he works for the fire brigade, Ari maintains an excellent site about his homeland, giving a thorough introduction to all aspects of the island, with plenty of detail and fine pictures.

Taiwan

Capital: Taipei
Population: 21 million
Language: Mandarin, Chinese dialects including Taiwanese and Hakka, and ten tribal languages
Currency: New Taiwanese dollar (NT$)
Religion: Buddhism, Daoism and Confucianism

Climate: Subtropical, with a rainy season in May and June
Best time to go: Good at any time but avoid festivals, especially Chinese New Year, as transport is booked solid and hotel prices soar at these times
Minimum daily budget: US$30/£20

Taiwan has had a turbulent history, with Chinese dynasties and foreign powers seeking sovereignty over the island in the past. Today its situation is ambiguous: at the end of the civil war on mainland China in 1949, with the communists set to win, the leader of the nationalist Kuomintang, Chiang Kai-shek, led an exodus of soldiers, merchants and scholars to Taiwan. They proclaimed the island the Republic of China, the name it retains today. China views Taiwan as a dissident province, while Taiwan has never declared independence from the mainland but views itself as the legitimate government of China. While relations have thawed to some extent, military intimidation by the mainland and a war of words between the two continue.

Taiwan today is home to some of the noisiest, most frantic cities in Asia, but also offers gorgeous mountain, coastal and inland scenery and a vibrant religious and cultural life. It's a startling mixture of a modern industrial nation, at the cutting edge of computer technology and production, alongside age-old beliefs and practices, with literally thousands of atmospheric temples.

There are also plentiful opportunities to get out into the countryside, either to take it easy and admire the views along with the rest of the day-trippers, or to get off the beaten track and take advantage of opportunities for trekking and camping. While the mountain scenery is serene and tranquil, bear in mind that Taiwan is one of the most densely populated countries in the world – you'll be hard pushed to get away from everybody. And as you won't come across many other Western tourists or a backpacker circuit, you'll have ample opportunity to mingle with and meet local people.

Main attractions

● **Taipei**. The capital is a congested place, with three million people in the city itself and another three million in the surrounding countryside. That said, Taipei has plenty of attractions to detain you for a couple of days, including atmospheric temples, museums, historic monuments and teeming night markets. If you do nothing else here,

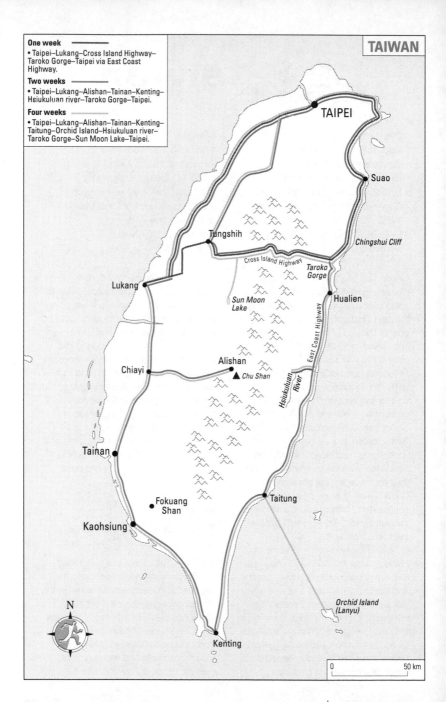

One week
• Taipei–Lukang–Cross Island Highway–
Taroko Gorge–Taipei via East Coast
Highway.

Two weeks
• Taipei–Lukang–Alishan–Tainan–Kenting–
Hsiukuluan river–Taroko Gorge–Taipei.

Four weeks
• Taipei–Lukang–Alishan–Tainan–Kenting–
Taitung–Orchid Island–Hsiukuluan river–
Taroko Gorge–Sun Moon Lake–Taipei.

TAIWAN

TAIPEI

Suao

Tungshih

Chingshui Cliff

Cross Island Highway

Taroko
Gorge

Lukang

Sun Moon
Lake

Hualien

East Coast Highway

Chiayi

Alishan

▲ Chu Shan

Hsiukuluan River

Tainan

Fokuang
Shan

Taitung

Kaohsiung

Orchid Island
(Lanyu)

N

Kenting

0   50 km

Mean Temperatures (°C) and Rainfall (mm)

Average daily temperatures (maximum and minimum°C) and monthly rainfall (mm)

	Jan	Feb	Mar	Apr	May	June	July	Aug	Sept	Oct	Nov	Dec
Taipei												
max °C	19	18	21	25	28	32	33	33	31	27	24	21
min °C	12	12	14	17	21	23	24	24	23	19	17	14
rainfall mm	86	135	178	170	231	290	231	305	244	122	66	71

visit the National Palace Museum, featuring the world's finest array of Chinese artefacts, moved here in 1948 by the Kuomintang. It's such a huge collection that only a tiny fraction is displayed at any one time. Also a must-see is Snake Alley, where fortune-tellers, tattoo parlours, fruit sellers and restaurants nestle alongside stalls where you can try a drink of snake blood and bile (and optional venom), removed from specimens freshly killed and skinned in front of you. This mind-boggling concoction is said to strengthen the eyes, spine and sexual vitality.

● **Taroko Gorge.** On the east coast, the island's main tourist attraction features a thundering river, towering cliffs and plenty of excellent opportunities for camping and trekking. The most picturesque route to the gorge is via the 200-kilometre-long Cross-Island Highway from Tungshih, with fabulous scenery – tropical valleys, mountain panoramas and lakes – all along the way.

● **Kenting National Park.** In the sunny, fertile lowlands of the far south of the island, the park, near the town of Kenting, has white beaches, forests, an attractive coastline, waterfalls, hot springs and plenty more to explore. On the beaches, there are plenty of water sports to try by day, and pubs, discos and karaoke bars to choose from at night.

● **Alishan.** At 2190m, the best of the island's mountain resorts doesn't merely offer an escape from the lowland heat; it's a gorgeous spot, surrounded by cedar and pine forests, with the blossoming of the cherry trees a special feature in the spring. Among the numerous treks here, the obligatory excursion is the one to the peak of 2490-metre Chu Shan (Celebration Mountain), where several thousand people jostle every morning for views of the sunrise. Some Westerners are disappointed by the misty weather, but local people are just as happy whatever the conditions, believing that mountain mists contain a high density of qi, the "life force". The narrow-gauge steam train from Chiayi to Alishan is an especially picturesque route there, taking three and a half hours to climb up through the rolling hills, negotiating 50 tunnels and 77 bridges en route.

● **Tainan.** Temples are the main reason to visit this city, said to contain around two hundred of them. The most famous is the Temple of the Jade Emperor, the oldest Daoist temple in the city, where a constant stream of visitors come to pray in a highly atmospheric setting: every wall, ceiling and door is adorned with detailed carvings and frescos, and spirit mediums here are often involved in rituals in which they attempt to contact the dead on behalf of the living.

● Taking the **east-coast highway** from Suao to Taitung. In places, the road is carved out of cliffs which drop a sheer

1000m into the crashing surf below. The most dramatic part is between Suao and Hualien, which includes a section called Chingshui Cliff where the drops beside the road are especially vertiginous. About halfway between Hualien and Taitung, the Hsiukuluan River is Taiwan's most popular white-water rafting area.

Also recommended

● **Lukang.** A major harbour from the seventeenth to twentieth centuries, this small west-coast town retains its tiny alleyways and historic atmosphere. In the centre of town, the Lungshan Temple, dating from the eighteenth century, has fantastically carved ceilings; it was dedicated to Kuanyin, the goddess of mercy, by Chinese settlers in thanks for their safe crossing from the mainland. The craftsmen here still produce furniture, fans, lanterns and incense using traditional techniques, and the Lukang Folk Art Museum is a good place to view fine, historic examples of their art.

● **Fokuang Shan.** These rolling hills northeast of the city of Kaohsiung are the centre of Taiwanese Buddhist scholarship. The largest Buddha on the island, a 32-metre, serene image, is surrounded by life-sized statues of 480 Buddhist disciples and the main prayer hall also features three huge Buddha images. Sadly, though open to worshippers, Fokuang Shan has been closed to tourists in recent years, but it's worth enquiring near the time of your visit whether this restriction has been lifted.

● **Sun Moon Lake.** Set 750m up in the hills, this popular spot was created by damming the valley here for a hydro-electric scheme. The surrounding forests

and bamboo groves contain many excellent treks.

● **Lanyu**, or Orchid Island. Just 45 square kilometres in size, this is home to just over 400 Yami people, the island's indigenous inhabitants, who still lead a seafaring lifestyle. Reached by ferry from Taitung, Lanyu has excellent coastal scenery and volcanic countryside, and is a great place to explore.

Routes in and out

There are international airports at Taoyuan (for Taipei) and Kaohsiung. Ferry services operate into Kaohsiung from Okinawa in Japan and from Macao, and into Keelung from Okinawa. To travel between mainland China and Taiwan, you'll need to transit in Hong Kong as there are no direct flights or ferries between the two at present.

Itineraries

One week
● After three days in Taipei, you can spend a day seeing Lukang, then use the Cross-Island Highway to reach Taroka Gorge. Finally, head back to Taipei up the east coast highway, via Suao.

Two weeks
● Stay a few days in Taipei, then head to Lukang, Alishan, Tainan and Kenting, spending a day or two in each. Return to Taipei along the East Coast Highway via Taroko Gorge (with an optional stop at Hsiukuluan river for some white-water rafting), then back across the Cross-Island Highway or around the north of the island via Suao.

One month
● Do the two-week itinerary at a far more leisurely pace, adding a visit to

Lanyu from Taitung and a side trip to Sun Moon Lake.

Taiwan online

Travel in Taiwan Ⓦ*www.sinica.edu.tw/tit* A monthly travel magazine featuring heaps of information for visitors, with articles and excellent photos covering every area and every facet of the island – from serious history through to sights, shopping and dining.

Tainan Ⓦ*taiwan.wcn.com.tw/en/tainan* Excellent introduction to the city of Tainan, especially its temples and their significance. Find out where local people go to pray for a mate or for a change of sex for their unborn child, and to communicate with the dead. It's also strong on local food – such as Coffin Cakes and Passing the Lean Months Noodles.

National Palace Museum Ⓦ*www.npm.gov.tw* Extensive and colourful site illustrating many of the treasures of this amazing museum – inspirational if you're thinking of a trip and some consolation if you'll never make it there.

History of Taiwan Ⓦ*www.leksu.com* Serious, detailed and readable introduction to Taiwan's history, both ancient and modern, with plenty of information about contemporary Taiwan.

Thailand

Capital: Bangkok	**Climate**: Tropical
Population: 61 million	**Best time to go**: November to
Language: Thai	February (but March–Sept for
Currency: Baht (B)	peninsular east coast)
Main religion: Theravada Buddhism	**Minimum daily budget**: $10/£7

The perfect place to start a cross-Asia trip, Thailand has a well-established tourist infrastructure, with good transport links, plenty of backpacker-oriented guesthouses and a thriving travellers' scene. Hard-core travellers dislike the place for those very reasons, considering it too easy, too popular, and over-explored – in short, not cool enough. But to most visitors it's simply a great holiday destination.

Bumming around on tropical beaches is the most popular tourist activity, with trekking in the northern hills a close second. Further south, swaths of intact rainforest have been conserved as national parks, offering a good chance of seeing monkeys, tropical birds, and even elephants from the trails. Thailand also has plenty of cultural highlights, including well-preserved ruined cities from almost every major period in its history, the finest of which are the Hindu–Buddhist temples built by the ancient Khmers of Cambodia a thousand years ago. In contemporary Thailand, a phenomenal ninety percent of the population are practising Buddhists, so there are also plenty of working temples to explore.

Thai food is another highlight – pungently laced with chilli and delicately flavoured with lemon grass and coconut, it's also deliciously inexpen-

sive. English is spoken by Thais working in the tourist industry, but not off the beaten track.

Main attractions

● **Bangkok**. Most people spend a few days in the Thai capital, but many find the pollution, traffic congestion and chaotic street life extremely wearing. There's plenty to take you off the street however, including the glittering Grand Palace, now used by the royal family only on ceremonial occasions; the National Museum; the massive Chatuchak weekend market; and a happening nightlife that runs the full range from cutting-edge clubs to depressing strip joints.

● **Beaches**. Thailand's beaches are among the world's best. You'll find the most developed and expensive resorts, and some of the finest sands, on the islands of Ko Samui, Phuket and Ko Phi Phi, while backpackers tend to head for the more budget-oriented Ko Pha Ngan, Ko Tao and Ko Chang. Ko Samet makes an easy and economical break from Bangkok, while Ko Lanta is low-key but well appointed, with accommodation to suit most budgets.

● **Trekking**. Unlike the organized treks in

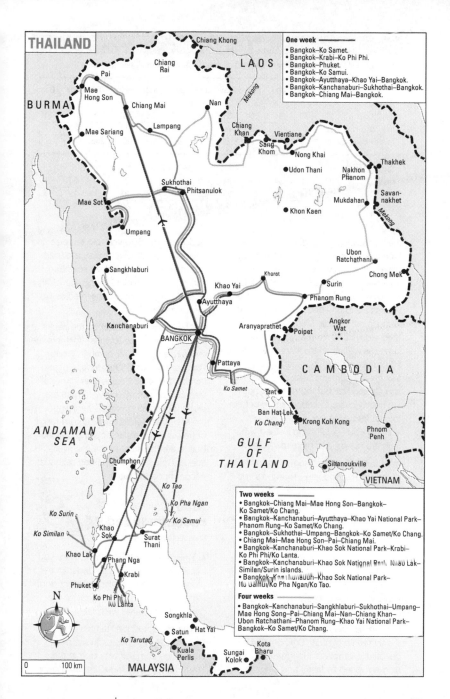

THAILAND

Chiang Khong

LAOS

Pai

Chiang
Rai

Mae
Hong Son

Chiang Mai

Nan

BURMA

Mae Sariang

Lampang

Chiang
Khan

Vientiane

Mekong

Sang
Khom

Nong Khai

Thakhek

Udon Thani

Nakhon
Phanom

Sukhothai

Phitsanulok

Mukdahan

Savan-
nakhet

Mae Sot

Khon Kaen

Umpang

Mekong

Ubon
Ratchathani

Chong Mek

Sangkhlaburi

Khorat

Khao Yai

Surin

Ayutthaya

Phanom Rung

Kanchanaburi

Aranyaprathet

Poipet

Angkor
Wat

BANGKOK

Pattaya

CAMBODIA

Ko Samet

ANDAMAN
SEA

Trat

Ban Hat Lek

Ko Chang

Krong Koh Kong

Phnom
Penh

GULF
OF
THAILAND

Sihanoukville

VIETNAM

Chumphon

Ko Tao

Ko Pha Ngan

Ko Surin

Ko Samui

Ko Similan

Khao
Sok

Surat
Thani

Khao Lak

Phang Nga

Krabi

Phuket

Ko Phi Phi

Ko Lanta

Songkhla

N

Satun

Hat Yai

Ko Tarutao

Kota
Bharu

0   100 km

Kuala
Perlis

Sungai
Kolok

MALAYSIA

One week ——————
• Bangkok–Ko Samet.
• Bangkok–Krabi–Ko Phi Phi.
• Bangkok–Phuket.
• Bangkok–Ko Samui.
• Bangkok–Ayutthaya–Khao Yai–Bangkok.
• Bangkok–Kanchanaburi–Sukhothai–Bangkok.
• Bangkok–Chiang Mai–Bangkok.

Two weeks ——————
• Bangkok–Chiang Mai–Mae Hong Son–Bangkok–
  Ko Samet/Ko Chang.
• Bangkok–Kanchanaburi–Ayutthaya–Khao Yai National Park–
  Phanom Rung–Ko Samet/Ko Chang.
• Bangkok–Sukhothai–Umpang–Bangkok–Ko Samet/Ko Chang.
• Chiang Mai–Mae Hong Son–Pai–Chiang Mai.
• Bangkok–Kanchanaburi–Khao Sok National Park–Krabi–
  Ko Phi Phi/Ko Lanta.
• Bangkok–Kanchanaburi–Khao Sok National Park–Khao Lak–
  Similan/Surin islands.
• Bangkok–Kanchanaburi–Khao Sok National Park–
  Ko Samui/Ko Pha Ngan/Ko Tao.

Four weeks ——————
• Bangkok–Kanchanaburi–Sangkhlaburi–Sukhothai–Umpang–
  Mae Hong Song–Pai–Chiang Mai–Nan–Chiang Khan–
  Ubon Ratchathani–Phanom Rung–Khao Yai National Park–
  Bangkok–Ko Samet/Ko Chang.

Mean Temperatures (°C) and Rainfall (mm)

Average daily temperatures (maximum and minimum°C) and monthly rainfall (mm)

	Jan	Feb	Mar	Apr	May	June	July	Aug	Sept	Oct	Nov	Dec
Bangkok												
max °C	32	33	34	35	34	33	32	32	32	31	31	31
min °C	22	24	25	25	24	24	24	24	24	22	20	
rainfall mm	8	20	36	58	198	160	160	175	305	206	66	5
Chiang Mai												
max °C	29	32	34	36	34	32	31	31	31	31	30	28
min °C	13	14	17	22	23	23	23	23	23	21	19	15
rainfall mm	0	10	8	36	122	112	213	193	249	94	31	13

the Himalayas, Thailand's so-called "hill-tribe treks" focus on the ethnic-minority villages that you walk to, rather than on the walking itself or the scenery. The hill tribes live way out in the sticks, but their villages are connected by tracks, so the hiking is not difficult. Most treks last two to four days and feature nights in the villages, as well as an elephant ride and some river rafting. The main trekking centres are the northern cities of Chiang Mai and Chiang Rai, but routes out of both are hugely oversubscribed, so it's better to start from Mae Hong Son, Pai, Kanchanaburi or Umpang instead, where trails are quieter and more rewarding.

● **Chiang Mai**. Best known as the hub of the trekking industry, Thailand's second city is also an attractive and popular destination in its own right, famed for charming traditional temples, its hill-tribe museum and delicious Burmese-style cuisine, which blends strong spices with sweet coconut cream. Guesthouses are plentiful here, and the night bazaar rates as one of the country's most rewarding shopping experiences.

● The ruined former capitals of **Sukhothai** and **Ayutthaya**. Dating from the thirteenth century, Sukhothai is a beautiful example of thoughtful city planning enlivened by lakes and elegant Buddhas. The 300-year-old temples and palaces of Ayutthaya display a refined mix of Hindu and Buddhist sculpture, and are fun to explore by bicycle. Both sets of ruins are now conserved as historical parks.

● **Kanchanaburi**. Sited on the banks of the River Kwai, the town is most famous for its role as a POW camp in World War II and for its bridge, whose destruction by the Allied Forces was immortalized in David Lean's movie. There are plenty of sobering World War II sights in the town, as well as a reasonable range of trekking, rafting and cycling options that make the most of the fine river scenery, plus some appealing rafthouse accommodation too.

Also recommended

● **Khao Sok National Park**. Here you can sleep in a tree house under limestone karst, wake to the sound of hooting gibbons, and spend a day at the park's eleven-tiered waterfall.

● The ancient Khmer temple of **Phanom Rung**. This exquisite pink sandstone complex was built in the tenth century as a blueprint for Angkor

Wat across the border in Cambodia.

● A **traditional Thai massage** at Bangkok's Wat Po temple.

● Snorkelling and diving off the remote **Similan Islands**. The turquoise water, powdery sand and banks of coral are regularly visited by sharks, rays and turtles.

● The **Southern Folklore Museum**, near Songkhla. Featuring plenty of intriguing household objects and some reconstructed rural homes, this unusual museum also occupies a fabulous spot on a hillside overlooking nearby fishing villages.

● A **kayaking tour around Phang Nga Bay**. The bizarre limestone karst that dots the area may be familiar – this was a location in the James Bond film, *The Man With the Golden Gun*.

● **Sang Khom**. It's great to chill out in this idyllic tree-shaded little town on the Mekong river, where you can rent bicycles to visit traditional local villages and mess about on the water in inner tubes and dugout canoes.

● **Khao Yai National Park**. Thailand's most well-organized national park has heaps of clearly marked trails and a couple of big waterfalls. You can either venture out on your own in search of the resident monkeys and tigers, or join an inexpensive ranger-led tour.

Routes in and out

Thailand's main international airport is in Bangkok, but a few international flights also use the airports in Ko Samui and Phuket in the south and in Chiang Mai in the north. There are lots of buses linking major cities and tourist resorts in Thailand and Malaysia, and you can also travel between the two countries by train. Overland travel to Laos is also

straightforward; the most popular border crossing is the Friendship Bridge which connects the Thai town of Nong Khai with Vientiane in Laos. Until the late 1990s, overland access in and out of Cambodia was dangerous, but the improved security situation means that this is gradually becoming more common. From Thailand, you can choose to cross either from Aranyapathet to Poipet, or from Trat to Sihanoukville.

Itineraries

One week
● Spend three days in Bangkok plus four days on a beach. If your budget is limited, choose the east coast island of Ko Samet, just three hours by bus from Bangkok; if you can stretch to a flight, your options are considerable, with airports in Krabi and on Phuket and Ko Samui all giving access to dozens of gorgeous beaches.

● Forget about Bangkok and spend seven days on the beach, learning to dive while you're there. You can get a connecting flight from Bangkok to Krabi, or fly via Singapore to Phuket or Ko Samui.

● Stay two or three days in Bangkok, plus a couple of nights each in two of the following: Ayutthaya, Sukhothai, the national park at Khao Yai, Kanchanaburi.

● After a couple of days in Bangkok, take a flight or overnight train to Chiang Mai for a two- to four-day trek through hill-tribe villages.

Two weeks
● Do the sights of Bangkok for a few days, then spend five days in and around Chiang Mai or Mae Hong Son, before rounding off with a stint on the beach.

● From Bangkok, head to Kanchanaburi for a couple of nights. Back in Bangkok, proceed eastwards to Ayutthaya for two days, then northeast for a couple of nights in Khao Yai National Park, followed by a day at Phanom Rung. Finally, take a bus down to the east coast and spend the last few days on the islands of Ko Samet or Ko Chang.

● Head north from Bangkok to the ruins of Sukhothai, then branch off west to Umpang, for some trekking. Finish off by getting down to an east-coast beach.

● Hire a motorbike in Chiang Mai for the Mae Hong Son loop, a 600-kilometre circular route via rolling hills and sleepy little towns. En route, organize a few days' trekking in Mae Hong Son or Pai.

● From Bangkok, set off for the southern beaches, stopping en route for a couple of nights in Kanchanaburi, then two or three days in Khao Sok National Park. Between November and April, continue down to one of the southwest beaches at Krabi, Ko Phi Phi, Ko Lanta or Ko Tarutao; alternatively stop off in Khao Lak and organize a three- or five-day snorkelling or diving trip to the fabulous reefs off the Similan and Surin islands. At other times of the year, head southeast to Ko Samui, Ko Pha Ngan or Ko Tao.

Four weeks

● From Bangkok, do a slow clockwise loop of the north and northeast, taking in Kanchanaburi and the little lakeside backwater Sangkhlaburi, then head up to Sukhothai, west to Umpang, and north to Mae Hong Song and Pai. Take a break in Chiang Mai before branching off east to remote and rural Nan, and then picking up the Mekong river route at Chiang Khan. From here, you can proceed in a leisurely fashion along the river, enjoying the tranquil little guesthouses that dot its course. Head west from the transport hub of Ubon

Ratchathani to Phanom Rung before exploring Khao Yai National Park and finally returning to Bangkok. Round off your month with a stint on the east-coast islands of Ko Samet or Ko Chang.

Thailand online

Bangkok Metro Ⓦ*www.bkkmetro.com* The online version of Bangkok's lively monthly listings magazine includes archives of features about contemporary Thailand, restaurant and club listings for the capital, plus a roundup of events in the main tourist destinations.

Bangkok Post Ⓦ*www.bangkokpost.net* Catch up on what's happening in Thailand with Thailand's leading English-language daily, which also carries interesting local travel articles.

Phuket Gazette Ⓦ*www.phuketgazette.net/gazette/* Southern Thailand's resort island of Phuket publishes a weekly independent newspaper, and their online version makes enjoyable reading, with editorials on a good range of Thailand-related subjects, as well as local and national news stories.

René Hasekamp's Homepage Ⓦ*www.hasekamp.net/thaiindex.htm* Constructed by a Dutch man who is married to a Thai woman, this site lists practical tips, dos and don'ts, info on certain sights, and an especially handy list of FAQs for travellers to Thailand.

Welcome to Chiang Mai and Chiang Rai Ⓦ*www.infothai.com/wtcmcr* This online version of the Chiang Mai listings magazine has some really interesting pages, including background info on hill tribes and northern Thai handicrafts, plus regularly updated news of forthcoming events and festivals in the region.

Vietnam

Capital: Hanoi	**Climate**: Tropical
Population: 77 million	**Best time to go**:
Language: Vietnamese	September–December, and March
Currency: Dong (d)	and April
Main religion: Mahayana Buddhism	**Minimum daily budget**: $10/£7

Although Vietnam has recently enjoyed a bit of a tourist boom, the country features on relatively few mainstream itineraries and so still feels like an adventurous destination, particularly in comparison to Thailand and Malaysia. Inevitably, the Vietnam War (which the Vietnamese refer to as the American War) of the 1960s and 1970s figures strongly in visitors' agendas. But when you've had your fill of crawling through guerrilla tunnels and posing beside downed helicopters, there are hill tribes, beaches and islands galore to check out, not to mention eleventh-century Hindu ruins and 300-year-old Confucianist temples.

Starved of contact with the West after a decade and a half in the wilderness, the Vietnamese people are welcoming and full of fascinating stories; it's a bonus that English is widely understood. War sights aside, contemporary Vietnam is very much looking to the future, and although the economic boom of the 1990s was all too brief, this is not at all the browbeaten country you may have been expecting.

Though the public transport system is as slow as it is extensive, budget tour operators are taking up the slack and making it easier to travel between major attractions. Accommodation, however, is taking longer to improve – for every comfortable room in a quaint

French colonial villa, there are five faceless cells in austere Soviet-style hotel blocks.

Main attractions

● **Hanoi**. Vietnam's capital, in the north of the country, enjoys a relatively cool climate and is a surprisingly pleasant place to linger. Highlights include the historic Confucian-style Temple of Literature, the chaotically traditional alleys of the Old Quarter, and the rather macabre Ho Chi Minh Mausoleum, where the body of the great man is displayed in a glass box.

● Taking a boat tour round the dramatic **Ha Long Bay**. This is the best and most popular way to appreciate the beauty and drama of the bay, which is peppered with hundreds of bizarrely shaped limestone outcrops and yawning caves. Most people start their boat tour from the resort town of Bai Chay, though the fishing island of Cat Ba makes a more interesting gateway.

● **Ho Chi Minh City**. More famously known as Saigon, the former capital of South Vietnam is a hectic city, stuffed with venerable temples, classy restaurants and hundreds of bars. Most visi-

VIETNAM

CHINA

Red River

Hekou
Lao Cai
Sa Pa
Da River
Dien Bien Phu
Son La
Mai Chau
HANOI
Haiphong
Ninh Binh

Nanning

Dong Dang

Mong Cai

Ha Long Bay

*Gulf
of
Tonkin*

LAOS

Vientiane

Cau Treo

Vinh

DMZ

Savannakhet
Mukdahan
Lao Bao
Dong Ha
Hué
Da Nang
Hoi An
My Son
Quang Ngai

THAILAND

Ubon
Ratchathani

Plei Ku
Qui Nhon

Tonle
Sap

Mekong River

Buon Me
Thuot

Nha Trang

CAMBODIA

Da Lat

*Gulf of
Thailand*

Phnom Penh

Moc
Bai
Cu Chi
Ho Chi Minh City
Phan Thiet

Long Hai
Vung Tau

*South
China
Sea*

N

Phu Quoc
Island

My Tho
Ben Tre
Can Tho *Mekong
Delta*

Ca Mau

0   200 km

One week
• Hanoi–Perfume Pagoda–Ha Long
Bay–Hanoi.
• Hanoi–Ha Long Bay–Hué–Lao Bao.
• Hanoi–Ho Chi Minh City–Mekong
Delta–Cu Chi tunnels–Phnom Penh.

Two weeks
• Ho Chi Minh City–Mekong Delta–
Long Hai/Nha Trang/Phan Thiet–
Hoi An–Hué–Hanoi–Ha Long Bay–
Hanoi–Sa Pa.

Four weeks
• Ho Chi Minh City–Mekong Delta–
Phu Quoc–Long Hai–Da Lat–Nha
Trang–Hoi An–Hué–DMZ–Hanoi–
Ha Long Bay–Hanoi–Sa Pa.

Mean Temperatures (°C) and Rainfall (mm)

Average daily temperatures (maximum and minimum°C) and monthly rainfall (mm)

	Jan	Feb	Mar	Apr	May	June	July	Aug	Sept	Oct	Nov	Dec
Hanoi												
max °C	20	21	23	28	32	33	33	32	31	29	26	22
min °C	13	14	17	20	23	26	26	26	24	22	18	15
rainfall mm	18	28	38	81	196	239	323	343	254	99	43	20
Da Nang												
max °C	24	26	27	30	33	34	34	34	31	28	27	25
min °C	19	20	21	23	24	25	25	25	24	23	22	20
rainfall mm	102	31	12	18	47	42	99	117	447	530	221	209
Ho Chi Minh City												
max °C	32	33	34	35	33	32	31	31	31	31	31	31
min °C	21	22	23	24	24	24	24	24	23	23	23	22
rainfall mm	15	3	13	43	221	330	315	269	335	269	114	56

tors make the "war sights" a priority, in particular the absorbing War Crimes and Revolutionary museums, and the former American Embassy.

● The Mekong Delta. Southeast Asia's greatest river, the 4000-kilometre-long Mekong, rises on the Tibetan plateau and runs down through China, Laos, Thailand and Cambodia before reaching journey's end in Vietnam, where it fans out into dozens of smaller rivers to water the vast alluvial plains of the Mekong Delta. The scenes here are quintessential Southeast Asia: emerald rice paddies, fruit orchards, sugar-cane fields and coconut palms, tended by conical-hatted farmers and criss-crossed by waterways that are chock-a-block with sampans and rowing boats. You can explore the area and its floating markets on day-trips from Ho Chi Minh City, or stay in one of the delta villages such as Can Tho, My Tho or Ben Tre.

● Hué. During the nineteenth century, this aristocratic city reigned as Vietnam's capital, and today it boasts the finest traditional Sino-Vietnamese architecture, a legacy of the inspiration the Vietnamese emperors took from Confucianist China. The walled citadel still contains relics from the Imperial City, while a short boat ride up the city's Perfume River brings you to the seven imperial mausoleums, where each Nguyen-dynasty emperor designed himself an elegantly land-scaped memorial of pagodas, pavilions and pleasure gardens. In complete contrast, Hué is also the most convenient departure point for day trips to the infamously bleak stretch of land known as the DMZ, or Demilitarized Zone, which once served as the border between North and South Vietnam.

● Hoi An. This captivating historic port town is characterized by narrow streets and a clutch of beautifully preserved 200-year-old merchants' shophouses, some of which are still inhabited by family descendants and can be visited.

● The Cu Chi tunnels near Ho Chi Minh. These are among the most visited sights from the American War. Scores of communist Viet Cong guerrillas lived for weeks on end in this 250-kilometre network of underground hide-outs, attempting to evade capture by the American forces. Tunnel facilities included rudimentary subterranean hospitals, kitchens and classrooms, relics of which can still be seen today.

Also recommended

● **Beaches**. Vietnam may not be renowned for these, but the sands that ring remote little Phu Quoc island, close to the Cambodian border, are splendid. Other low-key beaches that are easier to get to and reasonably near Ho Chi Minh City include modest Long Hai, and the beautiful, and rather more up-market, Cape Mui Ne, near Phan Thiet. Though less laid-back, the more famous municipal beach in the city of Nha Trang has plenty of fans nonetheless.

● **Trekking**. The region around the northern hill town of Sa Pa is inhabited by a variety of hill tribes and makes a rewarding destination for walkers. Most of the tribespeople arrived in the region about 200 years ago, when persecution in their native China prompted a mass migration into the northern hills of Vietnam, Laos and, most famously, Thailand. Although some of the hill-tribe villages around Sa Pa are now firmly on the tourist route, many are not, so encounters up here can be more authentic than in over-packaged Thailand.

● Meeting the **"mad monk" of Da Lat**. Artist, Zen poet and Buddhist monk Vien Tuc welcomes visitors to his pagoda-cum-art gallery, which houses thousands of his own abstract watercolours. Da Lat itself is a pleasant enough if rather self-consciously quaint hill-station town, surrounded by aromatic pine forests and enjoying a refreshingly cool climate.

● Drinking freshly brewed **bia hoi** (draught beer) in one of the makeshift streetside joints in Hanoi or Ho Chi Minh City. Pull up a stool and join the crowd round the barrel.

● The **Cham temples of My Son**. Dating back to the eleventh century, these evocative jungle-clad ruins of a group of Hindu temples still retain some carvings and statues despite the best efforts of countless American B52s.

Routes in and out

With Ho Chi Minh City and Hanoi both served by international flights, it's quite feasible – and very popular – to enter the country via one city and leave via the other. You can also enter (and depart) Vietnam overland – by train from China, departing from Beijing, Nanning or Kunming and arriving at Hanoi; by bus from Laos, via Lao Bao, to Dong Ha, and via Cau Treo to Vinh; by bus from Mukdahan in Thailand, via Savannakhet in Laos, to Dong Ha; and by bus from Phnom Penh in Cambodia via Moc Bai to Ho Chi Minh City.

Itineraries

One week
● Spend your first three nights in Hanoi, making a day-trip to the evocative Perfume Pagoda on the Red River Delta. Then head down to Ha Long Bay for two or three days before returning to Hanoi.

● It's quite feasible to treat Vietnam as a transit destination on an overland trip between China and either Laos or Cambodia. Beginning with a couple of nights in Hanoi, you can see quite a few major sights en route to either Laos or Cambodia:

● The route to Laos allows you to take in some northern Vietnamese sights.

From Hanoi, you can visit Ha Long Bay, then take the train down the coast to Hué for a pleasant few days' sightseeing and cycling. From here, strike west to cross the Lao border at Lao Bao.

● Heading for Cambodia, fly south to Ho Chi Minh City, basing yourself there for at least four days, making trips out to the Mekong Delta and the Cu Chi tunnels. From Ho Chi Minh City, take a direct bus to Phnom Penh.

Two weeks

● Spend a couple of days in Ho Chi Minh City, then head out to the Mekong Delta for another night or two. Start working your way northwards, stopping for a beach break at either Long Hai, Cape Mui Ne or Nha Trang, before spending a night in Hoi An and then two days in Hué. Continue north to spend three or four days in Hanoi , taking in a day and a night at Ha Long Bay en route. If you have time, make a side trip from Hanoi to the hill-tribe area near Sa Pa.

Four weeks

● With an extra fortnight you can follow the two-week outline at a more leisurely place and take in a few additional sights along the way. While you're in the vicinity of Ho Chi Minh City, take a few days

out on the lovely but rather time-consuming island of Phu Quoc. On your way north, stop off at Da Lat to enjoy the hill-station atmosphere. Once you've exhausted the main sights in Hué, make a trip north to see the notorious DMZ. Once you've reached Hanoi, take time to explore the hills of the northwest, particularly around Sa Pa.

Vietnam online

Destination Vietnam
Ⓦ *www.destinationvietnam.com* Highly recommended site with an especially good travel tips section, featuring dozens of recommendations from travellers to Vietnam, plus pieces on subjects as diverse as guidebooks and local music. Has a travellers' forum too.

Hitchhiking Vietnam
Ⓦ *www.pbs.org/hitchhikingvietnam* This enthusiastic homepage is a nice introduction to the country, with excerpts from the author's journal and photo album plus quirky tips and recommendations for different places.

Vietnam Adventures Online
Ⓦ *www.vietnamadventures.com* General site that looks at customs and culture, as well as featuring tourist destinations around the country.

First-Time Asia

The big adventure

Planning your route

opefully, the previous section has given you a taste of what's on offer in Asia. Now you have to decide which countries to head for, which ones to leave out, and what order to see them in. Later in this chapter you'll find some suggestions for popular and creative itineraries across Asia, and in Chapter Five there's a roundup of recommended guidebooks, travel literature and other travel publications that should also be a good source of ideas. But first, here are some elementary issues to consider:

- Your first task is to decide on the length of your trip. If money is the main consideration, check out Chapter Four to find out how far your budget will stretch.
- Do some research into the climate. Is it the right time of year to go trekking/white-water rafting/snorkelling and diving? Will it be raining all the time, or too hot to enjoy yourself? See Chapter Three for advice on this.
- Make some preliminary investigations into different ticket options, and check out relevant visa requirements, described in Chapter Two.
- Think about the pace of your proposed trip. Are you going to be whizzing through places so fast that you won't have any real sense of where you are or what each country is like? Are you allowing

yourself enough time and flexibility to add new places to your itinerary or linger in spots that you like a lot? Cramming too many destinations into your schedule means that you'll see far too much of the worst bits of a country, namely its bus stations and airports.

● Is your itinerary nicely balanced? Will you get bored if you see nothing but beaches for the next few months? Might you start longing for some hill walking after weeks of museums and temples?

A shared experience?

Now is also the time to think about who you want to go travelling with, or if indeed you want to share your trip with anyone at all. There are obvious pluses and minuses to both options. Travelling with one or more companions means you always have someone to chat to and plan things with; you can mull over your experiences together and share your enthusiasms and worries; and you may well feel braver about exploring and experimenting if you're with someone else. On a practical level, you will save money because double and triple rooms are better value and taxi expenses will be halved; and there'll always be someone to mind the bags while one of you looks for a hotel room or nips off to buy a pineapple in the market.

However, travel is a surprisingly stressful activity: the heat, the hassle and the sheer strangeness of things are bound to fray your nerves, and guess who's going to bear the brunt of your irritability? Expect to get on each other's nerves and to fall out every so often, and be prepared to split up during the trip – either for a few days because you've got different priorities, or for good because your differences seem to be insurmountable. Bearing this in mind, you and your prospective companion should take a long hard look at your friendship and try to imagine it under stress. Will one person be making all the plans and taking all the responsibilities, and will that annoy both of you? Do you have broadly the same expectations of the trip and share a similar attitude to mishaps and hassles? Does one of you have a lot more money than the other, and will that cause tension?

If travel puts a strain on friendships, then imagine what it does to relationships. A disconcerting number of romances crack during a long cross-Asia trip, but then perhaps they weren't meant to last anyway. If yours survives it, you will have been brought closer together and will have lots of great stories and photos to coo over for many years to come.

Going solo

Solo travel is a more extreme and intense experience. You have to face up to everything on your own, and find the motivation to move on, explore and be sociable all by yourself. There will be lonely times for sure, and scary ones, and you'll probably get tired of eating out on your own every night. But you will also be a lot more open to your surroundings and you'll make more effort to chat to new people – as indeed they will to you (twosomes often put people off because they seem so self-contained). Some people find they're more alert and receptive on their own, and most single travellers write much more interesting letters and journals simply because they're desperate to blurt out all their experiences. And, of course, you have no one to answer to but yourself, which means you can change your plans at a moment's notice or idle away your days without feeling guilty.

Finding a travel companion

If you're nervous about going on your own, but can't find anyone to accompany you, all is not lost. Travel magazines, university noticeboards, newspaper personal columns and Internet news-groups and travel forums are full of advertisements from people looking for travelling companions. Most advertisers have specific itineraries in mind and will want to meet and discuss plans quite a few times – if you don't find an ad that fits your bill, why not place one yourself? Just be sure to use your common sense when meeting any stranger for the first time, however genuine they sound on the net or on the phone: for example, arrange to meet in a public place, and don't give them your address too early. Travelling with an unknown person will bring its share of unpleasant surprises, so you should definitely discuss ground rules before you go and perhaps even set off on a dummy trip – a weekend away, for example

– before the big departure. But it can also be unexpectedly fun, and with any luck you'll have made a new friend by the trip's end.

Even if no one suitable turns up before you set off, you'll find it remarkably easy to hitch up with travel companions once you've actually arrived in Asia. The backpackers' scene is well established in major Asian towns, cities and beach resorts, and guesthouse noticeboards are usually thick with requests for travelmates. Bangkok's Khao San Road, the Paharganj area of New Delhi, and Thamel and Freak Street in Kathmandu are all fruitful places to look.

Joining a tour

For some people, joining an organized tour is the most appealing introduction to Asia. This takes away a lot of the more daunting elements – like arranging local transport and accommodation your-self – and often means that you're accompanied by an expert whose in-depth knowledge of the country can really enhance your stay. Hundreds of tour operators offer trips to Asian destinations (see Basics, p.358, for some recommendations) and the range of pack-ages is phenomenal: there are short city breaks, week-long beach holidays, cultural tours, walking tours, adventure tours (kayaking, trekking, wildlife-spotting), off-the-beaten-track tours, tailor-made tours and even culinary tours. Some tours whisk you around the highlights of two or even three countries in just a couple of weeks; others offer long, slow, overland journeys lasting anything up to six months. Most operators specialize in either up-market or mid-mar-ket packages, but there are a few economy packages, featuring homestay accommodation and local transport, and the long over-land ones are pretty basic, with participants sharing cooking chores and contributing to the food kitty.

One option worth considering if you're on your own or a bit apprehensive, is to start your trip by joining an organized tour from home for a few weeks, then branch off by yourself when you've gained more confidence and Asia know-how; many tour operators are used to this and offer tour-only prices so that you can arrange your own flights. This is also fairly common practice on the youth-oriented overland tours (run by Exodus, Encounter Overland and Explore Worldwide, for example), and gives you a good grounding as well as the chance to meet potential onward travel companions.

A sponsored holiday

A potentially interesting way of joining a tour and exploring a country while contributing something useful is to participate in a fundraising activity holiday in aid of a charity. Many of the major-league charities organize one or more of these events every year; recent examples have included a fortnight's cycle ride from Bangkok to Ho Chi Minh City, a trek through the jungles of Borneo, a fortnight's cycle tour around Vietnam, a trek into the Nepali Himalayas to help rebuild a Buddhist monastery, and treks in Nepal and Bhutan. Although participants have to be reasonably fit, the "challenge" element is generally minimal, and the idea is usually that you have an enjoyable and energetic holiday while simultaneously making some money for a good cause.

Each charity has a different way of organizing these events, but most ask for a minimum amount of sponsorship – which tends to be between £1500 and £2500 in the UK for a fortnight's trip. It's up to you how to get this money, though organizers usually offer advice and sometimes even practical help. Obviously some of your money is used to cover your holiday expenses – these are holidays after all, with reasonable board and lodging provided, as well as time off to go sightseeing where relevant – but not everyone is happy at the percentage of the fee which goes in the charity box, so check first before registering. In addition, not everyone feels comfortable that their friends, families and colleagues are effectively financing the trip.

If you have a favourite charity, contact them to see if they're planning any fundraising holidays. Otherwise, look for adverts in the travel sections of national newspapers, and in the travel magazines described in Chapter Five. The organization Charity Challenge ☎020/8557 0000, ⦿*www.charitychallenge.com* runs about twenty fundraising adventure holidays a year, including treks, mountain bike rides and canoeing trips, and has over fifty charities on its books, so you can choose which one to support. For information on working with a charity while you're in Asia, see the section on "Voluntary Work" (p.134).

Taking the kids

Many package tours are child-friendly and offer good deals. But it's also increasingly common for independent travellers, including single parents, to take their kids to Asia. Children are considered a huge blessing in most parts of Asia and yours will be no exception. They are great icebreakers with strangers and are often really interesting travel companions, noticing things that you don't and enthusing about all the weirdness and novelty. Outside the main resorts you're unlikely to find child-oriented entertainments, but there's usually so much going on that this shouldn't be an insurmountable drawback. And there's always the beach. As with adult travellers, certain countries or regions make for a smoother initiation into Asia than others – notably Singapore, Hong Kong, Bali, Japan and Taiwan – while China, India, Nepal and Pakistan may be better tackled after some acclimatization. Most of Southeast Asia falls somewhere in between.

The chief worry is how to keep your child healthy, but if you follow the advice given in Chapter Eleven, and contact both your own doctor and the travellers' health centres well ahead of your departure, there's every chance that the whole family will have a hassle-free trip.

Where shall I go first?

You probably won't have much trouble deciding where to start your trip – there'll either be an obvious geographical option, or your travel agent will twist your arm with offers of significant discounts if you go with their recommendation.

For Europeans, the usual gateway cities are Kathmandu, Delhi and Bangkok. These are the nearest entry points to Asia and generally the cheapest places to fly to. Australians generally begin somewhere in Indonesia, typically in Bali. Flying to Asia from America is a more long-winded process. From the East Coast, most flights go via London, Amsterdam or Frankfurt, and then on to Kathmandu, Delhi or Bangkok. If you're starting from the West Coast, the cheapest routes will probably be to Seoul, Taipei or Tokyo.

Saving money should not be the only consideration, though, and you'd be wise to think about the stress factor of your first days and nights in Asia:

● Start yourself off gently. Many travellers find the poverty, chaos and crowds of India, for example, a very tough introduction to Asia, so you might want to begin your cross-Asia trip somewhere calmer, like Malaysia or Bali.

FEAR OF FLYING

Not everyone relishes the idea of travelling to the other side of the world in a pressurized metal box that careers along at thirty thousand feet above sea level with no visible means of support. Fear of flying is a relatively common anxiety – apparently seriously affecting one in five adults – making overland travel a necessity rather than a choice for many people. But, while getting to Asia by land and sea can be a very enjoyable experience (see p.115), there are a number of courses and other resources to help those who would like to combat their dread of air travel. The self-help Web site ✪www.anxieties.com has a comprehensive section on fear of flying, with advice, practical step-by-step programmes and plenty of comparative statistics to impress upon you how safe air travel actually is. Several airlines run regular therapy workshops which aim to help you deal with your fear by taking you through a simulated flight – some even culminate in a short real flight. Prices range from £100–190 for a one-day course; in the UK, contact Aviatour ✪01252/793250, Britannia ✪01582/428001, or Virgin Atlantic ✪01293/744664. In the US, SOAR ✪1-800-FEAR FLY, ✪www.fearofflying.com offers courses on overcoming fear of flying, starting at $300. For advice on how to enjoy your flight, see Chapter Seven.

- For the gentlest introduction to a new country, consider arranging international flights to towns other than the capital cities. You can fly from Europe directly to Phuket in south Thailand, for example, which means that by the time you've worked your way up to Bangkok (or down to Kuala Lumpur) you'll be blasé about big noisy cities and will exude the confidence of an old Asia hand. Similarly, you can fly direct from New York to Goa, from Perth to Bali, from London to Kunming, and so on. See Chapter Two for information on the different types of air tickets available.
- If you've had a long flight, you'll probably be worn out when you arrive, so plan an easy schedule for the first week. Two or three nights in a pre-booked hotel near your place of arrival will give you a chance to sleep and acclimatize; then you might want to chill out on a beach somewhere, or relax in a smaller town or resort. See Chapter Seven for advice.

Across Asia by air

Most people choose to do their cross-Asia trip by air, simply because it's faster and easier than going overland. Travel agents sort out all the details for you and everything is booked in advance (which is reassuring for anxious relatives and one less headache for you). Advice on buying the best plane ticket for your trip is given in Chapter Two.

The best approach is to work out your ideal route before you have your final session with the travel agent, picking a few well-placed destinations that you're absolutely determined not to miss. Once you've got your core must-sees, be prepared to be flexible about the in-between bits, bearing in mind that some routes are a lot cheaper than others. If possible, leave some extra free time at strategic intervals so that you're able to be spontaneous and follow up other travellers' recommendations once you're on the ground.

Before making any firm decisions about your ticket, check out the section on overland routes within Asia beginning on p.118. There are all sorts of intriguing bus, train and ferry routes between countries in Asia, and this can save you a lot of money on your air ticket, as well as enhancing your adventure.

Round-the-world classic: UK–India–Nepal–Thailand–Malaysia–Indonesia–(Australia)–UK

This is a classic first-time Asia itinerary for anyone making their way there from Europe, giving you the run of the best of South and Southeast Asia with the added option of rounding off your trip in Australia. The route can be done on a round-the-world ticket, a multiple-stopover ticket or even on an open-jaw return – see pp.144–149 for details on which ticket would be most suitable for you. For Australians, the same route applies, but in reverse, with the option of extending to Europe if you want.

The first port of call on many round-the-world trips is Delhi, chiefly because it's only ten hours' flying time from London. Although the Indian capital is not necessarily an easy opener for first-timers, it is well positioned for trips to Rajasthan and the Himalayas. But if you're going to head south to the beaches of Goa, get an international flight to Mumbai (Bombay) instead. Calcutta is a more unusual alternative, but a useful one as you can get cheap routeings to Bangkok via Dhaka in Bangladesh. From any point in India you have the choice of flying or overlanding to Kathmandu (see p.117), but to continue to Bangkok you'll have to fly out, because it's currently impossible to cross Burma overland.

If you decide to leave out the Indian subcontinent altogether, your trip will begin in Bangkok. From there, you have a choice of flying in short hops through Thailand, Malaysia, Singapore and the islands of Indonesia (Sumatra, Java and then Bali), or making the long trek south overland. Travelling from Bangkok to Bali by bus, train and boat will save you heaps of money, but is obviously a lot more time-consuming. If you want to stop off for a while in all four countries then allow yourself at least two to three months for this part of the trip. There's a lot of ground to cover – Sumatra, for example, is the fourth largest island in the world – and the whole adventure becomes a real slog if you try to cram it all into three weeks.

In fact, the most popular route south from Bangkok is a combination of flying and overlanding. You can either weave a couple of flights into your round-the-world ticket before you go (for example, between Malaysia and Sumatra, and between Java and Bali), or buy flights in Asia as and when you get tired of long bus journeys. Bangkok is a good centre for cheap flights (visit **W** *www.thaifare.com* for a list of sample fares), and internal flights within Indonesia are both inexpensive and extensive. Long-distance overnight trains and buses cover the Thai–Malaysian–Singapore peninsula, and you can easily island-hop all the way from Malaysia to Bali and even on to Irian Jaya if you have the time.

Overland routes into Asia from Europe and Australia

For some travellers, the process of getting to Asia is a crucial part of the whole adventure. However, time is the major factor here, and the expense may be off-putting too – though trains, buses and boats are generally cheaper than flights, you will have spent a fair bit on accommodation and food before you even arrive in Asia.

The overland routes listed on pp.116–117 are just a handful of the possible options. Though we've described them as routes *into* Asia, they're quite feasible

Delhi to London on a motorbike

After six months exploring India on an elderly Enfield Bullet, bought in Delhi for £600, I thought the bike would make a good souvenir. Shipping it was an option, but somehow riding the 10,000-odd miles home across Asia seemed a lot more interesting . . .

My route was a fairly standard one, taking me through Pakistan (with a side-trip up the Karakoram Highway into the northern hills), and then on to Iran and Turkey. Over the next five months, I rode through some of the most stunning and least-touristed areas of Asia, beneath soaring mountains, through barren deserts and across fertile plains. All the way along, people were exceptionally hospitable – there was always someone around to help me decipher squiggly road signs, direct me to a mechanic or, frequently, invite me home to stay with the family.

The gradual transition from East to West was fascinating: the culture, climate and terrain changed imperceptibly day by day. On top of that, there was something immensely satisfying about tracing a line on the map across two continents and actually following it on the ground.

Nicki McCormick

when done in reverse. It's almost, but not quite, possible to travel all the way from Australia to Britain (and back) without resorting to an aeroplane; the only hiatus comes when you need to cross the sea between northern Australia and Timor, the Indonesian island that's closest to Australia – unless you cadge a ride on a yacht or a cargo boat, you'll have to get a flight from Darwin to Kupang, after which you can island-hop all the way to Singapore. In reality, most Australians choose the easy option and fly straight into Bali, beginning their journeys from there; the current instability in Timor means that even the most adventurous travellers may have to choose this route also.

On the whole, it's less hassle to organize overland trips from your own country, particularly if using your own transport. The bureaucracy involved in riding a motorbike back from India, for example, is so overwhelming that some travellers give up before they even get started.

Once in Asia you have the option of continuing your travels by road, rail and river (see "Overland routes within Asia", p.118), or you can buy a series of air tickets as you go.

The Trans-Siberian Railway

The Trans-Siberian Railway is *the* classic overland route into Asia. All its trains begin in Moscow and there are three possible routes. The Trans-Mongolian route and the Trans-

Manchurian route both end up in Beijing and take about six days to get there. If you are patient, have lots of time and have paid meticulous attention to visa requirements, you can then continue by train from Beijing to Hanoi in Vietnam; this takes about five days. For access to Japan, take the Trans-Siberian route from Moscow, via Khabarovsk, allowing seven days to reach Vladivostok; from here it's a two-day boat ride across to Niigata in Japan.

Providing you arrange relevant visas, you can stop off pretty much anywhere you like en route, so the trip can last for several weeks if you want. For a full rundown of everything you need to know about visas, life on the train and ideas for stopoffs, see the *Trans-Siberian Handbook,* published by Trailblazer.

The hippie trail: from Europe to Kathmandu via Turkey, Iran, Pakistan and India

The most common way to do this route is by car or motorbike – if you put your foot down and ignore the temptations of the countries en route, you can reach Delhi from London in 21 days. However, doing it this way obviously involves some serious preparation, both for yourself and your vehicle. The paperwork is the biggest headache – visas need to be sorted out well in advance of your departure date (especially for Iran) and you will also need a special document for your vehicle known as a *carnet de passage.* Bikers should check out *The Adventure Motorcycling Handbook* (Trailblazer), which contains full details of all these requirements; the closest equivalent for car drivers is currently Bradt's *Russia and Central Asia by Road*, which includes advice on vehicle preparation and the necessary documents.

Some tour operators (such as Encounter Overland and Exodus; see p.358) organize group overland trips along these routes in converted lorries. The trips take from four to thirty weeks, the age range is generally between 18 and 40, and the all-inclusive cost is quite reasonable. If you're nervous about setting off for Asia on your own, then this could be a good way to start. It's not uncommon for travellers from Europe to join an overland tour to Kathmandu and then continue on through Asia either alone or with a companion.

It's quite possible, if very time-consuming, to do the hippie trail by public transport. For specific advice, consult Trailblazer's *Asia Overland: A Route and Planning Guide.*

Be prepared

My trouble was I thought I
could just go where I liked
when I liked. I'll go to Cambodia today.
What do I need? Visa. Get that at the
border. Bus ticket. No problem. Can I
have a single to Phnom Penh please?

Ho Chi Minh bus station: No. Your visa
says leaving Vietnam from Hanoi. This
bus crosses the border at Moc Bai. Go
to the Ministry of Interior and change
your visa.

Ministry of Interior: Not possible. Go to
the Foreign Commission.

Foreign Commission: Can't do it. Go to
Vietnam Tourism.

Vietnam Tourism: Nope. Show me your
Cambodian visa first.

Cambodian Embassy:
Come back the day after
tomorrow!

Chris Humphrey

Overland routes within Asia

Before fixing your ticket routeing, think about spicing up your flight itinerary with some overland routes in between. It's a great feeling to watch from a train window as one country slowly metamorphoses into another – far more satisfying than whizzing over international borders at thirty thousand feet – and in nearly every case it will be a lot cheaper than flying. Sometimes it's also quicker and more convenient than backtracking to the airport in the capital city.

Having the right paperwork is absolutely essential for overland routes, as most countries demand that you specify the exact land border when applying – see Chapter Two for more advice on this, and be sure to check out the viability of your proposed overland route before making any firm flight bookings. You'll find a detailed list of the current designated border crossings in Asia on pp.120–121, and there's more detail in the individual country profiles on pp.3–102. See also the colour maps at the back of the book, which show border crossings and international ferry routes.

Overlanding under your own steam can also be an exhilarating way to travel across the continent. Some crazed intrepids do it by bicycle – see Josie Dew's *A Ride in the Neon Sun* (Warner), all about her two-wheeled adventures in Japan, and *Tea for Two*

. . . *With No Cups* by Polly Benge (Travellerseye), which describes a cycle trip through Nepal and India – but it's far more popular to zip around on a motorbike or in a car, as outlined on p.116.

Southeast Asia: Thailand–Malaysia–Singapore–Indonesia

By far the most popular overland route within Asia is the trip down from Thailand into Malaysia. You can cross between these countries quite effortlessly by train, bus or minibus, as nearly all major towns and resorts between Bangkok and Kuala Lumpur run long-distance cross-border transport. Not surprisingly, Bangkok–Kuala Lumpur is a common "surface sector" leg on round-the-world, Circle-Asia and open-jaw tickets (see Chapter Two). Sometimes this overland route is rounded off with a few days on the island of Singapore, which is connected to southern Malaysia by a causeway.

A relatively popular extension to the Thailand–Malaysia route is to continue on into Indonesia by sea. There are frequent ferries and speedboats from various ports in Malaysia to Sumatra, and from Johor Bahru and Singapore to Indonesia's Riau archipelago. Most of these ferries take just a few hours to travel between Malaysia/Singapore and Indonesia.

Indochina: Thailand–Laos–Vietnam–Cambodia–Thailand

The overland trail from Thailand across Indochina is becoming increasingly well travelled, and makes an interesting circular route that can be done without ever taking to the air. Bear in mind, however, that road transport in Laos and Cambodia is very slow and can be exhaustingly uncomfortable.

There are currently five crossings between northeast Thailand and Laos, the easiest and most popular of which connects Nong Khai and Vientiane. Laos has two gateways into Vietnam: both are served by buses. It's not possible to travel overland between Laos and Cambodia, but Vietnam does have a useful cross-border bus service that runs from Ho Chi Minh City to Phnom Penh. You can overland between Cambodia and Thailand at two points: the northern crossing runs from Poipet (a day's bus journey from Siem Reap/Angkor) to Aranyapathet in Thailand (a six-hour train jour-

BORDER CROSSINGS AND INTERNATIONAL FERRIES

All the border crossings listed below are served by public transport. In most cases you will have to get off the train or bus to walk over the border and show your relevant paperwork to both sets of immigration officials. Burma and Sri Lanka are currently the only two countries that are inaccessible to overlanders. Except where stated, all the following border crossings are accessible from both sides, but rules do change, so it's advisable to double-check the situation before making final decisions about your route.

Indian subcontinent

Pakistan–China. By bus along the Karakoram Highway from Sust (Pakistan) to Tashkurgan (China).

India–Pakistan. Bus or train via Amritsar (India) to Wagha (Pakistan) and Lahore.

India–China. No overland crossing allowed.

India–Bangladesh. From Calcutta via the border town of Benapal to Dhaka by train, rickshaw and bus; from Darjeeling via Haldibari to Chiliharti by train; from Shillong via the border town of Dawki to Sylhet by bus.

India–Sri Lanka. Owing to the unrest in Sri Lanka, the ferry service between Rameswaram in India and Talaimannar in Sri Lanka is suspended indefinitely.

India–Nepal. By bus from Delhi, Varanasi or Gorakhpur via Sunauli and Bhairawa to Pokhara or Kathmandu; by bus from Bodh Gaya, Calcutta or Patna via Raxaul and Birganj to Pokhara or Kathmandu; and by bus and/or train from Siliguri, Darjeeling or Calcutta via Kakarbitta to Pokhara or Kathmandu.

Nepal–China (Tibet). Currently not allowed for independent travellers on public transport (though it is permitted in the other direction). However, foreigners who have booked inclusive tours of Lhasa (these can be arranged in Kathmandu) are allowed to cross here; the tour companies organize the paperwork.

Southeast Asia

Thailand–Malaysia and Singapore. By direct train from Bangkok to: Penang, Kuala Lumpur via Hat Yai, or Singapore via Penang. By bus or share-taxi from the southern Thai terminal of Hat Yai to Penang or Singapore. By share-taxi from Betong to Butterworth via Keroh; by road from Ban Taba to Kota Bharu. By frequent ferry from Satun to Kuala Perlis and Langkawi.

Malaysia–Singapore. By bus, train or ferry.

Malaysia and Singapore–Indonesia. By ferry or speedboat from Penang to Medan in northern Sumatra; from Melaka to Dumai in northern Sumatra; from Kuala Lumpur, Johor Bahru or Singapore to Batam, Bintan and Karimun islands (in Indonesia's Riau archipelago). By bus from Kuching (Sarawak) via Entikong to Pontianak (Kalimantan). By ferry from Tawau (Sabah) to Pulau Nunukan in northeastern Kalimantan.

Philippines–Indonesia. Every week or so a cargo boat leaves General Santos for Manado in Northern Sulawesi. Owing to pirates and Filipino insurgents, the unofficial routes between Kalimantan (or nearby Sabah in Malaysia) and Mindanao are far too risky even to contemplate.

Indochina
Thailand–Laos. By bus from Nong Khai to Vientiane; and from Chong Mek via Ban Mai Sing Amphon to Pakxe. By ferry across the Mekong River from Chiang Khong via Houayxai to Louang Phabang; from Nakhon Phanom via Thakhek to Vientiane; and from Mukdahan to Savannakhet.

Thailand–Cambodia. By bus and boat from Trat to Sihanoukville, via Ban Hat Lek and Krong Koh Kong. By bus and train from Aranyaprathet to Sisophon, via Poipet.

Cambodia–Laos. No legal border crossing for foreigners in either direction. However, some travellers cross from Cambodia to Laos by travelling along the Mekong, making arrangements in Stung Treng.

Laos–Vietnam. By bus from Savannakhet and Xepon to Hué or Hanoi, via Lao Bao and Dong Ha. By bus from Lak Xao to Vinh, via Cau Treo.

Vietnam–Cambodia. By bus from Ho Chi Minh City via Moc Bai to Phnom Penh.

Vietnam–China. By bus or rail from Hanoi via Dong Dang to Nanning, and by bus or rail from Hanoi via Lao Cai to Kunming in Yunnan.

Laos–China. By bus from Vientiane to Kunming; by bus from Oudomxai and Louang Namtha to Jinghong; by bus and boat from Louang Phabang via Ban Boten to Mo Han (Yunnan).

China and Japan
China–India. No overland crossing allowed.

China–Pakistan. By bus along the Karakoram Highway from Tashkurgan (China) to Sust (Pakistan).

China (Tibet)–Nepal. Shared jeeps and buses via Zhangmu to Kathmandu, but not allowed going from Nepal into Tibet.

Hong Kong–mainland China. By train, bus or ferry from Hong Kong to Guangzhou (Canton).

China–Laos. By bus from Kunming (Yunnan) to Vientiane; by bus from Jinghong to Oudomxai or Louang Namtha; from Mengla via Mo Han to Boten.

China–Vietnam. By bus or rail from Nanning (Guangxi) via Dong Dang to Hanoi; and by bus or rail from Kunming in Yunnan via Lao Cai to Hanoi.

China–South Korea. By ferry to Inchon (near Seoul) from Tianjin (near Beijing), Qingdao and Weihai (both in Shandong), Dalian and Dandong (both in Liaoning), and Shanghai.

China–Taiwan. None.

Taiwan–Japan. By ferry from Keelung to Naha in Okinawa.

China–Japan. By ferry from Shanghai and Tianjin (near Beijing) to Osaka and Kobe.

Japan–South Korea. By ferry and hydrofoil from Shimonoseki and Fukuoka to Pusan.

ney from Bangkok); the southern route takes you from Sihanoukville to Trat in east Thailand.

Overland from China to Thailand via Indochina

As China has useful land borders with both Laos and Vietnam, the Indochina circuit on p.119 can easily be adapted into a smooth overland link between China and Thailand, and makes it feasible to do the entire journey from London to Hanoi by train.

The Beijing–Nanning–Hanoi train enters Vietnam at Dong Dang, where there's also a road crossing. Trains from Kunming in China's southwestern Yunnan province cross the border further west and terminate at Hanoi. Once in Vietnam, you can choose to travel to Laos or Cambodia, as outlined above.

To get to Laos from China, you can either take a bus from Kunming to Vientiane, or from Jinghong to Oudomxai or Louang Namtha, or from Mengla to Boten. From Laos you can head east into Vietnam or west into Thailand.

By bus from India to Nepal

Overlanding between India and Nepal is straightforward and popular, and a useful surface sector in Circle-Asia and open-jaw tickets (see Chapter Three). The easiest approaches are from Patna and Gorakhpur, which between them have useful train services to and from Delhi, Varanasi, Darjeeling, Gaya and Calcutta. Patna runs buses to Kathmandu via the Nepali border at Raxaul, and Gorakhpur runs buses to another border point, Sonauli, where you can get connections to Pokhara and Kathmandu. The seventeen-hour journey from the Kakarbitta border crossing to Kathmandu is more of a slog, but Kakarbitta is very handy for Darjeeling, and close to Silgiuri, which has good rail connections with Calcutta and Delhi.

India to China via Pakistan and the Karakoram Highway

This unusual trans-Asia route is longer and more challenging than the classic version through India and Southeast Asia, as travel is relatively difficult in Pakistan and China, and travellers rare. For many people, this is part of the route's appeal. The Pakistan–China section can be woven into all sorts of Asian and round-the-world itineraries. It can feature as the middle section of a major overland trip from Europe to Indonesia, following on nicely from the hippie trail to Pakistan (see p.117). It feeds easily into the China–Indochina route described above, becoming the meaty preamble to a more light-hearted Southeast Asian trip: the route from Thailand, through Malaysia, to Indonesia (see p.119) will almost certainly seem like a picnic after the bureaucracies of north Asia. Or you can treat it as the surface sector of an open-jaw return or a Circle-Asia flight (described in Chapter Three), buying a plane ticket that flies you into Delhi and then takes you out of Bangkok or Singapore a few months later, giving yourself the option of buying some internal flights en route if necessary.

Delhi is the obvious entry point to India if you're heading up to Pakistan, but it may be worth flying into one of the regional airports instead, such as Chennai (Madras) or Calcutta, if you want to explore southern or eastern parts of India first. You can either cross into Pakistan overland (via Amritsar) or fly into Hyderabad from Mumbai (Bombay) or Calcutta, or into Lahore and Islamabad from Delhi.

From Pakistan you can take a bus into China via the spectacular Karakoram Highway, which starts in Rawalpindi and goes via Gilgit to Kashgar in far northwest China. This should take about four days but is only feasible from May to October when the Karakoram Highway is not snowbound.

The direct overland route from Kashgar to Ali in western Tibet is closed to foreigners, so if you want to make a side-trip into Tibet you'll have to head east from Kashgar to Golmud and then southwest to Lhasa. From Lhasa you can fly east to Chengdu, which has good transport connections with Kunming as well as the main cities of eastern China.

By sea from China to South Korea and Japan

If you're in eastern China, it's quite possible and inexpensive, if time-consuming, to take a boat across to South Korea and then continue by ferry to Japan; or you could take a direct boat from China to Japan. Once you've seen your fill of Japan you could take the ferry from Niigata across to Vladivostok in Russia and make the long haul back to Europe on the Trans-Siberian Railway. The route works equally well in reverse.

“

Choosing to trek into the Kailash region of Tibet, I ruled out venturing near the city in order to avoid fellow "travellers". We saw no one for days, with the exception of sheep, yaks, and a few nomads. Not even a trace of civilization. An unforgiving wind swept across the plateau, and there were no trees, just low bushes, random rocks, high mountains and rolling hills. I had known what to expect: I knew the population was sparse, and that we would see no one until we reached Mount Kailash, but the desolate and almost Martian landscape made me long all the more for people.

The rivers we crossed were too cold for bathing, and plumbing was nonexistent. Thinking I was an eco-traveller, I carried plastic bags in which to dispose of my toilet paper. But I soon realized that trash and human waste were not confined to the towns. There was garbage scattered across the land, in the middle of nowhere, like it belonged there. Perhaps it had been dropped by pilgrims on their way to Kailash, or by Western tour groups from the windows of their Land Cruisers.

When we finally arrived at Mount Kailash, the sacred home of the Hindu god Shiva, and the centre of the Buddhist universe, happy pilgrims appeared. Finally, people! Pilgrims older than my deceased grandparents had walked 35 miles in a single day – at altitudes of over 15,000 feet. I was amazed. It took me three days to circumambulate the mountain, following a well-trodden path round the holy peak. Devout pilgrims prostrated themselves as they walked through incoming blizzards. One Hindu pilgrim had walked all the way from Delhi in India. He'd begun his journey two months earlier and had hitched rides, slept out in the open and crossed the Himalayas barefoot. In contrast, I wore heavy winter gear, walked no more than ten steps before having to gasp for breath, and slept inside a tent, wrapped in a down sleeping bag.

Karen Christine Lefere

There are regular boats to Inchon near Seoul from Tianjin (near Beijing), Qingdao and Weihai (both in Shandong), Dalian and Dandong (both in Liaoning), and Shanghai. The Weihai connection is the shortest, at fourteen hours, while the boat from Shanghai takes the longest, around forty hours. Hydrofoils to Japan run from Pusan in southern South Korea to Fukuoka (3hr) and Shimonoseki (3hr). To travel between China and Japan by boat takes around 48 hours; services run about twice a week between Beijing and Kobe and between Shanghai and Kobe.

Themes for travel

Rather than hang your trip round tourist sights and famous landscapes, you might consider planning your route around specific activities instead. We've selected some popular highlights below. You'll find specialist guidebooks covering some of these themes, though any decent travel guide should have at least some pointers on a country's most interesting activities.

Trekking and hiking

There's plenty of scope for interesting treks and hikes in Asia, and you don't necessarily have to be an experienced walker to enjoy them. In

Asia, you'll find the word "trek" used to refer to a long-distance walk, where you will spend the night or several nights en route. "Hike" generally means a walk taking a day or less.

In many cases you can do hikes and treks unassisted, so long as you have a decent route map and are dressed for the occasion. But in some places you'd be foolhardy to go without a guide: jungles, for example, are notoriously hard to navigate, even if you do possess a map, and high mountain passes are usually best negotiated with the help of a local expert. For long, arduous treks you'll probably need to hire a porter as well, to help carry tents and food. Travellers often join forces to arrange cheaper group treks, and in the more established places tour operators organize group treks along standard routes on a daily basis.

Don't forget to check on the climate (mid-June to late September, for example, is hopeless for trekking in the Himalayas), and remember to pack suitable clothes and footwear (see Chapter Six for specific advice). Here's a selective roundup of hikes and treks to whet your appetite:

- **China**. Highlights include the one- to three-day trek through the alpine scenery of Sichuan to the spectacular tongue of ice known as Hailuo Guo Glacier; hiking in the hills around Xinjiang's Tian Chi (Heaven Lake), surrounded by snowy peaks and pine forests and staying in Kazakh nomads' tents; and the two-day trek through Tiger Leaping Gorge in Yunnan, the world's deepest canyon. Much more arduous, but popular nonetheless, is the three-day circumnavigation of Tibet's sacred Mount Kailash, stopping at monasteries en route.
- **India**. There are challenging Himalayan treks of two to twelve days through forests and valleys, alongside mountain streams, past remote villages, and over sometimes snowy passes, with constant Himalayan views on all sides. The less difficult routes start from Dharamsala; the more strenuous ones – through the Zanskar and Ladakh regions – begin in Leh.
- **Indonesia**. There are plenty of one-day volcano hikes, including the sunrise walk up Java's Mount Bromo, the trek up to Gunung Rinjani's crater rim on Lombok, and the hike up Keli Mutu on Flores to see its famous three-coloured crater lakes. Irian Jaya's Baliem Valley offers scores of flatter trails to follow, taking you through cultivated land to interesting Dani villages. One of the most popular of the longer treks is the six-day route through

Gunung Leuser National Park in north Sumatra, from Ketambe to the orang-utan sanctuary in Bukit Lawang.

- **Malaysia**. Almost everyone who makes it across to Sabah on the East Malaysian island of Borneo attempts the two-day hike to the summit of Mount Kinabalu (4101m); neighbouring Sarawak offers some strenuous day-hikes in Gunung Mulu National Park, through rainforest to the razor-sharp fifty-metre-high limestone pinnacles, plus exploring parts of the largest cave system in the world. On Peninsular Malaysia, the biggest draw is Taman Negara National Park, which has a good selection of one- to four-day trails through the rainforest, some of them taking in observation hides en route.

- **Nepal**. The Nepal Himalayas are the most popular area in Asia for trekking; there are literally scores of possible options. Independent trekking is quite feasible, but guides, porters and organized tours are also available from Kathmandu and Pokhara.

- **Pakistan**. In the north of the country, where the Himalayas, Karakoram and Hindu Kush mountain ranges collide, you'll find some of the best, and least crowded, trekking in the world. The trekking centres of Shigar near Skardu, Gilgit and Chitral all offer treks that last from one day to several weeks, with the chance to take in glaciers and 5500-metre passes.

- **Philippines**. Highlights include the strenuous four-day climb up the country's highest mountain, volcanic Mount Apo, passing lakes, waterfalls, fine rainforest flora and hot springs en route; the steep four-day ascent and descent into sacred Mount Banahaw's thickly forested crater; and the picturesque day-long hike through sculptured rice paddy valleys to the traditional village of Batad in Ifugao.

- **South Korea**. This tiny country has seventeen national parks, nearly all of them offering scores of well-maintained trails. One of the best is Sorak-San National Park, whose tracks run via craggy peaks and forested slopes, taking in waterfalls, temples and hermitages along the way. Other good ones are Chri-san, which has long trails through the mountains, and the wooded valleys of Songni-san, where you'll come across lots of important temples and hermitages while hiking.

- **Thailand**. A huge percentage of visitors to Thailand go jungle-trekking in the northern hills, mainly to see hill-tribe villages but also for elephant rides and white-water rafting. There's more remote trekking from Kanchanaburi and Umpang, and in the southern jungles of Khao Sok National Park.

Wildlife spotting

Asia is home to some of the most unusual animals in the world, including the tigers and elephants of India and Indonesia, the snow leopard of northern Nepal, the yaks of the Himalayas and Tibetan plateau, and the orang-utans of Kalimantan, Sumatra and Sarawak, not to mention scores of extraordinary birds. Many of these creatures are now endangered, as the pressure from an expanding human population and the continued trade in rare species threatens their existence, so you're unlikely to happen across many of them on a random hike in the mountains or the jungle. However, Asia has a fair number of national parks where rare fauna and flora are, at least in theory, protected from poachers, and many of these places are accessible to tourists.

The places listed below are the cream of the crop, highlighted because you have a good chance of seeing wildlife there and can travel there independently without much trouble. You'll need to be careful about the timing of your visit to any national park, as birds and animals tend to be more social and therefore easier to spot at certain times of the year. For advice on this, and for an overview of Asian wildlife and where to see it, consult the two guides published by Insight: *Southeast Asia Wildlife* and *India Wildlife*, both of which are easy to read and full of colour photos; or check out *Wildlife Indonesia* and *Birding Indonesia*, both produced by Periplus. As for bird guides to the whole of Asia, try to get hold of *Where to Watch Birds in Asia* by Nigel Wheatley (Princeton University Press), or look at New Holland's *Photographic Guide to Birds* series, which covers China, India, Nepal and Malaysia.

- **Bangladesh.** An exceptionally rewarding country for bird-watching, Bangladesh is home to many species that are otherwise only found in either India or Southeast Asia, and is also a major wintering ground for migrant birds. The mangrove swamps and coastal wetlands of the Sunderbans are good places to spot cranes and golden eagles (and there's a very remote possibility of seeing a Bengal tiger here, too). The Madhupur Forest Reserve is renowned for its brown wood owl and the dusky owl, and you'll see rhesus monkeys and langurs here as well. Several species of pochards and teals visit the Sunamganj wetlands in Sylhet, as do crakes and various fishing eagles.

- **India**. The tiger population is famously in decline in India, but you've a reasonable chance of spotting one in Ranthambore National Park. Wild elephants are a little more common, and best looked for in the Periyar Wildlife Sanctuary and Corbett National Park. Kaladeo National Park is one of the most famous bird reserves in the world, with huge breeding colonies of cranes, storks, flamingoes and ibis, and the winter population of cranes in the desert village of Keechen is a similarly impressive sight.
- **Indonesia**. Highlights on Sumatra include the Bukit Lawang orang-utan sanctuary, and the hornbills, Argus pheasants and numerous other birds of Kerinci-Seblat National Park. On Komodo, everyone goes to gawp at the enormous and ferocious monitor lizards known as Komodo dragons; while Irian Jaya is famous for its spectacular birdlife, including birds of paradise (best seen in Pulau Yapen), and innumerable cockatoos, parrots and cassowaries that can be spotted almost anywhere, along with heaps of gorgeously coloured butterflies.
- **Malaysia**. There are common sightings of gibbons, macaques and monitor lizards in the easily accessible Taman Negara National Park on the peninsula. In Sabah, the big draws are the Sepilok Orang-utan Sanctuary, the flowers of Sabah's Mount Kinabalu – including a thousand species of orchid, 26 types of rhododendron, and various bizarre insect-eating pitcher plants – and the chance of seeing the proboscis monkey, found only in Borneo and most likely spotted along Sabah's Kinabatangan river. Gunung Mulu National Park in Sarawak is renowned for its phenomenal birdlife, which includes eight species of hornbill.
- **Nepal**. Trekkers rarely see any interesting mammals in the mountains; it's much more rewarding to head for the plains of the Tarai, where there's a good chance of spotting rhinos, monkeys and possibly bears at the popular Chitwan National Park. Langurs and wild pig are frequently sighted in Bardia National Park, where you also have a reasonable chance of encountering a rhino, a tiger, or even a Gangetic dolphin. Swamp deer, crocodiles and awesome birdlife, including heaps of cranes, cormorants and eagles, are good enough reasons to visit Sukla Phanta Wildlife Reserve.

Diving

Internationally certified scuba-diving courses are cheaper in Asia than in most other parts of the world and, once you've done your training, the potential for underwater exploration is phenomenal. The reef life is as diverse, prolific and fascinating as anywhere in the world, and as the water tends to be bath temperature you won't always need a full wetsuit. You will find reputable dive schools in all the major resorts listed below, and the same places also organize dive trips and rent out equipment. The worldwide Professional Association of Diving Instructors, or PADI, keeps an up-to-date list of PADI-approved dive centres around the world, which can be viewed at ❶*www.padi.com* The same is true of the National Association of Underwater Instructors, at ❶*www.naui.org* Expect to pay around \$200/£130 for the four-day open-water PADI course in Thailand, or around \$300/£200 in Bali. One-day dive excursions to local reefs cost from \$50/£35, including equipment and two tanks.

Though you can dive year-round in Asia, some seas become too rough and visibility drops during the rainy season (see Chapter Three), so check with a specialist diving guidebook before fixing your trip. Recommended diving guides, all of which describe and illustrate the marine life as well as detailing the best dive sites, include *Dive! Southeast Asia* and *Diving Indonesia* (both from Periplus); Fielding's *Diving Indonesia* and *Diving Malaysia, the Philippines and Thailand*; and the *Dive Sites* series published by New Holland, which covers Thailand, Indonesia, Malaysia and the Philippines. The online version of the divers' magazine *AsianDiver* ❶*www.asiandiver.com* is another good source of information, and includes travellers' reports.

- Boasting warm, clear waters and a breathtakingly diverse marine life, **Indonesia** offers masses of quality dive sites. The most accessible of these are found off Pulau Menjangan, Tulamben, Nusa Penida and Nusa Lembongan in Bali; off the Gili islands in Lombok; and in Sulawesi at the Bunaken-Manado Tua marine park. If you've got plenty of money, live-aboard charters open up areas off Maluku and Irian Jaya.
- **Malaysia**'s best diving facilities are centred on Pulau Tioman, but there are lots more dive centres on other east-coast islands. Aficionados head for Pulau Sipadan off Sabah.

- The dozens of islands that make up the **Philippines** archipelago are ringed by over four thousand square kilometres of reef which, not surprisingly, makes the country one of Asia's most important diving destinations. The main dive centres are at Moaboal, Puerto Galera and Boracay, but the cream of the reefs are off the Palawan Islands and Occidental Mindoro, and there are exciting shipwreck dives off Busuangra.
- Due to a volatile political situation, the most enticing reefs off east-coast **Sri Lanka** are currently too dangerous to visit, but Hikkaduwa in the southwest, and Unawatuna and Polhena near Matara in the south, are rewarding areas for diving and snorkelling.
- In **Thailand** there are numerous dive centres at the resorts on Phuket and in Pattaya, but the best reefs are around the outlying islands, particularly Ko Similan, Ko Surin, Ko Tao and Ko Phi Phi.

Chasing the adrenaline rush

For most people, a bus trip on the Trans-Sumatran Highway, a few hours in a tiny, overladen ferry boat in heaving seas, or a few minutes aboard some of the domestic airlines, generate quite enough excitement. But there are all sorts of other ways to spice up your trip, some of which are listed below. For more inspiration, and tales from the hot seat, have a look at the online version of the Hong-Kong-based *Action Asia* ✪*www.actionasia.com*, a lifestyle magazine that focuses on adventure travel in Asia. If you're planning on doing any of the following adventure sports, be sure to advise your insurance company before buying your policy.

- **Jet-skiing and other watersports**. Available at all the big tourist beach resorts, including Sanur on Bali, Pulau Tioman in Malaysia, Boracay in the Philippines, and Pattaya and Phuket in Thailand.
- **Kayaking**. Paddle your own canoe through mangrove swamps, jungle rivers and island caves in south Thailand, north Vietnam and the Philippines.
- **Mountaineering**. While most travellers go to Nepal to trek, the country is also the world's centre for serious mountaineering expeditions, as is the entire length of the Himalayas. The colossal Karakoram peaks of Nanga Parbat (8126m) and K2 (8900m) are both tackled from inside Pakistan. And at 5030m, Puncak Jaya in Irian Jaya (Indonesia) is the highest peak in Southeast Asia and one of only three snow-capped equatorial mountains in the world.

- **Rock-climbing**. The limestone karst that peppers the Krabi coastline of southern Thailand and Ha Long Bay in north Vietnam is just crying out to be scaled. Rock-climbing's quite a popular sport in South Korea too, particularly in Pukhan-san National Park, which is nicknamed "little Yosemite" because of its myriad perpendicular cliff faces. And in Laos, there's a newly developed set of bolted routes at Ban Pak Ou, near Louang Phabang.
- **Skiing, heli-skiing and snowboarding** in the Indian Himalayas. Take a very expensive helicopter flight out of Manali, then do spectacular runs from around 4000m. There are less dramatic, and less costly, opportunities for skiing and snowboarding in mountainous South Korea and in the Japan Alps.
- **Surfing** along the southern and western side of the Indonesian archipelago. The best facilities are in Bali but there are also top breaks off Sumatra, Lombok and Sumbawa, plus the world-famous G-Land breaks off the eastern end of Java. Check out *Surfing Indonesia* (Periplus), or *Fielding's Surfing Indonesia*, for more detail, or consult the excellent ⓦ*www.indosurf.com.au* In Sri Lanka there are surf centres in Hikkaduwa and Midigama and, in the Philippines, Luzon gets reliable waves, as does Siargao Island. The *Surfer Mag* Web site ⓦ*www.surfermag.com* carries surf news and tips for Asia and elsewhere.
- **White-water rafting**. In Nepal, you can race down choppy Himalayan rivers, through wooded canyons and jungle, past villages and beaches. It's less popular in the Indian Himalayas, but the scenery's almost as good – particularly around Leh, Manali and Rishikesh. And in Pakistan, there's some spectacular rafting around Gilgit. Alternatively, try the rivers of west Thailand, around Umpang, or the popular whitewater routes in Bali.

Spiritual quests

Westerners have been going to Asia on spiritual quests for decades, so there are heaps of foreigner-oriented courses to choose from. They're generally inexpensive and last from a few days to several weeks; most are residential. The usual procedure is to enrol on the spot for the next available course, so, unless you're very short of time, there's generally no need to book a place before you leave home.

Don't be put off by the fact that these courses are designed for visiting foreigners: the truly authentic programmes last for months (if not years), are conducted in the local language, and would be far too rigorous for first-timers. In most cases, the foreigners' courses are quite demanding enough: the daily programme generally starts around 5am; the food is healthy but hardly indulgent; sex, drugs and drink are all forbidden for the duration; and some course leaders ask you to stay silent for most of the day. With any luck you'll come away in a calmer and healthier state of mind and body and may also have learnt a bit more about the Asian way of looking at the world. It's quite feasible to practise your newly acquired yoga or meditation skills on your travels, especially if you're staying near a beach. We've selected a few of the most popular centres for yoga and meditation instruction, but there are plenty more.

- **India** is the spiritual heartland of much of Asia and the most popular place for travellers pursuing spiritual interests. Established centres (known as ashrams) for yoga and meditation courses include Rishikesh – famous as the place where the Beatles met the Maharishi – and Dharamsala, home-in-exile of the Tibetan Buddhist leader the Dalai Lama, and hundreds of his compatriots. The holy city of Varanasi is another good place to find yoga and meditation gurus. Also recommended are the Root Institute in Bodh Gaya (scene of Buddha's enlightenment), the Shivananda ashram in Trivandrum, and the ashram of Sai Baba in Puttaparthi. *Travels through Sacred India* by Roger Housden (Thorsons) is a mine of further information on religion in modern India and includes addresses of ashrams, or try Trailblazer's *Indian Ashram Guide*.
- **Japan** is the home of Zen Buddhism, and Kyoto the best place to find introductory Zen retreats catering for foreigners. For specifics, see *Zen Guide: Where to Meditate in Japan* by Martin Roth and John Stevens (Weatherhill).
- Like India, **Nepal** also attracts a large number of travellers looking for yoga and meditation courses, most of whom end up at ashrams in the Kathmandu Valley.
- In **Thailand**, the most popular meditation course is the ten-day Vipassana programme held every month at Wat Suan Mokh in Surat Thani. Other options include ten-day retreats on Ko Pha Ngan and month-long courses in Chiang Mai. *The Meditation Temples of Thailand: A Guide* by Joe Cummings (Silkworm) is worth consulting if you've a serious interest, or have a read of Tim Ward's first-hand experiences in *What the Buddha Never Taught* (Celestial Art).

Learning a new skill

With all that time on your hands, why not learn a new skill while you're in Asia? The places listed below are renowned on the backpacker circuit for their short, traveller-oriented courses, where you might learn batik painting in a couple of days, or the fundamentals of Mandarin in a couple of weeks. None of these courses require any special aptitude or prior knowledge, and most are informal and relatively superficial, but they're a fun way to get a little further under the skin of a country or a region. Backpackers' guidebooks usually carry details about course durations and prices, but you rarely need to book a place in advance, as most people just turn up in the town and find out what the schedule is.

- **Arts and crafts**. Design yourself a T-shirt or paint your own wall-hanging in Indonesia by taking a short course in batik design and dyeing in Yogyakarta (on Java) or Ubud (Bali). You can also learn batik making at Cherating and Kota Bharu in Malaysia. In Kyoto, the Japanese cultural capital, you can take workshops in all sorts of traditional arts, including woodblock printing, textile dyeing, calligraphy and ikebana flower arranging.
- **Cookery**. Learn how to re-create jungle curry and chilli-fried fish on Thai cookery courses in Bangkok and Chiang Mai. And bone up on Indonesian satay and a whole range of peanut sauces in Ubud and Lovina (Bali) and Yogyakarta.
- **Diving**. There are plenty of dive schools in Indonesia, Malaysia, Thailand and the Philippines, where you can do one-day introductory courses as well as internationally approved certificate courses. See p.128 for more advice.
- **Language**. All Asian capitals have language institutes catering for foreign students and interested tourists; contact tourist offices and/or embassies in your own country for details.
- **Martial arts**. A course in Chinese self-defence techniques may stand you in good stead on your travels – lessons for foreigners are held in the travellers' centre of Dali (Yunnan), and in Beijing.
- **Massage**. Become a hit with fellow travellers by learning the basics of traditional Thai massage in Chiang Mai or Bangkok, or of shiatsu in Kyoto, Japan.
- **Music and dance**. You'll get a lot more out of watching cultural performances if you've tried a few steps or banged out a few tunes yourself. Beginners' courses in Indonesian dance and gamelan playing are held regularly in Ubud and Yogyakarta.

A different kind
of trip

When I packed in my job, I decided to go travelling for a while, but I wasn't interested in just bumming around and wanted to try and get under the surface of things instead. Indian Volunteers for Community Service (IVCS) fitted the bill perfectly: a three-week visitors' programme at a small rural development project in northeastern India.

On our first day at the project, the ten new volunteers were all taken to the nearest town to buy traditional north Indian style dress: *salwaar kameez* for the girls and *pajama* for the boys. This was to make us feel and act like we weren't just tourists, and also to help us blend in better with the villagers of Amarpurkashi. Back at the village, we spent the next three weeks following an informal programme of yoga, Hindi lessons and cultural lectures in the morning, and rural development workshops in the afternoon. In between, we got involved with local projects like reorganizing the polytechnic's library and helping with the literacy campaign. And we helped out in the kitchens, and gave regular English lessons at the village school and the rural polytechnic. We also socialized with the villagers and were invited to join their festivities, including one which was held to honour the birth of a baby boy.

I couldn't have asked for a better introduction to India. Though there was quite a big group of us Westerners, we all got involved in community life and experienced things tourists rarely get to see and do. By the end of the three weeks I felt acclimatized, confident and eager to do some exploring, so I spent the next five months making informal visits to development projects in other parts of India, using contacts I'd made at Amarpurkashi.

Juliet Acock

- **Yoga and meditation**. Open up your mind, and loosen up your limbs – a huge variety of yoga and meditation courses are held in India and Nepal; see "Spiritual quests", p.131.

Voluntary work

Doing voluntary work gives you a special insight into a country and its people. As a volunteer you meet people you'd never come across on the tourist trail and may have a chance to do something useful for a community in need. Most international voluntary organizations (like VSO and the Peace Corps) employ people for a minimum of two years and require specific qualifications, but there are some shorter placements on offer.

Concerned tourists, however, can get involved in short-term voluntary projects such as coral surveying in the Philippines, caring for forest monkeys in China or tracking snow leopards in the Himalayas. There are also a few openings for work on archeological digs and community programmes. Projects last anything from a week to six months, and volunteers are expected to pay for their board and lodging and contribute towards the cost of the project. Established organizers of volunteer holidays are listed in Basics on p.360.

To get involved with any of these organizations you need to contact them in your home country before you set off. For a more comprehensive roundup, see *The Directory of Work and Study in Developing Countries* (Vacation Work), *The International Directory of Voluntary Work* (Vacation Work), or *Worldwide Volunteering for Young People* (How To Books). Two other useful resources are World Service Enquiry ☎44/20 7346 5956, ⓦ*www.wse.org.uk* whose Web site lists dozens of contact details for volunteer-placement organizations, and the specialist publication *Worldwide Guide to Voluntary Work in Nature Conservation*, which has information on 180 wildlife and environmental projects around the world (order on ☎44/1767262481 or at ⓦ*www.greenvol.com*). For a fee of $39/£23.50, the Swiss-based company Voluntary Work Information Service ⓦ*www.workingabroad.com* will compile a detailed list of projects that fulfil criteria you set, lasting one week to six months or more, in over 150 countries worldwide. All you do is fill in the online application form, giving preferred dates, type of project and countries of choice. For information on finding paid work in Asia, see p.182.

Some local charities are happy to accept volunteers who walk in off the street and have no qualifications except a desire to help out for a few days. A few random examples include Mother Teresa's Missionaries of Charity (hospices for the destitute and the dying) in Calcutta; Mother Teresa's Sisters of Charity (old people's hospice) in Kathmandu; and Empower (education for women in the sex trade) in Bangkok. Consult guidebooks for details on these and other projects.

2

Visas, tickets and insurance

Only a very few countries in Asia actually refuse entry to independent travellers, but in many cases you can only enter via certain air- and seaports unless you've obtained a visa in advance; in a few cases you're not allowed to enter by land borders at all. With all this in mind, it's essential to start researching the visa situation for all your intended destinations as early as possible – before you pay for your air ticket, and before it's too late to get all the paperwork done.

Though you need to find out about the visa requirements for all your intended destinations before buying your ticket, you shouldn't actually apply for your visas until you've got firm bookings for your tickets, as most visa applications ask for your arrival and departure dates.

Visas and borders

Lots of Asian countries are crying out for tourists to come and visit, so they make visas easy to obtain and often issue them free of charge as well. Indonesia, for example, grants visitors sixty-day tourist visas

VISA REQUIREMENTS

The following table indicates whether you need to buy a visa before you arrive. It's meant as a planning aid only and applies to entry via the most popular gateways. As rules change quite often, you should double-check by calling the relevant embassies. In the countries that let you in without an advance visa, the number of days you're allowed to stay is given in brackets; you may be able to get a longer visa by applying in your home country before you leave.

	EU	US/Can	Aus/NZ
Bangladesh*	no (15 days)	no (15 days)	no (15 days)
Bhutan	yes	yes	yes
Brunei	UK no (30 days) most EU no (14 days)	US no (3 months) Canada yes	yes
Cambodia†	no (30 days)	no (30 days)	no (30 days)
China	yes	yes	yes
Hong Kong	UK no (6 months) most EU no (3 months)	US no (30 days) Can no (3 m)	no (3 months)
India	yes	yes	yes
Indonesia	no (60 days)	no (60 days)	no (60 days)
Japan	no (90 days)	no (90 days)	Aus yes, NZ no (90 days)
Laos‡	no (15 days)	no (15 days)	no (15 days)
Malaysia	no (60 days)	no (60 days)	no (60 days)
Nepal	no (60 days)	no (60 days)	no (60 days)
Pakistan	yes	yes	yes
Philippines	no (21 days)	no (21 days)	no (21 days)
Singapore	no (14 days)	no (14 days)	no (14 days)
South Korea	UK no (90 days) EU yes	no (US: 30 days, Can: 18 days)	no (15 days)
Sri Lanka	no (30 days)	no (30 days)	no (30 days)
Taiwan	no (14 days)	no (14 days)	no (14 days)
Thailand	no (30 days)	no (30 days)	no (Aus 30 days, NZ 90 days)
Vietnam	yes	yes	yes

* Anyone intending to arrive by land should get a visa in advance.
† Anyone intending to arrive by land from Thailand or Vietnam should get a visa in advance.
‡ If entering anywhere other than Wattay Airport in Viontiane, Luuang Phabang Airport or the Friendship Bridge between Nong Khai in Thailand and Vientiane, get a visa in advance.

on arrival at major airports and ports. All you need do in such situations is show the immigration officials that your passport is valid for at least another six months and that you have a ticket out of the country (sometimes, you need only show you've got enough money to buy an onward ticket). However, if you want to enter the country through a less frequented route or stay longer than the statutory period granted upon arrival, you'll probably need to apply for a visa before you travel (in some countries, however, you can apply for an extension once you're there). Laos and Bangladesh sell fifteen-day visas at major entry points, and entering Nepal you can get up to sixty days. Less welcoming nations require visas to be bought in advance whatever the length of your trip; the Himalayan kingdom of Bhutan even refuses visas to any traveller who is not part of an organized tour. Rules change all the time, of course, especially in countries where the political climate is volatile. The table on p.137 gives a broad outline of visa requirements in Asia, but you should confirm details with the relevant embassies (see p.350).

Land borders are especially unpredictable – at the time of writing it was impossible to travel overland between Laos and Cambodia or between China and India. And while travellers can currently cross into Nepal from Tibet without difficulty, they cannot travel independently into Tibet from Nepal. You should also bear in mind that despite the very long border, there's only one crossing between India and Pakistan (between Wagah on the Pakistani side, east of Lahore, and Attari, west of Amritsar on the Indian side) and that to travel overland between Vietnam and Cambodia, and between Laos and Vietnam, you need to arrange visas in advance. Details of overland border crossings are given in Chapter 1.

On the whole, if you do need a visa, it's best to apply for one in your home country, with a couple of provisos: most countries require you to start using your visa within a specified time, usually within three or six months of it being issued, which is clearly hopeless if you'll be hitting India seven months after, say, leaving Australia. In such cases you'll have to get that visa from the relevant embassy somewhere en route. Also, not every nation has an embassy or consulate in every country (Laos and Cambodia, for example, have no representatives in the UK), which means you either have to arrange your visa through an agency or, if feasible, get your visa in Asia – in Bangkok, for example. Sometimes visas are *easier* to get en route: visas for China, for example, are simplest to obtain in Hong Kong; and Lao visas are quicker to get in Bangkok as all visa applications have to be sent to Laos for approval – considerably speedier when done from Thailand (it takes less than a week) than from Europe (about two months). On the other hand, getting an Indian visa is ridiculously bureaucratic in Nepal and much better done elsewhere.

Even when you have your visa, this doesn't necessarily give you *carte blanche* to roam wherever you wish. In some countries (like China, India, Laos, Malaysia and Vietnam) you also need special permits to visit remote or politically sensitive areas; trekking in parts of both Nepal and Pakistan is subject to restrictions; and many countries have areas where foreigners are not permitted at all – some parts of Tibet and border areas of India, for example. Permits for trekking and for visiting restricted areas are usually issued in the relevant country, but it's always worth checking with embassies before you go and maybe applying in advance. For example, Restricted Area Permits for the Indian northeastern hill states of Manipur, Mizoram, Nagaland and Arunchal Pradesh can be applied for in Delhi and Calcutta, or at Indian Embassies and High Commissions overseas.

Applying for a visa

Even in the most efficient embassies, applying for a visa is a time-consuming procedure – queues may stretch down the hallway, and most embassies and consulates keep unhelpfully short hours. It's worth contacting the embassy (use their 24hr information lines or Web sites if available) to check opening times, and do take national holidays into consideration, both yours and theirs – not only do embassies close on these days, but queues are twice as long on the days before and after. The same advice applies when picking up your visa. To minimize the hassle, find out in advance how many

Déjà vu on the Karakoram Highway

We reached the front of the queue and I handed the Pakistani officer our passports, open at the Chinese visa. He glanced casually at the first, then a little more deliberately at the second and finally scrutinized the pair together, side by side. Then he raised his head abruptly and peered over the lectern.

"What is this? These have not been signed! They must be signed, you cannot use them!" he barked.

"What? Surely not!" I protested. "Where?"

"There! Can't you read?"

"Well, actually, no," I admitted. "Not Chinese. Look, it's just an administrative error. These are genuine visas, they'll see that."

But it was no good, he was adamant the Chinese would not let us enter, and therefore he could not let us leave Pakistan.

"You'll have to go back to Islamabad and get them signed. Next!"

Slightly bewildered, I sat down and tried to come to terms with the appalling prospect of going all the way back. We had just spent three weeks exploring the Karakoram Highway and now we had to retrace our steps. In the end it took us four days and a catalogue of hassles, including an unpredicted holiday at the Chinese embassy, a bus breakdown, a randy fellow passenger and an awful lot of déjà vu.

Neil Poulter

photos you need, how much visas cost and whether you can pay by cash, cheque or credit card. Get to the embassy as close to opening time as possible, and take a good book.

If you've got plenty of time before your departure, it's easier to apply by post, though this might not be feasible if you've got several different visas to collect. Alternatively, you can always use the specialist visa service offered by major travel agents (see Basics, p.354, for a list of these). Expect to pay around $40 in the US or £20 in the UK for the service, in addition to the fee charged by the embassy. A few more points to remember when applying for visas:

- Be as accurate as you can about the date of your arrival in the country, as some embassies – eg Vietnam's – issue visas with exact dates on them; if you can't be certain, delay applying for a visa until later.

- If there's any possibility that you might be leaving a country and then going back there later (to catch a plane for example), make sure you apply for a multiple-entry visa rather than a single-entry one.

- In some countries, the authorities regard writers and journalists with suspicion, so it's advisable to be vague about these occupations on the visa form (they're unlikely to check).

- Some countries are hostile to passport-holders of particular nations. Islamic countries, for example, often refuse entry to Israeli passport-holders; this is true of Indonesia and Malaysia. Check with embassies for details.

● If you know that the statutory amount of time on a tourist visa is just not long enough for your trip, you could try applying for a special student or business visa. Sometimes it's enough to have a written invitation from someone in the host country; alternatively, try signing up with a language school or a meditation centre and getting a letter from the principal.

● When collecting your visa, check that all the details are correct, and that, if necessary, it has been signed.

Extending your stay

Some countries offer a way of extending your visa once you're there (the embassy in your home country should be able to tell you about this). In Thailand, for example, you can go to any of the provincial immigration offices dotted around the country and get a thirty-day extension for a reasonable fee. In Nepal you can get extensions of thirty days at a time for $1/70p per day in Kathmandu or Pokhara (though queues are often very long). You'll probably need two or three passport photos for this, and it always helps if you're dressed smartly when applying. In some countries, certain types of visa are absolutely non-extendable: for example, the sixty days given on entry to Indonesia, and Indian tourist visas.

All is not lost if you can't get a long enough visa. If you're planning to overstay by a few days, then – in some countries – you may as well just put aside some money for the fine that you'll be landed with when you fly out; in Nepal it's $2/£1.50 per day, in Cambodia around $5/£3.50 per day. In other countries, however, this is definitely not a great idea – China and Vietnam charge $50/£35 a day, sometimes more, for overstaying, and Indonesia penalizes anyone who overstays by more than two weeks by putting them on a blacklist prohibiting entry to Indonesia for the next few years.

Of course, you can always do what numerous expats do – cross the nearest border to get a new tourist visa and come back in again. In some places this is simple: in Indonesia, for example, you can either fly to Singapore, or take the two-hour boat ride there from Batam Island and then back again. In Thailand you can get a long-distance bus or train down into Malaysia or, much faster, take the hour-long flight to Phnom Penh; if you're in southern Malaysia you can zip across to Singapore; while from Japan the cheapest exit is by boat to South Korea. However, you shouldn't assume this is always a straightforward way to get a new visa; traditionally visitors to India who wanted to stay longer than the six months allowed on a tourist visa would head to get new visas in either Colombo in Sri Lanka or Kathmandu in Nepal, but in recent years numerous visa applications in those places have been turned down for no apparent reason. It pays to ask around among other travellers that you meet on the road.

Buying a ticket

The travel industry is a hugely competitive business, so it pays to shop around when looking for the best fare. It's unusual for travellers to buy air tickets direct from the major airlines – only business travellers can afford the standard airline fares; you'll probably be buying from a travel agent who, through dealing in limited blocks of seats that the airline doesn't think it can sell at full price, is able to offer discounts on air tickets. The Internet is also a fertile source of cheap flights, with Ⓦ *www.cheapflights.com* and Ⓦ *www.deckchair.com* among useful places to start looking; see p.354 for addresses of recommended agents.

When you've worked out some sort of itinerary, call up one of the major discount travel agents or, better still, go and see them, and ask the travel consultant's advice. Staff at these places are usually well travelled themselves; they know what they're talking about and generally aren't out to rip you off.

Having established a price for your proposed route, ring round a few other discount travel agents to see if anyone else can better it. Many newspapers and listings magazines carry advertisements for discount travel agents, and usually quote sample fares too. In London, try the *Evening Standard*, *Time Out*, or the free *TNT* magazine; in the US, there's *Village Voice* in New York, *LA Weekly* and the *San Francisco Bay Guardian*; and in Australia, try *TNT* magazine. Youth- and student-oriented travel agents give significant discounts to travellers who are under 26, and some places extend their deals to anyone under 35; student-card-holders of any age are often entitled to cut-price deals as well.

In the UK and Australia, always check that the travel agent you're dealing with is bonded with one of the big travel associations – such as ATOL Ⓦ*www.atoldata.org.uk* or ABTA Ⓦ*www.abtanet.com* in the UK, or AFTA Ⓦ*www.afta.com.au* in Australia – before you give them any money. If they are bonded you will be refunded if the agent goes bust before you fly out; if not you will lose your money and your ticket. There's no comparable organization in the US – here, and also in the UK and Australia, paying for your ticket by credit card is an alternative way to protect yourself against unreliable bucket shops, as the credit-card company is obliged to reimburse you if the agent doesn't.

Some Eastern and Central European airlines offer very cheap fares to Asia, but have notoriously poor efficiency (and, in some cases, safety) records and many major travel agents refuse to sell their flights. If you're looking for a rock-bottom fare and willing to take the chance, it may be worth contacting these airlines directly; alternatively, look through the classified ads for a travel agent that sells their flights.

How to save money on your flight

To help you get the best possible deal for your money, bear in mind the following:

- Ring round a dozen travel agents and write down their quotes so you don't forget them.
- Some travel agents have special discount arrangements with particular airlines, so ask several different agents the price of the exact same flight.
- Investigate several different types of ticket (see pp.144–149), even if you already think you know what you want.
- The early bird gets the worm, so book early. The best deals will be snapped up fast, leaving latecomers with the expensive flights. If you want to fly from Europe to India at Christmastime, for example, you should book your ticket by September to ensure a reasonable fare. And if you're heading from the US to Nepal for the popular October to November trekking season, you need to make your reservations around June.

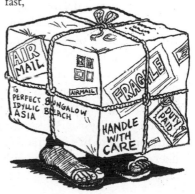

- Be as flexible as possible about your departure date. Airlines have high, low and shoulder seasons and prices vary accordingly, so you can sometimes make a significant saving by altering your schedule by a week or two. As a general guide, high season for flights to Asia covers the busiest holiday periods, namely mid-December to mid-January, and July to mid-September; shoulder season wraps around the peak winter season, usually from November to February (when most parts of Asia are enjoying their pleasantest weather); and the remaining months are low season.
- Be equally flexible about your routeing. It's generally more expensive to fly into less popular regional airports – such as Chennai (previously called Madras) in India rather than Mumbai (Bombay) or Delhi – simply because demand is low and competition slack. Perhaps an inexpensive overland connection (from Mumbai, for example) would do just as well, especially if it saves you $150/£100 or more. On the other hand, there's no question that spending your first night in Chennai is a lot less stressful than kicking off with Mumbai, so the extra cost might be worth every penny.

Which ticket?

Most discounted flights have restrictions on them, which your travel agent should explain. For example, once you've paid for your ticket, you probably won't be able to cancel it and may not be able to change your initial departure date (though return dates and the onward segments of round-the-world tickets are nearly always flexible). Most holiday insurance policies (see p.150) cover unavoidable cancellations and delayed departures. Many discounted tickets also have time restrictions on them, with a minimum stay of seven days and a maximum of thirty or ninety days, though this varies according to the airline.

Sometimes it's worth paying a little extra for your international flight to qualify for special perks. Some airlines offer good deals on domestic flights if you fly in and out of the country on the national carrier. Malaysian Airlines, for example, sells an inexpensive pass entitling you to five internal flights if you fly to Malaysia with them; likewise a couple of Indian airlines offer this sort of deal on flights around India (see p.258).

One-way tickets

One-way tickets always work out relatively more expensive than a return flight, so this is only a viable option if you're unsure when or how you'll be returning. On the plus side, one-way tickets are adventurous and liberating; overland transport in Asia is temptingly inexpensive, and airline tickets bought in Asia are good value, particularly in Bangkok, Calcutta, Delhi and Singapore.

However, buying a one-way ticket can create problems with getting visas, as most countries require proof that you are actually going to move on to another country within a reasonable time limit. In many cases, you will need to show evidence of onward or return travel plans, either when applying for a visa in your home country, or at the border when getting a visa on the spot. The easiest way to bypass this is to decide on an overland route out of the country and make sure you have the details and proof of sufficient funds when getting your visa. Of course, this only works if the route you have in mind is a legal way of exiting the country – verify this with travel agents, embassies and guidebooks before plumping for a one-way ticket. Some travellers get round all this by buying the cheapest return flight available and then getting a refund for the unused return sector, but read the small print before going for this option – certain tickets may not be refundable and even if they are, you'll only be able to collect the refund from the office that issued the ticket.

Open-jaw returns

Open-jaw tickets allow you to choose different airports for your arrival and departure, which means you can minimize backtracking during your trip. One example would be to fly from London into Delhi and then fly from Mumbai back to London, making your own way overland between Delhi and Mumbai. On some airlines, it's possible to buy an open-jaw that flies you into one country (eg Thailand) and out of another (say, Singapore), leaving you a fairly lengthy overland sector to organize yourself. Open-jaw prices are generally calculated by halving the return fares to each destination and then adding the two figures together.

Stopover returns

If you're only visiting one or two countries in Asia, then buying a return ticket with a stopover option will probably be your best deal, particularly as most stopovers are offered free of charge. Flying from Sydney to Delhi, for example, you can stop over in Kuala Lumpur, Bangkok or Kathmandu, depending on which airline you use; flying London–Kathmandu, you could stop in Karachi, Delhi or Dhaka. Most airlines allow you to stop over for up to three months, and you can usually choose whether you stop off on the way out or on the way back; you may even be allowed to do both. Not all airlines offer interesting stopover routes, but travel agents can advise on the best options. Don't forget to find out whether you need a visa for your stopover destination.

Circle Asia tickets

If you're planning a multi-stop route across Asia, your cheapest option is almost certain to be a Circle Asia ticket. This is in fact a whole series of tickets, generally put together by a travel agent using the cheapest flights they can find to construct a trans-Asia route via a series of key cities. It's up to you to choose which cities, of course, though agents generally offer very good deals on certain routes, which make them hard to ignore. Once you've decided on your key cities and paid for your ticket, the route is fixed and cannot be changed, although dates of component flights can usually be changed at any point along the way, free of charge. Circle Asia tickets are generally valid for one year.

The cheapest and most popular Circle Asia routes include one or more "surface sectors" – sections of the journey not included in your Circle Asia ticket, therefore requiring you to make your own way by land, sea or whatever means you feel like. A typical Circle Asia from London to Bali and back, for example, would include a flight from London to Bangkok, then a surface sector from Bangkok to Singapore, followed by flights from Singapore to Bali, then Bali back to London. You can get from Bangkok to Singapore as you please, either slowly, with several stops on the way, or in one swoop by overnight train or bus – or even a local flight – that you organize from Bangkok. The longer your surface sectors, the cheaper your Circle Asia ticket.

Sample Circle Asia prices

- Under £500: London–Beijing surface to Hong Kong–Bangkok–London.
- Under £550: London–Bangkok surface to Singapore–Bali–London.
- Under £650: London–Bangkok surface to Singapore–Delhi/Mumbai–London
- Under £700: London–Tokyo–Kota Kinabalu–Kuala Lumpur–London
- Under $1200: San Francisco–Tokyo–Singapore surface to Bangkok–Hong Kong–San Francisco
- Under $1300: New York–Hong Kong–Bangkok–Kathmandu surface to Hong Kong–Los Angeles–New York
- Under A$1600/NZ$2000 Sydney/Auckland–Bali–Singapore–Bangkok–Hong Kong–Manila–Auckland/Sydney.
- Under A$2000/NZ$2400 Sydney/Auckland–Bali–Singapore–Mumbai–Hong Kong–Beijing–Auckland/Sydney.

Round-the-world tickets

A round-the-world (RTW) ticket is a longer and more ambitious version of a Circle Asia ticket, with the added bonus of stops in Australia and the Pacific, North America, Europe or South Africa. As with Circle Asia tickets, RTWs are put together by a travel agent using the cheapest flights they can find; most travel agents offer a dozen or so set RTW routes at bargain rates. The route can't be altered after you've paid for your ticket, but again you can usually change the dates of component flights free of charge.

The more surface sectors you include in an RTW ticket, the cheaper the ticket. As internal and short-hop flights are generally cheaper to buy inside Asia than out, you may find it more economical to buy a skeleton RTW with long surface sectors and then add whatever extra flights you need once you've got there.

Sample RTW prices

- Under £900: London–Kuala Lumpur surface to Singapore–Perth–Cairns–Sydney–Los Angeles–New York–London.
- Under £950: London–Mumbai–Bangkok–Hong Kong–Vancouver surface to San Diego–Miami–Montego Bay–London.

- Under £1050: London–Cape Town–Johannesburg–Mauritius–Singapore–Langkawi–Ho Chi Minh City–Perth–Ayres Rock–Sydney–Christchurch–Auckland–Honolulu–Los Angeles–London.
- Under $1600: San Francisco–Bali–Singapore surface to Bangkok–Cairo–Athens surface to London–San Francisco.
- Under $2000: New York–Amsterdam surface to Paris–Ho Chi Minh City surface to Bangkok–Brunei–Perth surface to Melbourne–Auckland–Fiji–Tahiti–Los Angeles–New York.
- Under A$1600/NZ$2000 Sydney/Auckland–Bali–Bangkok–London–Jakarta–Sydney/Auckland.
- Under A$2000/NZ$2400 Sydney/Auckland–Kuala Lumpur surface to Bangkok–Vienna–Copenhagen–Toronto–Calgary–Sydney/Auckland.

Charters and courier flights

Charter flights to major holiday resorts (such as Goa and Bali) are sometimes cheaper than discounted fares on scheduled flights. Charters are sold through high-street travel agents and sometimes include accommodation as well (you're under no obligation to use the accommodation for any or all of the time if you want to move on), but you're generally limited to a two-week trip – a month at most. Some package tour operators also offer good last-minute discounts on any plane seats left unsold in the last week or ten days before departure. These are advertised in travel agent windows, in newspapers, on the Internet and, in the UK, on ITV's Teletext service.

One other way to get a really cheap flight is to become a courier. A number of courier companies offer heavily discounted international flights to travellers willing to accompany documents and/or freight to the destination for them. There's nothing dubious about these companies or their goods: it's just cheaper for them to subsidize a traveller's fare than send one of their own employees. Courier deals are advertised in the press and sold through special agents (see p.358 for a list); in some cases you'll need to pay a nominal joining fee to qualify.

Courier flights are only available to certain destinations (chiefly Hong Kong, Singapore, Japan and Malaysia), but can be up to fifty percent cheaper than advertised rates (eg Los Angeles to Hong Kong return for $350). Most have considerable restrictions attached: you will probably have to come back within a month, and might only be allowed to take carry-on luggage with you, as some courier companies use your luggage allowance themselves. Usually only one courier is needed per flight, which makes things more complex if you want to travel in a group. For the full lowdown on courier deals around the world, have a look at *Courier Air Travel Handbook: Learn How to Travel Worldwide for Next to Nothing* by Mark I. Field (Perpetual Press).

Booking your ticket

To make your arrival as hassle-free as possible, try to book a flight that touches down in daylight, remembering that it could take up to two hours to go through immigration and collect your baggage and that it gets dark around 6pm in South and Southeast Asia. This will give you plenty of time to sort out your ride into the city and your accommodation before it gets dark. Though things do not necessarily grind to a halt as soon as the sun sets, everything becomes more difficult – and unnerving – after dark. Not only is it safer to arrive during daylight, but the airport tourist information desk and cash exchange booths may not be open 24 hours a day. For more advice on planning your arrival, see Chapter Seven.

For long-haul flights and RTW tickets, it's nearly always acceptable to make provisional bookings on a ticket, though many travel agents ask for a small deposit – transferable but non-refundable – to deter time-wasters. You can always just grill the staff for information and then go home and think about it for a few days. Full payment on long-haul tickets is usually only due six weeks before departure.

Remember that ticket prices fluctuate according to the time of year (see p.144); it's always worth checking with your travel agent whether you could save money by going a week earlier or later than planned. Other things to ask your travel agent about:

- seat reservations. Some airlines let you book your actual seat (window/aisle, smoking/non-smoking, etc) when buying your ticket.
- ordering special food for the flight. All international airlines cater for a range of special diets (such as vegetarian, kosher and diabetic), but these must be ordered in advance, either through your travel agent or by calling the airline yourself.

- non-smoking flights. If you can't last a longish flight without nicotine, you'll need to avoid airlines that operate entirely smoke-free flights, as quite a few of the major airlines now do.
- reserving a room at your destination. Most travel agents can book mid-range hotels for you (from about $25/£16 a double in Bangkok, for example). Though more expensive than doing it yourself when you get there, this is a good idea for your first couple of nights in Asia as it's one less thing to worry about when you arrive. For more details, see Chapter Seven.
- travel insurance. Many travel agents offer their own travel insurance to customers (see below for advice on insurance).
- visa service. Major travel agents will get visas for you – especially useful if you're in a hurry, though it's much cheaper to obtain them yourself.
- vaccinations. The biggest travel agents have on-site health centres where you can get your jabs and buy first-aid kits and malaria pills. Though not cheap, these centres give extremely reliable advice and will sometimes see patients without an appointment.
- foreign currency. Agents sometimes offer competitive rates.
- first-class lounge facilities/arrangements. With many airlines you can pay (usually $10–20/£7–15) to use the first-class lounge, with free coffee, newspapers, comfortable chairs and sometimes even showers, even if you are travelling economy – invaluable if you have transfers or get delayed.

Insurance

Whatever the length of your trip to Asia and your itinerary, you'll need to arrange travel insurance – covering medical treatment and your personal possessions. Medical insurance is vital in case the worst happens and you are faced with serious illness or an accident. Some policies aimed at backpackers exclude baggage cover to keep costs down, but we would advise you to consider taking out a policy that also covers your belongings. You may only be taking your oldest, tattiest clothes with you, but the cost of replacing everything, including rucksack and perhaps sleeping bag and camera, can be very high.

Although some credit cards advertise travel insurance as part of their package, there are usually conditions attached – you must book the holiday using your card, and it is extremely unlikely that overall cover will be adequate. Check your individual policy as some aspects of cover start from when you buy the policy. If you need to cancel your trip due to emergency circumstances (illness, death in the family, civil war at your destination), then you may be covered.

With the huge number of policies on offer, it pays to start your research well in advance to make sure you get the policy you want at a good price. However, don't buy until you have fixed your dates of travel and itinerary. Things to think about when choosing a policy:

- If you are planning several trips over the space of a year, consider an annual policy, which usually works out cheaper than buying insurance separately for each trip. Check the maximum allowable length for each trip and the total maximum travelling time allowed. These policies are not suitable for those going on one year-long trip.
- For lengthy trips, head for travel insurers who specialize in longer deals (student insurance companies are worth checking even if you're not a student). You don't want to buy a policy from a company specializing in shorter trips and then pay to add on each week or month – it'll be more expensive.
- If it's possible that your plans will change, check whether you can add on time once you are travelling or reclaim money for unused time.
- Some insurance companies will allow travel companions or home-sharers to buy a policy for a couple, rather than two separate policies.
- What activities does your potential choice of insurance company classify as "hazardous pursuits"? These are usually excluded from cover and include bungy-jumping, paragliding and scuba diving, but some companies put riding a bicycle or trekking in remote areas under this heading. Paying a surcharge may get you cover for activities you want to pursue, or you may have to find another insurer, but either way you should think about all the exciting things you may do on your trip and buy your insurance accordingly.
- Make sure you note any limits on the value to which your possessions are covered. Most policies have single-item limits that don't cover camcorders or expensive cameras. It may be easier to add these items to an existing household insurance policy under an "all risks" clause that covers the item outside the home.
- Check how high the "excess" – the amount you have to pay on each insurance claim – is before you buy your policy. If, for example, the medical bill you paid in Thailand comes to $90/£55 and the excess on the policy is $50/£30, you'll only get $40/£25 back from your insurer.
- Make sure there is a 24-hour emergency medical line in case of accident or illness.

- Make sure you know what the claims process is – in cases of theft, for example, you must get a police report to submit when making a claim.
- Any claims won't usually get settled until you get home, so it is wise to have emergency funds – a credit card is the easiest – to cope with reimbursement costs on the spot.
- If you have particular circumstances (you might be over a certain age or have a medical condition, for instance), some insurers may be hesitant about covering you, so start your research early. The chances are that you will find a company who will offer cover, but it may take some time to track them down.

ROUGH GUIDES TRAVEL INSURANCE

Rough Guides offers their own travel insurance, customized by a leading UK broker and backed by a Lloyds underwriter. It's available for anyone, of any nationality and any age, travelling anywhere in the world.

There are two main Rough Guides insurance plans: Essential, for effective, no-frills cover; and Premier, for more extensive benefits. Each can be supplemented with a "Hazardous Activities Premium". Unlike many policies, the Rough Guides schemes are calculated by the day, so if you're travelling for 27 days rather than a month, that's all you pay for. You can alternatively take out annual multi-trip insurance, which covers you for all your travel throughout the year (with a maximum of 60 days for any one trip).

For a policy quote, call the Rough Guides Insurance Line on UK freefone ☎0800/015 09 06, or if you're calling from outside Britain on ☎(44) 1243 621 046. Alternatively, you can get a quote and buy your policy online at ⓦ*www.roughguides.com/insurance*

3

When to go

I f you've got no constraints on the timing of your trip to Asia, make good weather your priority. Contrary to the tourist-brochure image, the Asian climate is not all summery days and balmy nights – sometimes it's too hot even to venture outside the door, while in other regions you might get nonstop rain for a week or more, or even snow in the mountains. But with careful planning it's possible to organize an extended itinerary that follows the best of the weather across the continent – "best" here means least extreme, because that's when travel is generally easiest and most comfortable (see the box on p.160 for a list of the best times to visit each country). On the other hand, don't let the prospect of very hot or very wet weather deter you altogether – just be prepared for travel arrangements to be less reliable and for tempers to get more easily frayed.

There is no single time of year when the whole of Asia is out of bounds because of inclement weather, but in the main the northern hemisphere's winter (November to February) is considered to be the pleasantest time to visit the region and is therefore classified as peak season. Prices are at their highest then, for everything from international airline tickets to accommodation; the best-value hotels get fully booked and many places are uncomfortably crowded.

The weather is only one factor, of course. You might want to time your visit around a specific event instead – the blooming of

Travelling in extreme heat or cold can affect your budget as well as your state of mind and body. Most air-conditioned rooms cost at least a third more than fan-cooled ones, but sometimes that's a price worth paying when temperatures and humidity levels are unbearably high. If your finances won't stretch that far, take refuge in cafés and fast-food joints that can afford their own cooling systems; big supermarkets and modern shopping malls serve the same purpose. At night, wrap yourself in a wet sarong or sheet when you go to bed – that should keep you cool for long enough to get to sleep. Though air-con trains and buses are generally overrated (it's usually much more refreshing to throw the window open instead), taxis, whether air-conditioned or not, can be a real boon in the sweltering midday heat, so that's another expense to consider.

Conversely, you may be glad of heating in certain highland areas; again you will have to pay extra for this, though you might be able to get by with renting extra blankets and ensuring the showers have hot water. A cautionary note on primitive heating systems: it's essential that you check both your room and the bathroom for decent air vents before using any gas- or coal-fired heater. In January 1996 a young couple were killed by the carbon monoxide fumes from the charcoal fire they left burning through the night in their room in Darjeeling.

the metre-wide rafflesia, the world's largest flower, which blossoms in Sumatra, Java and Malaysia in August or September; the mango season in India (April–August) is well worth a detour, as are many of the major Asian festivals, detailed on pp.164–166. Or perhaps you want to be certain to catch the notorious full-moon party, held every month on the Thai island of Ko Pha Ngan. More prosaically, if you're hoping to pay for your trip by finding a job at the end of it – in either Europe or Australia – remember that timing is important here too. In Europe, May to September is the best time to find work in pubs, on building sites and on fruit farms; in Australia there's fruit and veg picking from November to April in the south, and from May to November in the far north, while in coastal Queensland, there's work available all year round.

The climates of Asia

Wherever you are in the world, the local climate is determined by latitude, altitude and continental position (distance from the sea), plus a whole assortment of microclimates. Within Asia, the two annual monsoons (seasonal winds) also play a crucial part.

The further a place is from the equator, the more defined its seasonal differences: northern Japan, for example, which shares roughly the same latitude as southern France or Quebec, has four distinct seasons. Summertime temperatures in Sapporo average 24°C, while winter ones average 2°C. As a general rule, this makes the northern hemisphere's spring and autumn the mildest and most pleasant time to visit the temperate regions of north Asia such as Japan, South Korea, China, northern India, Nepal and Bhutan. Spring and autumn are also the seasons for trekking in the Himalayas. Summer in north Asia varies from the pleasingly warm to the stiflingly hot, and winter days can get very cold, though skies are often invigoratingly blue.

As you move further south towards the equator, the weather gets warmer and the seasons become less distinct. By the time you cross the Tropic of Cancer – a line of latitude that runs just north of Vietnam and 450km south of Delhi – and enter the tropics (the zone that straddles the distance either side of the equator from the Tropic of Cancer in the north to the Tropic of Capricorn in the south), there is precious little change in temperature at any time of year: Kuala Lumpur is 31°C in December and 33°C in May.

Instead, seasons in the tropics are defined by the amount of rainfall and, to some extent, by the relative humidity. So you get a "cool" season (comparatively low humidity and little rain), a hot season (high humidity and little rain) and a rainy season (high humidity and lots of rain). These are only loose classifications, however, and are explained in more detail later in this chapter. Humidity also intensifies the closer you get to the equator, making central Sumatra and central Kalimantan, for example, sticky and sultry all year round, while northern Thailand and northern Vietnam (which lie close to the Tropic of Cancer) only get really humid just before the monsoon arrives.

Monsoons: tropical Asia

Though the temperature may not affect the timing of your trip to tropical Asia, you will probably want to avoid travelling there during the wet season. Wet seasons are relatively predictable in Asia, as the rains are brought to the continent by seasonal winds, known as monsoons, which follow a particular timetable and itinerary. Asia is hit by two monsoons a year, one bringing mostly wet weather (May–Oct), the other mainly dry weather (Nov–April). Monsoons are capricious, however, and although local lore has it that they should arrive in each place on the exact same date every year, they often turn up several days or even weeks late. Worse still, they can bypass whole areas altogether, leaving the farmers battling against drought for up to three or four years on the trot.

The southwest monsoon arrives in west-coast regions of Asia at around the end of May and brings rainfall daily to most of Asia (excepting certain east-coast areas, explained below) by mid-July. From then on you can expect overcast skies and regular downpours across the region till October or November. To get an idea of just how wet Asia can be during the rainy season, compare London's wettest month (64mm), or New York's (109mm), or Sydney's (135mm), with Bangkok, which gets an average of 305mm of rain every September – imagine what that does to the canals and rivers in the aptly named "Venice of the East".

That's nothing, however, compared to what happens to Mawsynram, a small town in northeast India that has been known to get over a metre of rainfall in a single day – for which it earns an entry in the *Guinness Book of Records* as "the world's wettest place". Across the border in low-lying Bangladesh, monsoons bring devastating floods every year, regularly rendering thousands of people homeless.

The wind direction is reversed during the northern winter when the land cools down, so the northeast monsoon brings drier, slightly cooler weather to most of tropical Asia (east-coast areas excepted) between November and February. This period is the best time overall to travel in tropical Asia.

The main exceptions to the above pattern are the east-coast regions of Vietnam, Peninsular Thailand, Peninsular Malaysia, and Sri Lanka, and the southeastern region of India. Due to various complicated factors, the most obvious of which is their east-coast location, these areas get rain when the rest of tropical Asia is having its driest period, but stay dry during the southwest monsoon.

Much of Indonesia, however, gets the worst (or best) of both monsoons, attracting the west-coast rains from May to October, and the east-coast rains from November to February. In some parts of the archipelago – like equatorial Sumatra – barely a week goes by without a shower or two, while the islands that lie relatively far south of the equator, like Timor, experience an annual dry season that usually runs from April to October.

Altitude: the Himalayas

Temperatures plummet by 6.5°C for every 1000m you gain in altitude, so the higher you go the colder the air becomes – worth bearing in mind when you're sweltering on the tropical plains (see box below for suggested upland getaways).

The Himalayas are Asia's major mountain range and, though the climate here is much cooler than on the lowlands, it too is affected by the southwest monsoon. The torrential rain that drenches the Punjab from June to August falls as several metres of snow in the Everest region – making this an unpredictable and potentially dangerous time to go trekking. At lower elevations, the rains can cause landslides on mountain roads during this time, so it's as well to keep travel plans flexible or to avoid the region altogether. The exceptions to this rule are the dry mountain areas of Ladakh and north Pakistan, where summer is the best time to go trekking.

The snow is heaviest, however, during the cold winter months, and mountain passes above 4000m are usually blocked between

IF YOU CAN'T STAND THE HEAT . . . GET OUT OF THE CITY

When the mid-morning mercury hits 35°C and the humidity averages ninety percent, it's time to think about cooling yourself down. If you can't get to the seaside, then consider heading up into the hills instead.

During the Raj era, the colonial Brits decamped en masse every summer to the Indian hill stations of Shimla, Ooty, Darjeeling and Kodaikanal, and these old-fashioned resort towns are still pleasant places to visit, many of them reached by quaint steam trains that trundle up through tea plantations to the refreshing forested hills. Further south, in Sri Lanka, the hill resort of Kandy (488m) makes a lovely cool lakeside retreat from the roasting plains, and for a full-on chill-out you can continue up to the former colonial outpost of Nuwara Fliya (1800m), at its best in March and April. In Malaysia, hot-season temperatures up on the Cameron Highlands are a good 10°C cooler than down in the sweltering capital. Other popular upland getaways include the hills around Chiang Mai in northern Thailand, the Bolaven Plateau in Laos, Da Lat in south Vietnam, Sylhet in Bangladesh, Baguio in the Philippines, and the volcanic highlands around Berastagi in north Sumatra and Lake Batur in Bali.

December and April, with the snow line descending to around 2500m during this period. October and November are therefore the most popular months for trekking in Nepal and northern India: skies are clear and daytime temperatures fairly warm, especially in the sun (nights are always cold in the mountains). Lower-level trekking is also popular from February to mid-April.

Throughout Asia, mountain areas become inaccessible to vehicles as well as trekkers and mountaineers during the winter months. Heavy snowfall makes the 5000-metre-high trans-Himalayan Manali–Leh Highway impassable between November and April (although the road is officially shut between September 15 and June 15, public buses plough on until the last possible moment). And the similarly dramatic link between Pakistan and China, known as the Karakoram Highway because it crosses a 5575-metre-high pass in the Karakoram Mountains (the range containing the famous K2 peak), is also closed between November and April.

If you're not trekking or driving at very high elevations, however, the northern winter is a lovely time to admire the snow-capped peaks from a warmer vantage point in the Himalayan foothills and valleys. Though days are brisk and nights extremely cold, the air is crisp and fresh in this season, the skies are a brilliant clear blue and the mountains at their most spectacular. So long as you're kitted out with the right gear, this can be an exhilarating – and peaceful – time to be in northern India, Nepal, South Korea and northern Japan.

Continental position: deserts and plateaus

A region's continental position also has a huge effect on its weather. Places far from the sea tend to have extreme climates, with very hot, dry summers, very cold winters, and precious little rain at any time of the year. The high Tibetan plateau and northwestern China, for example, get negligible rain, choking summer dust storms and bitterly cold winters – temperatures in Ürümqi, in Xinjiang province, northwest China, never rise above minus 1°C between November and March, sinking to minus 22°C during the daytime in January. In July, however, temperatures average 28°C. Rajasthan, in the Thar desert in northwestern India, experiences a less extreme version of the same climate, so expect some cold nights here in the middle of winter and avoid high summer if you can.

Travelling in the tropics

November to February: the best time to go

The pleasantest overall time to visit tropical Asia is from November to February. This is the so-called cool season, when lowland temperatures are at their most manageable, the humidity is relatively low, and there is hardly any rainfall. In December, you can expect maximum daytime temperatures of 31°C in Bangkok, 23°C in Delhi, 30°C in Manila, and 28°C in Vientiane. Unfortunately, prices are at their highest during this period, peaking over Christmas and New Year, and the classier hotels add a peak-season supplement to their already inflated rates.

However, most parts of Indonesia, southeastern India, and the east coasts of Vietnam, Peninsular Thailand, Peninsular Malaysia and Sri Lanka get the wet end of the northeast monsoon during this time; islands off these coasts are all best avoided between November and February, when boat connections are sporadic, beaches awash with flotsam and waves too high for a relaxed dip. Diving is unrewarding too, because the water gets quite cloudy. Eastern Malaysia (Sabah and Sarawak) is also subject to the northeast monsoon and some roads become impassable during this time. In Indonesia it's unsafe to climb many of the mountains in the wet season.

February to May: the heat is on

By February, the heat is starting to build up right across the plains of tropical Asia, reaching a crescendo in May. During this month, Bangkok temperatures peak at 34°C in the shade, and it's 41°C in Delhi, 34°C in Manila, and 32°C in Vientiane. Though travel is perfectly possible during the hot season, it can be hard work, not least because the humidity is so high that it saps your energy and

THE BEST TIME TO VISIT . . .

What follows is a very broad guide to the best season for travelling, assuming you want the weather to be as dry and mild as possible. Mildness is of course a relative concept: a mild maximum daytime temperature in Jakarta is 31°C, in Ho Chi Minh City it's 27°C and in Kathmandu it's 26°C. The summary below is meant only as an introduction to help with general route-planning and gear preparation; for fuller details, check with guidebooks or tourist offices. To find out what the next four days' forecast is for any major Asian city, call up Ⓦ*www.intellicast.com/weather/asia*

Bangladesh: Nov–Feb.
Bhutan: Oct–Nov; Feb–April.
Brunei: Feb–Aug.
Cambodia: Nov–March.
China: March–May; Sept–Nov; **Hong Kong**: Sept–Dec; **Tibet**: April–Oct.
India: Oct–March (except in the southeast); April–Sept (southeast only).
Indonesia: **Bali**: April–Oct; **Java**: June–Aug; **Kalimantan**: May–Sept; **Nusa Tenggara**: May–July; **Sulawesi**: Aug & Sept; **Sumatra**: June & July, Sept & Oct.
Japan: March–May; Sept–Nov.
Laos: Nov–March.
Malaysia: March–July (peninsular east coast, Sabah & Sarawak); Dec–Feb (for peninsular west coast).
Nepal: Oct & Nov; Feb–April.
Pakistan: Oct–Feb.
Philippines: Nov–Feb (except stretches of southeast coasts); March & April (for southeast coasts).
Singapore: Feb–Oct.
South Korea: April–June; Sept–Nov.
Sri Lanka: Nov–March (west coast); April–Oct (east coast).
Taiwan: Oct–Nov.
Thailand: Nov–Feb (except peninsular east coast); March–Sept (for peninsular east coast).
Vietnam: Sept–Dec; March & April.

can make you loath to leave the air-conditioning between 10am and 3pm. Heat exhaustion is more likely too (see p.302).

The weeks before the rains break are a notoriously tense time in tropical Asia: tempers are short, people are more likely to resort to violence, and the suicide rate goes up. Depleted water supplies mean many rural households struggle to keep their crops and livestock alive, and electricity in towns and villages is often rationed because there simply isn't enough water to run the hydroelectricity plants all day long. It's especially important to take a torch if travelling at this time of year, as budget hotels rarely have their own generators.

Many Asian cultures believe the rains are controlled by gods or spirits, so the end of the hot season is a good time to catch rain-making festivals. The people of Laos and northeast Thailand traditionally regard rain as the fruit of heavenly lovemaking, so in mid-May they hold an exuberant rocket-firing festival to encourage the gods to get on with it.

Places to avoid at all costs during the hot season include the Pakistani region of Baluchistan which, by the end of May, becomes one of the hottest places in the world, with peak daytime temperatures averaging 46°C; you won't get much relief across the border in India at this time either, where the Rajasthani town of Jaisalmer swelters in the low forties through May and June.

May to October: wet-season travel

As the southwest monsoon brings rain to most of Asia between May and October, this is overall the worst time to travel. Quite apart from getting soaked whenever you leave your hotel, you'll be uncomfortably sticky in any rainproof gear (use an umbrella instead) and may also have to ward off leeches, malarial mosquitoes and other wet-weather bugs. Diseases like typhoid and Japanese encephalitis spread faster in these conditions too (but are mainly confined to rural areas), and you'll be more prone to fungal infections and unhealthy skin.

Diving will be a complete waste of time as visibility will be minimal, surfing will likely be out of the question, and beaches languish under the garbage washed up by the storms. Some islands, such as Thailand's Ko Similan, are impossible to get to at this time, while other regions may be inaccessible because the roads have turned to mud.

Fierce tropical winds are also more frequent during the rainy season. Known as typhoons in the Pacific region, these hurricanes hit certain parts of Asia, notably the Philippines, Bangladesh and southeast China, at speeds of over 120km per hour, leaving a trail of flattened crops, dismembered houses and an inevitable toll of human casualties as well. Typhoons can be especially dangerous on the coastal plains where tidal waves cause additional destruction, so you should always heed local advice about places to avoid during a typhoon. As forecasters usually predict typhoons a few days in advance, you should have plenty of time to prepare and protect yourself (see p.329 for more typhoon advice).

However, rain needn't put a damper on *all* Southeast Asian itineraries. In some places (like west-coast Peninsular Malaysia) downpours are limited to just a couple of hours every day for two or three months during the wet season, and these storms are often so regular as to arrive at the same time every afternoon. Waterfalls spring back to life, rice paddies flood picturesquely, and this is often the best time of year for flowers.

The rainy season is usually low season for the tourist industry, and this can have all sorts of advantages, including discounted accommodation and more time to hobnob with local people. Note that, despite the weather, some airlines and swanky hotels treat July and August as a special peak season, because this is the time the northern hemisphere takes its summer holidays.

In most parts of Asia, the coming of the monsoon is cause for celebration – not only is it essential for the crops, but it also breaks the tension of the preceding weeks and is considered to have both healing and erotic properties (extramarital affairs are said to flourish during the rainy season). In India, middle-class city folk plan their holidays to coincide with the arrival of the first rains in the southwest, and in Bangkok men and women shampoo their hair out on the street in the first decent downpour of the season.

For travellers, east-coast beaches and islands that are not affected by the southwest monsoons come into their own during this time – that makes May to October peak season for Ko Samui, Ko Pha Ngan and Ko Tao in Thailand, and the best time to head for east-coast Sri Lanka; east-coast Malaysia is at its best between March and July. Off season for these coasts and islands is between November and April, during the northeast monsoon.

Special events and local holidays

Many festivals and annual events are well worth planning your itinerary around – or even changing your schedule for. Religious festivals can be especially fun, many of them celebrated with street parades, food fairs (Thailand), dance performances (India), shadow-puppet plays (Indonesia) and masked dances (Bhutan and Ladakh) which tourists are usually welcome to attend (though you should ask locally first). As Buddhists and Hindus operate on a lunar calendar (as opposed to the Western Gregorian one), these festivals occur on different dates every year, but tourist offices will be able to give you precise details.

The biggest festivals can draw huge local crowds as well, so be prepared for packed trains and buses and over-booked hotels. If possible, reserve transport and accommodation well in advance and expect to shell out up to double the normal price for food and lodging. Occasionally, the volume and exuberance of festival crowds can become quite scary, and so may be best avoided – the water- and paint-throwing festival of Holi, which is celebrated throughout India every February or March, is a typical example.

National public holidays tend to be more stuffy occasions, especially the ones commemorating political victories or rulers' birthdays, and are usually marked by military parades and speeches, if at all. Most businesses close on these days, as do markets and restaurants, though popular sights – particularly waterfalls, temples and public parks – will be chock-a-block with local people on their day off.

Soaking up the atmosphere, Indian style

It was Holi, the first day of spring, and the townspeople of Puri in east India were celebrating the day in traditional style, by taking to the streets with pails of water and armfuls of paint bombs, and chucking them at passers-by. The owner of the guesthouse advised us not to go out until after midday, when the water-throwing had to stop. Foreigners were popular targets, he said, and it would not be a pleasant experience.

But we had to go out, to buy tickets from the train station. From the safety of our rickshaw seat, we watched as people on the streets got sprayed, but we stayed fairly dry. Then the rickshaw driver turned down an alleyway and stopped, and the ambush began. A group of young guys rushed towards us, pelting us from all angles with buckets of water and handfuls of paint, which they rubbed into our faces and hair. It was pretty scary, and we got soaked. Our camera was sodden, I had paint in my eyes, and my clothes were stained for ever. Mission accomplished, they backed off and we drove on.

At the train station we stood soggily in the statutory queue. Just as we reached the sales counter, the ticket man's face dropped and we looked round to see another gang of water guerrillas bursting through the doors. This time everyone got soaked, not just the tourists, and files and papers were reduced to mush. Excitement over, the salesman proceeded with his form-filling, and we came away with our tickets.

Jo Mead

“

The Pushkar camel fair

Pushkar was hosting its annual fair, a combination of religious festival and huge camel market, with over fifty thousand animals brought in from all over Rajasthan. The streets were heaving with pilgrims, traders and tourists, and the bazaar spilled over into a labyrinth of dim, twisting alleys – market stalls a blaze of colour, the air thick with spices, dust and sweat.

A sea of makeshift tents, camels and assorted livestock stretched far out across the plain. Tall, regal men dressed in waistcoats and long, baggy loincloths wandered among the animals, inspecting, discussing, bargaining. Turbans formed bobbing multicoloured dots among the ochre-brown mass, and even the camels were decorated with vibrant bridles of twisted cord, tasselled and beaded. Most animals stood or lay quietly ruminating, surveying their surroundings disdainfully, but every now and then a screeching and a swirl of dust would signify a runaway, pursued by groups of stick-wielding men.

Nicki McCormick

Good days . . .

We've chosen some of our favourite festivals below, but any guidebook will offer heaps more. Or have a look at *Wild Planet! 1,001 Extraordinary Events for the Inspired Traveler* by Tom Clynes (Visible Ink Press), which includes details of dozens of small- and large-scale celebrations in Asia and the rest of the world. The Web site Ⓦ *www.whatsonwhen.com* offers a similar directory, with events around the world listed by country and by month.

- **Ice Lantern Festival in Harbin, northeast China**. From January 5 to February 5, when temperatures sink to an unbearably chilly minus 30°C, the excess snow and ice in Harbin's Zhaolin Park is carved into extraordinary sculptures and even replica buildings such as life-size Chinese temples.
- **Ati-Atihan harvest pageants, Kalibo, the Philippines**. This small town hosts a huge Mardi Gras-style extravaganza on the third weekend of January. The streets are packed with people in outrageous costumes and everyone joins in the dancing.
- **Buddhist New Year in Thailand, Laos and Cambodia**. The Buddhists of Indochina celebrate their New Year in mid-April with nationwide public water fights – once symbolic of a purification ritual, but now more of an excuse for

clowning about and drenching total strangers. The most organized people circulate town in pick-up trucks fitted with hosepipes and water cannons, while others limit themselves to more genteel sprinkling. Any passers-by, tourists included, will get a soaking, though it's quite refreshing at this time of year, April being the hottest month of the hottest season. The most exuberant New Year celebrations are held in Chiang Mai (Thailand) and Louang Phabang (Laos).

- **Cherry blossom picnics and maple-leaf viewing, Japan**. Cherry blossom season begins when the first flowers appear in spring in Okinawa, the southernmost island of the Japanese archipelago, and for the next few weeks national TV broadcasts a nightly *sakura* forecast, showing how far the pink wave has progressed up the country. When the main island of Honshu turns pink (towards the end of April), the parks are packed with blossom-viewing picnic parties. Friends and families settle under the trees, getting drunk on saké, belting out karaoke songs and composing maudlin haiku poems about the fragile petals. Seven months later, the ancient capital of Kyoto flames a brilliant red for the last couple of weeks in November, when the maple trees light up the hillsides in displays bettered nowhere but British Columbia. This is also your one chance to sample the bizarre local delicacy known as *momiji tempura* – fallen maple leaves fried in batter.
- **Spring fair in Dali, China**. For five days every April or May, thousands of people from all over Yunnan converge on Dali for horse-trading, wrestling matches, racing contests, dancing and singing.
- **Gawai Dayak harvest festival, Sarawak, East Malaysia**. Parties in the traditional Iban longhouses are always riotous, but the biggest celebration of the year happens in June to mark the end of the rice harvest. Expect all-night drinking and heaps of food, plus lots of jokes, pranks and party games.
- **Kandy historical pageant, Sri Lanka**. For ten nights every July or August, extravagant torch-lit processions of costumed dancers, drummers and elephants in full regalia parade through the streets of Kandy in what's thought to be one of the oldest historical pageants in the world.
- **Pushkar camel fair, northwest India**. For three days in late October or early November all roads seem to lead to Pushkar in Rajasthan, as crowds of 200,000 descend on this tiny desert town for India's biggest camel fair. Camels are paraded, raced and entered for competitions and the place brims over with market stalls and street entertainers. At night, visitors are housed in a spe-

cially erected tent city where huge marquees are equipped with camp beds and bush toilets.

● **Surin elephant roundup, northeast Thailand**. Surin's resident herd of working elephants is rounded up every November for a public display of their talents, and thousands of tourists come to watch them play soccer, engage in a tug of war and parade around the sports ground in traditional battle garb.

. . . and bad days

Though the tourist industry never grinds to a complete standstill, there are certain public and religious holidays when you'll be hard-pressed to find hotels and restaurants open for business. In Bali, for example, the Hindu New Year is celebrated in March or April with a day of complete silence and inactivity – shopkeepers are actually fined if they trade on that day, the chances of getting a taxi are very slim, and even the airport is closed for 24 hours.

Nor is it a great idea to land in China or Taiwan during the three-day Chinese New Year celebrations (in late January or early February) as everything will be closed, and you're unlikely to find a hotel room anywhere. The same is true of any town or city with a majority Chinese community – Singapore is an obvious example, but the hotels and restaurants in many Thai and Malaysian cities are also run by ethnic Chinese. If you want to be in one of these places for Chinese New Year (the firework displays can be unforgettable), then get to the city a couple of days early so you can stake your claim on a room and stock up on food. The same advice applies if you're in Sri Lanka over the Sinhalese New Year in mid-April, when lots of hotels and restaurants close down for a whole week.

Similarly, you might want to think twice about visiting an Islamic country during Ramadan, a month-long period of abstinence that falls during the ninth Muslim month (starting in mid-Nov in 2001, and subsequently starting about eleven days earlier each year), when practising Muslims do without food, water and tobacco during daylight hours. This makes for a very stressed-out population, par-ticularly by the third and fourth week, so you may not get the hos-pitality you were hoping for, especially in the more orthodox com-munities such as in Sumatra and Kalimantan. Many restaurants stay shut during the daytime throughout Ramadan, and in parts of Indonesia and Pakistan local bus services are less frequent during this month too. If you are in Indonesia, Pakistan, Bangladesh, India, Malaysia or southern Thailand during Ramadan, be sensitive to your hosts and don't flaunt your food, drinks and cigarettes in front of them.

Steer clear of big cities in the immediate run-up to elections too, particularly in India where rallies can turn nasty and curfews may be imposed on and around polling day. It's not unknown for election results to be greeted with riots, so head for safe havens in the hills or by the sea, and get your news from the *Times of India* instead.

4

How much will it cost?

udgeting is boring, but spending a bit of time thinking about it before you go will leave you more energy to enjoy Asia once you're there, rather than worrying about survival. Windswept and exotic as it may sound, there is actually nothing at all romantic about jetting off to the furthest place you can think of and realizing when you get there

EXCHANGE RATES AND CURRENCY FLUCTUATIONS

For an idea of how much your money will be worth once you're on the road, you can check conversion rates for the most popular destinations in the financial pages of newspapers, at the exchange counter of your local bank, or using Web sites such as ⓦ*www.oanda.com/convert/classic*, which gives you up-to-date rates for 164 currencies and can compile wallet-sized conversion tables.

It's worth bearing in mind that economic conditions in Asia can change and change fast. Keep a close eye on currency fluctuations prior to your departure.

Inflation in Asian countries can be equally volatile and anyone operating on a shoestring budget with no room for manœuvre can find themselves in serious trouble as prices rocket – for example, at the time of writing, annual inflation in Laos was estimated at 85 percent.

that you can't afford to eat or drink or sleep in a decent bed, that you've got a ticket that won't let you return home early, and you have to spend the first week working out how you can get money wired out to you. If you are seriously strapped for cash, it's worth planning a shorter trip – we guarantee you'll have a better time than if you embark on a longer, penny-pinching haul. This chapter will help you calculate your costs, give you ideas for making your cash go further and provide practical advice on how to take your money with you.

However carefully you work out your budget, though, there will be unexpected expenses along the way, so try to take more money than you think you'll need. Global incidents such as war and the collapse of stock markets can cause serious currency fluctuations, which will wreck your conversion calculations, while the insatiable urge to ship a divine granite elephant home from Bali or the pressing necessity for a white-water rafting trip down the Sun Kosi in Nepal will throw inflexible finances into chaos.

Budgeting

One thing to remember is that generalizations are dangerous. "Oh, Asia's cheap," you'll hear again and again. It is true that, compared with the major expense of your plane ticket, prices in Asia can seem cheap. But while you can find a basic beach hut in Goa or on the islands off the southeast coast of Thailand for about $5/£3 a night, you'll be looking at at least $10/£7 for a bed in Singapore, $20/£14 in Hong Kong; in Tokyo anything less than $25/£17 is very rare indeed. In fact, you'll find all extremes across the continent. A night in the *Raffles Hotel* in Singapore will cost you well over $450/£300, which buys almost six months' accommodation in parts of Indonesia; in India, a twelve-hour train trip costs about $5/£3.50 second class and a cup of tea beside the road is just a few cents, but it's equally possible to spend $200/£130 a night on accommodation in luxury hotels in the big cities, or $240/£160 flying between Delhi and Chennai (Madras). And while the Japan National Tourist Office

SAMPLE BUDGETS

Here is a rough indication of minimum daily costs in all the countries we cover (if you are planning internal flights or adventure activities, add these on top):

Top-end countries will cost you $35/£25 a day upwards:

Bhutan	China (east coast)
Brunei	Japan

Mid-range countries should be manageable on a budget of $20—35/£13—23:

China (interior and Hong Kong)	South Korea
Singapore	Taiwan

The **cheapest** countries can be coped with on under $20/£13 a day:

Bangladesh	Nepal
Cambodia	Pakistan
India	Philippines
Indonesia	Sri Lanka
Laos	Thailand
Malaysia	Vietnam

Three months in India

While it's possible to manage on around $10/£7 a day in India, this would mean staying in the cheapest hotels, eating only rice and dhal and travelling second class on all train journeys. If you bump up your luxury quotient, have a room with your own bathroom, vary your diet slightly and throw in a few first-class train journeys, then you're looking at $20–25/£12–15 a day, $140–175/£85–105 a week. Go further up the scale – book into mid-range hotels, eat in moderately priced restaurants and rent a car and driver for a few excursions – and a better estimate is around $35/£25 a day, $225–250/£140–175 a week. To travel cheaply but realistically, we recommend reckoning on covering around half the trip at the lowest rate – say six weeks at $70/£45 – and the remainder at the middle rate – say seven weeks at $175/£105 – giving a much more realistic total of $1645/£1100.

A three-month trip through Thailand, Malaysia and Indonesia

To spend a month in each country, you'd need $1020/£720 if you work out your costs using a minimum daily budget of $10/£7 for Thailand and for Indonesia, and $14/£10 a day for Malaysia. However, long-distance travel costs increase this figure significantly, especially if you fly, as does white-water rafting, clothes shopping and/or bar-hopping in Bali. Allowing for half the trip at the basic rate, and the other half at double this, reckon on at least $2000/£1400 to cover long-distance travel, the occasional splurge and some (restrained) souvenir shopping; and at least double this if you are intending to fit in the entire Indonesian archipelago and do your island-hopping by plane.

do their utmost to entice you there, giving information on economical accommodation, food and travel in all their brochures, the truth is that you can manage there on a New York or London budget – but not on a Bangkok one.

How much you spend naturally depends on the sort of holiday you want to have. While rock-bottom accommodation, local transport and food from simple roadside stalls in Vietnam is likely to set you back about $12–15/£8–10 daily, once you start considering a bit more comfort, a few beers, better-quality food and the occasional minibus tour, then $25–30/£17–21 is more realistic. It's relatively easy to sit in comfort at home and swear you'll manage without air-conditioning, bathe in cold water and love it, and never want a private toilet, but after a week in 45°C heat and ninety-percent humidity, a few cold showers at 3000m or three days with chronic diarrhoea, your perceptions will certainly alter. Even if you plan to have the budget holiday to beat all budget holidays, it makes sense to plan for the occasional splurge. Most first-time visitors to Asia aim for a low weekly budget as far as living costs are concerned, but allow themselves the occasional treat such as a few nights in air-conditioned accommodation, some hot water every so often or perhaps a couple of local flights.

Generalizations about individual countries can be misleading, as some Asian countries are so vast that you'll find different price "zones" in different parts of the country. In China, the east-coast cities have prices on a par with cities in the West, and you'd be hard pushed here to find a bed for less than $40/£26. Inland, the picture changes hugely; in Sichuan, for example, there are decent beds available for a couple of dollars.

It's worth bearing in mind that throughout Asia, prices can escalate sharply in peak season; hotel rooms can even double in price. Peak seasons vary locally, but Christmas and New Year are popular pretty much everywhere. On Bali, June to September – coinciding with the European holiday season – is very busy, whereas in Nepal, it's October and November that see a tourist rush to take advantage of the ideal trekking weather.

Saving money before you go

Some of the biggest savings you'll be able to make are those before you go. The best flight deals sell out early and you'll find that certain routes, eg to Goa for Christmas and New Year, are booked solid several months in advance. If you're rushing to fit visas, vaccinations and shopping into a few hectic weeks, you'll have to make hurried decisions and may end up paying to cut corners. The following tips may help:

- Shop around for your flight tickets and plan your itinerary with your budget in mind. You may well be better off visiting a few places in one region than racing across the continent – even in Asia the cost of train/ferry/internal-flight tickets adds up. A free stopover in Tokyo may seem like a good idea, but can you afford several days of high city prices? Taking a cheaper ticket that leaves you to travel from Bangkok to Singapore overland can sound appealing, but make sure you budget for the train or bus fare and the extra days on the road.

- Although there are plenty of visa services who will arrange visas for you (your travel agent may even offer to do this), it is always cheaper to do it yourself. However, you will need to allow plenty of time, especially if you are applying by post. See Chapter Two for more information on visas.

- For certain countries, you'll need an armful of inoculations (see Chapter Eleven). Travel clinics provide excellent specialist information and are a time-saving and hassle-free way to get all your jabs. However, many injections are cheaper, even free, from your own doctor.

- If you're booking your first couple of nights' hotel accommodation before you leave home (see Chapter Seven), contact a few hotels directly and compare their prices with those on offer through your travel agent. Also check online accommodation booking agents (listed on p.362) for good deals.

- By all means shop around for a good deal, but do *not* skimp on your insurance. Knowing that your medical costs and replacement gear will be paid for doesn't make a disaster OK, but it certainly makes it a whole lot more bearable. Don't consider going without insurance, lying about where you're heading or what you're intending to do, or underestimating the value of your stuff just to get cheaper premiums – it isn't worth it. You could end up with tens of thousands of dollars of medical bills if you tell the insurance company you are going to Europe but end up being airlifted out of Irian Jaya, or insist you are not taking part in any hazardous sports, but are injured whitewater rafting in the Himalayas. Similarly, don't expect to be able to claim the full amount for your $200 camera if you tell the insurance company it's only worth $50. For more on insurance, see p.150.

Be economical

Don't assume you have to take everything with you from home. Some equipment that will be essential for your trip (see Chapter Six), such as lightweight clothes, insect repellents and mosquito nets, are cheaper once you are in Asia. Sarongs, those all-purpose coveralls, are cheap across the continent, as are Tiger Balm (a local ointment – useful to soothe insect bites), soap, shampoo, stationery, mosquito coils and detergent. However, sun block, tampons and deodorant are pricey throughout Asia, and hair conditioner is expensive and difficult to find outside tourist areas.

One item to consider taking if you're going on a long trip is a water filter. The price of bottled water, particularly in tourist resorts, can be surprisingly high and could use up a substantial part of your budget over a long period.

Don't assume everything you bring from home has to be sparkling new – it certainly won't be after a few weeks on the road. Trekking equipment shops often have a board advertising second-hand gear, and outdoor sports magazines usually include a classified ads section. Try local thrift and charity shops for cheap cotton clothes, rucksacks, waterproofs and even boots, though do check the merchandise carefully – you don't want a pack with holes, broken zips and detached straps. Look for good value and don't get carried away by cheap prices.

Spending wisely while you're there

While many of the major savings can be made before you even leave home, there are plenty of ways to save money on the road. These tips may be handy:

- Take your International Student Identity Card if you have one. The response to this is variable – in some places it'll simply get a bemused look, but in others it can get you reduced entrance fees to museums and performances.
- Eat as local people do. Western food and drink cost much more than local food throughout Asia.
- You'll save money by eating in groups of two or more – many restaurant dishes come in family-sized portions, especially in

China and Thailand, the idea being that diners share several dishes.

- Take advantage of the thriving secondhand market among travellers on the road – you can sell or swap items of equipment or guidebooks rather than buying them new. Many travellers' hotels and restaurants have noticeboards advertising goods for sale or swap.
- Hone your bargaining skills (see opposite) so that you don't pay over the odds for goods and services.

Indulging yourself

It's worth bearing in mind that cheapness isn't everything. Asia is probably the best chance most people have of affording some five-star luxury – so why not make the most of the opportunity to join the jet set for at least a few days? For example, a slap-up buffet

IT'S NOT FAIR?

Don't be too distressed if you see local people being charged less than you are – in several Asian countries there is a two- or three-tier pricing system in operation. Vietnam has a three-tier pricing policy, with foreigners paying more than local people for accommodation and train tickets, and *Viet Kieu* (overseas Vietnamese) paying somewhere between the two. In China the same principle applies to plane tickets and entry charges for museums and famous sights, while some hotels slap a foreigner's surcharge onto their prices. In Thailand and Sri Lanka, foreigners are charged more than local people for entry to all national museums and historic places.

The reasoning behind all this is simple: foreigners can afford to pay more, therefore they should be charged more. It's a philosophy you will encounter time and time again throughout Asia, from the woman selling mangoes in the market to the national airline company. There is usually little you can do in official situations (rail and air tickets, entrance charges, etc), except pay up. Some travellers feel it's a fair cop, others fume against it at every turn. However, when dealing with local people (in the market, in a rickshaw), try to find out a fair price from those around you and endeavour not to pay more (or at least not too much more). If foreigners consistently pay way over the top for something, the danger is either that prices will also rise for local people or that traders will prefer to provide services to foreigners. Accept that you'll end up paying somewhat over the odds on many occasions, but try not to get totally obsessed and distressed about it and feel you are being "ripped off" at every turn – especially when the amount involved may be just a few pennies.

lunch in a top-flight Manila hotel will cost around $15/£10, and a night in the *Lake Palace Hotel* in Udaipur, one of the world's most spectacular hotels – it's an ex-maharajah's palace on an island in the middle of a lake – will set you back $240/£160 or more. You can see Bali in style, with your own car and driver for the day, for $30/£20, or have a tailor-made cashmere suit run up in Bangkok for around $160/£100.

And, whenever it's a toss-up between spending a bit of extra cash and putting your own safety at risk, you should always part with the cash. Spending money wisely will ensure you have a far more memorable trip than trying not to spend any at all.

Bargaining

This is an aspect of Asian life that is very alien to visitors from the West. Some people take to it like ducks to water; others find it hard to cope with, no matter how long they stay on the continent.

It's important to remember that bargaining over the price of something is as much a ritual of social interaction as it is about saving money. Essentially it means that, with a few exceptions, the price of anything on offer is open to negotiation. However, if you

SPECIAL PRICE FOR YOU, MADAM

You might like the look of a pair of trousers in an Indian market. You enquire the price, the vendor asks five hundred rupees. You shake your head regretfully and offer two hundred (somewhere in the region of a third or a half the initial asking price is a good starting figure in India). He or she throws their hands up in horror – they have a family to support, how can you expect them to make a living when you are taking the profit out of their business and the rice out of the mouths of their starving offspring, and how about four hundred? You nod sympathetically, but you notice a tiny fault in the material, can't really see your way to paying that much, but could perhaps go as high as three hundred. The fault is nothing; here, he has another pair that are perfect, three-eighty? Ah, but you have seen some similar ones at a better price down the road, what about three-fifty? He agrees, smiles, this is a special price for you, Madam – the transaction is done. All this may well have taken place over five minutes, an hour or even a week! However, it's always accompanied by smiles, gentle voices and good humour. Even if you can't reach an agreement, and often you can't, you can shake your head regretfully and walk away. This in itself can be a useful ploy in the process – many a bargain has been struck halfway down the street.

offer a price and it is accepted, you are morally bound to go ahead with the purchase – so don't haggle if you haven't made up your mind whether or not you really want the item. It's perfectly acceptable, though, to wander around a market asking the prices just to get some idea of the starting figures.

If you're really into bargain-hunting, it can be worthwhile doing your shopping early in the day. In Bali, for example, the vendors believe that a good early sale establishes their fortune in trading for the rest of the day, so start bargaining at lower "morning prices".

Fixed prices and discounts

The real difficulty in Asia is knowing when and when not to bargain. Basically, prices are fixed (non-negotiable) in restaurants where prices are displayed; in supermarkets and large department stores; on official public transport with tickets; in metered taxis; and in museums, parks or temples where entrance charges are displayed and tickets provided. Even in shops with prices labelled, such as CD and tape shops, you may be able to negotiate a better rate for purchases of ten or more or get a free tape thrown in.

As you move upmarket, the jargon changes slightly. So, for example, in a small guesthouse you might simply enquire whether they can let you have the room they offered you at 100,000 dong for 80,000 dong, whereas in a luxury hotel you could enquire about the availability of discounts, perhaps producing a business card for a bit of extra effect. You are far more likely to get discounts on accommodation during the low season than when the place is packed out. It's always worth bargaining if you're staying longer than a couple of nights: many places do good weekly and monthly rates.

How to take your money

However short your trip, *never* simply take a huge wodge of cash hidden about your person. You want flexibility and easy access to your money, but you also need security against loss and theft, and ideally some kind of backup or emergency funds. The best solution is to travel with a combination of cash, traveller's cheques and credit cards. In case the exchange counter at the airport you're flying into is closed or out of cash when you touch down, it's a good idea to change a small amount of cash into the currency of your first Asian landfall before you leave home. However, there are cases where this isn't possible: for example, you cannot legally buy rupees outside India; Vietnamese dong are not available outside the country; and other currencies are partially restricted, meaning you can only change very small amounts abroad.

Cash

The US dollar is the hard currency of choice throughout Asia, as long as the notes are clean and in good condition. Even little hotels in the back of beyond may be willing to change a few dollars into local currency if you get caught short, but they're unlikely to look at any other form of foreign currency. And in Cambodia, you will be expected to pay in US dollars rather than *riel* at guesthouses and restaurants, and for most entrance fees to tourist sites. Always take small denominations ($1 and $5), as small businesses are unlikely to keep large cash reserves. The advantage of cash is that it's usually exchangeable even if you lose your passport. The big disadvantage is its vulnerability – if stolen, cash is untraceable and most insurance policies expressly exclude the theft of cash from their cover.

Traveller's cheques

Still an essential part of travelling in Asia, traveller's cheques are issued in a variety of currencies, usually at 1–1.5 percent commission, which is essentially the price you pay for peace of mind. However, you do need to be careful about whose cheques you carry. Whatever the other companies say, American Express is the most widely acceptable traveller's cheque in Asia. However, every now and again there is a localized scare about fraud involving one brand or another, and if you are relying totally on traveller's cheques you should think about taking cheques from two or more companies.

Although traveller's cheques in most major currencies are happily accepted at moneychangers and banks in tourist centres, get a bit off the beaten track and you'll find that only US-dollar cheques are acceptable. It pays to do some research before heading too far off into the wilderness, as in the remotest regions – in parts of Indonesia, Laos and Cambodia and in northern Vietnam for example – no traveller's cheques at all are exchangeable.

Traveller's cheques need careful handling. You must record the numbers of the cheques and tick them off on your list as you use them. Keep this record separate from the traveller's cheques themselves, because if the cheques are stolen or lost you must be able to report the missing numbers to the company. Also keep the emergency telephone number separate from the cheques – directory enquiries in a foreign language when you're upset isn't much fun. In general, traveller's cheques will be replaced at the nearest representative within a day or two, provided you have the missing numbers, information about the date and place of purchase, and some form of ID. However, if you're exploring the river systems of southern Sarawak in a longboat, the nearest Amex office could be a long trip away. You'll be very glad of a $50 or $100 emergency stash kept somewhere apart from your main money supply should the worst happen.

You always need your passport as identification to change traveller's cheques, so if your passport gets stolen, your traveller's cheques are useless. In addition, some banks, in an attempt to avoid fraud, insist that you also show them the receipt – it has "Agreement to purchase" written on the back.

Credit cards

The extent to which credit cards are acceptable as payment varies hugely across the continent. Though most top-class hotels, restaurants and shops are happy to accept them (and you often get a very favourable rate of exchange when the bill comes in), they're not

much use in establishments at the budget end of the market.

Credit cards are particularly useful for major outlays such as internal flights, the occasional hotel or restaurant splurge, or for very large souvenirs and the cost of shipping them home. They can also be useful when booking and prepaying for a hotel room over the phone or fax (very handy at peak times of the year), though only at mid-market and top-end places.

Even if you don't plan on using

it, a credit card is a great emergency stand-by, since you can obtain cash advances against credit cards. Visa and Mastercard are the most widely accepted throughout Asia, both at banks and moneychangers; you can also use their cards to withdraw cash at ATMs (cash dispensers) once you are on the road – check the Web sites ⓦ*www.visa.com* and ⓦ*www.mastercard.com* for the locations of machines accepting their cards. American Express offices even provide a free cheque cashing service for Amex card-holders.

Make sure you carry with you the phone number to report theft of the card, and *never* let the card out of your possession, even stored in a so-called safe while you're away trekking for a few days (see p.327). Bear in mind that, if the card does get lost, getting a replacement sent out to you is likely to take at least four days, and that you'll need someone at home to organize the paying of the credit-card bill if it's going to reach home before you do.

Debit cards

Debit cards that are part of the Cirrus and Maestro network can be used in ATMs worldwide. It's pretty clever stuff: you pop the card in, key in your PIN (personal identification number) and the system immediately accesses your bank account back home and flashes messages to you in your own language. Needless to say, you have to have the funds in your account at home to support the withdrawal, and all the security warnings about credit cards also apply to debit cards. There's a charge of around two percent for each transaction, although this varies; it's worth checking how much your bank charges before you leave home.

In Asia, you can use cards bearing the Cirrus or Maestro logos in cities and larger towns in China, Hong Kong, India, Indonesia, Japan, Malaysia, the Philippines, Singapore, South Korea, Sri Lanka, Taiwan, Thailand and Vietnam; the Mastercard Web site ⓦ*www.mastercard.com* contains lists, organized by country and town, of ATMs that accept Cirrus and Maestro.

Changing money

Whenever you change money you should check the exchange rate being offered and the commission charged on the transaction. Just as

" "

Ready cash?

I'd arrived in Sumatra from Singapore, where changing money is absolutely straightforward. I was in Bandar Lampung, a big city of several million people in southern Sumatra, and down to my last few rupiah. It was time to hit the bank. I left the guesthouse saying I wouldn't be long, but there were a few things I hadn't counted on.

The banks were all closed. Today was a national holiday on account of a Hindu festival in Bali, over 1000km away. Nobody in Bandar Lampung was Hindu, but who were they to turn down a day off? Well, three days off to be precise. Well, really five, if you add the Saturday and Sunday that followed.

I borrowed some cash off other travellers to tide me over and returned to town on Monday to try the bank again – actually several of them. In the first three branches they didn't do foreign exchange and directed me to a main branch across town (funds were getting low again and I had to walk). When I presented my sterling traveller's cheques rather than nice desirable US dollars, however, they didn't want to know, and directed me to another bank, who were equally uninterested in my cheques but took pity on my plight and found me a bank up the street that would exchange them.

By the time I got there it was lunch time. Myself and my rumbling stomach (no money for food) settled down for a long wait. The security guard was very apologetic, but I couldn't wait in the lovely cool air-conditioning – the bank had to be locked. I sat on the steps and dreamed of how many ice-cold drinks and outrageously exotic lunches I would buy when I got my hands on some cash.

When the bank reopened, I was first at the counter. Did I have my purchase agreement for the traveller's cheques? Owing to some recent frauds, head office insisted that this piece of paper must be presented as well as a passport. I didn't know whether to laugh or cry. Yes, I had it, but it was back in the hotel. I raced back across town, starving hungry and dehydrated, collected the agreement and scurried back to the bank with ten minutes to spare before it closed for the day. Together the bank staff and I negotiated the forms in triplicate, they photocopied my passport and purchase agreement, they phoned head office twice to check the day's exchange rate, the supervisor checked everything and handed it all over to the cashier, who checked it all again and then, finally, handed over the money – six full days after I wanted it.

" "

Lesley Reader

rates vary from bank to bank, so can the commission on the deal. In some cases you'll need to do your sums to decide on the best place to go. For example, £100 of Thai baht at B63 to the pound with a one percent commission fee is a better deal than a rate of B62 to the pound with no commission. One disadvantage of traveller's cheques is that you pay commission on them when you buy them and you usually end up paying again to cash them. However, the same applies to a cash advance obtained with a credit card: you'll be charged commission when you get the money, but it also attracts a 1–1.5 percent cash transaction fee on your bill.

Wherever and however you change money, at banks, moneychangers or hotels, shop around carefully, and do keep your exchange certificates. This is your proof that you changed the money legally and in many countries it's vital if you want to change unspent local currency when you leave the country, or want to pay for tourist tickets – for example, on Indian railways or internal flights in China – with local currency.

Follow a few sensible precautions when changing your hard currency into local money and you'll be a few baht, rupiah or dong better off:

● In some countries (for example China, India, Vietnam) there is a black market in the local currency offering better rates than the banks for hard currency. However, bear in mind that the local police or security forces often "sting" foreigners in this way: they set up the deal and then either arrest you for black-market trading or extract a bribe to avoid criminal proceedings. There is also a risk you'll get caught up in a crackdown on local operators, become the victim of sleight-of-hand tricks or receive counterfeit notes. The black market probably isn't worth it – especially as the difference between the official and unofficial rate is usually ridiculously small.

● The best rates are usually found in travellers' centres, such as Kuta in Bali or Khao San Road in Bangkok, where there's plenty of competition.

● Don't be unduly suspicious of moneychangers. They are licensed by the local authorities, offer competitive and often better rates than the banks, have more flexible opening hours and often require less paperwork than banks (see box on p.180). The last resort is to change money at hotels, where rates are usually the poorest.

● If you are passing through a country more than once, don't get rid of all your local currency until you leave the final time, as you'll only have to get more each time you come back.

● Get rid of coins before you leave a country, as they are not exchangeable outside.

● At border crossings the chances are that rates will be poor. Change only what you need until you can get to a more competitive dealer.

● Always count your notes before you leave the cash desk, however long and tedious the process. It's worth it to be sure you've got the right amount. There are plenty of scams in operation – one involves folding notes in two so that you actually get half as much as appears to be being counted out. Another ploy is distracting you while counting out the money, so stay alert.

● Make sure you never run down to your last few cents before you change money.

Running out of money?

It is possible to get money wired out to you from home – especially useful in an emergency. However, hefty fees are charged for this, and the efficiency and speed of the service varies across the continent; it's easier if someone in your home country can make the arrangements. Not surprisingly, it is relatively straightforward to transfer money to banks in Hong Kong (even so, it can take the

best part of a day to arrange), but more time-consuming and haphazard to banks in Nepal and India, while in China it can take weeks. If you think you might need this service, have a chat with your home bank before you leave. You'll need to find a bank in the country you're visiting that has an agreement with the bank you wish to transfer funds from at home, and you'll need your passport as ID to collect the money once it has arrived. Most banks charge a flat fee for transfers, which makes it more economical to send larger sums. From the UK, expect to pay £15–20, in Australia A$25–40.

More straightforward, but more expensive, are Moneygram Ⓦ *www.moneygram.com* and Western Union Ⓦ *www.westernunion.com*, which transfer money to their overseas offices in a matter of minutes. This needs to be initiated by someone at home. Currently Western Union has agents in all the countries covered in this book, except Bhutan, Japan, Laos, Malaysia and South Korea, but it is extending its network all the time. Charges (around 10–30 percent) depend on the amount sent, with small amounts attracting a larger percentage charge.

Earning money while you're away

There are ways of profiting from your trip. No, we're not talking drug-running or importing gems from Thailand; however, it may be possible to supplement your money supply with a temporary job of some sort while you're away, or to sell the story of your journey and/or photos of your trip when you get back. It's worth looking into these before you leave home because a bit of planning is required.

Getting a job on the road

Discretion is the order of the day here, as many tourist visas expressly prohibit employment. Depending on the job, and the employer, you might get away with working on your tourist visa for a month or two; to work any longer entails regular "visa runs" across the nearest border. For official employment you'll need a working visa; contact the relevant embassy about this (see p.350 for addresses). Information on doing unpaid, short-term voluntary work in Asia is given on p.134.

Before you travel, have a look at *Working in Asia* by Nicki Grihault (In Print), a hugely detailed handbook with contacts and advice on job possibilities ranging from volunteer work, through bar and restaurant work and working as a film extra or model, to English teaching. It also includes tips on getting accustomed to working life in individual countries. You could also check out the Asian sections in *Work Your Way Around the World* (Vacation Work/Petersons Guides) by Susan Griffith or *The Directory of Jobs and Careers Abroad* (Vacation Work/Petersons Guides) by Jonathan Packer. Once you start travelling, look for adverts in English-language newspapers and on noticeboards in travellers' areas; also talk to other travellers or approach potential employers directly.

In Japan, many young Western women get work as hostesses in bars

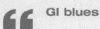

GI blues

The plan was to travel from London to Perth – I had $400. I sold my camera in Delhi, but by the time I got to Bangkok I was broke. Somehow I had to get to Bali. I wasn't particularly worried about it; something would turn up. And it did – I landed a role in a movie called *Saigon*. The screen test required a crew cut as I was to be a GI, and I got one by marching around and saluting a bemused Thai hairdresser and saying loudly in English, "Shorter, shorter."

Heading to Lop Buri, however, where some evacuation scenes were to be filmed, I was singled out. I'd been surviving on $5 a day in India and it showed. The hard-as-nails American drill sergeant took one look at me and said, "Get him out of uniform." As I sloped off in scrawny shame, he called out, "You can play a civilian, son." Still, I was officially a GI (I had the haircut to prove it), and when the GIs went on strike for higher wages I got a rise too.

Chris Taylor

where they entertain male customers. Whilst there is nothing inherently seedy about most of these places ("hostess" is not a euphemism for "prostitute"), drunken fumblings are not unknown, and the same risks apply as in any situation where you might find yourself alone with a relative stranger. If you're considering this sort of work, be sure to sound out other Western women already employed in this way before you sign on.

Teaching English

One of the more common jobs is teaching English; Asia is swarming with people learning the language who yearn for a native speaker with whom to hone their skills. Most employment for foreigners is in private language schools, found in every city and catering for the full range of pupils, from beginners to pre-university students; the best pay for this is to be found in Japan and Taiwan. Classrooms are often small and the hours antisocial, as many students want classes in the evening or at weekends, but students are invariably eager, especially when they have a native speaker as a teacher, and the work is a good stepping stone to employment as a private tutor or better-paid jobs in the more established schools or universities.

Everywhere you will find a TEFL (Teaching English as a Foreign Language) qualification very useful and it will give you access to better rates of pay. The most basic qualification is the RSA/Cambridge Certificate in English Language Teaching to Adults (CELTA), which takes four weeks' full-time study (it is also available part-time) and is recognized throughout the English-teaching world. Courses are widely available in the UK and cost around £950, but are well worth it if you are seriously contemplating teaching while you're away. In the US, Cambridge EFL **W** *www.cambridge-efl.org.uk* offers CELTA courses, which last four weeks and cost around $2300. The Australian TESOL Training Centre, P.O. Box 82 Bondi Junction, NSW, 2022, **T** 02/9389 0249, offers a similar accredited course for about A$2100.

For details of where to study and how to find work abroad, consult the *ELT Guide* (EFL Ltd). *Teaching English in Southeast Asia* (In Print) by Nuala O'Sullivan is also worth a look, and includes language school addresses in every country in Southeast Asia. Web sites such as **W** *www.jobs.edunet.com* and **W** *www.englishexpert.com*

advertise jobs at language schools all over the world, including a good selection in Thailand, South Korea and Japan. When you travel, don't forget to take photocopies of your qualifications with you and references from previous employers.

Working as a diving instructor

There is a good living to be made in Asia as a diving instructor especially as – rightly or wrongly – many novice divers prefer to be taught by a Westerner than a local person. Diving is especially popular in Indonesia, Malaysia, the Philippines and Thailand, and this is where most opportunities are.

To become an instructor, you need relevant experience and certificates from one of the internationally accredited dive organizations. Alternatively, many travellers get the diving bug while they are overseas and quite a few end up taking all the necessary courses while they are on the road. For information about the training necessary for PADI qualifications, which are accepted throughout Asia, take a look at Ⓦ *www.padi.com*, which also gives the locations of diving centres and resorts.

5

Guidebooks and other resources

Once you've planned a skeleton route, you can enjoy filling in some of the detail by scouring guidebooks and tourist brochures, reading travelogues and talking to old Asia hands. Check out the various travel-related sites on the Internet (see the online sections on pp.3–102, and Basics, p.367) and contact relevant tourist offices (pp.347–349). And try asking your travel agent for first-hand recommendations – the bigger student-oriented travel agents advertise the fact that their consultants have been all over the world, and advising prospective travellers is part of their job.

Guidebooks

In an alien culture where you can neither speak the language nor read the signposts, a guidebook will be a real comfort to you in the first few days. You don't have to use it slavishly, but a good guidebook can make all the difference to your trip by showing you what to leave out of your itinerary and what to include. Don't buy your guidebook at the last minute, however, as it will also contain crucial advice on all sorts of travel preparations, including what visas you'll need, which inoculations to organize, and what gear to take along. See Basics, p.366, for a list of recommended travel bookstores.

On the other hand, you could waste a lot of money if you splash out on a set of guidebooks before you've settled on a definite route. It's probably best to start off by borrowing a few guides from a library (even out-of-date editions are usually perfectly adequate for planning purposes), and then invest in a couple of new editions when your itinerary becomes more certain. If you're planning a long trip, there's no need to buy a guidebook for every country you're going to visit: you'll save money and luggage space by buying secondhand guides on the road, or swapping a guide you've finished with for a book on your next destination.

Choosing a guidebook

Personal recommendation is unbeatable, but you can also make your own judgement in bookshops by comparing the way Guidebook Series A describes a certain town and the way Series B does it. Look up a few things you're particularly interested in – wildlife, for example, or budget accommodation – and see how different books approach the topics. Do not be swayed by sumptuous photographs, and remember that you'll be lugging your chosen book around with you for quite a few weeks, so it shouldn't weigh too much. (Whatever the size of the book, you can save weight by ripping out and discarding the sections you know you'll definitely not need.)

Never expect your guidebook to be infallible: new editions are generally only published every two or three years, and in between things *do* change – prices rise; hotels shut down. Guidebook authors also have their own preferences (some series emphasize this, others play it down), so you may not always agree with their choices. And it can be worth getting a second opinion on certain things – for example, the specific direction of a moun-

Good guides
and bad guides

"We're going to die."

"I know," I replied. We sat on the mountain ridge in silence. There was nothing more to say.

Dawn was approaching. The sun was rising leisurely over Lake Batur, northern Bali. I remember thinking it was the most beautiful sunrise I had ever seen. Oranges and purples filled the sky. Down below, specks of brown dotted the white sandy beach: men had risen early to prepare for the day's fishing. Life was going on as usual, unaware of our predicament. I laid back in the sun and closed my eyes.

We had begun to climb Mount Batur in the early hours of the morning, misled by a guidebook which had stated that the route was easy and a local guide unnecessary.

Two hours later, with a bruised back and a twisted ankle, we found ourselves stranded on a rock ledge. A sheer rock face loomed above us, and a steep drop onto boulders lay below. No one knew where we were. I really believed this could be the end.

Some time later, our knight in shining armour arrived in the form of an 8-year-old boy, wearing flip-flops and balancing a bucket of iced drinks on his head. We would have paid anything to have been led off the mountain but, crazily, in true Indonesian style, the bargaining began. We settled on 5000 rupiah, approximately $3; a bargain.

For the next nerve-racking three and a half hours, we scaled precipitous rock faces with no ropes or safety equipment. A couple of times we slipped, but somehow managed to hold on. To this day I cannot believe we made it.

At the summit we learnt that we'd taken the wrong path up the mountain. It was sheer luck that a local villager had spotted us and summoned our guide. I felt someone was watching out for us that day. Guidebooks contain lots of useful information, but local knowledge should always be consulted too.

Sasha Busbridge

tain trail – either from other travellers, or from local people.

Bear in mind, too, that there are many types of guidebook. Books that cover several countries in one volume are easier to carry than a set of individual books and include specific information on travelling between the countries contained in the book; on the down side, you may find that the smaller and less mainstream islands, towns, hotels and restaurants have been edited out because of space considerations. If, on the other hand, you know that you'll be sticking to just one city, region or route, comb the shelves carefully to see if there's a detailed guide on that area. The *Rough Guide to Goa*, for example, contains a lot more local information than the general *India* guide, and also includes access and accommodation details for Mumbai (Bombay), the gateway city to the region. There are also a useful number of activity guides, some of which, like *Trekking in Ladakh* (Trailblazer), are self-contained and include enough details on gateway cities and accommodation options for you to do without any other guidebooks; others, such as *The Dive Sites of Indonesia* (New Holland), are best used in conjunction with general guides.

Lonely Planet

Ⓦwww.lonelyplanet.com
Lonely Planet is the best known guidebook series for independent travellers in Asia. *South-East Asia on a*

Shoestring (first published in 1975) is their longest-running title and regarded by many as the backpackers' bible for the region. They also publish a huge number of single-country guides to Asia, as well as trekking and city guides, plus a few Asian food titles. Lonely Planet's strengths lie in their attention to practical detail, and they're good on how to make your money stretch as far as possible. You will find Lonely Planet readers dominate the Asian travellers' scene, and that's beginning to have its own drawbacks, with certain listed guesthouses monopolizing all the local business, so that staying in these places can feel like being at a Lonely Planet readers' convention.

Rough Guides

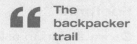**www.roughguides.com**
Rough Guide authors pride themselves on giving detailed practical information for independent travellers across all budgets, and include good write-ups on culture, history and contemporary life as well. Many travellers prefer Rough Guides because they're not Lonely Planets, appreciating a fresh perspective on well-trodden routes as well as distinct alternatives. Rough Guides to look out for include guides to Bali and Lombok, China, India, Indonesia, Japan, Laos, Malaysia, Nepal, Thailand and Vietnam, plus several city guides, and a new guide to the whole of Southeast Asia.

> ## " The backpacker trail
>
> Guidebooks can have a huge influence on a town's tourist trade. If a hotel, restaurant or tour agent in a popular travellers' centre is given a favourable review in a Lonely Planet guide, for example, that business is almost guaranteed to receive a steady flow of backpackers. In a North Indian town, a tout runs through the normal routine: "Where you from? How long you been in India? Where you stay? I know cheap hotel." When we say that we've already decided to go to *Dreamland Hotel*, he smiles. "Ah, you must have the *Rough Guide*. All *Rough Guide* readers go to *Dreamland*; *Lonely Planet* readers go to *Uphar Hotel*, next door."
>
> If an establishment does not appear in the guide, it will have to try harder to attract customers, possibly by resorting to touts or by making itself more competitive. On the door of a small restaurant in a tiny, but touristed, Indian village is pinned a sign that reads, "We're not mentioned in the *Lonely Planet*, but please give us a try anyway." "
>
> **Lucy Ridout**

Footprint

W www.footprintbooks.com

These budget-traveller guides have a good emphasis on contemporary issues such as politics, economics and ecological concerns, and the practical information is well laid out and easy to digest. The series covers most of Asia, including Cambodia, Indonesia, Laos, Pakistan, Sri Lanka, Tibet and Vietnam.

Moon

W www.moon.com

Moon's *Indonesia Handbook* is regarded as a classic because of its phenomenal attention to cultural detail, but it's not updated very regularly, so you probably wouldn't want to use it as your only source. Their *Tibet Handbook* is also as comprehensive as you could want, and is essential reading for anyone intending to trek in Tibet. Other Moon guides to Asia include books on Thailand, Japan, South Korea and the Philippines, as well as the whole of Southeast Asia, all of which feature practical information geared mainly towards low-budget independent travellers.

Let's Go

W www.letsgo.com

Written, researched and edited by students, these American guides are aimed specifically at budget-conscious travellers. Although they carry extensive practical information, updated every year, they can be short on details about the sights and cultural background, and some readers find the studenty tone a bit wearing. Areas covered by Let's Go guides include Southeast Asia, India and Nepal.

Trailblazer

W www.trailblazer-guides.com

This small but respected publishing house produces specialist guidebooks for independent travellers and is especially good on Himalayan trekking guides, with individual titles on the Everest Region, the Annapurna Region, the Langtang Region and Ladakh. Also worth looking out for are their *China by Rail* and *Vietnam by Rail*, plus the exhaustive 34-country guide, *Asia Overland*.

Insight

Ⓦ**www.insightguides.com**

Insight guides are thick glossy handbooks with lovely pictures and text written by cultural experts. They have little practical information and nothing for low-budget travellers, but they do make inspirational pre-departure background reading. The Insight Pocket Guides are much handier, and livelier, than the parent series, but are only good for short-stay visits and have no practical information on hotels and transport.

Periplus

Ⓦ**www.tuttle-periplus.com**

Periplus only publishes guides to the various islands of Indonesia and to Malaysia, Brunei and Singapore. If you want a specialist guide to a specific part of Indonesia (eg Sulawesi or Maluku), this is the series to go for. Their activity guides on surfing and diving in Indonesia are also worth checking out. Like Insight, Periplus specializes in combining stunning photographs with thoughtfully written descriptions of sights and local issues, but the books are not that strong on practical detail.

Maps

Most guidebooks include useful enough maps of major towns and resorts, but you might want to invest in a larger, more detailed map of the whole region or country you're planning to visit as well, particularly if you're going to be renting a car or a motorbike, or if you're planning to do some long-distance cycling. If possible, buy this before you leave home, as you can't rely on being able to find good maps when you're in Asia – check your guidebooks for specific advice on this.

Very large-scale maps for independent trekking should also be bought before you leave home (the best selection of trekking maps for Nepal and Tibet, however, are available in Kathmandu). Detailed town and city street maps, on the other hand, are often best bought on arrival, particularly big city maps that include bus routes.

Only a few maps cover the whole of Asia and the scale is so small on these (1:12,000,000) that they're only useful for a general overview. Better to invest in one or more of the major regional maps – Southeast Asia, China, the Indian subcontinent – published by Bartholomew, Nelles or Geocenter. The same publishers do maps to a comprehensive range of individual Asian countries as well. See Basics, p.366, for a list of recommended travel-book and map stores.

Background reading

Other people's travel stories are full of good ideas on where to go and what to do – and will help prepare you for what lies in store, too. National newspapers and specialist travel magazines are fruitful places to look for first-hand, up-to-date travel narratives, often accompanied by inspiring photos, and below you'll find a roundup of recommended publications that are well worth a browse. We've also included a highly selective list of some of our favourite books about Asia, both nonfiction and fiction.

If you've got plenty of time, consider reading up on Asian religions before you go – in Asia, most people's lives revolve around their faith, and many of the sights and festivals that you'll be visiting will be religious ones. Icon Books publishes two enjoyable cartoon-and-caption introductions to Asian religions: *Ancient Eastern Philosophy for Beginners* and *Buddha for Beginners*. Hodder and Stoughton's *Teach Yourself World Faiths* series takes a more serious approach, but its paperback books on Hinduism, Sikhism, Buddhism and Islam are all clearly written and easy to understand.

Magazines

All the following magazines are aimed at independent travellers and, while none of them deals exclusively with Asia, you're guaranteed to find some sort of feature on Asia in every issue. Unless otherwise stated, they're all monthly publications, and all of them accept overseas subscriptions. Most have fairly interesting Web sites, with a selection of news items and main features from current and back issues. Specialist diving magazines and Web sites are covered on p.129, and surfing resources on p.131.

In the UK, *Wanderlust* ⓦ*www.wanderlust.co.uk* focuses on fairly mainstream destinations for the independent traveller, with well-written travel stories plus lots of useful items on equipment, visas, tour operators and related TV and radio programmes; it also carries classified ads for people who are searching for travelling companions. As you'd expect, *Adventure Travel* is aimed at the more active and intrepid traveller, so the emphasis here is on hiking, biking, kayaking and the like, though the featured activities are by no means too extreme for the average independent traveller.

In North America, the long-running *Outside* ⓦ*www.outsidemag.com* is a huge glossy tome, with heaps of readable articles on worldwide destinations for backpackers and independent travellers, plus plenty of ads for gear specialists and tour operators. *Escape* ⓦ*www.escapemag.com* centres on more adventurous trips and activities and is a similarly good read. Other mags worth dipping into include the consciously unglossy and low-key bi-monthly *Big World* ⓦ*www.bigworld.com* and the quarterly magazines *Outpost* ⓦ*www.outpostmagazine.com* and *Trips* ⓦ*www.tripsmag.com*, all of which run articles on fairly unusual and adventurous destinations.

In Australia, the wilderness adventure magazine *Wild* ⓦ*www.wild.com.au* covers activities such as climbing, trekking and rafting, and has information on training courses and on buying specialist gear. The adventure travel magazine *Action Asia* ⓦ*www.actionasia.com* published in Hong Kong, is also widely available in Australia.

For a more detailed take on the realities of daily life in the countries you're planning to visit, you could browse through some of the special-interest magazines that carry a more in-depth coverage of Asia than national newspapers at home. The *New Internationalist* ⓦ*www.oneworld.org/ni* focuses on areas such as environmental concerns, women's issues, education and poverty action; *Far Eastern Economic Review* ⓦ*www.feer.com* does hard-hitting, readable reports on the political and economic stories in the region, and its Web site gives access to a mine of interesting background information; and *Asiaweek* ⓦ*www.asiaweek.com* is a lighter-weight version of the *Far Eastern Economic Review*. Many of Asia's main national newspapers, such as the *Times of India* and the *Bangkok Post*, also have online versions; see the online sections of pp.3–102 for their Web addresses.

Travellers' tales

- *Women Travel* (Rough Guides). If you're feeling a bit nervous about setting off on your own, or just setting off full stop, this edition of real-life travellers' experiences will cheer you up and give you heart. It's an inspirational collection of travel stories and anecdotes from about eighty different women – tourists, long-term travellers, expats and volunteers – but is as relevant to male readers as to female ones. Though the book covers the whole world, there are plenty of tales about Asia.

- *Travelers' Tales* (Travelers' Tales Inc) are also highly enjoyable anthologies, full of lively extracts from contemporary travelogues, magazines and guidebooks. They make perfect pre-trip reading matter. Asian titles include separate volumes on Thailand, India and Hong Kong.

- Alexander Frater's account of *Chasing the Monsoon* (Penguin) will revolutionize your attitude to rain and make you long to be in Asia during the monsoon. As the author – a self-confessed weather nut – follows the annual rains north through India, he goes to monsoon parties, interviews harassed meteorologists and listens to rainy-season tales.

- If you want to know what it's like in the jungles of Southeast Asia, look no further than Redmond O'Hanlon's *Into the Heart of Borneo* (Penguin/Vintage), the hilarious true story of two erudite, but not terribly fit, Englishmen as they search the impenetrable Borneo jungle for the elusive two-horned rhinoceros. There's a memorable passage on an encounter with the local tribespeople at a typical Dyak party (involving much drunkenness and buffoonery) and offputtingly graphic descriptions of leeches, Dyak cuisine and jungle trekking.

- And for a fine account of trekking in the Himalayas, read Peter Matthiessen's *The Snow Leopard* (Vintage), which describes the author's two-month hike into the remote Inner Dolpo region of northwest Nepal. Alongside beautifully written passages on the changing scenery, the tracks, rivers, peaks, and bird, animal and plant life, Matthiessen also talks about his own emotional ups and downs, as he oscillates between exhaustion and exhilaration and tries hard to make sense of his Zen Buddhist training.

- Peter Hopkirk's *Trespassers on the Roof of the World: The Race for Lhasa* (Oxford/Kodansha) tells the amazing story of how, at the start of the twentieth century, a group of Brits and Indians charted every nook of the vast High Tibetan Plateau, the most inaccessible – and hostile – place on earth.

Under the skin

- Even if you've no intention of visiting Bhutan, Jamie Zeppa's *Beyond the Sky and the Earth: a Journey into Bhutan* (Pan) makes an enthralling and moving read. It tells of her years as a teacher in the remote Himalayan kingdom, and is both an intriguing introduction to this secretive country as well as a very open account of the highs and lows of life in an unfamiliar culture.
- *Touch the Dragon* by Karen Connelly (Black Swan) is another exceptionally warm and observant tale of life in another country. In 1986, as a seventeen-year-old Canadian schoolgirl, she joined a Rotary Club programme which sent her to a small town in northern Thailand for a year. She spoke no Thai and was the only foreigner in town, and this is the enjoyable story of how things turned out.
- For some idea of what it's like to be a woman in India, dip into Elizabeth Bumiller's *May You be the Mother of a Hundred Sons* (Fawcett). This American journalist spent several years listening to the life stories of all sorts of different Indian women – young brides, housewives, widows, film stars, even a traffic cop – and in this collection she draws together their experiences, putting some into context, expressing her own horror or amazement at others. Well worth reading, even if you're not going to India, as many of the stories have relevance to other parts of Asia too.
- You'll get another, more controversial, peek behind the scenes of Asian women's lives in *Patpong Sisters* by Cleo Odzer (Arcade Publishing), an American anthropologist's funny and touching account of her life with the prostitutes and bar girls of Bangkok's notorious red-light district. It's an enlightening and thought-provoking read, and a surprisingly enjoyable page-turner.

Real lives

- Forget the dry analytical history books and turn instead to Jung Chang's emotionally charged story of her family's experiences in twentieth-century China *Wild Swans* (Flamingo/Doubleday) paints a harrowing picture, with vivid accounts of her grandmother's days as a concubine, of her mother's struggle to fulfil her obligations to the leaders of the Cultural Revolution, and of her father's victimization under a new regime. It's even more sobering when you realize that this is probably not an unusual story, and that the people you meet in China may well have similar histories. Don't take the book with you, however, as it's banned in the People's Republic.

- A stark reminder of Burma's parlous human rights situation, Rory Maclean's *Under the Dragon: Travels in a Betrayed Land* (Flamingo) tells the story of the author's trip through Burma in the late 1990s, a decade after the killing of over 5000 peaceful demonstrators by the ruling junta who are still in power today. The bulk of the book is about four very different women he meets, all of whom have had their lives decimated by recent events in their country.
- The trilogy of depressing real-life atrocities in Asia is completed by Pin Yathay's *Stay Alive, My Son* (Bloomsbury), the grim and graphically described autobiography of a highly educated Cambodian civil engineer. His story is a horrifyingly typical one, chronicling the terrorization of him and his family by the Khmer Rouge from 1975 to 1979. Essential pre-trip reading.

Fiction

- Now a Hollywood blockbuster, Alex Garland's immensely popular novel *The Beach* (Penguin) is a very entertaining piece of fiction inspired by the Southeast Asian travellers' scene. It tells the story of a group of travellers living a utopian existence on an uninhabited Thai island. Tensions rise as people start to reveal their true personalities and, when the idyll begins to sour, the book turns into a mesmerizing thriller.
- Vikram Seth's addictive mega-tome *A Suitable Boy* (Phoenix/Orion) will have you travelling long distances without so much as a yawn. This is the rollicking saga of a young Indian woman, her extended family and all their acquaintances, set just after Partition in 1947, when the subcontinent was divided and, amid great sectarian violence, the separate Muslim country of Pakistan was created. Hilarious and engaging, it's full of characters that you'll bump into all over India.
- Vikram Chandra's slim volume of short stories, *Love and Longing in Bombay* (Faber & Faber), is similarly engaging and makes a perfect introduction to the complexities of 21st-century India. His evocative tales of modern life look at how contemporary concerns with sex, art, gangsters, computers and movies are underwritten by ancient traditions and entrenched religious and ethnic divisions.
- What does war do to people? Novelist Tim O'Brien has made his name as an eloquent, thoughtful chronicler of the emotional, physical and moral effects of the Vietnam War on the people involved on both sides and the land it destroyed. All his books are moving and thought-provoking, his gaze is unflinching. *Going After Cacciato* (Flamingo) starts with the notion that one American soldier in Vietnam, Cacciato, would, all things considered, prefer to be in

Paris than fighting in Vietnam; he sets out to walk the 8600 miles necessary to get there, pursued by the men in his squad.

Learning the lingo

Wherever you go, people will appreciate your efforts to speak their language. You'll probably be giggled at, but that's as good an ice-breaker as any and, in the more remote spots, knowing a few local phrases can make the difference between having to cope with a plate of beef brains and enjoying a tasty bowl of noodles.

Luckily, English is the language of tourism throughout Asia, so it's quite possible to do a six-month trip without ever consulting a phrase-book. And, in India, one of the greatest delights is the sheer number of Indian English speakers who take great pleasure in debating local and international issues with English-speaking travellers. French is also understood in parts of Indochina by the older generation who lived under French rule, and some elderly Indonesians can speak Dutch.

However, as only a tiny percentage of Asians can speak or understand any Western languages, it is well worth learning at least a few phrases. For travel off the beaten track, a basic vocabulary is essential, and will also give you access to people who are not involved in the tourist industry – a reason in itself for struggling through a few unfamiliar verbs.

Though some languages are guaranteed to turn you into a tongue-tied fool (Mandarin Chinese with its four tones and everyday alphabet of 10,000 pictograms springs to mind), others are relatively simple to master. Bahasa Indonesia, for example, is generally considered to be the easiest language in the world. It's written in roman script, has a straightforward grammar, and is very similar to the Malay language that's understood throughout Malaysia and Singapore.

If you have the time, it's very satisfying to give yourself a proper grounding before you go. There's a huge range of teach-yourself language tapes available for most Asian languages now, including Hodder and Stoughton's *Teach Yourself* series, and other options from Routledge, Berlitz, Hugo and Lonely Planet. The Linguaphone tape courses are the most comprehensive, but are also expensive.

Alternatively, fix yourself up with some face-to-face language classes. Expatriate Asians quite often advertise lessons in local papers, or you might try setting up an informal language exchange via a community centre or even a neighbourhood Asian restaurant. Should you be planning a lengthy stay in Asia, the very best way to learn the lingo is to attend a course once you're there – check the local English-language press for details or ask at tourist offices, embassies or universities.

Choosing a phrasebook

The easiest way to make yourself literate in an Asian tongue is to travel with a good phrasebook. Rough Guides, Lonely Planet, Berlitz and Hugo all publish a good range of handy pocket-sized phrasebooks and, as with guidebooks, you should compare several different ones before you buy. Think of a few situations – asking the price of a double room, for example, or saying that you're vegetarian – and look for them in the three or four rival phrasebooks. A user-friendly layout is also important and, where relevant, you'll probably want words and phrases to be written in local script – especially important for China, Japan, South Korea, Laos and Thailand.

Background viewing: Asia on film

Why not round off your Asia education the easy way – by watching a few videos? The films we've recommended have been chosen not necessarily because they're great works of art, but because they evoke the feel or character of a place, or provide an easy or unusual history lesson.

In addition, you might want to check out some of the numerous natural history documentaries and travel programmes now available on video. Videos produced by National Geographic and by Lonely Planet are recommended.

China

- For sheer aesthetic pleasure you can't beat the films of Chinese director Zhang Yimou, with his stunning attention to visual drama, his glorious use of colour and his alluring portrait of traditional rural China. *Red Sorghum* (1987), *Ju Dou* (1989) and *Raise the Red Lantern* (1991) are all set in the 1920s and all variations on a similar theme, each concerning a young woman who is sent against her will to marry an elderly and intransigent man, the elderly husbands symbolizing the inflexible Chinese state. Yimou's more overtly political *To Live* (1994) follows a single family from the end of the old, aristocratic regime, through the crazy, dehumanizing twists of Communist rule, to the present day. His more recent work, *Not One Less* (1999), highlights the terrible failures of the education system in modern China by describing the lives of one young teacher and her pupil.

- *Farewell My Concubine* (Chen Kaige, 1993) takes a more unusual approach to modern Chinese history, filtering it through the melodramatic and often heart-rending experiences of two (male) stars of the Peking Opera; one a sensitive, gay, interpreter of female characters, the other his macho leading man.

Vietnam

- Vietnam figures in dozens of movies – from *Rambo: First Blood* (Ted Kotcheff, 1982) to *Born on the Fourth of July* (Oliver Stone, 1989) and *Apocalypse Now* (Francis Ford Coppola, 1979) – but few of these films have anything very interesting to say about Vietnam itself, or about the effect the Vietnam War had on the Vietnamese people. Most focus instead on the American experience in and after 'Nam, and Vietnam is generally depicted as a land of hellish bug- and mine-ridden jungles inhabited by a bunch of crazy savages.

- Balance out the American view of the Vietnam War with an attempt to see the conflict from a Vietnamese point of view. Though *Heaven and Earth* (1993) was made by US director Oliver Stone, the film is based on the autobiography of Le Ly Hayslip, who grew up with the war, was tortured by the Viet Cong and forced to flee, eventually ending up in Saigon. The film ends with Le Ly in rural USA, struggling to cope with life as the wife of a damaged and violent former GI.

- And to complete the picture, you should definitely rent a copy of *Cyclo* (Tran Anh Hung, 1995), a shockingly graphic thriller set in 1990s Ho Chi Minh City. Uniquely among all the films about Vietnam, this paints a recognizable portrait of modern-day city life – though you're unlikely to encounter the underworld inhabited by its hero, a desperately poor young cycle-rickshaw driver who gets drawn ever deeper into S&M prostitution, drug smuggling and gang warfare. Dubbed by some critics the Vietnamese *Pulp Fiction*.

Cambodia and Thailand

- When the Vietnam War spilled over the borders into Cambodia, and the Khmer Rouge began their terrifying campaign of re-educating the Cambodian people, journalist Dith Pran was forced, along with millions of others, to deny his past and work for the Khmer Rouge in labour camps. His story is told in *The Killing Fields* (Roland Joffe, 1984), a harrowing, if Hollywoodized, portrait of life under Pol Pot's tyrannical regime.

- *Swimming to Cambodia* (Jonathan Demme, 1987) makes a good companion piece to *The Killing Fields,* as it's about – at least in part – the making of *The Killing Fields*, which was filmed on location in Thailand. In fact, it's a monologue, a hugely entertaining *tour de force* by actor and raconteur Spalding Gray, who had a minor role in Joffe's film. He tells some funny stories – about his first encounter with a hallucinogenic Thai stick, about the bar girls of Bangkok, and about his perfect moments on the beaches of Thailand – and in between these anecdotes he tells us what he learnt about the Cambodian War.

- As with the novel that inspired it, the travellers' thriller *The Beach* (Danny Boyle, 2000) is a gripping, hi-energy story with plenty of recognizable characters and scenes from the Southeast Asian backpackers' scene. Most of it was filmed on location in Thailand, so it's hardly surprising that tourist numbers have soared since the film was released.

India and Tibet

- Richard Attenborough's *Gandhi* (1982) is an epic blockbuster, but none the worse for that. His biography of the famous man of non-violence is both an inspirational tribute to the power of civil disobedience and a very watchable lesson in twentieth-century Indian history.

- The Raj era has been romanticized, and criticized, by dozens of film-makers, but *A Passage to India* (1984) is one of the most interesting movies about colonial tensions in early twentieth-century India. Director David Lean evokes a tangible sense of unease as the good-hearted but ignorant and suggestible young English heroine becomes overwhelmed by the sheer strangeness of India. The film is a fine exploration of (extreme) culture shock (and colonialism), still relevant to modern-day travellers.

- *Bandit Queen* (Shekar Kapur, 1994) was so controversial that it was initially banned in India and denounced by the woman whose life story it tells. She is Phoolan Devi, a young woman from a village in northeastern India, who endured a forced marriage, domestic violence and several rapes before fleeing to the hills and becoming a much-feared bandit leader. The film shows how cruel life still is for some women in caste-ridden rural India.

- Based on the experiences of a hot-headed young Western doctor in the slums of Calcutta, *City of Joy* (Roland Joffe, 1992) captures the atmosphere of life on the street better than any other mainstream film about India. The film shows the daily struggles of a rickshaw puller as he races round the city trying to earn enough money for his daughter's dowry, and the frustrations of the Irish nurse as her clinic is repeatedly trashed by the local mafia. And, though the young doctor is a typical Hollywood hero, he is also a typical Westerner in India, angry at his inability to change things for the better and frustrated at the slum dwellers' apparent acceptance of their lot.

- Directed by the Bhutanese Buddhist lama Khyentse Norbu, and the first full-length feature ever made in Tibetan, *The Cup* (aka *Phörpa*; 1999) is one of Asian cinema's most unusual and delightful films. The engaging and witty story, acted entirely by a cast of Buddhist monks, centres on the World Cup mania sweeping a tiny monastery in the hills outside Dharamsala (home of the exiled Tibetan Buddhist community), and is also well worth watching for the depictions of monastery life, the haunting chants, and the religious ceremomies.

6

What to take

You could quite happily set off for Asia with all your belongings stuffed into a plastic bag and stock up on clothes and extra bits as and when you need them. Contrary to popular stereotypes, most of Asia is absolutely brimming over with merchandise, so you don't need to pack a lifetime's supply of T-shirts or shampoo.

Of course a few things are best bought at home, as the quality of Asian goods is variable, and certain items will be difficult to find when you're away. But apart from these essentials, we'd advise you to take the very minimum you can and improvise on the rest. Buying on the road is nearly always cheaper and, more importantly, means that you'll be able to travel light; a heavy load is a real hindrance and can spoil your trip by making you less keen to stop off at places because you just can't face dragging your huge pack along with you. Things really are bad when your pack begins dictating your itinerary, so start how you mean to go on and get your baggage under control right away. A few tips on how to lighten the load:

- Mail stuff to the place where you think you'll need it most. For example, if you're doing a three-month overland from Australia to Europe and you're planning to look for office work when you get to London, send your smart work clothes direct from home to a UK poste restante. Use surface mail, as poste restante/general delivery is usually only held for two months.

- Plan to send excess baggage back after you've finished with it (eg your thermal underwear and wool sweater after you leave Kathmandu) or, better still, buy your woollies when you get there and then sell them, junk them or send them home. Surface mail from Asia generally takes about three months and costs around $35/£20 for 5kg to the UK or the US; a bit less to Australia (see Chapter Twelve).
- Rent or buy any special gear on the ground rather than taking it with you. You can rent diving and surfing gear in Bali and southern Thailand, for example, down jackets and sleeping bags in Kathmandu, sleeping bags (but no down jackets) in Lhasa and Chiang Mai (northern Thailand), and camping equipment in Malaysia's Taman Negara National Park; consult your guidebook for details. You may also be able to buy secondhand equipment from departing travellers – check guesthouse noticeboards.

Rucksacks

If you haven't already got a rucksack, this is the one item that it's worth splashing out on. Choose a recognized-brand-name pack (such as Berghaus, Karrimor or Lowe-Alpine) as they are hard-wearing and ergonomically designed. A rucksack can cost anything from $80/£50 to $250/£150, but think of it as an investment: a good pack could last you for many years and will certainly make your trip a more comfortable one. For details of recommended suppliers of rucksacks and other travel equipment, see Basics, p.369.

Rucksack capacity is measured in litres or cubic inches – not that helpful really as it's hard to visualize your socks and T-shirts in liquid form. Our advice is to buy the smallest one that looks practical for you: a 40- to 55-litre one if possible, but certainly no bigger than 65 litres. Buying a smaller pack forces you to travel light, and there's no question you'll be grateful for that when you're battling with overflowing Bangkok buses or wandering up and down a roasting Columbo street.

Some travellers, on the other hand, claim you should buy as large a pack as you're ever likely to need, presuming that if you don't fill it to the brim on your way out, you'll certainly pick up enough trinkets on the trip to make it worth its massive size. In the end, though, it's not the capacity that matters so much as the weight of stuff that you cram into it. Nearly all airlines specify a 20kg maximum for hold baggage, so that should definitely be your limit; a realistic optimum weight lies somewhere between 10kg and 15kg – it's definitely worth jettisoning stuff once the scales go over the 17kg mark.

Once you've decided on the size, check out the extra bits, particularly the pockets, compartments and additional strap attachments. Packs with more than one compartment are easier to use. And side- and lid-pockets are perfect for stashing bits and pieces you need to get at quickly – soap and a toothbrush for example, so that you don't have to root right through to the bottom of your pack in the sleeping compartment of an overnight train – as well as your map and guidebook, or your rain gear. Some rucksacks have detachable front pockets which are actually daypacks, of which more on p.206. Bear in mind, though, that the more compact your pack, the easier it will be to lug on and off buses and trains, and to squeeze onto luggage racks and into left-luggage lockers. Fully stuffed side-pockets can add a good 30cm to the width of your pack, and attaching boots, sunhat and umbrella to external loops only makes your load more difficult to carry.

Choosing a rucksack

You won't regret the time and care you take in choosing the right rucksack. Always try them on before buying, and think about the following:

- The best packs are made from heavy-duty synthetic fabrics; avoid the ones that feel flimsy and might tear easily. Zips should be sturdy, too.
- Most travellers' rucksacks are constructed round a lightweight internal frame. This gives shape to the pack but, most importantly, it helps spread the load across your back. The smaller packs – under 40 litres – are often considered too small to warrant a frame, but they should come with thickly padded and contoured backs which also help distribute the weight and make the whole thing more comfortable. These days, uncomfortable, external frames are the province of serious, long-distance trekkers and backpacking travellers don't need them.
- A thickly padded hip belt is essential for carrying any load over 10kg. This transfers most of the weight off your shoulders onto

your hips and legs – the strongest and sturdiest part of the human body. By channelling the weight down to your lower body, you're also making yourself more stable: a full load resting solely on your shoulders will quickly tire you out.

- If you're not average size and build, check out the packs with adjustable back systems, where you can change the position of the shoulder straps in relation to the frame.
- Some packs are designed especially for women, with shorter back lengths and a differently contoured back shape and hip belt.

Is it a rucksack? Is it a suitcase? . . .

. . . No, it's a travel sack. Some rucksacks can also be turned into suitcases: a special flap zips over the straps and, with the aid of a handle, you can carry it like a suitcase or a shoulder bag – a useful feature for plane, bus and train journeys where dangling straps can get tangled up or ripped off. This also means that you can walk into a smart hotel without necessarily looking like a scruffy, impecunious backpacker. Most travel sacks can be unzipped all the way round to open like a suitcase, which is much more convenient than a conventional rucksack, especially for overnight stopovers. They are also easier to lock.

Though all these features make travel sacks versatile, they won't provide the long-distance support of a properly contoured rucksack and their traditional-suitcase shape makes them much bulkier to carry on your back. If you choose this option, go for a travel sack with an internal frame, not just padding; external compression straps also help secure the load.

Packing up and locking up

It's worth customizing your pack to make it as user-friendly, resilient and secure as possible. These ideas may be useful:

- Most rucksacks are showerproof, but that doesn't make them monsoon- or tropical-storm-proof. To keep your stuff dry, you can either buy a special rucksack liner, or make do with a large dustbin liner or two; alternatively, just wrap your most precious items in individual plastic bags.
- Pack your rucksack so that you are not being pulled backwards all the time. This means distributing weight as evenly as possible from

top to bottom, and keeping the heavier stuff as close to your body as possible. Be careful where you pack sharp or angular objects as you don't want them jabbing into your back.

● As well as tagging your pack on the outside, stick an address label to the inside of one of the side-pockets, so that there can be no dispute about whose it is. Tie a brightly coloured ribbon to one of the outside straps to make it easily identifiable in airports and bus stations.

● Though most rucksacks are non-lockable as bought, a lot of them come with useful devices like double zips on the side- and lid-pockets so that you can use a small padlock on them. If not, you might think about getting a couple of small holes punched into your rucksack fabric above the zip fasteners, so that you can use a mini-padlock to lock the zip to the hole; shoe-repairers and key-cutters will do this for you, and will reinforce the hole with a metal ring. To lock the straps you can use specially designed little ladder locks or sacklocks (available from camping shops) and attach mini-padlocks to them. None of this prevents someone slashing your pack with a blade of course, but mini-padlocks are certainly a deterrent to opportunist thieves. The bottom line, however, is never to leave your most valuable or important items in an unattended pack – that's what money belts are for (see opposite).

● Some travellers take a small chain and a spare padlock for securing their pack to luggage racks on overnight trains and buses (see pp.262 & 266).

Daypacks and shoulder bags

Unless your planning's gone seriously awry, you won't be carting your rucksack around every day of your trip, so you'll probably need a much smaller bag for daily around-town necessities like your camera, guidebook, map, water bottle and sunblock. Many travellers like to use a daypack for this purpose, but there are advantages to using a shoulder bag instead, not least because shoulder bags are smaller and less unwieldy, and can easily be folded away into your main pack or worn comfortably at the same time as your main pack. They are also easier to access while you're walking along, and do not mark you out so obviously as a tourist, particularly in bars and clubs. Advice on what to carry in your daypack or shoulder bag on long-haul flights is given in Chapter Seven.

Choosing a daypack

You should be just as fussy about choosing a daypack as you are with your main pack. After all, the daypack is what you're going to be carrying around all day every day, so it needs to be comfortable and well designed. For comfort, you'll need padded, adjustable shoulder straps, a padded back and an overall size and shape that's not too cumbersome.

For convenience, you should look at how the pack opens up and the number of pockets. Some daypacks zip open all the way round; although this is handy for digging out a wayward pencil or whatever, it also makes the daypack easier to drop things out of when you're opening it up, and the pack can come unzipped if you don't keep it locked. The top-opening drawstring system is a more user-friendly alternative. External pockets can be useful – some are large enough to accommodate a one-litre water bottle on each side – but an internal pocket is more useful, ideal for documents, a wallet, a map or a bus ticket.

Remember, too, that you will sometimes have to wear both your rucksack and your daypack at the same time. This can be awkward, and a security hazard, so the best solution is to empty your daypack and stuff it inside your main pack. If that's not possible, you're probably best off wearing your daypack across your front; this helps your balance a bit, and discourages pickpockets.

Some main packs are designed with built-in, detachable daypacks, which zip onto the outside of your main pack. If you go for this option, be sure not to carry valuables in the zipped-on mini-pack as you probably won't be able to tell if a pickpocket slashes it when you're on the move.

Money belts

Most travellers like to keep their valuables on their person at all times, and the safest and most convenient way of doing this is to wear a money belt. This is essentially a long flat pouch, made of fabric, plastic or leather, attached to a belt and designed to be worn around the waist. It should be worn *under* your clothes, and should be as discreet as possible – preferably invisible – so that it does not attract the attention of muggers and pickpockets. To keep it slim-line, it should be used only to carry stuff that you don't need to access every twenty minutes. Keep your passport, your airline ticket, your credit card, travel insurance policy and the bulk of your cash in the money belt, but leave your petty cash, notebook, lip balm and pocket torch for your daypack.

Be sure not to confuse money belts with bum bags. A bum bag is a larger and an altogether more ostentatious item; it's worn over your clothes and can usually hold a small camera as well as sunscreen and dark glasses. As a security item the bum bag is useless and may as well be inscribed with flashing lights announcing "Valuable items inside, help yourself". It just takes one deft swipe of a knife for your bum bag to drop to the ground and into the hands of an opportunist thief.

Some people prefer neck wallets to money belts. These are similar pouches, designed to be worn either round the neck or over the shoulder. As with money belts, they should be kept under your clothes and out of sight. The main drawback with neck wallets is that they swing around more than money belts and therefore feel less safe and possibly more uncomfortable.

Choosing a money belt (or neck wallet)

A few points to bear in mind:

- It should be wide enough to accommodate your passport and long enough for your travellers' cheques. Take these along with you when making your purchase.
- Cotton is the most comfortable fabric: it absorbs the sweat and does not irritate the skin – and you can wash it when it gets dirty or smelly. Nylon and plastic are not recommended. When wearing a cotton money belt, it's a good idea to keep something waterproof – eg your free plastic-coated traveller's-cheque wallet – at the back of the money belt nearest your skin, so that any excess sweat will not obliterate vital documents such as airline tickets.
- If you're planning to spend a fair amount of time on the beach, consider buying – as a supplement to your money belt – a little waterproof canister that you can wear when swimming. These come in varying sizes (with names like "Surfsafe") and should be able to hold your room keys and/or security box key so that you don't have to worry about leaving your money belt with all its valuables unattended on the beach.

Clothes

Once you're on the road you'll almost certainly end up wearing the same two or three outfits week-in, week-out. Ideally you'll want to work that out before you leave home, but there's always parcel post to send back any excess. Nonetheless, it's well worth being brutal with yourself at the packing stage. Ask yourself: do I *really* need five T-shirts and three pairs of jeans?

Your clothes will deteriorate faster than they do at home because of the heat, the extra sweat, and the pounding and mangling they'll go through at local laundries. To some this is a reason for taking new clothes: the newer the item, the better its chance of survival.

THE MODESTY FACTOR

Most Asians do not enjoy seeing acres of exposed Western flesh displayed in public. They find revealing dress offensive and cheap, so you'll get a much better response from local people if you respect their views and adapt your attire accordingly. This is particularly important when visiting temples, mosques and shrines – if you're unsuitably dressed in these places you'll probably be refused entry.

Prudish (and sweaty) though it sounds, this means wearing long trousers or skirts for most day-to-day activities and keeping shorts for beach resorts. Singlets are also considered low-class, especially for women, who will get a lot of unwanted attention if they reveal their cleavages or are obviously not wearing a bra. The notice above the entrance gate to Bangkok's Grand Palace sums up the (usually unspoken) rules; it's illustrated with photos of unsuitably dressed men and women, and forbids "leggings, shorts, singlets, fishermen's trousers, torn and dirty clothing and flip-flops".

Lots of travellers ignore local clothing etiquette and may not even notice that it's an issue. This is quite easy to do if you're sticking to heavily touristed ghettos – Bangkok's Khao San Road, for example, or Sudder Street in Calcutta. But as soon as you deviate from the beaten track you'll almost certainly start to feel more self-conscious. One young female traveller got stones thrown at her in Medan (a Muslim town in Sumatra) for walking around in shorts; another adopted local Indian dress (cotton pyjama-style tunic and trousers) for her six-month stay and found that this made villagers much less nervous of her – in fact, they would often start a conversation by complimenting her for wearing a *salwaar kameez*.

For first-hand advice on acceptable clothing for women in about one hundred different countries, check out the "What Should I Wear?" section of the Journeywoman Web site (🅦*www.journeywoman.com*) which has sartorial tips and comments from dozens of women travellers.

On the other hand, why waste your money if things are only going to get ruined anyway? Whatever you decide, don't take your smartest gear, or anything that's of irreplaceable sentimental value.

And remember: Asia is full of clothes shops selling stuff that's ideal for the local climate. Note, however, that Asian sizes rarely go above men's UK/US trouser size 36 and women's UK size 16/US size 14, though you can get Western sizes in touristed towns. Also bear in mind that tailoring in Asia is extremely inexpensive, and Asian fabrics are stunning, so you can always get new clothes made up, particularly in Bangkok, Hong Kong, Singapore and almost any big town in India (a tailored cotton shirt costs about $8/£5 in India). You may end up wanting to replace your entire wardrobe anyway: Asian men and women tend to dress far more colourfully than Westerners so you might feel rather drab in comparison if you wear nothing but sober blues, blacks, greys and browns.

Packing for the heat

For tropical Asia you will need clothes that are long, loose and light:

- Long trousers and long sleeves are good because of the modesty factor (see box, p.209), but also for sun protection and, curiously enough, for coolness as well. The more skin you expose to the sun, the faster your body moisture evaporates and the more dehydrated and, therefore, hotter you become. You only have to picture the flowing robes of an Arab sheikh to be reminded of this.
- Long sleeves and long trousers are also good protection against mosquitoes.
- Loose, baggy clothing improves ventilation and cuts down on sweat.
- Lightweight fabrics are faster to dry and smaller to pack.
- Cotton and linen are the most comfortable, as natural fibres are absorbent and let your skin breathe.
- Artificial fabrics such as nylon and rayon tend to encourage sweat and itchiness, and may even cause heat rash and fungus.
- Lycra is a guaranteed heat trap and crotch-rotter – and it contravenes the modesty code too.
- T-shirts are quite heavy to wear and to carry, and take a long time to dry. Consider taking short-sleeved cotton shirts instead – or buy some on the road.
- Jeans are heavy to carry, hot to wear and take a long time to dry, though some travellers find they make them feel comfortably at home.

- Light-coloured clothing will help to keep you cooler (it reflects rather than absorbs the sunlight), but will also get dirtier faster.

Packing for a cold climate

The best way to pack for a trip that is to include a few weeks in a cooler climate is to go for the layers technique. This means you can make the most of your tropical clothing by wearing several items at the same time (two short-sleeved T-shirts under a long-sleeved shirt for example), though you should also think about topping up with some of the following:

- Consider taking a fleece jacket; these are warm and weigh surprisingly little.
- Thermal underwear is a good idea: ideally long johns and a long-sleeved undershirt, but woollen tights or thick leggings and a long-sleeved brushed cotton top will do instead. If you have money to spare, buy some silks (100 percent silk thermals), which feel incredibly light (and slinky) but are extremely warm.
- Warm socks are a must: go for the hard-wearing, double-thickness ones sold in camping shops. They're good for wearing with hiking boots in hot places as well.
- Woolly hat and scarf, or Balaclava, plus gloves are easily bought when you arrive; the yak-wool ones sold in Nepal are especially popular.

A clothing checklist

- Two pairs long trousers/skirts/dresses.
- Two T-shirts/short-sleeved shirts.
- One long-sleeved shirt.
- One lightweight fleece jacket, sweatshirt or similar item for moderate warmth.
- One pair shorts.
- A sarong.
- Swimwear. Stripping down for swimming and sunbathing is a Western practice that bemuses most Asians. When the Thais go swimming they walk straight into the water in their jeans and T-shirts; Indian women do the same in their saris or *salwaar kameez*.
- Underwear. Natural fibres are most comfortable. Easily replaced all over Asia, except for bras over size 38B. Don't bring too many, as you can wash and dry them in no time at all.

Cracking the dress code

A friend of mine and I were in Amritsar and decided to walk from the hotel to the Golden Temple. We were both wearing ankle-length skirts and decently modest tops, but we may as well have been sporting sequined bikinis for all the anonymity that gave us. No sooner had we stepped out of the lobby than the stares began, levelled unashamedly and unmistakably directly at crotch level. It took us a while to realize that this was not the impolite lunacy of one or two individuals, but rather the local pastime for any male aged between 10 and 80. Our skirts were neither see-through nor hip-hugging, but maybe that was the attraction: what could be hiding behind those draped floral pleats? Which just goes to show that, whatever you wear, as a foreign female you will always be an object of fascination for local men.

Lucy Ridout

- Socks. Handy armour against mosquitoes at night.
- Rain gear. A PVC poncho or cagoule might be useful and squashes into a small space. But in the tropical heat that comes with monsoons you'll feel more comfortable using an umbrella instead (PVC makes you sweat). Buy your umbrella when you need it; don't take one with you.
- Sunhat. Not many people wear them, but they do keep you cooler and prevent sunstroke. Broad-brimmed straw hats are a pain to carry when you're on the move, so either buy one there and then dump it, or opt instead for a baseball cap or squashy cotton number.
- A smarter option. You might find yourself invited to a wedding, a festival, or even a circumcision ceremony, so you'll want to at least look like you've made an effort. Smart gear is also useful when dealing with Asian bureaucracy. Something light that doesn't crumple is best.

Shoes

The footwear of choice for the perfect backpacker is the sports sandal or reef-walker, of which Teva are the best known: a go-anywhere sandal with adjustable straps, and sturdy, contoured rubber soles. With a pair of sport sandals on your feet, you can negotiate rough terrain, go swimming, wade through rivers and wander the streets, without having to take them off. They are, of course, not as protective as walking boots, though not nearly as heavy either. Genuine Tevas are pretty expensive in the UK (from about £30 to £75), although in the States you should find them for $40–80. If you're considering trying one of the numerous copies, be warned that the $8/£5 lookalikes sold in Bangkok and Delhi are nothing more than glorified paddling shoes.

Each extra pair of shoes adds a kilo or two to your load, so, sports sandals or not, you need to keep your shoe quotient down. Ideally this means you should take just one hardy pair for daily walking, plus a pair of thongs or flip-flops for beach and hotel. If you're planning to do any sort of overnight trekking, hiking boots will probably be useful enough to justify that extra space and weight, and you can always wear them rather than pack them whenever you're moving on, though some people find trainers an adequate substitute. A few pedi-points to bear in mind:

- You may be wearing these shoes every day for the next six months, so they must be comfortable and strong.
- Your shoes need to be airy too, as, not only do sweaty feet stink, but they can also fester and give you unpleasant flesh-rot in tropical climes.
- Leather sandals (Indian chappals) are the foot uniform of the East: do as most Asians do and wear sandals.
- In Asia, you will find yourself forever taking your shoes on and off to go into temples and mosques, and when visiting people's homes. Laces and other fiddly fastenings can become extremely annoying after a while.
- If you have big feet (that is, bigger than the Asian maximum size – men's 44/US 9¹/2, UK 8¹/2; women's 40/US 8¹/2, UK 7¹/2), be sure that your shoes will last you the whole trip, as you may not be able to buy any more off the peg. But you will be able to get some made for you – Bangkok, Delhi and Yogyakarta in Java all have reputable shoemakers.

Essentials

An alphabetical list of things you will definitely need.

Batteries

Put new batteries in your watch, camera, alarm clock, flashlight and any other vital item before you leave home. Consider taking replacements as well: although you will be able to get most brands in major cities, you may not be near a major city when yours run out.

Contact lens stuff

You can get standard brand-name contact lens solutions at opticians and pharmacists in Asian capitals and major cities, so you don't have to take a huge supply along with you. Take a pair of glasses as a backup, as your lenses may get damaged by dust and sand and it would be a shame to travel all that way and then not be able to see anything. Also, should you get an eye infection, you'll need to do without lenses until the infection clears up.

Contraceptives

Condoms are available over the counter in nearly every Asian nation, but try to buy them from air-conditioned shops or places where they keep them in the fridge so the latex doesn't perish; women may feel uncomfortable buying them because many Asian women don't. Do not rely on being able to buy other contraceptives in Asia: take enough to last you for the whole trip. See Chapter Eleven for more on this.

First-aid kit

Basic first-aid kit, medicines, antimalarials and insect repellents: see Chapter Eleven for details.

Flashlight (torch)

Head-torches, which are like mini miners' lamps on an elasticated headband, are much more practical than conventional hand-held ones, leaving your hands free to wrestle with keys and padlocks in the dark, say, or to hold up your skirt while pissing in the pitch black – and they're a godsend for taking out or putting in contact lenses when the guesthouse power supply suddenly packs up.

Glasses

Take your prescription with you. Any optician should be able to fit your frames with new lenses, or supply a new pair if required.

Guidebooks, phrasebooks and maps

See Chapter Five for advice on choosing the most useful guide-books, phrasebooks and maps.

Padlocks and a chain

Small padlocks serve as a good deterrent to anyone considering pilfering stuff from your rucksack, and are also useful as extra security on hotel doors. Keep two sets of keys in different places, or take combination padlocks instead, so you don't have to worry about losing the key (just about forgetting the number). A chain can also come in handy for securing your pack to luggage racks on overnight trains, or to roof racks on long-distance buses.

Sarong

It's amazing what you can do with a 2m x 1m length of cloth: you can use it as a bath and beach towel, as a sleeping sheet or blanket, as a turban-style sunhat or a temple headscarf-cum-shawl. You can turn it into a shopping bag, an awning on a shadeless beach, or even a rope for hauling your friend up a mountainside. And, of course, like the women and men of Thailand, Indonesia, Laos, Cambodia and Bangladesh, you can also wear it! Sarongs are easy to buy in the West now, but you'll get a much bigger selection if you wait for

your first port of call. You should be able to pick one up for around $8/£5 anywhere in Asia.

Sunglasses

Tropical light is intense, so you'll be glad to hide behind some dark glasses. The same goes for high-altitude glare in Pakistan, Nepal, Tibet, Bhutan and northern India. Buy them at home, as the quality is not as good in Asia.

Sunscreens

Take sun block and a bottle of high-factor suntan lotion (15 for average white skins) for the first few weeks, plus a lower-factor lotion for use once your skin's adjusted to the rays. Don't forget that you can get burnt just as easily in the mountains as by the sea: do not be deceived by the cooler air, as the UV rays are just as strong and the risk of getting skin cancer just as high.

Tampons

Available in most major cities across Asia, though check with your guidebook. Southern Sumatra, for example, is an exception, as is most of Laos outside Vientiane.

Toilet paper

Toilet paper is only sometimes supplied in backpackers' accommodation in Asia. You can buy it in tourist centres and big cities, but take a small roll with you anyway.

Toiletries

Unless you have very special requirements, you'll be able to restock your toiletry supply anywhere you go. And there'll be plenty of new lotions to experiment with, too – like the ochre-coloured face powder that some Thai women plaster on themselves to prevent sun damage, or the pure coconut oil used in India to ensure supple skin and lustrous hair. However, beware the large number of moisturizers, very popular with Asian women, that have a "whitening" effect on the skin, as they contain bleach.

Towels

Towels get disgustingly smelly very easily, take ages to dry and use up far too much valuable rucksack space. Use a sarong instead. Or, if you must, take a tiny hand towel.

Optional odds and ends

An alphabetical list of bits and pieces that you may or may not need.

Alarm clock or watch

For early departures.

Binoculars

Worth considering if you're going to be wildlife-spotting in national parks, or even trekking.

Books

New, English-language books are relatively expensive in Asia (India and Nepal are the exceptions), but second-hand bookstores and book exchanges are usually plentiful in travellers' centres, so there's no need to carry a whole library around with you. See Chapter Five for a list of novels and travelogues about Asia that will make enjoyable travelling companions.

Cigarette lighter

Useful even for non-smokers, for lighting mosquito coils, candles (dur-

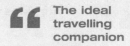

The ideal travelling companion

When I'm travelling on my own, I find it comforting to have a reminder of people at home, so I always take Reggie, a tiny teddy bear, along too. We have shared many adventures, but it was in India that his talent as an icebreaker came to light – children and adults seemed to find him so irresistibly cute that they just had to start talking to me!

The most memorable Reggie-encounter happened when I was trekking in Kinnaur, in the Himalayas. I was following a path up through the forest, heading for the snow line, when I heard a man's voice beckoning from below. I wandered down to the clearing, greeted the old man and his wife, and introduced Reggie, emphasizing that his Hindi was much better than mine. Beaming from ear to ear, the old man immediately grasped hold of Reggie with both hands and began to have quite an animated conversation with him. Ice duly broken, we all sat down and shared a cheroot, after which I helped them with their wood-collecting.

Juliet Acock

“

Earplugs

Earplugs are essential for
screening out the routine din
of Asian hotels. Until you've been to
Asia, you just can't imagine how noisy
everyone is. We regularly had building
work going on in the next-door room or
in the one directly above us – and it
always continued through the night
because that's the coolest time to work!
Then there's the morning throat-clearing
chorus – at 5am – when the night's
phlegm is hawked and spat out by every
man in the locality. And in Indonesia, it's
impossible to stay out of earshot of the
early morning muezzin calls at the
neighbourhood mosque; in Padang, our
hotel had its very own
mosque – in the room
adjacent to ours!
”

Jo Mead

ing power cuts), and campfires;
matches get soggy from the humidity and are more of a hazard.

Comfort food

Some travellers swear by Marmite,
Vegemite, peanut butter or whatever –
a little taste of home to soothe their
stomach and their taste buds. Whatever
you take, it should be small, non-per-
ishable and hard to break or spill.

Compass

Only necessary if you're trekking
without a guide.

Earplugs

To block out snoring partners, roaring
all-night traffic, video music on
overnight buses and other annoyances.

Games

For all those exhausting thirty-hour
bus and train journeys. Pocket
Scrabble, playing cards, Game Boy
and Connect 4 have all been road-
tested by the authors.

Gluestick

For recalcitrant Asian envelopes and
stamps.

Handkerchief

Hopefully you won't be getting a
cold, but you will be sweating a lot –

and a hanky is useful for mopping your brow. Also practical for drying your hands after washing them in restaurants or public toilets (generally, only posh hotels and airports provide paper towels or dryers). A soaking wet handkerchief tied around your neck has a refreshingly cooling effect on your whole body.

Mosquito coils

Buy them when you arrive, where they will be much cheaper. Some hotels provide them free. See p.302 for more on this form of mosquito repellent.

Mosquito net

Can be useful anywhere in Asia, though most tourist accommodations will provide nets or screened windows. Nets are much cheaper in Asia than in the West, but, if you do buy one from home, choose one which is impregnated with mosquito repellent. They're available from camping shops in the UK for between £20 and £40, although you should find them cheaper in the States ($25–40). Also pack a handful of hooks and a small roll of heavy-duty tape so that you can fix your net to beams, bedposts, window frames and ceilings.

Notebook or journal and pens

For all your profound observations and amusing anecdotes. (Don't for-

Together forever

The problem with travelling with a keyboard in your rucksack is that you don't have any room for normal things like clothes or insect repellent. But you could never make as many friends with a pair of Levi's as you could with a Casio. My keyboard was a brilliant way of meeting people and a positive effort on my part to communicate in a language other than the ones we speak.

Sometimes I used to carry my keyboard around in a bin-liner. One time, during a hand-luggage check in Vientiane Airport, Laos, they threw my money belt on top of the keyboard, setting off the demo button. Everyone stopped in their tracks and stared as this black bag emerged from the X-ray machine singing Rick Astley's "Together Forever". Naturally, I was arrested.

Chris Humphrey

get to send in the best ones for the next edition of *First-Time Asia*.)

Penknife

If you take one, make it a Swiss Army knife (or a good cheap copy), as you might be glad of the blade and the bottle opener.

Personal stereo

A personal stereo is great for long bus journeys and for entertaining people in the more remote villages. Consider taking a pair of mini-speakers as well. Bootleg tapes are sold all over Asia, often for as little as $3/£2. If your personal stereo has a record button, you can also make interesting audio-diaries – and audio letters to the folks back home.

Photos of home

A good icebreaker, and just as weird and interesting to the people you'll meet on buses and trains as a picture of a Dyak longhouse or a Vietnamese rickshaw would be to you.

Radio

If you're away for a long time, a short-wave radio can be a comforting link with home, especially if you're travelling alone. See p.324 for advice on tuning in overseas.

Sewing kit

Safety pins, needle and cotton, plus a couple of buttons for emergency repairs.

Sheet sleeping bag

More useful in tropical Asia than a down sleeping bag, but by no means essential: if you're worried about the cleanliness of the hotel sheets you can always use your sarong instead – or change your guesthouse. If you do want to take one, you don't need to buy one: either sew two sheets together, or use a lightweight duvet cover instead.

Sink plug

Asian sinks tend not have plugs, so this can be useful, especially for wet shaving. On the other hand, most hotels provide buckets for you to do your laundry.

Sleeping bag

Unless you're going to spend a long time camping or trekking in the colder and more remote parts of Asia, there's no point lugging a sleeping bag around with you. In popular trekking centres (like Kathmandu and Lhasa) you can rent four-season bags for as little as a dollar a day.

Stamps from your home country

No, not because we assume that everyone's a closet collector, but because Asian post is not always that speedy (see Chapter Twelve), so you might want to give pre-stamped letters to travellers you meet who are heading home in the next week.

String

To use as a washing line and to suspend mosquito nets from. Some travellers swear by dental floss instead of string – it comes in a tiny box, and as well as helping to keep your gums healthy is strong enough to support your wet laundry and to tie up parcels.

Tent and other camping gear

Accommodation and food is so inexpensive in most parts of Asia that you won't need a tent, sleeping bag and camping stove to eke out your budget – and the weather in tropical Asia is so warm anyway that you can sleep out under the stars with no canvas protection. Exceptions include Japan and Hong Kong, where hotel rooms will take a big slice out of your budget and campsites are plentiful (if a bit far from major tourist attractions). Camping gear is essential if you're heading into remote wilderness areas anywhere in Asia and are not planning to take a guide (guides usually provide food and bedding). In South Korea, for example, there are lots of mountain huts dotted over national park trails, but they provide nothing more than floor space and a roof. Before lugging your equipment halfway round the world, check relevant guidebooks for local places that rent out camping gear.

Travel plugs

If you're taking a hairdryer, laptop, or any other electrical appliance, you'll need a set of travel plugs/electrical adaptors so that you can plug in wherever you are. Guidebooks will tell you what the local voltage and usual socket formation is, or check out the Help for World Travellers Web site ⓦ *www.kropla.com* which has a very helpful list, complete with pictures, of the different sockets, voltage and phone plugs used around the world. You can buy sets of three or four travel adaptors from any of the travel equipment suppliers listed on p.369.

Wallet

Most Asian currencies are based on notes and, in countries where the denominations are very big, you'll find a wallet much handier than a purse because you'll have far more notes than coins. In Indonesia, for example, there's even a note for 100 rupiah, currently equivalent to about one and a half US cents. Inexpensive leather and fabric wallets are available all over Asia, so you might want to buy one when you get there.

Washing powder (laundry detergent)

Camping shops sell expensive travel-wash suds in tubes, but you're better off buying cheap individual portions of washing powder when you get there.

Water bottle and water purifier or tablets

If you stick to the beaten track, you shouldn't need your own water bottle, as bottled water is sold in all touristed areas. You should definitely take your own water bottle and purifying equipment if you're going trekking or venturing into remote areas. Buy a bottle that holds a litre and has a belt or shoulder-strap attachment. More information on water purification is given in Chapter Eleven.

Wet ones (baby wipes)

Not just for babies, but for sweaty travel-worn adults too. Good for cleaning yourself up on buses and trains, and for wiping hands before eating.

Cameras

Photos are a great way to jog your memory when you get home, and the best way to share your experiences. Weigh up the advantages of taking a bulky top-of-the range SLR (single lens reflex) with a variety of lenses against a point-and-shoot compact or the compromise zoom-compact option. Be realistic about what you intend to do with the pictures once you get home: if you're planning to sell them for publication or use them in slide shows and lectures, then an SLR is probably essential. But, if you just want them for your personal satisfaction, you may be happier with a smaller and less ostentatious camera (cameras draw a lot of attention wherever you are and can make you feel self-conscious – they also attract thieves). The third option is to invest in a digital camera, though be

---

PICTURE ETIQUETTE

Remember that not everyone you see in Asia, no matter how photogenic, will want their photo recorded by you for posterity. Some tribal people in Thailand and Indonesia hate to be photographed as they believe that a tiny fragment of their soul dies with every snapshot taken; and, for many orthodox Muslim women, to be photographed by strangers is almost tantamount to being indecently assaulted. You should therefore always ask before taking someone's picture – gestures can usually convey the idea.

Festivals and religious events may also be off limits, so check with local people first: masked festival dancers in Nepal believe they embody the deities during their performance, so taking photos of them is sacrilegious; and filming the sacred cremations in Varanasi, India, could easily get you lynched by mortified onlookers. Be equally sensitive when photographing temples, mosques and other shrines, and don't whip out your camera at an international border, airport or military checkpoint.

You'll even find that some people – like the Padaung "long-neck" women of northern Thailand, the Ifugao people in the Philippines, and certain Nepalese sadhus – are now so used to having their pictures taken by tourists that they charge a per-picture fee.

aware that there are currently very few cybercafés in Asia that will let you download your pictures on their terminals.

Accessories

- Take a UV or skylight filter if you have an SLR camera, as the ultraviolet light in the tropics and at altitude can give an unnatural cast to pictures that makes them look washed out.
- Pack cleaning equipment, at the very least a little brush and air-cleaner, and use it daily: dust will quickly ruin both your camera and your pictures.
- Carry some silica gel in with your camera lenses and film. This will absorb excess tropical moisture.
- Take spare batteries, as they're not always available in Asia.
- Consider taking a compact tripod.

Film

- Take a range of film speeds as the speed of the film determines its ability to cope with different light conditions. Much of Asia is very bright, so ASA100 film is generally fine. But for darker subjects, like a tropical rainforest, or the inside of certain temples, where you may be allowed to photograph but not use a flash, you'll need ASA400 or 800.
- You can buy print film all over Asia, but slide film is less easy to find. Do not buy film that looks as if it's been stored in damp or humid conditions, and avoid film kept in a hot place or in direct sunlight.

- Many Asian baggage-check machines are film-safe. However, you should always pack your films (new as well as exposed) in carry-on baggage, as hold baggage gets a heavier dose of radiation, which can fog films. The higher the film speed, the more vulnerable it is to X-ray damage. X-rays are cumulative, so one X-ray incident isn't fatal, though if you are doing a lot of air travel consider keeping your films in a special lead bag (available from all decent camera shops), which will protect them from the rays.

Developing film

Film should be processed as soon as possible after being exposed; a couple of months is fine, but you don't want films rolling about in the bottom of your pack for a year before getting them developed. Process-paid slide film can be sent air-mail to the processor for the pictures to be returned to a home address. If you decide to get film developed while on the road, you should definitely check the quality first, either by asking other travellers or by getting just one roll developed first. Sending film, prints or negatives home is often a good idea (see p.318).

Documents

Your most essential documents are your passport (with appropriate visas), airline tickets, traveller's cheques, credit card, and insurance policy. These should all live in your money belt (see p.207), which should be in permanent residence around your waist. Make two sets of photocopies of all your vital documents, including the relevant pages of your passport, your airline tickets, travellers' cheques receipt and serial numbers, credit card details and insurance policy. Keep one set of copies with you, but in a separate place from the originals (eg passport, etc in your money belt; copies in your rucksack), and leave the other set at home with friends or relatives In case of loss or theft. All the better if those friends or relatives have a fax machine, so they can get them faxed to you or the relevant issuing office straight away. You can store credit card numbers, passport details and the like using Lonely Planet's ekno service 🟢 *www.ekno.lonelyplanet.com* which allows you to retrieve the information online; these details can also be stored with Rough Guides Travel Insurance 🟢 *www.roughguides.com/insurance* if you take out a policy with them. Some travellers recommend scanning all your important documents and then emailing them to your own Web-based address, so that you can get hold of them almost anywhere on your travels, cybercafé availability permitting. If you want to do this, try it out before you leave home so you can make sure your documents convert into an attachment format that you can read online. For more on using email while you travel, see p.321.

Take an international drivers' licence if you're eligible, and a student card and international youth hostel card if you have them. Don't buy a hostel card just for the trip, though, as guesthouses tend to be cheaper and more convenient than hostels in most parts of Asia (Japan, Hong Kong and Singapore are the exceptions – see Chapter Ten). In Bangkok you can buy fake student ID cards and press cards; no one will accept them in Thailand, but you may find them useful elsewhere in Asia. Take eight passport-size photos with you to use for visa applications, visa extensions and any passes you might need to buy while you're travelling.

7

Your first night

There's nothing quite like a foreign airport for freaking you out and making you wonder why on earth you left home. Illegible signs, confusing instructions, and crowds of unfamiliar people chatting incomprehensibly can be bewildering, even scary, especially when you've just spent a night without sleep. On top of all this, you'll perhaps be anticipating extortionate taxi fares, sleazy hotels, and "friendly" helpers who turn out to be predatory touts or worse.

Rest assured, however, that even the most laid-back travellers find their first night in a new country a challenge, something that needs to be approached with a clear head and a sense of humour. After thirty hours on the move you'll probably be lacking both, so this chapter is designed to help you cope without them and ensure that your first experience of Asia is a positive one.

Planning your first night

If you follow only one piece of advice in this whole chapter, then this is it: plan your first night before you leave

A cautionary tale

Three intrepid young men of my acquaintance set off for their year-long travels around the world, first stop Delhi, touching down at around midnight. In their enthusiasm to begin their adventure they abandoned their original plan to wait in the airport until daybreak and rushed outside to join the queue for taxis, which was a mile long. A driver and his friend approached from the side and offered them a cab. They accepted keenly: surely this would be better than hanging around waiting?

Once in the taxi they told the driver they had no idea where to go, but they needed a hotel. He knew just the place. Off they set through the dark Delhi streets. The first hotel was full. No matter, he knew another place. Yet more meanderings through the dark Delhi streets to learn that the second hotel too was full. They became concerned that he would charge them for all this useless ferrying around and pointed out they wouldn't pay for his mistakes. He replied it wasn't his fault and demanded the equivalent of $50 for the trip so far.

Thinking this was too much they eventually, after much heated argument, handed over the equivalent of $30, suggested the cab driver and his chum called the police if they were unhappy, hoisted themselves and baggage into the dark Delhi streets and set off on foot. They flagged down a motorized rickshaw and, having learnt at least one lesson, asked how much it would cost to take them all to a hotel – forty cents! They loaded themselves and luggage aboard and were whisked away to an acceptable hotel where they got a bed for the night.

The next morning they were having breakfast and another foreigner approached them. He was leaving India; did they want to buy his guidebook? They definitely did. They read that the official fare from Delhi Airport to town was less than $8; they also found out about backpackers' places in the city. "Why didn't we buy one of these before?" they wondered.

Lesley Reader

home. The decisions and preparations you make in advance can go a long way to reducing the chances of trouble once you arrive.

Even if your aim for the trip is to wander where your fancy takes you, it isn't really advisable just to amble off the plane that first night in Shanghai, Singapore or Seoul trusting that something will turn up. It probably will, but the chances are you won't like it. You should know where you are planning to stay and how you are going to get there.

As part of the planning, make sure you have all the right paperwork (tickets, passport and visas; see Chapter Two) and a rough idea of how long you intend to stay – you may need to stipulate this on arrival.

Choosing where to spend your first night

Stage one is to work out in which area of the city you want to spend your first night or two. To have your destination clearly etched in your mind is absolutely essential, whether you decide to book ahead or just take potluck on the ground. Any reliable, up-to-date guidebook will help you decide (see Chapter Five), but here are a couple of extra tips:

● Choose an area that has a lot of budget hotels close together, so that if you don't like the first hotel it's easy to change to a different one.

- Select a district that's close to the sights that interest you, and/or convenient for any onward transport connections you might be needing in the next few days.
- Check out how easy this area is to reach from the airport and, with the help of your guidebook, decide what method of transport you plan to use. Bear in mind that the cheapest options (eg some of the youth hostels in Hong Kong) may be significantly less accessible than pricier alternatives.

Once you've picked your area, draw up a list of three hotels you like the sound of so that you have a ready-made contingency plan should one of them fall through. Consider booking in for two nights, which gives you your first day to sleep, clear your head and plan your next move. Plus, if the hotel's too expensive, or just not right, you've plenty of time to explore alternative options without having to repack your bags by midday and lug them round the neighbourhood.

Booking a hotel room before you leave home

If you wish, you can book your hotel before you leave home. Your guidebook should list phone, fax and email details of recommended hotels; alternatively, contact the relevant tourist office (see p.347) to get some details of places to stay. The disadvantage of booking from home is the price. In Asia, the cheaper hotels and guesthouses rarely accept bookings without advance cash payment (youth hostels are an exception; see p.362), so you will probably find yourself booking a moderately priced room for your first night or two. But remember that prices are much lower in Asia than in Europe, the US and Australia, and that you can always move to a cheaper place later. Even though you may be planning to do your entire trip at subsistence level, your first night is not really the time to start – saving money takes time, local knowledge and alertness, and you'll lack all three when you first arrive.

Plenty of Asian hotels employ English-speaking staff, so you shouldn't have too much difficulty making yourself understood if you phone. Give them your flight number and the approximate time you expect to arrive at the hotel (allowing up to two hours to get through airport formalities, plus whatever time it takes to get into town) – and enquire about hotel courtesy buses as well. You might be asked for a credit card deposit. Once you've made your booking, confirm it in writing by mail or fax.

If you can't face phoning the hotel yourself, you could either make your arrangements online, through Internet-based accommodation booking agents (see p.362), or you could use a travel agent instead. Both these options could be a little more expensive, as your choice will probably be limited to mid-range and expensive hotels.

The best budget option may well turn out to be the youth hostel (if there is one) in the city of your arrival. Some youth hostels can be booked from overseas using the IYHF Booking Network (see p.362). Women might also consider a homestay with a local woman for the first couple of nights: contact the Women Welcome Women organization (see p.362) for details.

The plane journey

If you're coming from Europe or America, the flight into Asia is almost certain to be a long slog – NYC to Hanoi, for example, lasts a good thirty hours, and London to Mumbai (Bombay) can't be done in less than eight. If you're doing things on a budget, chances are your journey will be convoluted, involving several touchdowns and possibly even a couple of long waits while changing planes. There's nothing you can to do to speed the trip up, but here are a few suggestions on how to make it as bearable and comfortable as possible.

Hand baggage

Don't just throw all your backpack overflow into your hand baggage, but think about what you might need for the time you'll be in transit. If you pack too little into your hand luggage, you might freeze or go out of your mind with boredom; too much, and you might not be allowed to take it into the cabin (many airlines specify a 5kg maximum weight for hand baggage, while some others refuse anything that won't fit under your seat). Also, if you're wandering round transit lounges for several hours en route, you don't want to be dragging too much with you. Airlines also have regulations about batteries, blades and knives – anything deemed a potential weapon in a hijack will be removed from you and returned at your destination.

Handy items you might want to include in your carry-on baggage:

- something to read (don't rely on the in-flight movies being riveting).
- a guidebook so you can plan your arrival strategy (see p.186).
- socks and a sweater. Even planes in tropical climates get cold when they're cruising at 36,000 feet; airline blankets are often in short supply.
- all valuables and fragile items, including your camera. Your checked-in baggage is not only more likely to go astray than your hand baggage, but is also treated much more roughly.
- films. Checked-in baggage is treated to higher doses of security X-rays, which can fog film.
- some basic toiletries, including a toothbrush: a quick wash and brush can improve how you feel very quickly and put that freshness back into your breath after a surfeit of airline food.
- contact lens case and spare specs so you can sleep without waking to permanent haloes around your eyeballs.
- moisturizer to combat the dry cabin atmosphere; cooling eye-gel, eye drops and a moisturizing face spray are stand-bys for many flyers for the same reasons.
- chewing gum and/or sweets to help clear your ears during takeoff and landing.
- a small bottle of water so you don't dehydrate either on the plane (you can fill it up when you run out) or in transit lounges where you might otherwise have to shell out for soft drinks in local currency. Even if transit lounge facilities accept hard currency, you will usually be given local currency as change, which is a waste of time since you're heading somewhere else.
- clothes appropriate for your point of arrival. In other words, it's a good idea to wear or take several layers of clothing so that you don't perish in your home country and boil when you arrive (or vice versa); also remember the modesty factor (see p.209).
- one set of clean underwear. You never know when you or your baggage may get delayed or separated – you don't want to be trying to buy new underwear on your first morning in Vientiane.
- medicines. Include any medication you take regularly. A few painkillers are a good idea, as flying is very dehydrating and headaches are common. Air sickness is not unusual: if you know you suffer, dose yourself with your favourite medication. If you don't know, but fear you might, put some in your hand baggage – they do take a while to work, but it's better to take them late rather than never.

- a pen, for filling in immigration forms.
- an inflatable neck pillow, eye shades and ear plugs if you're intending to sleep during the flight; these should effectively shut out the rest of the world and make sure you don't wake up with kinks like the Hunchback of Notre Dame.

Some people fly with far more – a Game Boy and/or Walkman, and snacks or more substantial food in case of foodless delays, but also in case your appetite goes haywire on arrival (see p.242), causing you to venture out at 3am looking for munchies. If you know you're going to spend a few hours in transit at Singapore's Changi Airport, you might even consider including swimwear – the airport has its own swimming pool.

Checking in

At check-in you'll present your ticket and passport to the airline for inspection, and hand over your main baggage, which shouldn't weigh much if you take our advice in Chapter Six. If you haven't yet ordered your special meal, such as a vegetarian or diabetic option (see p.149), this is your very last chance, though don't bank on a positive outcome.

When you check in your bag, a baggage coupon will be clipped to your ticket or handed to you. Keep this safe. In the event that

MEMORABLE LANDINGS

Flights into parts of Asia offer some of the most spectactular scenery in the world, with the Himalayas being the most breathtaking. Planes arriving in Kathmandu of necessity make their descent within spitting distance of soaring peaks, including Everest. After flying across Sichuan's western mountain ranges, the landing at Lhasa seems like a miracle of faith over logic as the ground appears to rise up to meet the plane instead of the plane making a normal descent. The flight along the Himalayas towards Bhutan is spectacular enough, but the most remarkable part is the landing at Paro airport, as the plane circles down below the mountains and then twists and turns along the Paro valley, passing isolated farms and temples on the cliffs on either side and finally the enormous medieval fortress, Paro Dzong, before crossing the river, apparently a hair's-breadth above the water, and eventually touching down. In other parts of the continent, it's ocean views that are spellbinding: flying in to the Philippines, you get a great view of the sparkling South China Sea and the seven thousand plus atolls that make up this island nation.

the worst happens, and you have lunch in London and dinner in Delhi but your baggage goes to Bangkok, you will need this counterfoil to complete the lost-luggage paperwork at your destination. You may also need the counterfoil if officials want to check that you are the owner of the baggage – this tends to happen in, among other places, Hanoi in Vietnam and Lhasa in Tibet.

Most airlines specify that for intercontinental flights you should check in a minimum of two hours before departure – there are exceptions to this (eg Air India and El Al both require longer), so you should ask your travel agent, or call the airline in advance. Whatever the minimum time given, it is advisable to check in as far ahead as possible.

Though it's a pain having to wait around for a couple of hours after you've checked in, the earlier you do so the more likely you are to get your preferred seat, which can make all the difference to your state of mind – and body – on arrival. If the plane isn't full, it is possible to change seats once you're on board, but it's much better to ask for what you want initially. If you have long legs, then go for the aisle seat, or make a special request for an exit-row seat where there are no seats immediately in front of you. Alternatively, the seats at the front of the cabin also have plenty of leg room, but you're likely to find yourself in among the babies as that's where the cots get put. Aisle seats have the advantage that you can get up and stretch your legs as often as you like without disturbing anyone, but you do get disturbed by everyone else in the row going in and out. A window seat, on the other hand, guarantees you extra in-flight entertainment. You get good views during takeoff and landing (some destinations are especially memorable – see box, opposite), and the views at 30,000 feet can be extraordinary, particularly at sunrise or sunset, or during flights over mountain ranges (like those that dominate western Iran), or azure-fringed archipelagos (such as the islands of Indonesia) during daylight hours.

Even if you are a smoker, you might want to waive your right to a seat in the smokers' section simply because the air is stale and fuggy enough on the plane as it is, without being choked full of fumes. If you want the occasional cigarette it's nearly always possible to sit, or stand, in the smokers' section for ten minutes before returning to the non-smoking part of the plane. Note that an increasing number of flights are totally non-smoking.

Coping with the flight

One way to ensure that the flight passes happily is to make full use of the in-flight bar service, offered free on most long-haul flights into Asia. Free drink can make the time go quickly, help you to sleep and calm your nerves if you're scared of flying. However, anyone who's ever got seriously drunk on a plane will know just how magnified the usual side effects become. Your head aches violently, your heart pounds incessantly, and your body temperature soars to an unnatural high – not much fun. Whether or not you get drunk, dehydration is a major cause of discomfort on long flights, so you need to combat this by drinking lots of soft drinks and water. You'll be a regular visitor to the toilet, but in any case it's a good idea to use the toilet on the plane before you get off at your destination. Tackling foreign public toilets with some or all of your baggage to worry about, and possibly having to pay for the facilities in local currency, is an avoidable extra hassle.

There is increasing publicity about the potential health risks of flying. It's a good idea to get up and walk around every so often and even while you are in your seat do some flexing to keep the circulation going; not only will you feel better but in rare cases, blood clots can form due to the cramped conditions. Discuss this with your doctor if it is of concern; some recommend taking a small dose of aspirin while flying. Investigations are also ongoing about the air quality in aircraft cabins and the extent to which air-conditioning systems can spread airborne diseases among passengers. For those interested in complementary healthcare, echinacea is often recommended as a boost to the immune system to help you ward off anything that comes flying your way; speak to a qualified practitioner.

Every now and again the media lurches into a brief flurry about the phenomenon of "air rage" and we're treated to stories of drunkenness, assaults and offenders dumped off on foreign soil to find their own way home. Psychologists suggest that alcohol, stress, fear of flying, too little oxygen plus too much carbon dioxide in the cabin air and the fact that habitual smokers can't get their regular nicotine fix all lead to exaggerated human reactions which in some cases go over the top. Bear in mind that these types of incidents are rare and when they do happen the pilot has full power to land at the nearest airport and offload the offenders.

The transit experience

Should you be turfed off the plane for a couple of hours' refuelling en route, or have to wait for a connecting flight, the transit experience doesn't have to be an unpleasant one, though sometimes you can't avoid being holed up in the transit lounge from hell: Moscow, for example, offers hard seats, dim lighting, no refreshments in the middle of the night, the most miserable cleaners in the western hemisphere and, on occasion, resident refugees inhabiting cardboard boxes. However, some of Asia's airports are simply wonderful.

- Singapore's Changi Airport Ⓦ *www.changiairport.com.sg* has a highly browsable English-language bookshop full of publications on Asia that you rarely see in the West. There's also an Internet centre, a swimming pool and showers, and free two-hour city coach tours are available for transit passengers. The airport's transit hotel rents rooms out for short periods (with wake-up calls provided) so you can get some proper sleep.
- Kuala Lumpur also has an excellent transit hotel Ⓔ *airsidehotel@po.jaring.my* costing around US$21–25/£14–17 for six hours in a double room, with toiletries, luxury towels and hairdryer provided.
- Jakarta's Soekarno-Hatta Airport is pleasingly laid out in pagoda-style buildings, connected by walkways that lead you through tropical gardens. There's a well-priced Asian food court and a *McDonald's* too.
- Dubai's is also a good airport – a huge white dome dominated by dramatic fountains, with shops selling reasonably priced duty-free electrical goods.
- Hong Kong's gleaming new airport has a spa lounge, with massage chairs to ease out the kinks after long flights, as well as showers, sofas, free email facilities and free food and drink. It costs US$25/£16 to get into the lounge though.
- In the transit lounge at Osaka's Kansai International Airport, you can rent therapeutic massage chairs that vibrate gently to ease away your in-flight stiffness – a bargain at $5/£3.50 an hour.

Don't forget to find out from your airline whether it is possible to pay to use the first- or business-class lounge – it's much quieter than the rest of the airport, the chairs are more comfortable and there'll be free coffee and newspapers.

No harm in asking . . .

I was nervous about doing the big cross-Asia trip on my own, but as there was no one else to go with, off I went. Standing by the luggage carousel at Denpasar Airport in Bali (my first port of call), I got chatting to a couple of hip-looking American women, and asked if I could share a ride with them into town. It turned out we got on really well and we spent the next two weeks together, travelling as a threesome all round Bali. After that I was much more confident and happy to continue through Indonesia on my own.

Debbie King

Arriving

While some Asian international airports – eg Tokyo – have the look and the seamless efficiency to match anything in Europe, North America or Australasia, others, such as Tribhuwan in Kathmandu, are more basic. However, the days of grass landing strips and tin shacks operating as international airport terminals are largely extinct in Asia. Remember that airports the world over, even in your own country, can be soulless, confusing, intimidating places and certainly don't reflect the country as a whole. They are, literally, a rite of passage to be gone through by every traveller – ideally as painlessly as possible.

New arrivals are prime tout fodder; you'll be amazed just how many services you can be offered in the short walk between customs and the taxi rank – hotels, hash, sex, diamonds, tour guides, you name it. The slightest flicker of interest, or even friendly eye contact, is encouragement enough to continue the encounter and, if this is your first time in Asia, it will be written all over you, from your face to the way you walk. Not only do you feel vulnerable, but this is the time when you *are* most vulnerable. Much as you may hate to be unfriendly, in arrivals you should keep your eyes angled unflinchingly forwards, your rucksack strapped firmly to your back, and your plan of action bleep-

ARRIVALS

ing loudly inside your head. It's a mad zone out there and right now you can't afford to be soft-centred.

Hopefully you're following our advice on p.149 and planning to arrive in daylight, so that you have plenty of time to sort out your ride into the city and your accommodation before it gets dark. A lot of the lowlife of any city emerges after sunset; with your senses and fears heightened by the shadows it is perfectly possible, and even sensible, to assume that absolutely harmless and helpful people are out to rip you off. If the worst comes to the worst and you do arrive in the middle of the night and don't know what to do, just wait in the airport until daybreak.

Daylight or not, if you're on your own, think about linking up with other travellers who look as if they might be on the same budget as you and therefore heading to the same area of town – there's usually plenty of time to size people up in immigration and baggage collection queues. This will save money on taxi fares and will probably make you feel more confident about the whole arrivals procedure. Nonetheless, it makes sense to retain some of your healthy scepticism in encounters with fellow travellers, too.

Formalities

In general, the sequence of airport formalities is: immigration, baggage collection, customs, and then into the arrivals hall. If you follow the advice about paperwork given in Chapter Two, you shouldn't have too many problems, but the thing to bear in mind is to keep your cool, whatever happens: the queues may be a mile

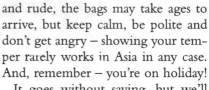

Anarchists in the UK

The only time I've ever had trouble at immigration is when I went to Japan with my friend John. John is an archivist, which is what he told immigration officials when they asked. Unfortunately, they misheard, or at least misunderstood, and, thinking he'd said "anarchist", hauled us both off for a thorough baggage check behind closed doors. Moral of that story: either give a simple version of your job title or make one up.

Bob Williams

long, the officials may be obstructive and rude, the bags may take ages to arrive, but keep calm, be polite and don't get angry – showing your temper rarely works in Asia in any case. And, remember – you're on holiday!

It goes without saying, but we'll say it anyway. You shouldn't be trying to bring anything inappropriate into the country. Most countries stipulate a duty-free allowance for alcohol or tobacco, some countries do not allow the import of certain food items (eg chewing gum into Singapore), and all prohibit the import of hard and soft drugs. In some Asian countries the penalty for smuggling drugs is death and, in the remainder, lengthy jail terms are the norm. It is up to you to find out what the regulations are in each country and obey them.

Solo travellers should be especially vigilant when collecting baggage. Many a lone traveller has left their hand baggage on a trolley while lunging for their pack on the carousel only to turn around and find their precious hand baggage gone. Keep at least one hand on your hand baggage at all times – even if it means sacrificing your trolley.

Changing money

Unless you manage to buy some local currency before you leave home (see p.176), you'll need to change money before you leave the airport. Keep your eyes peeled for exchange facilities as soon as you get off the plane, as some airports keep them hidden away on the air side of immigration in other words, between the runway and passport control; you won't be able to re-enter this area once you've left, so change your money while you're passing through. Rates will probably be less favourable at the airport than in town, though, so you might only want to change enough for the first couple of days. A few other things to bear in mind:

- However hard it is to get your jet-lagged brain into gear, it is important to look at the exchange rate, work out how much local cash you should get and check while you are still at the counter that you've been given precisely that – unscrupulous exchange counter clerks all over the world know that passengers just off long-haul flights aren't on the ball.
- Make sure you get plenty of small-denomination notes; you don't want to end up arguing with a taxi or bus driver who has no change.
- Make sure you get and hold onto your exchange receipt. Because of the proliferation of black-market moneychangers across Asia, you will probably be asked to show at least one official exchange receipt when you want to change back leftover local currency at the end of your stay.
- Stash some of your cash in an easily accessible place so that you do not have to unzip your clothes and bare all to half the population of Kathmandu while trying to retrieve a taxi fare from your money belt.

Finding a place to stay

If you haven't pre-booked a place from home (see p.229), it's not too late! Many international airports have a counter for booking local hotel rooms, though these charge a booking fee. The booking clerk rings the hotel and makes the reservation, then issues you with a voucher, which will either be the receipt for payment made at the counter or specify the price you will pay at the hotel. He or she should also be able to advise you on the best way of getting to your hotel. The main drawback with this option is that only certain hotels – generally mid- to upper-range establishments – feature on their booking lists and may not be described in your guidebook, so you won't have any idea of what the place is like until you get there.

If you're up to tackling the local telephone system and language, there is nothing to stop you ringing hotels yourself and finding a bed, although you should come armed with a list of options together with phone numbers – most public phones don't sport directories. Remember to establish the price and make sure you get them to hold the room for long enough for you to get there and claim it.

Probably the least desirable situation on your first night is to be tramping the streets with your pack on your back looking for a place to stay. If, for whatever reason, this happens, then you should head for an area where there is plenty of accommodation so you'll have a few alternatives and short distances to tramp between places. This means that you won't be unduly concerned if your first is full and your second closed down – particularly crucial if you arrive late in the day or if your visit coincides with the peak tourist season or a local holiday. For full details on accommodation, see Chapter Ten. If there are two or more of you travelling together, it's easier if one of you sits in a café, bar or restaurant with the bags while the others do the trailing around to find a place.

Getting into town

The golden rule here is to put personal safety above everything, and that includes price. If you do not feel comfortable waiting an hour for a bus in a dark underground car park or sitting in an unlicensed cab on your own for forty minutes, then don't do it. You will have plenty of chances to save money later. On your first night, do what feels safe.

Airports always seem to be a long way from where you want to go. The possibilities for getting into town obviously vary depending on where you are. In a few cases there is a rail link (for example, Don Muang in Bangkok, Chek Lap Kok in Hong Kong and Narita in Tokyo have these), but more likely you'll be looking at road transport. The variety can be overwhelming: you might find motorbike taxis and three-wheeled sidecar taxis, air-conditioned limos and special luxury six-seaters, vans and family cars, and even cycle-rickshaws, and it'll be up to you to decide! Your most likely options for getting into town are:

- official taxis. In some cases you join the taxi queue and get the next metered cab from the rank. In others there are prepaid taxi counters with fixed prices (often displayed on a noticeboard): you tell them where you're going, pay your money, collect a coupon that acts as a receipt (and may have your destination scrawled on it), and they find an official cab to take you. This is generally the most expensive but most reliable method: the cabs and drivers are licensed and, in theory at least, know the area well.

- unofficial cabs. Touts for these hang about at most major airports and try to entice customers away from the official cabs. They may well be cheaper – providing you can haggle effectively over the price – but you'll end up at the mercy of a car and driver with no official recognition and uncertain local knowledge. *Always* agree the price before you get in.

- courtesy buses. Many of the upmarket hotels operate courtesy bus services for their customers. If you are booked into a more expensive hotel, check whether this service is available.

- airport buses. Many airports operate bus services which, if available, are probably the most hassle-free and cost-effective means of getting into the city. Though slower than taxis, the buses usually have plenty of space for luggage, and often follow routes that are conveniently close to the main tourist and hotel areas. Sometimes you prepay your ticket inside the arrivals hall and sometimes you pay on board.

- local buses. These are the slowest but the cheapest of the lot. You'll need to have small change to pay the fare and you should be prepared to be rather unpopular if you're hauling a mountain of luggage, even a small mountain, while commuters are trying to get to or from their workplaces. Some bus conductors might refuse entry if you've got piles of stuff; others may charge extra. Make sure you know where to get off! Our advice is to leave your first brush with Asian buses until the next day – at least then you'll have a better chance of seeing the funny side (there's more on the delights of local buses in Chapter Nine).

Guidebooks are probably the best way to weigh up, and budget for, your options but you might also like to take a look at the Web site Ⓦ *www.concierge.com/travel/c_planning/06_airports/intro.html*, which exhaustively details and costs transport links between more than a hundred worldwide airports and the closest city. The site includes several airports in China, India and Japan plus Manila, Kuala Lumpur and Singapore. Getting this sort of information in advance is pretty vital: for example, it's useful to know that in Tokyo a ninety-minute, seventy-kilometre, taxi ride into town will cost no less than $200/£140, whereas the ninety-minute train trip costs $16/£11.

Jet lag for beginners

You're wide awake and feeling peckish at 3am. Try as you might, your body just does not seem to understand that it's time for sleep right now. Though it's dark and most right-minded citizens of Manila are fast asleep, you're just not tired. Chances are you've got jet lag. It happens because we travel too far, too fast – in days of old when travellers went by land or sea, nobody suffered from the effects of zooming across lots of time zones and arriving at a strange time of day or night with their body clock still operating on home time.

Some of the possible effects of jet lag are disturbed sleep patterns, hunger pangs at weird times and severe fatigue and lethargy for several days. In general, the more time zones you go through, the worse the effects are likely to be. Received opinion says that for every hour of time change it takes a day to adjust (in other words, flying from London to Delhi should theoretically take you five and a half days to adjust). If you are exhausted before you leave home the effects are likely to be worse. The younger you are, and the less rigidly timetabled your life at home is, the more adaptable you're supposed to be.

Some people find that flights leaving home at night are better for minimizing jet lag, and that eastbound flights are worse than westbound (supposedly because your body clock adapts more easily to a longer rather than a shorter daily cycle). Also, being obliged to disembark during middle-of-the-night refuelling stops makes readjustment harder – try to find out if you'll be subject to this when booking your flight.

To combat jet lag you might want to try doing one, or all, of the following:

- Adopt the timetable of your new country as soon as you land there. In other words, go to bed at 11pm Manila time, not 11pm Eastern Standard Time. If you're dozy at 3pm, have an espresso or go for a run round the block, but whatever you do don't lie down and have a nap – doing so will only lead to your taking longer to adjust.
- Take a couple of strong sleeping pills an hour before local bedtime.
- Try melatonin tablets (not yet licensed for sale in the UK), an active herbal remedy treatment that dupes the body into believing it's night.

- To avoid late-night hunger pangs, eat high-protein foods at breakfast and lunch, and high-carbohydrate (low protein) foods such as pasta at dinner.
- Do a short (five to ten minutes' worth), gentle, exercise programme before bed. A few bends and stretches will get the kinks out of your body after the flight and help you wind down and relax ready for sleep.
- Try the aromatherapy method. Geranium and lavender oils should help you sleep, whereas eucalyptus and rosemary keep you awake. For further advice, consult Jude Brown's *Aromatherapy for Travellers* (Thorsons).
- Switch on Star TV, the less-than-riveting Asian cable station.
- Soothe yourself with the thought that you'll be fully adapted in a couple of days, and meanwhile lie back and enjoy the coolness of the (very) early morning.

8

Culture shock

Do not be surprised if you don't enjoy your first few days in Asia. You might feel self-conscious, paranoid or just plain exhausted. You might even find yourself wishing you'd never come, hating the heat, sickened by the smells and appalled by the poverty. This reaction is quite normal and is called culture shock. Everyone experiences it in some form, and anyway it's all part of the challenge of dropping yourself into an alien environment.

● Be kind to yourself for a few days after arrival. You may well be jet-lagged (see p.242), extremely tired, and overwhelmed by the unbearably hot and humid climate. Check out the acclimatization guidelines in Chapter Eleven.

● Venture out gradually. It takes time to find your bearings and get used to the ways of a new country. Start off by exploring the closer, more accessible places you want to see and save the more adventurous outings for later.

● Buy a decent map of your new city; you'll feel far more confident if you know where you are.

● However haltingly, try speaking a few words of the local language. It will make you feel much less alien and you might even make some friends. (See Chapter Five for some language-learning tips.)

● Do not feel obliged to have a completely "authentic" experience right from the start. If you feel like drinking milkshakes and eating nothing but cheese sandwiches for the first few days, then why not? There'll be plenty more opportunities to experiment with local cuisine, so ease yourself in slowly.

And now for something completely different

Though your first brush with Bangkok, Beijing or Jakarta may well be disappointingly banal – a Western-style cityscape of neon Coca-Cola ads, skyscrapers and middle-class office workers – it won't be long before you realize that the *McDonald*-ization of Asia is only cosmetic.

Traditions run deep in Asia and, though urban fashions come and go, community life continues to revolve round religious practices and family units. From a Western point of view, traditional Asian

TRAVEL TALK

Once you have arrived in Asia, you'll find that the most useful, up-to-date information about where to go, what to see, where to stay, how to get there and what to avoid – in fact, stuff about pretty much every aspect of your trip – comes from other travellers. Sitting chatting in the guesthouse or over a beer you'll hear the latest from people who have already done it. They'll be more clued in than a guidebook, more impartial than the tourist office, and they won't be getting commission for sending you to cousin X's restaurant, shop or hotel.

However, it pays to assess the person you're talking to fairly carefully. Sooner or later, you'll bump into the long-time-on-the-road-been-there-done-it-all-on-one-cent-a-day-macho-man (yes, most of them *are* men), who gets his jollies by insisting to newcomers that the only way to have a really authentic Asian experience is to stay in a particular rat-infested flea pit tottering on stilts over a mosquito swamp where breakfast is a grain of rice and a lentil, if you're lucky, and the toilet is guarded by a pit of writhing black mambas who can kill with a droplet of venom from twenty paces.

This kind of traveller also loves to assure you that whichever place you thought of heading for is now spoilt; you should have been here five, ten, fifteen or twenty years ago to see the real Asia. In addition, he'll claim you really need to speak the local dialect to get even a glimpse of the local culture, and any fool with half a brain could have bought whatever you've just purchased for a tenth of the price. He never takes precautions against malaria, drinks the water from the tap, doesn't believe in travel insurance and has never had an inoculation or day's illness in his life. He's also a dangerous liar who will spoil your holiday if you let him – avoid and/or ignore as necessary and watch out that you don't fall into the same sad trap of self-aggrandizement after a few months on the road.

values can seem stiflingly conservative, especially in relation to gender roles and social conformity. Many Asians find travellers' behaviour just as strange, not least because the whole idea of an unmarried youngster (or even a long-married oldster) sloping off around the world seems bizarre if not downright irresponsible.

Women in the traditional Muslim and Hindu communities of India, Nepal, Pakistan, Indonesia and Malaysia are encouraged to be economically dependent on fathers and husbands, and to keep a low profile in public, often hiding behind veils or scarves. This can be a shock to Western travellers, who will miss having contact with local women – and of course it has an effect on how local men see Western women, too. Asian men often address all conversation to a Western woman's male companion (if she has one), while solo women may be jeered at or worse. Advice on coping with sexual harassment is given in Chapter Thirteen.

Asia is the most populous continent in the world and your first bus ride in China or India will etch that fact indelibly in your mind. Crowds and queues are the norm and there's no point protesting when five more people try to cram onto an already overloaded share-taxi. Time to dust off your sense of humour and start a section on "quaint local customs" in your journal.

The same goes for the bureaucratic tangles involved in simple transactions like cashing a travellers' cheque, and for the haphazard timetables of most Asian buses. Indonesians have a great phrase for Asian timekeeping that translates as "rubber time" – sometimes it stretches, sometimes it doesn't.

Being an alien

As an obvious outsider (or "alien", as foreigners are known in Japan), you will arouse a lot of interest, for your novelty value as well as your commercial potential. What's considered nosy in the West is often acceptable in Asia, so try not to get offended by the unflinching stares, or by women stroking your oddly coloured skin and feeling your strangely fine hair. And, if you're blond-haired or black-skinned, get ready for movie-star treatment!

Be prepared to answer endless questions about your marital status and also about your children (in most parts of Asia to be single is a calamitous state of affairs and to be childless a great misfortune). In fact, be prepared to answer questions about absolutely any private matter at all: how old you are, how much you earn and how much your air ticket cost are common conversational openers. People will read your letters over your shoulder, and eavesdrop quite blatantly too, even if they can't understand what's being said.

Sometimes it can be easier to lie about yourself – depending on who you're talking to, it may be less controversial to pretend that you're a Christian (or whatever), as agnosticism is incomprehensible to many Asian communities and atheism almost offensive. Lies can sometimes get you into more trouble of course, as the box on p.248 illustrates only too well.

You may well be asked for your home address by complete strangers who like the kudos of collecting exotic Western pals, and you'll probably have your photo taken a few times too – now there's a cultural somersault to make you think. In short, you're as fascinating to them as they are to you – and that must have some positive influence on global relations.

Curiouser and curiouser

We've all been stared at and had our hair stroked and muscles squeezed before, but I do remember a rather more significant experience on a long-distance bus journey in Vietnam. We had a toilet stop after about two hours, and this "toilet" just so happened to be a very large open field. Naturally I was rather surprised to find a man standing only 10cm away from me in such a spacious latrine. As I was going about my business he certainly wasn't minding his, and he saw nothing wrong in leaning over and staring directly at my penis during my efforts to relieve myself. "That's OK," I thought and looked straight ahead as if I hadn't noticed. It was only when he bent over and started touching it and wiggling it that I really had trouble ignoring him. This unbridled curiosity and complete absence of the concept of privacy is one of the hardest things to adjust to.

Chris Humphrey

Telling tales

Charles and I talked a lot about his travels in Indonesia. As in most parts of Asia, English-speaking Indonesians almost always ask the same four questions of every tourist: "(1) Where are you from? (2) How old? (3) You married? (4) How many babies?" Charles, already 62, never married, and childless, sometimes got tired of these questions. So, one day, when someone came up to him at a bus station in Sumatra and started firing away, Charles decided to make sure the guy would go away. He told him, "Yes, I *was* married, and sir, the reason I'm in Sumatra now is that I murdered my wife and I'm running away from the police!" The guy looked at him in awe and quickly left. Charles was satisfied, almost thrilled; he had found a way to avoid more personal questions.

An hour later the same guy came back with his whole family – about fifteen people in all – and he said to Charles, "Now you're going to tell me the story of how you murdered your wife, and I'll translate for my family!". Unfortunately, Charles' bus was delayed for ten hours, not the one hour he'd expected, and he was trapped there making up stories for the rest of the day.

Laura Littwin

"Where are you going?"

It's amazing how quickly you tire of being in the public eye so much. One surprising irritation is being asked the same question – in English – again and again. In India the line is nearly always "What is your mother country?", while in most parts of Southeast Asia it becomes "Where are you going?". The questions aren't meant to annoy, but are intended as friendly greetings: "Where are you going?" is simply the literal translation of "Hi!" or "How're you doing?". Just as in the West no one expects a full rundown on your state of health, no one in Asia really wants to know where you're heading; they just want to make contact.

Instead of getting irked by the constant chorus and more incensed still when they ignore your answer, try responding as local people do. In Indonesia, for example, you should reply "jalan jalan", which means "walking walking"; in Thailand "bpai teeo" means "I'm out having fun"; and in Malaysia the even more cryptic retort, "saya makan angin", literally translates as "I'm eating the wind".

On your best behaviour

However much you dislike the notion of being an ambassador for your country, that is how local people will see you. Similarly, your view of their country will almost certainly be coloured by how they treat you. So it pays for everyone to respect everyone else. No one expects you to traipse around Asia dressed in local fashions, but it is polite – and in some places expedient – to adapt your Western behaviour to suit the local culture. Because social rules tend to be more rigid in Asia, it's relatively easy for tourists to do the wrong thing – nine times out of ten, you'll be forgiven for being ignorant of the niceties, but there are a few behaviour codes you should definitely follow.

- Asian men and women dress modestly and find exposed flesh an embarrassment anywhere but the beach (and even when swimming they plunge in fully clothed in the more conservative countries). For more detail, see the box on p.209. Shoes are never worn indoors at home or inside temples and mosques, so remember to take them off in religious buildings and when entering people's homes – this includes some small guesthouses.
- Getting angry at anything is a very un-Asian thing to do. In fact, it's considered to be a loss of face and therefore an embarrassment for both the perpetrator and the recipient – a bit like being heard farting loudly in a posh restaurant. Always keep cool when expressing displeasure or making a complaint, trying to be as dispassionate as possible.
- Canoodling in public is frowned upon in most parts of Asia (even Japan). It's quite common for friends of the same sex to wander about with their arms round each other, but passionate embraces with the opposite sex are considered rather gross, regardless of the couple's marital status.
- Throughout Asia, the head is considered the most sacred part of a person's body, and the feet are the most profane. Try not to touch anyone on the head (even kids) or to point at anyone, or anything, with your feet.
- Avoid making eye contact with members of the opposite sex – in some Asian cultures it's seen as an unabashed come-on.
- Take special care not to offend when visiting temples and mosques or attending religious festivals. Dress modestly, observe the behaviour of local devotees, and never come between people at prayer and their altar, or take photos without permission.
- Be sensitive when discussing religion and politics with local people. In most parts of Asia, a person's faith is inviolable and should not be questioned. Censorship is rife in some Asian countries and penalties can be severe for a resident who goes public with unfashionable views. This is very much the case in China at the moment,

and in Tibet. Even in happy-go-lucky Thailand, anyone who makes disrespectful remarks about the king is liable to be put in jail. In India, on the other hand, opinionated political debate is standard fare on train journeys and in newspaper columns.

- For tips on avoiding embarrassing situations in Asian bathrooms, see Chapter Ten.

Eating and food

Strange foods and bizarre eating habits are a major feature of the Asian experience, and can often be one of the highlights. After all, Asia is home to two of the world's greatest cuisines – Indian and Chinese – and you can be sure that tandoori chicken and Peking

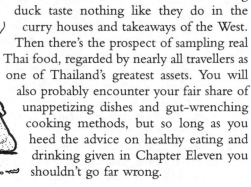

duck taste nothing like they do in the curry houses and takeaways of the West. Then there's the prospect of sampling real Thai food, regarded by nearly all travellers as one of Thailand's greatest assets. You will also probably encounter your fair share of unappetizing dishes and gut-wrenching cooking methods, but so long as you heed the advice on healthy eating and drinking given in Chapter Eleven you shouldn't go far wrong.

- Lots of Asian food is eaten with the hand (rather than a knife and fork). Sticky rice in Thailand is rolled up into tiny balls and then dunked in spicy sauces, and most meat and veg dishes in India, Nepal and Pakistan are scooped up with pieces of flat bread. Local people always use their right hand for eating because the left hand – which is used for washing after going to the toilet – is considered unclean (see Chapter Ten). There's often a washbasin in the restaurant for diners to use before and after eating, or at least a pail of water and a scoop.
- Japanese and Chinese food is eaten with chopsticks, as are noodles in all parts of Asia. But don't panic! Though it's a good laugh to watch a hapless tourist wrestling with the equivalent of two pencils and a slippery piece of spaghetti, most restaurant owners take pity on foreigners and offer spoons and forks as well.
- Asian dishes can be unbearably spicy – just one mouthful of a Lao chicken salad or a green Thai curry could be enough to send you hopping round the room in a blaze of oral agony. Water won't cool your palate down, but yoghurt is a great palliative, and so is beer, as

both contain chemicals that dissolve the chilli oils. It is possible to retrain your taste buds to actually enjoy chilli-rich food, but if you can't face that, be sure to learn the local phrase for "not spicy, please".

● Despite the strong religious culture, vegetarians get a mixed reception across Asia. With nearly all its restaurants categorized as either "Veg" or "Non-Veg", India is by far the most veggie-friendly nation. Chinese chefs, on the other hand, regard meat-free meals as unbalanced and lacklustre. The best approach is to learn the phrase for "without meat or fish" and to be prepared either to compromise when it comes to stocks and soups (which are nearly always made from fish or meat) or to eat mainly fresh market produce.

Some harsh realities

Poverty is a lot more visible in most parts of Asia than it is in the West, and in some places a lot more prevalent too. Asia is home to some of the poorest people in the world, destitute people who live in slums or on street corners, who sometimes disable their own children so that they can be sure of earning something from street-begging. It is also home to some of the wealthiest people in the world, and the rich–poor divide is distressingly pronounced in many Asian cities – beggars congregate outside the most upmarket hotels, for example, and in

> ## The Mumbai shuttle
>
> The airport shuttle bus between Mumbai (Bombay) International and Mumbai Domestic drives through seemingly endless shantytown slums, a whole suburb constructed out of cardboard boxes, rice sacks and corrugated iron. As the bus slows down at traffic lights, the noses and outstretched arms of the people who live in these slums press against the bus window, chorusing "one rupee mister, one rupee". Travellers lock the windows shut and turn the other way. It's a distressing experience – and one that you'll have again and again in Asia.
>
> **Lucy Ridout**

Hong Kong it's hard not to be shocked by the sight of glossy banking headquarters built right next door to squalid tenement slums.

For Hindus, Buddhists and Muslims of all wage brackets, the giving of alms to the sick, the disabled and the very poor (as well as to monks and holy men) is almost an obligation, a way of adding credit to your karma. These donations serve as an informal welfare system, as in most parts of Asia there's no national health service or financial support for the unemployed.

Western tourists tend to be less used to dealing with beggars, and you would not be the first one to mask your discomfort with averted eyes and a purposeful stride. Giving is a personal decision, of course; you might prefer to donate to a charity instead or, better still, get actively involved with a local charity for a few days – see Chapter One for some suggestions. Supporting local small businesses is also a positive way of preventing the encroachment of poverty; see the section on responsible tourism (opposite) for more about this. And it's always worth going out of your way to pay for small services – like giving kids in India a few rupees to stand in your bus queue for an hour, or agreeing to have your shoes shined by an elderly Malaysian man even though they don't really need a clean.

Being a wealthy tourist

All over Asia, people will express amazement at the price of your air ticket – it will seem an absolute fortune to them. Regardless of how impecunious you are, or feel, to an Indian factory worker on less than a dollar a day or a Thai waiter on the daily equivalent of $3, you are quite literally a millionaire. And your camera, watch and sunglasses will do little to change his or her opinion. Small wonder that Asians can't understand why travellers dress in torn and dirty clothing – surely if they can afford an air ticket they can stretch to a new outfit?

It's always worth trying to put money matters in context when people ask the price of your ticket, and to emphasize how hard you had to save to buy it. For example, your ticket probably cost you the equivalent of three months' rent, or about three weeks' wages. On the other hand, there's no question that you are comparatively rich – and that was probably one of the reasons why you chose to go to Asia (just as Arabs and Japanese choose to do their shopping in Europe).

Be aware that as a person with cash you can easily pump up local inflation just by paying over the odds for a taxi ride or even a mango.

Traders then overcharge the next customer and so prices rise and rise. The worst-case scenario is when goods and services become so expensive that local people can no longer afford them and so traders start catering solely for foreigners. Ask locals about prices before buying, and do some bargaining – this is an age-old Asian practice and there's advice on how to do it in Chapter Four.

Responsible tourism

Culture shock works both ways and, with Asia playing host to tens of millions of tourists every year, it's impossible to overestimate the impact that the tourist industry is having on indigenous cultures. One of the most alarming things is the way in which big businesses and multinational companies have taken over local enterprises and begun mopping up all the profits. It's not uncommon for villagers to be forced off their land because a major investor wants to build a hotel or a golf course there. Hotel complexes make a massive demand on local infrastructures and regularly wipe out village water supplies. In some cases, as in Burma, it is government officials who are forcing villagers to co-operate with their tourist projects. Many politically aware tourists are choosing to boycott Burma for this reason. For further information on this campaign, and on organizations concerned with

" Bitter moon

Full moon over Hoi An, an ancient port town in Central Vietnam. I gazed off into the heavens from my café table; Hoi An had me feeling mystical. I smiled dreamily at nothing. Enter Don, all energy and intellect, clever not merely for his mastery of the English language, but for his sharp wit and precocious insights. He plopped into the empty chair across from me and I waited for the standard shoeshine pitch. Instead this beautiful 12-year-old boy asked me if I was in love. I pulled the picture of a new boyfriend (my "fiancé" for the trip) from my notebook. I kept the picture handy to ward off prospective suitors.

After twenty minutes of fluent chatter about Vietnam, America and tourism, it was clear that little Don had a crush. In the following days we shared discussions, lunches and laughs; he enjoyed practising his English and I enjoyed his energetic company. He took me to drink my first sugar cane and insistently paid for both drinks. It never occurred to me to ask Don where he got the money.

Later in my stay, I was out with a friend when we noticed Don. "Here comes my conscience," I laughed. My friend grimaced. "Don't look now, your conscience just disappeared with that German man." It was in that moment of rage and close-to-the-bone pain that I realized Don was a prostitute. He resurfaced a little while later with a fistful of money and disappeared into the night. "

Andrea Szyper

Just say no

One of the main tourist attractions in southern India is a six-hour boat trip along the narrow waterways of Kerala. Local kids are so used to the tourists that they now race, in relays, along the river banks yelling "one pen, one pen" at the boats. What began as a game on the boat that I took soon turned into a depressing case of bear-baiting as the tourists started to chuck pens into the water just so the little boys would dive in to grab them. The kids were just normal village boys, not destitute slum-dwellers, but they knew they could get some trinkets if they "performed" for the tourists – and that's how a demeaning relationship between locals and tourists begins. Though it's natural and generous to want to give little presents, the last thing you want to do is *create* a culture of beggars.

Lucy Ridout

encouraging responsible tourism in Asia, see Basics, p.365. And for an introduction to organizations concerned with the rights of indigenous peoples, see Chapter Fourteen.

As a budget traveller, you're unlikely to be patronizing the *Hiltons* and *Sheratons* of Asia – but you may be stopping off at *McDonald's* and *KFC*. Try to support local restaurants, shops and hotels instead. That way, profits stay within the community, local residents still have power in their own neighbourhoods and the place keeps its original character – which is, after all, what you've come all this way to experience.

Try to eat local food too, so that you're not promoting a two-tier culture: one for the tourists, another for the locals. It's in your interest, anyway, as local produce is always much cheaper than imported brands. If you're very saintly you will also avoid buying bottled water – which creates tonnes of unrecyclable plastic waste every year – and filter your own from tap water instead (see Chapter Eleven).

It's also important to support local initiatives when it comes to visiting ethnic villages, so that the people you go to see – such as the hill tribes of Thailand and Vietnam, the Dyaks of Borneo and Sarawak, or the Torajans of Sulawesi – profit from your curiosity. All too many tour companies advertise trips to see "the primitive people" without giving travellers any chance to communicate with them. The ethnic communities then become little more than human zoos and exotic photo opportunities (many Thai hill-tribe villages are a classic example of this). If possible, try to organize a tour with someone from within the community, or at least make a big effort to meet the people you've travelled so far to see. Tourism has a huge effect on these remote communities, thrusting them suddenly into a cash economy they have existed without for centuries. If you can't find any useful leads from the Web sites listed on p.365, have a look at the *Community Tourism Guide*, published by Earthscan for the campaigning organization Tourism Concern, which lists and reviews a selection of locally initiated tours in Asia and the rest of the world.

It's not all bad, however. Some minority groups – like the Sakkudai of the Mentawai Islands off the coast of Sumatra – see tourist interest as a way of keeping traditions alive, of encouraging young people to learn the old ways. In Bali, too, young and old can now make a good living out of traditional performing arts. The difficult thing is for them to keep control of their own cultural heritage in an increasingly voracious tourist industry.

As a responsible tourist, you should also try to minimize your impact on the environment. In practice, this can mean anything from being careful about rubbish disposal – in particular, don't dump non-biodegradable stuff like plastic bags and bottles and dead batteries in rural areas – to sticking to marked trails when you're hiking. The Himalayas have suffered a lot from inconsiderate trekkers, and the same is true of coral reefs throughout Southeast Asia, where snorkellers and divers have broken bits off, and souvenir-buyers have encouraged local fishermen to do the same on a larger scale. Advice on getting involved in conservation projects in these areas is given in Chapter One, and there's a list of relevant organizations in Basics on p.360.

Getting around

Travelling in Asia can be both wonderful and frustrating, often at the same time. As the entire continent is teeming with people, so it is teeming with the means of getting them around. It's not so much a matter of discovering whether the journey you want to do is possible or not, but a question of deciding if it's better done by plane, train, high-speed ferry, slow boat, share-taxi, tourist bus or local bus. The huge plains of India and China are ideal for rail systems; the mountains of Nepal and northern India dictate road and air travel; the island states of the Philippines and the huge Indonesian archipelago, the mountainous jungle rivers of Borneo, and the mighty Asian waterways of the Mekong and Yangzi are served by ferries and boats in all shapes and sizes. Within some cities you even have the option of rickshaws and bullock carts. However, this exciting variety should be set against discomfort, lateness, some of the most terrifying driving on the planet, and unreliability, which are all enduring characteristics of Asian transport. Look on the travel itself as part of your adventure and you'll stand a better chance of keeping it in perspective. One way to do this is to allow plenty of time to get around. Hold-ups and delays are almost inevitable at some point, and you'll be far less stressed if you've allowed for them in your schedule. The golden rule is that distance does not equal time.

Even within individual countries the variations can be huge and you shouldn't make too many assumptions. There may not always be a direct service between two points for instance; instead your journey could involve two painfully slow local buses, a ferry and a rickshaw. On the other hand, trips that you assume to be mundane can turn out to be extremely memorable. The Shimla Toy Train, for example, winds its way through the Himalayan foothills in northern India from Kalka up to the hill station of Shimla while you sit aboard in armchairs, reading the morning newspapers and sipping tea served by uniformed waiters.

Despite initial impressions in some cities, car ownership is not widespread; instead, bicycles are common. Most Asians rely on public transport, and though systems may appear hideously complex and grotesquely overcrowded, they are cheap and often far more comprehensive than services at home. Be sure to check your guidebook for the journey you want to do and, if you are fascinated by the adventure of it all, take a look at the *Thomas Cook World Timetable* (Thomas Cook Publishing), available in good travel bookstores, which details trains and ferries across the globe; the sheer enormity of the possibilities makes for exhilarating reading.

Planes

Most countries have an internal air network of some sort. This is the fastest, but also the most expensive, way of getting around, with the added disadvantage that you are flying over the country rather than exploring it. Still, when it's too much to contemplate the sixty to a hundred hours (it can take far longer) the bus takes to do the bone-rattling 1800-kilometre Trans-Sulawesi Highway in Indonesia, spending a few short hours doing the same route in the skies looks decidedly appealing (and excellent value at around $100/£65). If the 35-hour train trip between Beijing and Chengdu is more than you can bear, then the two-and-a-half-hour plane journey begins to look attractive at $150/£100. It's worth bearing in mind that air fares are generally a lot lower than at home, so don't rule out buying plane tickets once you've arrived, especially if time is tight.

It's also worth remembering that in some countries a short plane ride can flip you into the wilderness, which might otherwise take days or weeks to reach on foot. For example, the forty-minute flight between Kathmandu and Lukla in the Everest region can save you an extra five to seven days' walking, and access to many of the highland valleys of Irian Jaya is virtually impossible without flying.

Several airlines offer internal air passes at good rates to tourists, although the passes are probably only worthwhile if you are intending to cover a huge amount of ground in as short a time as possible. For example, Indian Airlines offers a fifteen-day Discover India fare for $500/£330, allowing unlimited use of their flights throughout the country during the period, as long as you only pass through each airport once. Others restrict their concessions to travellers who have travelled into the country with them, such as Malaysia Airlines and Garuda in Indonesia. If you are thinking of buying an air pass, it pays to do your research and see how much the flight would cost if you bought it locally. For example, the Garuda deal is that each flight on the air pass costs $75/£50, $125/£80 or $150/£100 (depending on the precise route), which represents a small saving on longer trips but means you end up paying over the odds if you use it for short hops; furthermore these internal flights must be booked from abroad if you're using the air pass, which ties you down. At certain times however, national airlines may offer a free internal flight or two to tourists travelling internationally with them. It's worth checking what deals are available at the time of booking your international tickets.

If you are travelling to more than one Southeast Asian country, the ASEAN Pass sold by national airlines in Brunei (Royal Brunei Airlines), Indonesia (Garuda), Singapore (Singapore Airlines), Malaysia (Malaysia Airlines), the Philippines (Philippine Airlines), Thailand (Thai International Airlines) and Vietnam (Vietnam Airlines) is an excellent deal. The pass allows you to buy three to six flights between and within those countries for around $100/£65 each. You must buy the pass outside the countries concerned, and book and confirm your flights at that time (though you can change the dates later) and complete travel within a two-month period. There are certain other restrictions; contact the airlines for details.

When using Asian airlines, the following tips should make your trip easier:

- Some of the airlines flying internal routes are small setups with minimal backup both on and off the ground. Don't expect quite the organization or efficiency of the airlines at home.
- It's worth avoiding certain domestic Asian airlines which have poor safety records; check with ⓦ *www.airsafe.com*, which lists safety records of many Asian airlines, or your embassy before you book.
- Make bookings in person and get confirmation in writing, especially if your ticket will be issued later. Take a note of the name of the person you dealt with, in case of problems later
- Don't let the booking office keep your passport overnight – it can be useful to have photocopies of the key pages ready for them .
- Having booked a seat, you often need to reconfirm with the airline before travel. Check the rules when you book.
- If the airline seems to have lost your booking despite all the evidence you can produce, get them to look under your first or even your middle name, as misfiling is common.
- Some airline offices find it virtually impossible to issue confirmed tickets for flights from a city other than the one they are in. If you get a ticket under these circumstances, be sure to reconfirm with the airline when you get to the place you'll be flying from.
- Flights are often overbooked, cancelled or delayed at short notice due to monsoons, typhoons, heavy snowfall and lack of aircraft. The more flexibility you can build into your timetable, the better.
- Check in as early as possible; if flights are overbooked, boarding passes are often given out on a first-come, first-served basis.
- Follow the advice on hand baggage on p.230 – just because a flight is internal doesn't mean you can't get delayed and/or your baggage lost.
- Certain items are banned on Asian planes. Penknives and Swiss Army knives are often confiscated from hand baggage and returned at your destination; some items are banned not because they could be dangerous but because they smell so bad – the stinking fruit called durian, and fish sauce, are the most notorious.

Long-distance buses

Bus travel in Asia is one of the most flavoursome experiences the continent has to offer: all of human life is jammed together, often with a few animals as well, passing through the landscape slowly enough to appreciate it. Inside, many drivers personalize their vehicles with pictures of their favourite gods and goddesses, flashing

Room on top

"

It is important to have the
right attitude when travelling
Asian-style, eg hanging from the side of
a vehicle, teetering from the top like a
flagpole in the wind or – if you are lucky
enough to be inside – cramped in a fetal
position with your knees in your face.
These situations need meditation;
releasing the mind from the perils of
travel is an absolute necessity for
psychological survival.

We'd stepped on a few hands on the
climb to the last free spaces – on the
roof, but the other passengers didn't
seem to mind. It took a few minutes to
get the overstuffed truck moving at a
reasonable clip down a one-lane road
with barely a shoulder on either side and
a sheer drop into the marshlands. I
hoped the luggage I was holding on to
was firmly attached to the roof. Several
times as we moved over to the side of
the road we tipped until I could see my
reflection in the water all too clearly. I
figured if the truck rolled over I'd be fine
in the water – until the truck and other
passengers landed on top of me.
Swaying like a willow tree in the wind,
the vehicle recovered again and again
from potentially disastrous situations
and continued on its way in
its charmed state of
existence.

"

Shannon Brady

fairy lights and an incense stick or
two on the dashboard. For some drivers the bus is their home and they
eat and sleep on board when it's not
in use.

The quality of the buses, however,
is very variable – the best ones have
air-conditioning, comfortable reclining seats and toilets on board; the
worst feature cracked or missing
window glass, ripped seats and minimal suspension. Try to look at the
bus before you book a seat, whatever the ticket-seller may tell you about
his pristine speedmobile that will
whisk you to your destination faster,
and more safely, than any other operator's. The back seats are the bumpiest, the front seats give a grandstand
view of the driver's technique and an
earful of his choice of music and/or
video.

Many cities have separate bus stations for local and long-distance destinations, and the larger the city the
more likely it is to have several long-distance terminals, often on opposite
sides of town far from the city centre
– Bangkok, Ho Chi Minh City,
Jakarta and Beijing are among the
most confusing. A good guidebook
will provide you with enough information to orientate yourself and get
into town, or vice versa.

Tickets are extremely economical
when compared to travel at home –
for example, the 2200-kilometre,
three-day, three-night trip from
Medan on Sumatra to Jakarta on Java
costs $15–40/£10–25, depending

on the degree of comfort you want. In many cases your ticket includes a ferry crossing or two between neighbouring islands. However, it can sometimes appear totally impossible to get a ticket or seat on a bus – there are just too many people and they are all far more adept at forcing their way through the crush than you. Try booking through an agency for a small fee (often  your accommodation will do this for you). As departure time gets close you could consider paying a small boy to climb through a bus window and occupy a seat for you until you can get to it.

Asian buses are built for generally smaller Asian physiques, so don't underestimate the stamina needed to cope with several days and nights jammed on board. Consider booking two seats if you are quite large in any dimension and can afford it, although you'll have to be pretty assertive to keep both seats to yourself as the bus gets steadily more packed along the way. In countries with extensive train systems – India and China are prime examples – it's usually faster and far more comfortable to do long-haul trips on the train.

Tourist buses

In some countries where the tourist infrastructure is developing, private companies have started operating special tourist bus services exclusively for foreign visitors. On these buses, there's always plenty of space for luggage, including pushchairs and wheelchairs, though in other respects the vehicles themselves aren't particularly different from regular buses – many aren't even air-conditioned. However, they do offer a direct, hassle-free, though more expensive, service between main tourist centres. To get from Kuta to Ubud on Bali by public transport, for example, you have to change at least three times in a part of the island where routes are especially confusing, but a tourist bus will get you there in one go for around three times the ordinary fare. In Nepal, tourist buses ply between the main tourist destinations, are generally safer than local services and have bigger seats. It pays to do your research, though – on the more straightforward routes you'll be paying a lot for very little.

Is it safe?

There is no escaping the fact that much road travel in Asia is extremely hair-raising. Buses often travel far too fast for the conditions – overtaking on blind corners is a regular occurrence – and drivers frequently take some form of stimulant to stay awake as a lot of long-distance services travel at night. Not surprisingly, accidents do happen. Remember that even once you've bought a ticket it's still your choice whether or not to climb on board any particular bus.

Having a pleasant journey

These suggestions may improve your journey:

- Baggage is often put on top of the bus where there may well be other passengers riding alongside it. As a security measure, you might consider chaining your pack to the roof rack (see p.206 for more) so you won't be anxiously craning your neck out of the window at every stop to see if your stuff's still there.
- Make sure you have plenty of water, food and toilet paper. Stops are often at weird times when you may not want to eat and at places with limited facilities.

KARMA ARMOUR

Most Asian people have a rather more fatalistic approach to accidents and misfortune than we do in the West. We are increasingly of the view that we can, and indeed have the right to, control anything nasty happening to us. In contrast, Buddhists and Hindus believe in karma, whereby a previous existence influences the events in their current life. Thus a traffic accident is more likely to be seen as preordained karmic retribution than as a direct result of irresponsible driving. Muslims presage most plans with the word *Inshallah* ("if God wishes"), showing they accept that they do not have ultimate control over the future. This can be infuriating or even downright terrifying if you're on a bus with a maniac driver who seems intent on killing you all. It's unlikely that any of the other passengers will try to moderate any lunatic behaviour; you may want to try or even get off and wait for the next bus.

- Consider packing earplugs, as Asian buses usually travel with music tapes or videos turned up full volume for the entire length of the journey.
- A neck-pillow is an excellent idea on long bus journeys – much better than jolting up and down on the shoulder of the person next to you.
- A blanket, sarong or jacket is useful for warmth, especially on overnight trips.
- However uncomfortable, you should keep your money belt on and well hidden: you are vulnerable when sleeping, and theft isn't unknown.
- Never accept food or drink from strangers – unfortunately this can be a means of drugging travellers before robbing them.

Best bus rides

- Riding the Halsema Highway. One of the most awesome roads in Southeast Asia, this rough, potholed highway shadows the twisted course of the Chico river valley from Baguio to Bontoc in the Philippines, snaking its way up into the Central Cordillera mountains and affording panoramic views over the white-water river valleys below. The trip takes seven hours and tops 2000m at its highest point. Sit on the right-hand side of the bus, have your camera to hand, and take travel-sickness pills before setting off.
- The Karakoram Highway. The sheer scale of the 1300-kilometre road which links Islamabad in Pakistan with Kashgar in China is impressive enough, but the stunning and ever-changing scenery as the bus twists and curves through the Karakoram mountain range is equally magical, as is the fact that such an incredible feat of engineering was ever achieved.
- Manali–Leh Highway. The two- to three-day marathon trip between Manali in Himachal Pradesh and Leh in Ladakh, both in India, offers spellbinding mountain passes, massive and apparently endless valleys, gorges, plains and cliffs as it winds its way through the Himalayas and up onto the Tibetan plateau.
- The Cross-Island Highway. The scenery as the highway heads up and across the central mountains of Taiwan is impressive enough, with misty valleys fading evocatively into the distance between fold after fold of wooded mountains. At the end of the journey, Taroko Gorge is justifiably one of Taiwan's most popular tourist attractions, as the road edges between the cliffside and the river thundering below.

Hard seat hell

We boarded the train to Chengdu and our expectations for the coming journey were high. We were well stocked with fruit, chocolate and enough biscuits to see us through the coming twenty hours. We were also naively optimistic about the chances of upgrading our seats.

Tickets for hard seats were the only ones available. No amount of charm, joviality or bare-faced begging could persuade our stony-faced ticket vendor to part with the more comfortable hard sleeper or even the ludicrously overpriced soft sleeper options usually reserved for party cadres. "No," he informed us, "no have."

Later we discovered that a hefty hard-currency "present" would have secured a comfortable passage. Instead I waited in vain for a non-existent legitimate bed to become available at the "next station . . . next station . . . next station". Sweat mingled freely with grime and smoke as the day turned into night and day again. My companions slept and my frustration and anger rose, aided by the neighbouring cherubic Chinese child clearing his sinuses, gulping and with an almighty hoik landing a dribble right on top of my big toe. His father looked on proudly.

Daniel Gooding

Trains

Trains offer a memorable and often safer means of travel across large tracts of Asia. Although often distressingly crowded and rather dirty, especially in the cheaper classes, train travel thrusts you into the company of local people. You'll get brilliant views too: the sun setting over rice paddies in central Thailand and southern India; soaring cliffs and white-sand beaches along the coast between Da Nang and Hué in Vietnam; and dizzying drops between the peaks en route from Peshawar to the summit of the Khyber Pass.

When booking a train ticket, make sure you know whether the service is a stopping one or an express. Stopping services can literally stop at every sign of human habitation along the way, with hawkers plying tea, snacks, books and toys continually hopping on and off even during the night. While these slow trains are a lively experience with plenty to keep you entertained, they can take twice as long as the express without a corresponding halving of the fare.

You don't necessarily have to wait until you are in-country to get train information. For example, Indian Railways, one of the most remarkable setups in the world, shifting over 11 million passengers daily, has a Web site Ⓦ *www.indianrailway.com* supplying information on the entire network (in English or Hindi) in as much detail as anyone could need.

Tickets

Ticket options vary from system to system – Indian Railways has seven different classes – but you'll usually have a choice between hard and soft seats or berths and between carriages with and without fan and air-conditioning. Generally, the longer the trip, the more advisable it is to go for a bit of comfort.

Fares are good value, with the very cheapest seats often the same price as the equivalent trip on a bus. For the twenty-hour journey between Beijing and Shanghai, expect to pay from $40/£25 to $120/£75 depending on the class, while in Vietnam, the two-day haul from Hanoi to Ho Chi Minh City costs between $45/£30 and $90/£60.

Actually getting hold of a ticket can be a major hurdle; for long-distance, sleeper and first-class travel, these invariably need to be booked several days in advance (short-hop and third-class tickets can often be bought on the train). Although foreigners' ticket offices can cut down hassle in larger cities in China, Thailand and India, and women-only queues in India can help, you may spend hours fighting your way through a mass of people only to find the train you want is already fully booked. Many travel agents and hotel staff can buy tickets for you for a small fee – this is money well spent. You won't find many ticket barriers on Asian rail networks (Japan is an exception), but your ticket will be checked on board, often several times.

Sleepers

Remember that if you book a sleeper service you'll be saving on accommodation costs, so it can be worth splashing out to get a good night's sleep. The sleeping areas usually consist of two or three tiers of bunks that may run the length of the railway carriage or be broken up into compartments by curtains or hard walls. Top bunks are marginally cheaper in some countries, China for example, and are the safest for your luggage, but cigarette smoke tends to gather up there and you may be next to a blaring radio, a light that stays on permanently, or right under a fan, which can be chilly. On the bottom bunks you'll often get people sitting along the edge and talking, smoking, eating and playing cards while you try to sleep. Thai trains are a pleasant anomaly – staff fold sleepers down out of the seats at night and make them up with fresh linen for you. Sleeping compartments can get surprisingly chilly at night, so remember to keep your warmer clothing handy. In India, though, you can rent extra bedding very cheaply on board.

Safety

The security issues on trains are pretty similar to those on long-distance buses, except that you'll have all your stuff with you and your fellow passengers have more chance to move around. In addition, the following may help:

- Lock your bags and padlock them to something immovable, like the berth or seat.
- Keep small bags away from windows so they can't get rifled at stations.
- Solo women travellers in India and Pakistan may feel more comfortable in the women-only compartments, especially on long trips.

Train passes

Train passes are available for travel in India, Thailand, Malaysia and Japan. You should check details before you leave home as the Japan Rail Pass, for example, is only available outside the country. Consider the individual passes carefully to work out whether they are good value or not. You'd need to travel a huge amount to make India's Indrail Pass – available for periods of one to ninety days in first or second class – financially worthwhile, but its chief advantage is that it saves you queueing for tickets, you get priority for tourist quotas on busy trains and you can make and cancel reservations free of charge. Similarly, the Thai and Malaysian passes may not be worthwhile unless you are travelling a great deal. On the other hand, the seven-day version of the Japan Rail Pass pays for itself in just one return trip from Tokyo to Osaka.

Top train rides

- The Death Railway – so called because thousands of the World War II prisoners-of-war who built it died during its construction – from Kanchanaburi to Nam Tok in Thailand is a stunning feat of engineering. The track was blasted through mountains and rock faces and traverses numerous amazing bridges, passing along and over the River Kwai and stopping at flower-decked villages.

- The most scenic way of getting to Ooty, the former colonial outpost in India's Blue Mountains, is to take the Toy Train, a coal-fired, narrow-gauge, three-carriage antique that travels at around 11km per hour. You're treated to gorgeous views of the hills as you pass through forested slopes and tea plantations.

- The steam railway that links Peshawar and the Khyber Pass in Pakistan, passing through dramatic, barren, tribal land, is pretty unmissable. The British-built railway has 34 tunnels and 92 bridges along the fifty-kilometre route, and is so steep in places that trains need another engine at the back to push them up.

- If money's no object, consider treating yourself to a ride on the Eastern & Oriental Express. This deluxe train is modelled on the original Orient Express, with wood panelling, cordon-bleu meals and first-class service throughout the 41 hours it takes to travel from Singapore via Kuala Lumpur and the River Kwai to Bangkok at a cost of around $1400/£850 per berth. It also does a shorter, cheaper, run between Bangkok and Chiang Mai.

- With an average speed of 261.8km/hr, the *Nozomi-503* is the fastest train in the world, and also one of the smoothest. It's the star of the famous fleet of Japanese bullet trains or *shinkansen*, and races along the coast from Tokyo to Fukuoka (via Kyoto, Osaka and Hiroshima) in just five hours.

Boats

One of the highlights of travel in Asia is the opportunity to make some spectacular boat journeys. The island nations of Indonesia, with over thirteen thousand islands, and the Philippines, with seven thousand, offer countless long- and short-distance trips, but in most Asian countries you'll have the chance to cruise on rivers and across lakes and lagoons as well as between islands. Boat travel is a convenient and economical alternative to flying, with the bonus of great views and the chance to see marine and river wildlife at close hand.

In some areas of Kalimantan in Indonesia, Sarawak in Malaysia and Laos, for example, river transport is the only way to get around, whereas in many cities, such as Bangkok, river ferries and taxis are considerably faster than road transport, as well as being a cooler and more pleasant way to travel.

Bearing in mind that long-distance trips can last several days, it pays to make some advance preparations:

- If you're travelling deck class, take a waterproof sheet to lie on as the floor gets very damp.
- Keep precious things, especially your camera and film, in waterproof bags. Particularly in smaller boats, ocean waves or wash from other river craft can sometimes drench you.
- Take your own food and water, as the quality of what's available on board – and there might be nothing – is often variable. Boats break down or get delayed or diverted due to bad weather conditions, and your journey may take longer than anticipated.
- It gets cold at sea – keep warm clothing near the top of your pack.
- Equally, the sun can be scorching, so keep sun protection, hats and lotion to hand.
- Put some sea-sickness tablets in your pack even if you don't normally suffer. The combination of big swells and deafening engines belching noxious fumes can affect even the most hardened stomach.

Best boat trips

- The Star Ferry across Hong Kong Harbour gives you the city's best views of the skyscraper skyline.
- Arriving at Puerto Galera on Mindanao in the Philippines. Although most of the two-hour journey from Batangas City is unspectacular, the approach to Puerto Galera itself is incredible – a tiny entrance through a narrow strait fringed with tropical palms before opening out into a huge and picturesque bay.
- Backwater trips in Kerala, South India. The two-hour public ferry service between Allappuzha and Kottayam takes you along water-lily-choked canals and across lagoons, slicing through farmland and coconut plantations, past temples, mosques and waterfront houses. It's much more interesting than the eight-hour tourist ride from Allappuzha to Kollam.
- Across the Brahmaputra (Tsangpo) River to Samye Monastery in Tibet. Amid stunningly cold, high-altitude scenery, a noisy, smoky flat-bottomed boat weaves between sandbanks for well over an hour. Unforgettable.
- The Bangkok *khlongs*. A ride on these inky-black and stinky canals gives an unsurpassed insight into Bangkok's watery suburbs, including teak houses where longboats are the family car, half-submerged temple grounds, kids playing in the water, men bathing

and women doing the washing-up as you swish past.

- The towering limestone outcrops in Ha Long Bay, Vietnam: sixteen thousand islands in 1500 square kilometres of water.
- The two-day journey by slow cargo boat down the Mekong River from Houayxai to Louang Phabang is one of the most popular things to do in Laos. It's not exactly a luxurious way to travel – there are no seats and no cabin accommodation – but the trip gives you plenty of time to appreciate the shifting panoramas of rice fields, limestone karst, temples and villages along the waterside.

City transport

It's in the cities that you'll see the full and glorious range of Asian transport, and here that you can witness the incredible juxtaposition of traditional and ultramodern. As well as buses, taxis and subway systems, be prepared for minibuses, motorcycle taxis, rickshaws, three-wheelers and even horse carts. You'll be flung into close, sometimes very close, proximity with your fellow passengers, who'll possibly be travelling together with their vegetables, goats and chickens for market, babies for the clinic and kids for school. A sense of humour is a prerequisite for travel this way.

Make it a point to find out how to get around a city, as this is a great

Monsoon miracle

Thai ferries are always full and always run on time, or close to it. Broken gadgets are usually repaired with random pieces of wire, shoelaces or just held together manually. This is the miracle of Thai transportation. You're always going somehow – storms, rain and floods be damned.

I hopped on the boat headed for Ko Tao. As we waited for passengers to board, I established myself on a wooden bench and watched a Thai official remove all the life jackets on board. I breathed deeply. My blind faith in Thai efficiency kicked in – we'd get there somehow, some time.

It began to rain and off we went. We dipped and trundled into the open sea, away from land, warm hotel beds and everything safe. After half an hour we encountered not waves anymore, but swells the size of two-storey buildings which rocked and crashed our little ferry from side to side, playing with us as a cat might bat a mouse around the room. We were reassured by the crew when the engines cut for a spell, that it was only engine trouble, nothing more. I sat on my bench and attempted to read as water crashed through the doorways onto backpacks and eventually onto me.

The swells grew higher, meaner and quicker. Book forgotten, I looked at my white knuckles, straining to keep my body on board and in an upright position. Around me, the other passengers held on as I did to whatever they could to prevent themselves from being catapulted out of the boat. I thought of my mother. She'd be devastated to learn of my demise. No glory, no excitement. Another drowning in a raging sea. My story would end up in the obscure international section of newspapers.

Our prospects looked grim. So I began to pray and remembered, as words failed to flow, that I knew no prayers whatsoever. I wished I had been raised in some religious setting. Nonetheless, I continued: "Holy Mother of God," I chanted, "please save us." And after one hour she did. I watched the swells change from assaulting us head on, to broadside, to coming in from the stern as we slowly turned to Ko Pha-Ngan, an island between Ko Samui and Ko Tao. I was alive and thankful to walk on land.

Nicole Meyer

BEWARE WOMEN!

Monks in Thailand, Laos, Cambodia and Vietnam are allowed no physical contact at all with women. If they accidentally touch or are touched by a woman they must engage in a lengthy series of purification rituals. On public transport monks often congregate in particular places such as on the back seat of buses. No matter how crowded the vehicle, women travellers should not sit next to a monk and should be very careful if passing close to one. Local people will give up their seat for a monk and you'll be appreciated if you offer to do the same.

In Laos, it's taboo for women to sit on the roof of a bus or a boat. The Lao believe that a woman has the power to ruin the potency of the amulets carried by Lao men simply by placing herself physically above him. Furthermore, boats are thought to possess a guardian spirit, and a woman riding on the roof offends this spirit, which is to invite dire consequences for passengers and crew.

way to increase your confidence in a place and helps you begin to feel less alien. You may adore Calcutta but be daunted by Delhi purely because you've worked out a couple of the central Calcutta bus routes, whereas the Delhi system remains a mystery, resulting in constant aggravation with taxi and rickshaw drivers.

Local buses

Most Asian cities have a mixture of large and small buses supplemented by a whole host of smaller minibuses, vans or motorized three-wheelers. The general rule seems to be that the smaller the vehicle, the less rigid the route and the greater the linguistic and geographical skills needed to find out where they are going; the smaller ones also stop wherever passengers want to get on and off. All these vehicles are cheap, but are very slow and packed solid with passengers, and, if the driver fancies a lunchtime break at the market en route, you'll have to wait the twenty minutes or so it takes him to buy and eat his noodle soup. You'll see all of Asian life on the buses, and depending on your mood they are either great or intensely frustrating.

In some places, such as Bangkok, it is possible – well nigh essential – to get a map of local bus services. Otherwise, get directions at the tourist information office, from your guidebook or at your hotel. Ask again for your destination when you're on board, just to be sure the bus is really going there. The following tips will help you negotiate the confusion more easily:

- Before you set off, find out the fare schedule (prices are generally incredibly cheap) and how to pay.
- Take a pocketful of small-denomination coins or notes as getting change is a nightmare.
- You'll find that drivers, conductors and other passengers are generally helpful and concerned to get you where you want to go, although rush-hour commuters the world over aren't the most patient of folks and Asia is no exception.
- Give yourself as much time as you can and keep calm, and you'll soon be hopping around town like a local. Remember, it doesn't really matter if you get lost. You're on holiday!
- Be very wary of pickpockets and slashers with razor-sharp knives who cut through material, canvas and the straps of shoulder bags.
- Women travelling on crowded city buses are, unfortunately, prime targets for sexual harassment ("Eve teasing" as it's called in India), and you may well experience groping hands, men squeezing past and "accidental" touches and brushes against you.

Taxis

Most cities and built-up areas have official taxis, a convenient and usually very reasonably priced way to get from door to door. Find out what they look like and whether they should have meters or not, and you're ready to go.

There are, though, a few complications associated with using cabs. Most Asian taxis are supposed to have meters; however, these may or may not be a true indication of the full cost. Sometimes when prices go up the meters don't get adjusted until much later. In these cases, drivers carry official charts to convert from the meter price to the new fare. In other places there may be legitimate additional charges, such as entry to the central area of Singapore, tunnel toll charges in Hong Kong and surcharges after midnight. At many Asian airports the meter is officially suspended and taxis operate on a fixed price tariff to nearby destinations.

On occasions when the taxi meter is not working, drivers will negotiate a fare with the passenger. You may well experience taxi drivers claiming that the meter is not working or simply refusing to use it because they believe, usually correctly, that they can get a higher fare out of ignorant tourists than they can by using the meter. The situation varies from place to place: in some it is worth holding out and flagging down cab after cab until you get one to use the meter; in others you might as well start your negotiation with the first one that comes along.

If the meter isn't working, negotiate the price before you get in. The price is per cab, not per person, and this is a good place to hone your bargaining skills (see p.175); the tactics are the same whether you're getting a ride or buying a mango. This is one area where a bit of research among other travellers is very useful indeed; but generally speaking, cabs in Indonesia, Thailand and India are so cheap – well under $5/£3 to get across town – that if there are three or four of you with luggage, it's hardly worth bothering with a crowded bus. On the other hand, prices in Japan are sky high, around $165/£110 for a sixty-minute ride from Central Osaka to Osaka International Airport; though taxis in Singapore and Hong Kong aren't so exorbitant, you'll still need to have plenty of spare cash to jump into them regularly.

Motorbike taxis

In many areas, motorbikes operate as taxis. They are a high-risk, big-thrill way to get around – a few minutes screeching through the rush-hour Bangkok traffic on the back of one and you'll understand the real meaning of fear. Bikes are especially useful in busy cities, though, as they can nip in and out of traffic jams and even zoom up one-way streets the wrong way.

Negotiate the fare before you get on and, no matter how derisory the helmet offered or the means of keeping it on your head, you should still wear it. The drivers may or may not be able to manage a backpack – you might have to wear it, which is very uncomfortable after a while, or get it balanced between the handlebars.

Cycle-rickshaws

Rickshaws are particularly useful for backroads where there is no other form of public transport, and for finding obscure addresses – many of the drivers know every inch of their territory. They are also a lovely sedate

way to travel, although you should be prepared to hop out at the foot of the most daunting hills, and if you're stuck in any traffic you'll be breathing in the exhaust fumes of every larger vehicle on the road.

A variety of different incarnations of rickshaw are found across Asia. The most ancient form, with a single man running on foot between two poles, pulling a seat perched above two wheels, has thankfully all but died out. Calcutta is the last outpost of such vehicles in Asia, and by the time you get there they may well have been replaced by cycle-rickshaws. It can feel morally uncomfortable sitting on the shaded, padded seat in a rickshaw while the wallah exhausts himself ferrying you around in the midday sun: are you shortening the poor chap's life, ensuring he suffers a chronically painful old age with wrecked joints, or are you making sure his children at least get a meal to eat that evening?

Cycle-rickshaws have different designs and names depending on the country: *cyclo* in Vietnam and Cambodia, *samlor* in Thailand and *becak* in Indonesia. With all rickshaws, negotiate the price before you get in and make sure it's clear whether it is for the vehicle or per person. The price will depend not only on distance but also on the number of hills, amount of luggage and the effort the man thinks he'll have to put in. You can also negotiate an hourly rate if you plan to visit several places.

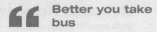

Better you take bus

I had always refused the Calcutta rickshaws despite their bell-ringing blandishments every time I set foot outside my hotel. However, one day after wandering all over the backstreets of the city I was foot-sore, worn out by the heat and flies, and found myself well off the beaten track. I approached the nearest rickshaw driver and named my hotel. He looked me up and down, took in my height and likely weight at a glance, and looked at the sun blazing down. Then he raised an arm towards the nearest main road: "Better you take bus," he decided.

Lesley Reader

Motorized rickshaws

More sophisticated versions of rickshaws are motor-rickshaws, also known as auto-rickshaws (*auto* in India, *bajaj* in Indonesia, *cyclo mai* in Vietnam and *tuk tuk* in Thailand). They are noisy (*tuk tuk*s are so named because of the sound they make), smelly, unstable three-wheelers with the driver in front and enough space for a couple of passengers behind (but that doesn't stop four or five crowding aboard on occasion).

Driven by a grossly underpowered two-stroke engine, motor-rickshaws are extremely useful if you want wheels from A to B but balk at taxi fares. Like taxis they are usually supposed to have meters though – as with taxis – it's often difficult to get the drivers to use them. Rides can be hair-raising, as these little vehicles are very nippy. Received wisdom in Bangkok is to find an elderly *tuk tuk* driver, the theory being that in this notoriously manic profession he has survived to drive again. There's only one problem – it seems virtually impossible to find a single driver of these machines who looks older than sixteen.

Vehicle rental

Throughout Asia the law is variable on foreigners driving rental cars. In China, for example, foreigners may only drive in certain areas: Beijing, Shanghai, Hong Kong and Sanya on Hainan Island. However, in most countries an International Driver's Licence (get this before you leave home) will give you full access to the roads. Expect to pay the equivalent of $20/£14 per day in India, $40/£25 in China, $10/£7 in Bali and $25/£16 in the remainder of Indonesia (insurance and petrol not included) for a jeep or small saloon car. Most capital cities have international rental companies such as Hertz, Budget, Avis and Europcar, which means you can book your vehicle in advance, but these places are almost always more expensive than local firms.

If you want to travel by car, you should consider the (often minimal) additional cost of hiring a local driver as well (even though you'll have to pay his food and, if you're touring overnight, his lodging costs as well, though the additional expense is usually not significant). The advantage of a local driver is that you can spend all your time enjoying the scenery, he'll probably know the way (or at least be better at asking if he gets lost), will often have good suggestions about side-trips and will hopefully offer a useful insight into the local area and people. And, if anything goes wrong, he carries the can: killing a cow in Nepal carries roughly the same penalty as killing a person – up to twenty years in prison. An alternative is to rent a local taxi for a day, a week or whatever – a popular and economical idea in India. It's a good way to see a lot quite quickly, visit outlying districts and do it all in a bit of comfort. If you decide to drive yourself, the following tips may help:

- Make sure you know the legal speed limits and other requirements. In Indonesia you must carry the vehicle's registration papers as well as your own. Balinese police love to stop tourists and issue on-the-spot fines if they aren't carrying the right documentation.
- Inspect the vehicle carefully before you accept it and make a note, signed by the owner also, of any scratches or dents, or you may get blamed for these.
- Check things you would take for granted in a rental vehicle at home: the lights, horn, windscreen wipers/washers, door locks, petrol cap.
- Make sure you know how to get the bonnet up and check the spare tyre (is there one?), tool kit and jack.
- In some parts of Asia, insurance is not available for rental vehicles; if it is available, it's pricey. You should definitely buy insurance if you can, but make sure you know what's covered. In particular, check how much the excess is – the amount you will have to pay if there's a crash.
- Find out the local rules of the road. The official version should be in a comprehensive guidebook, but spend some time observing what goes on around you – there's often a big gap between the legal and the habitual. In Beijing, nobody seems to obey red lights, while in Sumatra they are ignored if you are turning left.
- Be alert and considerate. Hardly a week goes by on the island of Phuket in Thailand without one foreign driver racing him or herself into a crumpled smash on the roadside. Island roads are not racetracks.

Motorbikes

Motorbikes are available for rent in many places and are a great way to travel independently to out of the way places at reasonable cost. All the tips for car drivers above apply to motorbikes, with the additional proviso that, whatever the local laws dictate, driver and passenger should both wear helmets and always cover up. However tempting it is to feel the wind on bare limbs, it's madness not to have some sort of protection in case you come off, and you also

Respect

To stay safe you must be respected. When I walked through the bazaar of one town in Pakistan, even fully robed, I was stared at, catcalled by giggly young men and felt a little vulnerable – a shameless foreign woman unaccompanied in male territory. The next day I rode into the same market on my motorbike. No giggles. No lechery. Previously disapproving old men decided I was worthy of a nod. Young men approached to make intelligent conversation and ask about the bike. Suddenly I became a person; I had respect again. The bike takes the focus off you and your marital status, opens doors and is a great conversation starter.

Nicki McCormick

need to be especially careful of exhaust pipes – many a pillion passenger ends up with a nasty burn on their calf, which is no fun especially in the tropical heat. Be aware that unpaved roads can be unpredictable, varying from sand to mud depending on the weather conditions – motorbike riding in Asia is not for novices.

Bicycles

A bicycle is the only vehicle that millions of Asians will ever own, and bikes are available for rent pretty much everywhere. Levels of sophistication vary from mountain bikes to bone-shakers that barely hold together. If you want to rent a bike, ask at your guesthouse or at local shops; you'll get better rates for longer rents. Security can be a problem – the exception is in Chinese cities where there are official bike parks – and you should always use a chain or lock.

A few words of warning:

- Try out the bike before parting with your money. Wonky front wheels, seats with springs sticking through and clunking chains get a bit wearing after an hour or so. Be especially careful to check the brakes. A working bell is essential for riding all over Asia.
- Be aware that most bikes come without a helmet and without efficient lights, so you must be home by dark.
- Most other road users will behave as though you don't exist.

- Carry plenty of water – cycling is thirsty work.
- Protect yourself from the sun.
- Don't be overambitious in tropical conditions and overdo it. In Beijing, where distances are enormous, it doesn't cost much to get a taxi to take you and your bike back to your accommodation if you get too exhausted.

Hitch-hiking

The cost of travel in Asia is so low that hitching isn't really necessary for tourists, though in out-of-the-way places, with the last bus gone, not a taxi in sight and still 40km to go to your hotel, it sometimes becomes the only option. Most drivers will expect payment from their passengers. Hitch-hiking carries the same risks wherever you are, and just because you're on holiday, don't suspend the instincts that keep you safe at home. If you do decide to hitch a ride, bear in mind that in some areas (Tibet is one example) drivers of trucks and other private vehicles are not legally permitted to carry foreigners, and risk heavy penalties if they are caught doing so.

Walking

With the dizzying range of forms of transport, don't forget the pleasures of simply walking around – just get out of the guesthouse and wander where the fancy takes you. Asian life is lived on the streets – yes, there are beggars, hawkers and hustlers galore, but there are also millions of people going about their everyday lives, commuting to work, shopping at street markets, praying at tiny shrines, having a snack at food stalls, gambling or simply watching the world go by. Bear in mind that:

- Asian roads can be terrifying to cross. Walk with a local person between you and oncoming traffic. When they move, you move; when they stop, you stop.
- jaywalking is illegal in many places – Singapore is one; Indonesia, another. You must obey pedestrian signs and use footbridges and underpasses if they exist.
- pedestrian survival can depend on knowing the rules of the road: remember which way oncoming traffic is approaching from and be aware that drivers may interpret stop signs differently from you.

Tours

Just as tourist bus services can take the strain out of complicated connections, so there are plenty of travel agents and tour companies in Asia offering organized trips, which can make things a lot smoother. You may leave home vowing to see it all and do it all independently, but it's worth bearing a few things in mind:

- A day or half-day city tour can be an excellent way to orient yourself. You'll see far more than you could on public transport and it'll help you decide what you do and don't want to spend more time exploring on your own.
- In some places, a tour is very often the only way to get to certain parts of the country – for example, some areas of Tibet, and upper Dolpo in Nepal, are only accessible to trekkers on organized trips.
- Not all tours are super-luxury – there are plenty of less expensive trips aimed specifically at backpackers.
- Going on a tour with a group can be an economical way to see harder-to-reach regions, eg the Mentawai Islands off the west coast of Sumatra, where you can take an all-inclusive, five-day tour for around $150/£100 from the mainland. Arrange individual porters, guides and some charter boats, and you'll be looking at around double this figure.
- With longer trips, make sure you find out the full details of the itinerary and what is included, as well as departure and arrival times. One common complaint is that a "three-day trip" turns out to leave after lunch on Day One and arrives home in the early morning on Day Three.

10

Accommodation

ccommodation in most parts of Asia is astonishingly
inexpensive. It's quite feasible to set aside $5/£3 a day
or less for your accommodation budget in India,
Nepal and many of the countries in Southeast Asia –
though you'll get little more than a single bed and four
walls for that money. You can scrape by on less if you share a double
room, and less still if you sleep in dormitories with several others.

Although making the most of your money is important, you'll
probably find that you're willing to pay a little more than rock-bottom rates in return for extra comforts like an attached bathroom, a
quieter location, air-conditioning or more attractive surroundings.
After a day-long bus ride in the sweltering heat or a marathon tour
of every last Kathmandu temple, a comfortable room can restore
your mental health faster than a bottle of Kingfisher beer. Good
value for money is a factor right up the scale in Asia – for $40/£25
in Vietnam you'll get a double room with TV and minibar as well
as shower and air-conditioning, while for $75/£45 you can stay in
an Indian maharajah's palace.

Some hotels in China and Vietnam are not allowed to take foreign
guests (simply because the manager hasn't submitted the requisite
paperwork), so don't take offence if you're rejected on sight. Hoteliers
in other countries, however, can be prejudiced – some mid-range and
upmarket hotels in India won't take backpackers, regardless of how

Lowering the tone

The staff at the five-star Bombay hotel took one look at my scruffy T-shirt and well-travelled rucksack and said, "Sorry sir, the hotel is fully booked." I'd just finished a five-year contract in Bhutan – a country not noted for its designer clothes shops, or even its laundrettes – and was desperate for a few days of luxury. Though I waved wads of cash at the receptionist and flashed my credit card, he was just not willing to lower the tone of the establishment by admitting a backpacker: "Sorry sir, the hotel is fully booked." So I strolled down the street, found a public phone and called him up from round the corner. He didn't recognize my voice and answered, "Yes, sir, we have a room; how many nights?" Ten minutes later, I was back at the five-star, picking up the keys to my deluxe accommodation.

Gerry Jameson

much cash you have. The suitcase-style travel sack is a useful disguise in such instances (see p.205); putting on your smartest gear helps too.

Accommodation in Asia is not confined to hotels. You may well find yourself sleeping in a rafthouse on the infamous River Kwai, dossing down in pilgrims' *gurudwaras* at the Golden Temple in Amritsar, or even sharing a tent with other trekkers at the foot of Mount Everest. More prosaically, major Indian train stations all offer "retiring rooms" for early-morning travellers, and there's always sleeper-car accommodation on the trains themselves.

In some countries, it's also possible to organize a homestay with a local family. You can do this officially, through tourist offices (in India, Korea and Malaysia, for example), through specialist organizations (Japan, China, Korea, India, Nepal), or for women, via the Women Welcome Women World Wide network (see Basics, p.362 for details). Or you can do it on the spur of the moment, simply because you have no alternative, as in remote reaches of Tibet or in Sarawak (East Malaysia), where tribespeople welcome overnight visitors at their longhouses.

Finding somewhere to stay

Any decent guidebook will list a range of accommodation, and these recommendations are useful starting points – bearing in mind that prices go up, hotels change managers, and guidebook writers have preferences that you may not share. For your first few nights in Asia we strongly recommend reserving a hotel room before you leave home (advice on how to do this is given in Chapter Seven). After that, you'll probably do what every other traveller does and trawl the streets yourself, especially if you're looking for budget places.

Because accommodation is so inexpensive, youth-hostel culture barely exists in most parts of Asia, and most backpackers head instead for traveller-oriented budget hotels known as guesthouses. There is usually quite an obvious distinction between places that call themselves guesthouses and those in the same price bracket that call themselves hotels. Inexpensive hotels are generally set up for local travellers (usually businessmen and sales reps), rather than foreign ones, which can mean that rooms are too soulless for any more than a one-night stop.

If you're in a city, start your search in an area that has several hotels or guesthouses close together. That way you won't feel obliged to stay in the first fleapit you come across just because you've taken two buses to get there, nor will you be unduly upset if your first choice is fully booked or has closed down. Get there by mid-morning, if you can, as most guesthouses have a noon

> ### ❝ All that glitters . . .
>
> Looking for somewhere to stay in a small town somewhere between Bombay and Goa, I was directed into a gloomy bar full of tatty pin-up calendars and racks of bottles. "Aah," said the manager nervously, "this is, errmm, men's club."
>
> With my short hair, androgynous clothes and large motorbike parked outside, no one dared to question my gender, so I took the room and hoped I wouldn't be asked to prove my manliness. In the brothel's communal bathroom next day, I kept my head low, grunting a deep "Mornin" to the night's revellers. However, I was soon spotted as female by a sharp-eyed client, and the chatter of excited, astonished Hindi rattled through the corridors as I slipped away quickly, honour intact. ❞
>
> **Nicki McCormick**

checkout time and, during peak season, will have an impromptu waiting list established by about 10am. If there are two of you, get one person to sit down and guard the packs while the other checks out two or three places to find the best deal.

Don't ignore a hotel just because it doesn't feature in your guidebook: it's not uncommon for some books' recommendations to be overflowing while the equally pleasant outfit next door is half-empty. If you don't have a guidebook, or want to get right off the beaten track, then the most obvious places to look for inexpensive hotels are around bus and train stations. Though in some cities these hotels may well double as brothels, business is generally discreet and you may not even realize that most of your fellow guests are booking in and out within the hour.

Finding a room in high season or at festival time can be a real problem in some places, and prices always rocket when demand outstrips supply. During the Sound and Light Festival at the River Kwai in Thailand, rooms are so oversubscribed that travellers doss down on guesthouse floors, in corridors and even restaurant areas, while in Pushkar, northwest India, the local authorities erect a special tent city to house the thousands of visitors who come for the annual camel fair.

Lots of guesthouses employ touts to bring in new customers and, though you might find their persistence incredibly irritating, they sometimes come up with useful leads, especially during peak season. Touts generally hang around bus and train stations (though they have been known to ride the most popular routes into town to get the choicest pickings) and will flash various cards, photos and brochures at you until you agree to go and see a place with them. In some cases the tout's commission is invisibly added onto your room rate. Before going off with a tout, always get an assurance of price, facilities and, crucially, its exact location on the map.

The guesthouse circuit

Most big towns on the tourist circuit in India, Nepal, Thailand, Malaysia, Vietnam, Cambodia, the Philippines, Java and Bali have a backpackers' enclave where you might find anything from ten to a hundred guesthouses packed cheek by jowl into a few hundred square metres. Such concentration ensures prices are kept low and gives you a range of options to check out without having to lug your rucksack too far. It's also a good place to meet new travel companions, especially if you're by yourself or in Asia for the first time. Travellers often say that the real highlight of their trip was the range of characters they met on the road and in the guesthouses: an interesting crowd can transform a dull guesthouse into a memorable experience.

On the downside, backpackers' centres do tend to take on a peculiar ghetto character of their own, a strange medley of watered-down Asian practices and cheapskate Western ones, which not only insulates travellers from the real Bangkok/Delhi/Kathmandu, but makes Bangkok, Delhi and Kathmandu seem indistinguishable. The same is true of popular backpackers' beach resorts, where travellers may hang out for weeks, if not months, without even venturing to the nearest town.

A typical no-frills guesthouse (like the ones in Bangkok's Khao San Road) has about thirty rooms packed into three or four storeys, most of them little more than white-walled cells with one or two beds and a ceiling fan – some don't even have a window; bathrooms are shared with other rooms on the floor. Though basic, rooms are generally clean and functional and, best of all, cheap – from $3/£2 a single (less if you share with several other people, dorm-style), so you can hardly complain about the decor. Some guesthouses also have more expensive rooms with en-suite bathrooms and air-conditioning.

In smaller towns, guesthouses can be far more appealing, with tropical gardens, cool central courtyards and much more spacious rooms. They're often more welcoming than hotels too, being family-run businesses offering just a handful of rooms. Beach accommodation is generally just as basic and cheap as city guesthouses, but looks a lot more idyllic. A standard beach bungalow (the usual term for guesthouses by the sea) on Malaysia's Pulau Tioman island, for example, is a rickety wooden A-frame hut built on stilts right on the beach, with a palm-frond roof and a veranda that looks out to sea.

Most people only use their rooms for sleeping and storing their packs, and spend their hanging-out time in the guesthouse café. These cafés serve Western food like cheese sandwiches and milkshakes, but are used mainly as a common room, a place to write journals and postcards and to swap anecdotes and recommendations with other backpackers. A genial café or roof terrace with good views can do a lot to compensate for a depressing room.

Some guesthouses also keep a noticeboard for travellers' messages and may offer a poste restante service and Internet access too. The most efficient ones operate like small hotels and will sell bus and train tickets, do your laundry and store left luggage as well (though beware of leaving credit cards and other valuables in these; see Chapter Thirteen).

A few great guesthouses

Below is a very selective taster of some of our favourite places to stay, where you'll pay under $15/£10 a night for two people:

- At the rural riverside eco-resort Lao Pako, 50km northeast of **Laos's** capital, Vientiane, you can either sleep on a bamboo platform in the woods, or bed down more conventionally in bungalows or dorms. And when you wake up, you can spend the day swimming in the river, bird-watching, or hiking to nearby villages.
- The thirty simple bamboo huts at *KC Beach Resort,* on the island of Ko Chang off **Thailand's** east coast, are built right on the beach and strung out at wide intervals under the palm trees, so each has an uninterrupted sea view from its rattan veranda.
- *Mount Davis Youth Hostel* boasts eye-popping views over **Hong Kong** harbour – a treat by day or night. It's set right on the top of a hill, so getting there's a trek, but you couldn't find a calmer or more panoramic spot on Hong Kong Island.
- A stiff two-hour climb from Altit village, *Eagle's Nest* is a no-frills dorm with stupendous views along **Pakistan's** Hunza Valley. Most people wake before sunrise to catch the first rays of dawn lighting up the surrounding peaks.
- Though the bungalows at *Puri Widiana* in Ubud, **Bali**, are simply furnished, each has its own veranda where you get served banana pancakes and coffee in the morning and can sit quietly and watch the birds flitting round the tropical flower garden.
- At the backpackers' resort of Cherating in **Malaysia**, the small, basic chalets at *Greenleaves Inn* are hidden away in the trees beside

the river, which makes this a perfect place to chill out and enjoy doing absolutely nothing. And when you feel energetic, the beach is just a few minutes' walk away.

- In Dharamsala, northern **India**, the best rooms at the hillside *Kalsang Guest House* look down over the village, and from the roof terrace upstairs you get perfect views of the snowcapped Dhauladhar mountains.

- Set plumb in the middle of a spectacular valley of sculpted rice terraces, *Hillside Inn* is one of just a few perfectly located guesthouses in the traditional **Philippines** village of Batad.

Room rates

Standards of budget accommodation vary quite a lot across Asia, so it might take you a while to work out whether or not you're getting good value for money. Most travellers rave about the guesthouses in Bali, for example, where it's quite normal to be housed in a pretty setting and to have a good breakfast included in the price; for around $10/£7 a double, that's a great bargain. At the other end of the scale, Chinese hotels in all price brackets are generally a disappointment, being mainly faceless blocks lacking atmosphere or appeal; they're not that cheap either.

Expensive countries such as Singapore, Hong Kong, Japan and Brunei charge relatively large sums for even the most basic double room ($35/£20), so most budget travellers opt for dorm beds – although even these will set you back around $10/£6 a bed. Youth hostels can be a useful alternative in these countries and camping is cheaper still, though official city campsites tend to be inconveniently located in the suburbs; elsewhere in Asia, camping is only appropriate in national parks and on treks. See Chapter Six for advice on whether or not to take camping equipment. The following tips will help you make the most of your accommodation budget:

- A good way to save money if you're on your own is to use dorms, where a bed will be at least thirty percent cheaper than a single room. If no dorms are available you might want to split a double room with another traveller, again cheaper than a single room. Obviously you should only do this if you feel comfortable with the other person.
- Beds in many Asian hotels (as opposed to guesthouses) are very large, so it's quite acceptable for two people to book into a single room; a double room will have two double beds in it.

- In some places you can bargain over the price of a room (especially in low season); others might offer discounts for stays of a week or more.
- If travelling long distance, you can save a night's hotel costs by taking the overnight train or bus and making sure you get a reclining seat. Second-class berths on trains usually cost about the same as a single room in a guesthouse.
- Watch out for "luxury" service charges and taxes in mid- and up market places (up to 21 percent extra in Indonesia, for example), and for ridiculous room-service charges as well as overpriced food in the hotel restaurant.
- Using the phone in your room is just asking to get ripped off, as most hotels add a huge surcharge to phone bills.
- Unless you pay by credit card in many up-market hotels (in India, for example), you may have to put down a deposit against your possible phone bill and minibar tariff.
- An unorthodox way of finding cheap accommodation in Japan is to check in to a "love hotel" after all the lovers have departed for the night (usually around 10pm). These hotels are designed for secret and extramarital liaisons, but are definitely not brothels. They're completely legal and unsleazy, if a little kitsch – rooms tend to be plastered in mirrors, fake fur and romantic images – and are scrupulously clean. Because most clandestine liaisons take place during the day, overnighters get a huge discount.

Can I see the room please?

Always look at the room you're being offered before paying for it – this is normal practice throughout Asia and, though time-consuming, is definitely worth it. Once you've checked out a few places you'll be able to size up a room in five seconds, but for first-timers here's a checklist of essential points to look out for.

- If you like the hotel but aren't sure about the room, always ask to see another one: the view might be better, the neighbours quieter and, who knows, the fan might even be working in that one.
- Is the room clean? Check the sheets for blood spots (blood means fleas or bedbugs), the floor for cockroaches and the walls for squashed mosquitoes. Look under the bed for rat traps (squares of cardboard sprinkled with food and smeared with glue) and scour the window screens and mosquito nets for holes (which render them useless, unless you want to spend the whole

night doing repair jobs with Band-Aids).

- Does everything work? Try out the lights, the fan/air-conditioning/heater, the flush toilet (if there is one) and the shower (ditto).
- Do the taps run fresh or salt water? If you asked for hot water, check that it works.
- Is the room secure? Can you put your own padlock on the door? (Not applicable in China, where hotel rooms are locked and unlocked for you by the floor attendant.) Are the windows safe? Are there any peepholes in the door or walls?
- Is it quiet? Rooms on the main road will be noisy, but so will any place near a morning market, a night market, a disco, a hotel kitchen or an electricity generator – which you may not discover until the next morning. The same goes for rowdy neighbours (snorers and squabblers), and 4am cockerels; even temples can be noisy if there's an all-night prayer session or festival.
- Is it comfortable? Check the bed for springs and the mattress for lumps. Are you certain it's worth saving a dollar a day by staying in a place with no window or somewhere with paper-thin walls and a creaking fan?

Checking in

In most parts of Asia, you'll be asked to register when checking in to any accommodation, however small. This usually entails writing your

❝ Peeping toms

Jill and Danny were lying naked in their room in Danang, Vietnam when they spotted a hole in the wall with a dirty great eye behind it, staring at them. Completely amazed, they told the person in so many words to mind their own business, and blocked up the hole with tissue and tape. Ten minutes later, they looked up to see a long pair of chopsticks penetrate the hole, free the space and the big eye return. **❞**

Chris Humphrey

name, passport number and several other details in a ledger – a legal requirement in most countries which, in theory at least, enables the authorities to trace travellers in cases of emergency. For the most part, this should be quite straightforward, though registration forms in China are a notable exception, being painfully long-winded and sometimes written entirely in Chinese script.

Wherever you stay, you should avoid leaving your passport with hotel staff unless you absolutely have to do so. This is unavoidable in some parts of Vietnam, however, where hotel managers have to present their guests' passports at the police station. If you're asked to surrender your passport as security against your bill, offer to leave a monetary deposit instead. Your passport is your only official means of identity in a strange land and should be kept on your person at all times – besides which, you'll need it for changing money and other transactions.

Most people keep their passport, airline ticket and other valuables with them whenever they leave their hotel, not least because hotel security can be quite lax. However, you could also leave these items in your room and use your own padlock on the door (if you can), or put them in a hotel safety box, again secured by your own padlock. Bear in mind, though, that sawing through a small padlock is not so difficult, and be aware that not all hotel staff are scrupulously honest.

Security should also be an issue when you're inside your hotel room with your valuables. Always lock the door from the inside, even when you're awake (people have a habit of drifting in for a chat at the most inopportune moments; see the anecdote on p.334). And check on window access too, in case a thief decides to climb in while you're asleep.

Bathrooms and how to use them

Though many guesthouses and hotels have Western-style showers, the traditional scoop-and-slosh method of bathing is also common right across Asia. Known in travellers' speak as a *mandi* (Indonesian for "to wash"), this basically involves dipping a scoop, jug or small bowl into a large bucket or basin of water and then chucking it over yourself – very refreshing in a chilly kind of way. The cardinal rule of the *mandi* is never to put your soap or shampoo into the basin of water and, though it often looks like a big stone bathtub, *never, ever* to get into it as this water might have to supply the next two weeks' worth of guests.

Washing in cold water is the norm throughout most of Asia, but in the high altitudes of Nepal, northern India, Tibet, Bhutan, Pakistan and north China, you'll definitely need a hot shower, so make sure it's operational before paying for your room. Some places only turn on the water heaters at certain times of day. You'll come across some intriguing bathing habits depending on where you are in Asia:

- In rural parts of Asia, the local river, lake or well doubles as the village bathroom and everyone congregates there at the end of the day for their evening wash. Men and women nearly always have separate bathing areas and, though they may be within sight of each other, there's absolutely no ogling or communication between the two groups. Both sexes wear sarongs in the water and no one strips off to wash. If you bathe in the local river, you should do as they do, or find a place much further upriver.

- Traditional Japanese hotels generally have old-fashioned bathtubs. These have no running hot water, but work instead by heating up the full tub with an element, like a kettle – enabling you to sit in the water and keep warm for hours on end. The same bath water is used by several hotel guests one after the other (not as unhygienic as it sounds if you think of it like a public jacuzzi), so it's essential to wash yourself clean, using the scoop-and-slosh method, before hopping into the tub.

- In Bali, the most stylish guesthouses and hotels have beautifully designed "garden bathrooms" with roofs that are open to the sky, sculptured water flues and tropical plants growing round the *mandi* area.

- Most small towns in Korea have public bathhouses – a national institution that should definitely be experienced. In these you wash yourself on the side of the main pool and then climb in for a soak and a chat with your neighbours. Most have separate pools for men and women.

- Traditional Bhutanese baths are heated with huge stones, which are first cooked to a high temperature in the embers of a fire and then thrown into the tub.

Toilet habits

Flush toilets and toilet paper are relatively new concepts in most parts of Asia and, apart from in tourist hotels and the wealthiest

homes, it's usually a question of hunkering down over a squat toilet like everyone else does. Asians wash their bottoms rather than wipe them, using the bucket of water provided and their left hand. This explains why eating, shaking hands and giving things is always done with the right hand – see Chapter Eight for details.

Traveller-oriented guesthouses often provide sit-down toilets that are plumbed in but don't flush. In these you're expected to do the flushing manually by pouring a bucket of water down the bowl. These plumbing systems are very sensitive and get blocked up easily as, unlike Western ones, they're not designed to take paper or tampons. Many guesthouses have signs telling you to throw your waste in the bin instead and it's selfish not to obey the rules. Even if there's no sign and no bucket, you should chuck any paper waste into a plastic bag: a blocked drain in your en-suite bathroom will attract mosquitoes and all sorts of germs, and the stink will permeate your dreams.

The obvious way round all this is to adopt the Asian habit and wash instead of wipe. If that sounds too unpalatable, then travel with your own roll of toilet paper as most places won't provide it. The one situation where it's hard to either wipe or wash is when you're out trekking in the wilderness. If you don't want to use leaves, either burn your paper with a lighter or dig a little hole and bury it – there's nothing like a ribbon of pink toilet paper for ruining a spectacular view.

Be prepared to come across a good percentage of gut-wrenchingly vile public toilets, particularly in bus and train stations, and on trains in China and India. Try and get into the habit of using hotel and restaurant facilities when you can, and don't be surprised by the following:

● Indoor bathrooms are considered unhygienic by many rural Asian communities, for whom the idea of having a toilet just a metre or so from the kitchen is quite disgusting. Indian villagers, for example, will set off for the fields every morning to do their ablutions away from the home or, if they live near the sea, they will do them on the shoreline so that the sea washes everything away. With that in mind, it pays to be careful where you swim and sunbathe on Indian beaches.

- Public toilets in China are often very public indeed – with only a low partition between squatters, and sometimes no partition at all.
- All Chinese and Japanese hotels provide special plastic slippers for wearing in the bathroom.
- Some public toilets in Japan play piped music to mask the sound of pissing, which is considered embarrassing for Japanese women. If you're lucky, you might even come across a singing toilet-roll holder, which plays *Für Elise* every time you yank the paper.
- In Thailand, toilet attendants in up-market restaurants massage your neck and shoulders while you stand at a urinal.
- In Singapore, there's a S$500 fine for failing to flush a public toilet and, should you be caught urinating in a public space, you get your picture splashed over the front page of the national newspaper.

11

Staying healthy

There's no advice that we can give and nothing that you can do that will absolutely guarantee you don't fall sick in Asia. You are subjecting your body to different food and water, extreme heat or cold, tropical sun and a whole host of new creepy-crawlies. Even the air you breathe will be carrying different cold and flu viruses from those at home. This chapter presents the straightforward facts that every visitor to Asia should know, gives advice on precautions and has suggestions to help you to cope should you get ill.

These points may help to put things in perspective and prepare you before you travel:

- Millions of travellers go to Asia every year and millions return home safely, the vast majority having suffered nothing worse than a few days of travellers' diarrhoea.
- Almost everyone gets sick at some time during a lengthy Asian trip. The last thing you'll feel like doing if you're unwell is boarding a massively overcrowded bus for an overnight journey or subjecting yourself to any other form of travel. Make sure you build enough leeway into your itinerary to allow you to rest up for a few days if you need to.
- Read up about diseases prevalent in Asia, as symptoms that probably just indicate flu at home may be something far more serious in the tropics. There are several good books on travellers' health – some people take them along, and they can make interesting if

Many of the items listed here are available in Asia, but it's better to have them to hand and replace them later. You'll save money and get a more individualized pack if you put your kit together yourself rather than opt for a commercially packaged one. If you're trekking you should consult a specialist guide/trekking book for additional items.

Anti-diarrhoea tablets.
Anti-fungal cream.
Antiseptic cream.
Aspirin/paracetamol.
Band-Aids, small and large (if you take the fabric ones they work well for blisters also).
Bite cream. (Tiger Balm, available throughout Asia, is a good soothing alternative; it is also useful for aching muscles and headaches.)
Cold remedy.
Gauze pads.
Insect repellent.
Lip salve/sun block for lips.
Rehydration salts.
Scissors.
Sterile dressings.
Sterile needles and syringes.
Surgical tape.
Thermometer.
Throat lozenges.
Tweezers.

Prescription drugs

The following items need to be discussed with your doctor as, in the West, they are only available on prescription. He or she may be willing to give you a course of tablets to take with you if you explain where you are going. Make sure you know how and when to use them:

Antibiotics, for throat and bronchial infections, and for intestinal bacteria.
Diamox (acetazolamide), for the treatment of mild altitude sickness. However, this is somewhat controversial and medical opinion varies.
Tinidazole, for giardia (see p.306).
Emergency treatment for malaria (see p.298).

gory reading while you are squatting over the toilet for the twentieth time that day. Check out Dr Richard Dawood's *Travellers' Health: How to Stay Healthy Abroad* (OUP/Random House), an extensive and detailed book intended for those living overseas, but full of invaluable information for travellers, and Dr Jane Wilson

Howarth's *Bugs, Bites and Bowels* (Cadogan/Globe Pequot), a splendidly titled book, small enough to carry easily, outlining simply and clearly the illnesses you may get in the tropics, likely symptoms and what to do about them. Rough Guides' *Travel Health* features an A to Z of possible diseases, a first-aid section and particularly useful tips on safety during adventure activities. Lonely Planet's *Asia and India*, in their Healthy Travel series, is compact but packed full of vital information for before, during and after your trip, and is small enough to take with you. Alternatively there are several excellent Web sites; see Basics, p.364, for details.

- Go for a dental checkup before you leave home and have any recommended treatment. Dental pain is unpleasant at the best of times, and finding dental treatment in Asia on a par with that at home is even more difficult than finding other forms of medical care (see p.309).
- Carry a first-aid kit (see p.293), though hopefully it will be used very little. Though it will probably be bulkier and more extensive than you have at home, it will be worth its weight in gold if you do actually need it. Also take with you any medication you use regularly.
- Make sure you have adequate medical insurance (see p.150).
- Some Asian illnesses don't show themselves straightaway – if you get sick within a year of returning home from Asia, make sure you tell the doctor treating you where you've been.

Vaccinations

As early as possible, you should get advice about which vaccinations you require for your trip, as many jabs are given as a course of two or even three in order to be maximally effective. Some cannot be given within a certain time of others because they cancel each other out; in any case, you won't really want to subject your arm to four needles in one sitting. Similarly, you need to find out early about the type of malaria-preventive medication that is recommended for the areas you are visiting; you'll need to start taking the tablets in advance of departure. Even if your itinerary is not finalized, compile a list of places you are planning to visit (as well as any others you may visit) and think about whether you are planning to stay in tourist resorts or the countryside, to travel during the monsoon, and whether you'll be camping. All of these will affect the advice you are given.

While your family doctor will be the cheapest for injections (many of these are free), you may want to contact a private specialist travel clinic to make sure you get the most specific information available. Many travel clinics have telephone information lines, are quick and convenient and, though expensive, provide information that's up-to-date and extensive (see p.363 for contact details).

Vaccinations don't offer lifelong immunity, so keep a record of your injections to know when you need a further injection – called a booster. Some jabs can cause reactions – unpleasant but much better than getting the disease.

Different countries vary in what inoculations they insist upon for visitors, but the only time you are likely to be asked for documentation is if you have recently travelled to a country in South or Central America, where yellow fever is endemic. In this case, you must have had a yellow fever jab (and have the certificate to prove it). It's worth bringing your medical card, showing which vaccinations you've had, with you, as scams are not unknown: for example, border officials on the Thai/Cambodia border at Aranyaprathet/Poipet have been known to ask travellers who can't show what jabs they've had to swallow unidentified pills – and pay 200B for the "medication".

Diseases you should know about

Below is a rundown of diseases you might be exposed to and what vaccinations are available. Don't be unduly alarmed, however, as some of these are confined to limited regions or seasonal (usually more prevalent during monsoon time):

- **Cholera**. Being vaccinated against this extremely severe diarrhoeal illness, transmitted via contaminated food and water, used to be recommended for travellers, but is now thought to be too ineffectual and short-term. The best advice is to follow the guidelines given in this chapter regarding what you eat and drink, and steer well clear of any areas where you hear there's an epidemic.
- **Dengue fever**. This viral disease gives rise to severe fever and joint and muscle pain. It's spread by mosquitoes which, unusually, bite during the day. Dengue fever is painful and unpleasant, but the more serious, life-threatening dengue haemorrhagic fever can

Even in paradise

On approaching the small Thai island of Koh Tao, I was mesmerized. Across the water I could see a mountainous mass of trees, surrounded by white sands, coconut palms and rickety thatched huts. As we stepped off the boat, hordes of touts appeared clutching wooden boards advertising their beach resorts. Bewildered, we followed a young, stocky Thai man by the name of Chet. He walked us to his truck and we clambered into the back, to be driven to a resort.

During many weeks on the island, poker playing with Chet developed into riskier games, and we started sleeping together. Armed with condoms, I didn't worry about health issues. However, the seduction of our utopian surroundings resulted in increasingly neglected safety. I asked Chet if he had been tested for HIV and we discussed the chances of pregnancy. But the reality of the risks never truly set in; condoms were fast becoming an inconvenience and the belief that nothing could harm me grew. What can happen to you in paradise?

In the New Year I left for Australia but sometime in March, I began to feel ill. I spent my days huddled in bed trying desperately not to throw up. One morning looking in the mirror, I discovered the whites of my eyes were turning yellow. This was followed by my stomach and slowly the rest of my body. I was losing weight, my hair was falling out, and I could barely stand. The doctor ordered an exhaustive series of blood tests. At last the results came: I had been diagnosed with Hepatitis B, the worst strain of the disease and one which you're destined to carry – and suffer from – for life. Hepatitis B attacks the liver – brutally; liver cirrhosis is a distinct possibility, as is liver cancer.

My world collapsed. I was treated with countless pharmaceuticals, and, feeling partially recovered, I left for Britain three weeks later with a batch of statistics and a handful of leaflets. Back home was worse: I faced hospital appointments, HIV tests, and family hysteria. I contacted Chet, afraid that he too might be ill, or perhaps that he might pass on the condition to someone else, but he denied any knowledge of the disease and I felt angry, rejected, naive – and incredibly foolish.

I've got used to things now, and have learned to live with the disease. But it dominates my life to an extent I could never have imagined possible. The cost of my trip feels enormous and will continue to do so, but at least I know now that you have to be on your guard – even in paradise.

Vicky Nicholas

also occur, although the latter is most usually associated with a second or later bout of the illness. There is no vaccination and the disease is currently on the increase in Asia – see precautions for avoiding mosquito bites, pp.298–302.

● **Hepatitis**. There are several strains of this disease (Hepatitis A, B, C, D and E) in which viruses attack the liver, causing a yellow colouring of skin and eyes (jaundice), extreme exhaustion, fever and diarrhoea. More seriously, hepatitis can result in either cirrhosis of the liver or liver cancer in the long term. One of the most common of the serious illnesses that can afflict travellers, it can last for many months. Hepatitis A is transmitted via contaminated food, water or saliva; the long-term vaccine against it is a course of two injections, six to eighteen months apart, giving ten years' protection. A gamma globulin injection, giving three to five months' protection, is cheaper and is useful if you haven't time to fit in the other course or are going on a one-off, short trip. The more serious Hepatitis B is transmitted through contaminated blood, needles and syringes and by sexual contact; the vaccine is given as a course of three injections over six months. For increased convenience, a combined vaccine for Hepatitis A and B is just becoming available in the USA and is already available in

Australia. Hepatitis E, which is especially dangerous for pregnant women, is transmitted by the same route as Hepatitis A. There's no vaccine against the C, D or E strains.

- **Japanese encephalitis**. A viral illness resulting in inflammation of the brain, it is found across Asia, although largely restricted to rural areas. It's transmitted via mosquitoes from infected animals and is very dangerous – the death rate is high, and so is the danger of brain damage if you survive. Inoculation provides only partial protection, and involves three injections spread over a month.

- **Malaria**. There are several strains of malaria, most causing recurring bouts of fever, headache and shivering. All are serious, debilitating and difficult to treat successfully. The parasites which cause malaria are carried by night-biting mosquitoes. All travellers to Asia should consider taking a course of preventive tablets and do everything to stop themselves being bitten, as none of the drugs available is one hundred percent effective. See pp.298–302 for more details.

- **Meningococcal meningitis**. Caused by airborne bacteria, this disease attacks the lining of the brain and can be fatal; epidemics occasionally affect parts of the continent, though it's generally rare. The vaccine (different from the injection given to children) is given by a single injection and does not protect against all strains of meningitis. It takes two weeks to reach full immunity after having the injection.

- **Polio, diphtheria** and **TB**. Most people will have been inoculated against these in childhood and, while they are rare in the West, they are still common in Asia. You should make sure you are still covered – you need a booster every ten years.

- **Rabies**. Spread via the saliva of infected cats, dogs and monkeys, rabies is prevalent throughout Asia, with ninety percent of the world's deaths from the disease occurring in India. You'll probably want to take specialist advice on this one as, although there is a vaccine, you'll need a course of three injections before leaving home, and a booster is required every three years. Even then, you'll still need urgent medical help and further injections should you get bitten by an animal suspected of carrying the disease. Without previous vaccination at home, you'll need more injections if you do get bitten abroad.

- **Tetanus**. Also known as lockjaw, the disease is contracted via open wounds (for example, a cut caused by stepping on a rusty nail). Make sure your jabs are up to date before you leave home – you need a booster every ten years.

- **Typhoid**. Spread by contaminated food and water, typhoid is characterized by extremely high fever, abdominal pains, headaches, diarrhoea and red spots on the body; patients need urgent medical help. Protection (which lasts two to five years) is either given by injection or a course of more expensive capsules. Be prepared for some pain, discomfort and possible fever after certain types of typhoid jab.

Mosquitoes

Given the number of diseases carried by mosquitoes (malaria, Japanese encephalitis, dengue fever), not to mention the unpleasantness of mosquito bites, you should do whatever you can to avoid getting bitten. This means wearing long sleeves or sloshing mosquito repellent on exposed skin during the dusk and darkness hours when the malarial mosquito operates, and sleeping under a mosquito net or with any open windows covered by a fine wire mesh. It's a good idea to have a shower and get changed for the evening before it gets dark – mosquitoes adore sweaty skin.

You might decide to take your own mosquito net with you – they are light and compact, and you can guarantee one brought from home won't be full of mosquito-sized tears and cigarette burns. Some nets now come impregnated with Permethrin insecticide as an additional barrier against the bugs, and you can also buy Permethrin sprays to treat older nets.

Malaria

Malaria is one of the nastiest and most common tropical diseases worldwide – it affects between 300 and 500 million people each year and kills up to 2.7 million of them. Though most of these deaths occur among young children in sub-Saharan Africa, the disease is a serious risk for anyone travelling to Asia, where some of the most dangerous forms of malaria lurk, especially in the Thai-Cambodian and Thai–Burmese border areas where the parasites which cause the disease have developed resistance to several drugs.

There is currently no vaccine against the disease, but there are a range of drugs that can cure malaria or prevent you contracting it, though none is one hundred percent effective. You must start taking them at least a week before you arrive in a malarial area and, even more importantly, continue taking them for four weeks after you leave. It is possible to develop malaria back home if you ignore

MALARIA IN ASIA

This is a broad overview of the malaria situation in the countries covered in the book. Be sure to check the current situation and appropriate preventive medication and emergency treatment with a medical specialist before you travel.

Bangladesh	Malarial
Bhutan	Malarial along the southern borders
Brunei	Not malarial
Cambodia	Malarial in all forested and hilly rural areas, but Phnom Penh, Sihanoukville and Battambang are malaria-free and Siem Reap is low risk
China	Malarial between the Yellow and Yangzi rivers in Yunnan Province, along the borders with Laos and Vietnam and on Hainan island
India	Malarial all year in areas below an altitude of 2000m; not malarial above
Indonesia	Malarial, but Bali is malaria-free
Japan	Not malarial
Laos	Malarial
Malaysia	Malarial, though the Peninsula is low-risk
Nepal	Malarial all year in areas below 1300m; the risks are minimal above this altitude and In Kathmandu
Pakistan	Malarial all year in areas below 2000m; not malarial above
Philippines	Malarial only in the southern tip of Palawan and in the Sulu Archipelago
Singapore	Not malarial
South Korea	Malarial in rural areas in the far north otherwise minimal risk
Sri Lanka	Malarial except Colombo, Kalutra and Nuwara Eliya
Taiwan	Not malarial
Thailand	Malarial, but high-risk only along the Burma and Cambodia borders, including Ko Chang
Vietnam	Malarial in the highlands and rural areas, but low risk in Hanoi, Ho Chi Minh City, the northern Red River delta and coastal regions of the south and centre

this regime – typically about two thousand British travellers contract malaria every year and ten of these die from the disease. Another consideration is that all drugs have potential side effects and travellers need to weigh up the potential risks of taking preventive drugs against the potential risks of the disease itself.

There is considerable difference between countries in their recommendations for travellers and in the drugs that are available. For many decades the most commonly used prevention against malaria has been chloroquine (sold as Nivaquine and Avloclor in the UK, and Aralen and Resochin in the US), taken weekly together with daily proguanil (sold as Paludrine). However, as strains of chloroquine-resistent malaria have evolved, other drugs have come into use in some areas. Mefloquine (sold as Larium) is probably the best known due to considerable controversy that continues to rage over serious side effects in some users. Before you travel, seek advice from your doctor or a specialist travel clinic about which drugs are recommended for malaria prevention in the areas you plan to visit, and treatment options should you contract the disease. If you are heading a long way off the beaten track, it is worth discussing with your medical adviser whether you should carry an emergency course of treatment – though this should be used until you can get to medical help rather than instead of it. If you develop any fever up to a year after you get home, be sure to get medical advice and make sure the doctor is aware that you've been to a malarial area.

The books on p.293 and Web sites on p.364 all carry information about malaria; in addition, ⓌⒶ*www.malaria.org,* Ⓦ*www.actmalaria.org* and Ⓦ*www.geocities.com/aaadeel/malaria.html* (the last of these contains a vast number of links to associated sites) are all worth checking out for the latest information. And keep your eyes peeled for news of qinghaosu, a derivative from the plant sweet wormwood that has been in use against malaria in China for over a thousand years; it's proving highly effective, especially in areas where resistance has developed to everything else.

Mosquito repellents

Hopefully all of the above has convinced you of the importance of avoiding mosquito bites. One way to do this is by applying mosquito repellent to exposed skin; the most renowned is called DEET (Diethyl Tolumide). You can buy repellent containing up to 95 percent DEET, and wrist and ankle bands pre-soaked in the chemical are also available. However, it's strong stuff and can cause skin reactions after extended use. You also need to be careful with anything plastic (sunglasses, watch straps, shoes), as it tends to melt on contact with DEET. Locally bought repellents are often very good and much cheaper than ones bought at home. They may even be the same brand as the ones at home – Autan, for example, is widely available throughout Asia. One advantage of using a mosquito repellent is that it will ward off leeches, ticks and sandflies as well.

There's also a range of natural products that work fairly well. These substances aren't quite as repugnant to mosquitoes as DEET, but avoid its disadvantages. Most commercially produced natural insect repellents are based around citronella, a substance found in certain plants, such as lemon grass. Eucalyptus oil is another natural repellent and is used in the brand Mosi-guard. Some travellers believe that vitamin B1 tablets or garlic capsules, taken on a regular basis, make the blood offensive to insects and so protect against bites, though there isn't much evidence for or against this.

LEECHES

Any forays into the jungle, especially near the equator (or anywhere in the rainy season) mean potential encounters with leeches – tiny, thread-like blood-sucking creatures that attach themselves to your skin, zap you with an anaesthetic and anticoagulant, slurp away at the red stuff and, when they've had enough and expanded to many times their normal size, drop off and leave you dripping blood for a long time afterwards. The good news is they don't carry any nasty diseases; the bad news is that they can get through the tiniest holes, such as between the threads in most socks (they love the eyeholes of boots). One glimpse of your ankle with a dozen or so of them attached is a short cut to hysteria.

To stop them attacking, silk socks, insect repellent and tobacco leaves in your socks are all useful, plus regular checks of your feet when you are walking. If you do fall victim, dab at the creatures with salt, a lighted cigarette or chewing tobacco (widely available across Asia) to get them to let go. Don't just pull them off in a panic – easier said than done – as this is likely to leave their sucking parts embedded in your skin.

At some point in your trip you'll encounter mosquito coils, which you can buy cheaply there in boxes of eight or ten. Bright green and impregnated with chemicals, they are the main Asian way of deterring mosquitoes. To use a mosquito coil, light it, let the flame burn for a second or two and then blow it out – to be effective coils should be smoking rather than burning. They also need to be suspended above the floor, and so come with a tin stand, the prong of which goes through the slit in the centre of the coil. Each coil smoulders for about eight hours. They're useful for protecting your ankles if you are sitting out on a verandah at night, or you can put coils beside the bed while you sleep; thoughtful restaurants put them under their tables. The coils are effective as long as you keep close to them, but you may find that after a few nights' sleeping near them you end up feeling suffocated by the pungent smell.

Also available are several brands of electrically powered machines, making use of vapour tablets that release a repellent into the air when heated up. The disadvantages are that they rely on having a mains supply, need a fairly confined space and don't operate too well if there's a draught.

The heat

The opportunity to experience a tropical climate is one of the big attractions of a trip to Asia, yet exposure to extreme heat is one of the major causes of illness for many travellers. Once you arrive, it's important to:

- respect the heat. It isn't only mad dogs and Englishmen who go out in the midday sun, it's plenty of other travellers as well; but it's far better to stay in the shade during the extreme heat of the day, as most local people do.
- dry yourself carefully after bathing – use medicated talcum powder (available throughout Asia) or antifungal powder if you fall victim to heat rashes, prickly heat or fungal infections that adore the damp, humid conditions of the tropics.
- dress sensibly – see p.209 for ideas on clothing that will help you keep cool in hot climates.
- protect yourself from the extreme sun and be especially careful at high altitude, where you may be cool but still exposed to huge

amounts of sunshine. Use plenty of high-factor sunscreen, even if you are just walking around (don't forget the tops of your feet, tops of your ears and backs of your hands, especially if you are fair-skinned). A hat or umbrella can stop your brains frying.

- drink plenty of water. The heat will make you sweat, so you need to increase fluid intake to compensate. If you stop peeing or your urine is becoming very dark, then you're not drinking enough.

- increase your intake of salt – you also lose this when you sweat. Many travellers add a pinch of salt to fruit juices and shakes (see rehydration advice on p.305). Muscle cramps are a sign that you are lacking salt in your diet.

- be aware of the symptoms of heat exhaustion, which is common in hot, humid places and characterized by exhaustion, cramps, a rapid pulse, reddened skin and vomiting. Anyone with these symptoms needs a cool place to recover, plenty to drink and even wrapping in sheets or sarongs soaked in cold water. Hospital treatment is sometimes necessary.

- get enough rest. It is very easy to get exhausted and run-down if you are racing round sightseeing in the heat all day and sampling the nightlife after dark. If you're tired, you're more open to illness in general.

Water

With a couple of exceptions – Singapore and Japan – tap water in Asia is not safe for tourists to drink (for this reason you should avoid ice in your drinks). However, bottled water is widely available in all but the most out-of-the-way places. Check the seals of the bottles before you buy, as some unscrupulous dealers collect empty bottles and refill them straight from the tap; such bottles have the seal missing or have obviously been tampered with. Bottled water can make a surprising hole in your budget and you'll need to allow for it in your pre-trip calculations. In the cheapest countries, a couple of litres of bottled water will only set you back a dollar or so a day, but this is $90/£55 over a three-month trip, and you'll also have deposited a small mountain of nonbiodegradable plastic bottles into the largely ineffectual Asian rubbish system.

One alternative is to boil drinking water to sterilize it – five minutes' boiling (ten minutes at high altitude) will kill off anything that is likely to harm you. While this is fine if you are camping or have access to cooking equipment, it is not really convenient in most situations. Another option is to sterilize the water using chlorine or iodine tablets (available from outdoor-equipment shops or travel clinics). While these are cheap and easy, they are not effective against all the harmful organisms in the water (amoebic dysentery and giardia, to name a couple), and they leave the water with a definite chemical taste. Water filters also only do a partial job, and do not remove viruses (such as those that cause hepatitis). The most effective solution is to take a water purifier, which will both filter and sterilize the water. There are several on the market; before buying one, you should compare their different sizes, weights, the speed at which they process water, and how often replacement cartridges are needed.

Food

The sight, smell and taste of the massive variety of Asian food is one of the greatest pleasures of any visit to the continent. A few minutes among the fruit and vegetables of even the smallest town market and you'll be dying to try out the unfamiliar breadfruit, rambutans and mangosteens as well as the new variations on old favourites, such as red bananas. A walk through any Asian night market where cooks behind tiny stalls conjure up enticing, spicy meals of rice, noodles, seafood and soups, will set your taste buds tingling. Head down any Asian street and the chances are you'll stumble across carts selling tea, soup or ice cream, women peeling pineapples to order or tiny neighbourhood restaurants wafting succulent odours into the air. Though not everyone will want to tackle the crunchy cooked grasshoppers of Thailand, the liberal chilli-

fest of Sumatran Padang cuisine or the dog-meat delicacies of southwestern China, we guarantee you will make some unforgettable culinary discoveries.

While you should enjoy the new tastes and eating experiences to the full, it pays to exercise some control over what you eat and where you eat:

- Avoid food that has sat out in the midday heat assaulted by flies, and food that has had to be reheated. One of the reasons Indian food can have such a disastrous effect on foreign bowels is the cooking style: slow-cooked casseroles and stews are common. Western food is often the most hazardous – ask yourself how long that cannelloni has sat around before its brief interlude in the microwave. In contrast, in a place like Thailand, stir-fries are whipped up on the spot and have no chance to languish all day in the tropical heat.
- Fruit that has been peeled for you or doesn't get peeled, such as pineapples, papaya or grapes, can be a hazard, but fruit you peel yourself should be fine.
- Similarly, raw vegetables, including salad, are suspect, either because of the water they have been washed in or the human excrement that is used for fertilizer in some parts of Asia.
- Surrounded by so many unfamiliar foods, it can be difficult to get a balanced diet, especially as in some places, such as Nepal and parts of China, fresh fruit and vegetables are scarce. You may want to consider taking vitamin tablets with you.

Diarrhoea and dehydration

There are numerous causes for the diarrhoea and vomiting that strike travellers in Asia, from a straightforward reaction to a change of water and diet to more unpleasant bacteria and viruses. Whatever the cause, the main problem you'll face is dehydration, which will make you feel exhausted and dizzy, and give you a splitting headache. It's important to focus on rehydrating the moment any stomach problems start; worry about a diagnosis later.

You should be drinking two or three litres of water a day just to cope with being in the tropics, but if you get diarrhoea, you'll need a lot more. In addition, your body will be losing important minerals and so you should always carry sachets of oral rehydration salts (ORS) with you. These just need dissolving in clean drinking

water and are available under a variety of names (such as Dioralyte) in the West and throughout Asia. Even if you're vomiting, you should sip small amounts of the solution. If you can't get hold of commercial brands, dissolve approximately half a level teaspoon of salt and eight level teaspoons of sugar in a litre of water; it's important that the resulting mixture shouldn't contain too much salt – it mustn't be any saltier than the taste of tears.

Diarrhoea and vomiting caused by changes to diet and water should run their course in two to three days, and as long as you keep drinking you'll be OK until you can start eating again (start with bland food such as boiled rice). If the diarrhoea and vomiting are particularly severe, persist for more than three days without abating or are accompanied by blood or mucus in your faeces, or by fever, then you should seek medical help. There are several illnesses you should be aware of, including bacilliary or amoebic dysentery, typhoid and a particularly common one called giardiasis (or giardia), which produces rotten-egg belches and farts – not guaranteed to help you make friends.

Anti-diarrhoea tablets should be used extremely sparingly. Diarrhoea serves a purpose in ejecting poisonous toxins from your body. These tablets, which effectively halt the movements of your digestive system, stop the diarrhoea, but they block you up, don't attack the microorganisms responsible for the problem and can actually make you feel worse. They are useful, however, if you absolutely have to travel.

As bizarre as it may sound, after a few months on the road you'll be gleefully swapping stories with fellow travellers of "the yellow frothy diarrhoea I had in Nepal" – probably while tucking into a pizza in Thailand.

Altitude

The problem of altitude is a serious one for anyone planning to trek in the Himalayas or visit Tibet or other high-altitude regions such as Ladakh in India; some parts of Xinjiang, Sichuan and Yunnan in

China; the Karakoram region in Pakistan or Mount Fuji in Japan.

The higher you go above sea level, the less oxygen there is in the air and the lower the air pressure that drives it from your lungs into your bloodstream. Your body needs time to adapt to this, and while this process is under way – probably for the first three days at altitude, especially if you have flown in – you are likely to experience headaches, shortness of breath, tiredness, loss of appetite, aches and pains, sleeping problems and nausea (collectively known as acute mountain sickness, or AMS). Relax totally and drink plenty of water and the symptoms should pass, although having acclimatized you must still ascend slowly – no more than 300m per day. If you go too fast the symptoms will return.

If your symptoms worsen, however, and especially if you start vomiting and experience loss of co-ordination, delirium, rapid heartbeat, breathlessness and blueness of tongue and lips, you must descend as rapidly as possible. Just a few hundred metres of vertical descent can be life-saving and usually brings about immediate recovery. Serious cases of AMS are very rare, but anyone planning a trek over 3000m should inform themselves fully of the potential risks before setting off.

AIDS and contraception

Unprotected sex is as unwise in Asia as it is at home. Reliable figures are not easy to find, but HIV and AIDS are prevalent across the region. As an indication, there are an estimated five to ten million HIV-positive people in India and 50,000 to 100,000 with AIDS. The level of AIDS education is very variable throughout Asia and all travellers should assume they will be the one taking responsibility for the supply and use of condoms in any sexual encounter.

Condoms, often locally manufactured, are widely available throughout Asia in pharmacies and supermarkets, although local brands have a fairly mixed reputation – you'd be well advised to check use-by dates and buy from air-conditioned suppliers as far as possible, as extreme heat can rot the rubber. Expatriate residents in Asia usually keep theirs in the fridge – not a service most budget hotels offer – but it is worth trying to keep them in the coolest part of your pack along with your films. Women travellers may feel very conspicuous asking for condoms, especially in traditional Muslim areas such as Indonesia, and may prefer to carry some from home, particularly bearing in mind the quality concerns.

Not sure of the word in the local language? It may not be as tough as you think. While condoms are the fairly tongue-knotting *bao cao su* in Vietnamese, they are *kondom* in Indonesian and Malay, *kandom* in Hindi and Urdu, and are informally known as *meechai* in Thailand after the charismatic former Minister for Health, Mr Meechai.

Women travellers using the contraceptive pill should take a sufficient supply for the entire trip; your brand may not be available locally. However, the pills can be affected by the extreme heat and if you have diarrhoea or vomiting their effectiveness is reduced, so you'll need other protection.

Marie Stopes International produce a great booklet that is small enough to pack (and also accessible online at Ⓦ *www.mariestopes.org.uk*) and details potential men's and women's sexual health problems and the availability of contraception, emergency contraception and abortion across the globe.

Travelling with children

Health is the most serious concern for anyone thinking of taking children to Asia. As every parent knows, kids can get very sick very quickly, and although they very often recover equally fast, it means that you need to think long and hard about taking them too far off the beaten track where medical treatment may be hard to find. You also need to brief yourself fully about all the potential health hazards you might encounter and get advice from a specialist travel clinic as soon as you begin thinking about the trip, especially as vaccination and malaria prevention and treatment are more complicated for children. Once you are travelling, don't underestimate the stress and exhaustion that kids experience from too much hurtling around, which can make them run-down and more prone to illness. Be sure to include plenty of chilling-out time – you'll all have a better trip that way.

All of the general publications on p.293 and Web sites listed on p.364 have sections devoted to travelling with children, and the malaria Web sites on p.300 are also useful. A few publications offer sensible, down-to-earth advice about children's health. In the UK, the Nomad Medical Centre ☎020/8889 7014 publishes a special information sheet on keeping kids healthy when abroad, full of extremely sensible tips. Other useful resources include the books *Your Child's Health Abroad* by Dr Jane Wilson-Howarth and Dr Matthew Ellis (Bradt Publications); Maureen Wheeler's *Travel with Children* (Lonely Planet) and the Travelling with Children bulletin board at Ⓦ *thorntree.lonelyplanet.com*

Health care in Asia

Millions of people in Asia have only limited access to the good-quality, local, affordable health care that we take for granted. Of course, the situation varies from country to country, but don't be surprised if health facilities are few and far between, staff don't speak English, have only limited training and their equipment for diagnosis and treatment is woefully inadequate.

However, throughout much of Asia there are private hospitals that exist alongside the underfunded and overstretched public facilities. In some cities with a large expatriate population or plenty of tourists, such as Kathmandu, you'll even find specialist travellers' clinics. Check in the guidebook if you get sick, but private places are often the best places to go.

You should make it clear on arrival that you can pay (many hospitals accept credit cards) and set about contacting your insurance company (see p.150 for more on medical insurance). In most cases, you'll end up paying the bill and reclaiming the costs later. In Singapore a visit to a general practitioner will cost you around $20/£13, while in Vietnam, for example, a consultation in an international hospital will be about $40/£27.

Throughout Asia there are plenty of pharmacies and even local corner shops selling drugs that in your home country would only be sold on prescription and/or by trained personnel. This means that on the surface it is apparently easy to self-medicate, although you'll need to know how to take the drugs, as the person who sells it may not. One potential hazard is that many of the drugs distributed in Asia are fakes and possibly below strength, useless or even potentially poisonous. If you do need to buy medicine in Asia, it pays to:

- buy from large, efficient-looking operations, whether hospitals, pharmacies or doctors.
- check that the packaging and labelling looks correct and intact.
- check the expiry date of the drugs you're given.

At the crossover between health care and beauty treatments, there is an increased availability of spa treatments throughout Asia, especially in the more upmarket hotels of Bali, and also in Thailand, where everything from mud wraps to aromatherapy massages and reflexology is on offer to soothe and cossett the body and mind.

Traditional medicine

Many Asian countries have their own traditional health systems, and clinics are invariably willing to treat foreigners, although you may need to take an interpreter with you unless you're pretty fluent in the local language.

Ayurvedic medicine has flourished in India for five thousand years and is a holistic medical system that looks at the whole body and detects imbalances in the system. The body is believed to be controlled by three forces – *pitta*, the force of the sun; *kapha*, associated with the moon; and *vata*, linked to the wind. An imbalance in these is regarded as leading to disease; treatment, often with herbal remedies, concentrates on restoring the balance.

In Tibetan medicine, which derives from ayurvedic medicine, health depends on the balance of the three humours – *beken* (phlegm), *tiba* (bile) and *lung* (wind). A diagnosis is made by examining tongue, pulse and urine and by diagnostic questioning; treatment may be by herbal remedies and/or changes of diet and activity.

China has another ancient holistic medical system with largely herbal remedies, though the often apparently bizarre ingredients in traditional Chinese medicine – such as snake gall bladder and scorpion oil, not to mention the notorious rhinoceros horn – have served to give it a somewhat besmirched reputation outside the country. Acupuncture, where needles are inserted at various "vital points" in the body, is available in clinics across China and Japan – try to make certain that sterile needles are used. There are also non-invasive forms of Asian treatments, such as massage in Thailand and shiatsu in Japan, where finger pressure is used to work on a lot of the same parts of the body as acupuncture.

While opinions in the West vary about the efficacy of such treatments, a considerable body of anecdotal evidence suggests Eastern medicine can help in some situations where Western medicine offers little; for example, ayurvedic medicine can provide useful relief of symptoms in travellers with hepatitis.

12

Keeping in touch

Not only is it fair and reasonable that your friends and family at home will want to keep in touch with you while you're away, but you may be surprised at the extent to which you are delighted by contact with them. Travelling abroad is huge fun and wildly exciting, but it can also be stressful, disorienting and at times depressing, and communication with familiar people is very comforting.

You'll find the quality of most mail and telephone services in Asia very high. However, costs vary – you'll notice a big difference across the continent in the cost of that six-minute phone call home to your bosom chum.

How will we know where you are?

Parents and friends are naturally concerned that there will be periods when, literally, they have no idea where you are. If you do some of the following before you go, it can help to reassure them that you have at least a tentative schedule and aren't as inaccessible as they fear:

- Provide them with a copy of your flight schedule (include carriers and flight numbers), and notify them of any changes as you go. If there should be an Asian plane crash while you are away, they will naturally fear you are on board unless they know otherwise.

- Give them a list of poste restante addresses and dates, a few fax numbers for hotels or American Express offices (they accept faxes for their customers) and dates, a list of cybercafé email addresses and dates and/or, best of all, a free email account that you can access from Asia (see p.322).

- Establish a phoning-in schedule – for example, every four weeks or so. Don't promise to phone at an exact time or even on a specific day though, as if you can't get to a phone for a genuine reason (late bus, phone lines busy, post office closed) you will cause a great deal of worry with the folks back home, who will be imagining newspaper headlines rather than the day-to-day irritations of Asian travel.

- Consider joining a voice-mail scheme, which gives you access to a private answerphone. You leave your message for callers; they call in and leave their own messages, which you can call in and listen to (and you can change your own message at the same time). When you enquire about a scheme, make sure you check whether it is easily accessible from public phones in the countries you are visiting; most schemes rely on tone phones for access.

Mail

To see Asian society in microcosm, get along to the post office. In Indonesia you'll see the hi-tech types heading upstairs for the public Internet access, while downstairs old men struggle to address letters to relatives a couple of islands away, parents queue to send cash to needy children studying away from home, and large businesses register piles of parcels to their overseas customers. Essentially, Asian post offices perform pretty much the same functions as their Western counterparts and come in all sizes. In the larger ones, you'll find different services available from different counters, usually with a jostling crowd

Bhutan postal runners

I lived for some time in a remote village in Bhutan. There was no road to the village and mail was delivered every two or three weeks by a "runner" whose job was literally to run between the nearest post office and all the outlying villages, delivering and collecting mail. He operated on a two-week circuit, travelling across mountain passes, over rivers, through sparsely populated forest, and sleeping wherever he was given hospitality at night. In the old days, runners carried spears to fend off bears (still a considerable hazard in the area), but these days they are more likely to carry transistor radios for company. These also have a bear-scaring purpose, as it is widely believed that if a bear hears voices approaching it will run away – you only get attacked if you scare a bear that hasn't heard you coming.

Lesley Reader

around them rather than a queue. Even the tiniest villages have some system of postal collection and delivery, albeit sometimes bizarre.

Mail is quicker and more reliable from towns and cities, although variability in speed is a common complaint among travellers. Why should my postcard to the UK take three weeks when another traveller reliably reports that his took four days? Such things remain one of the mysteries of the East. Generally, mail does seem to reach its destination (although avoid posting anything other than letters from Nepal). However, it pays to be vigilant – stick the stamps on yourself and ask for them to be franked while you wait, as there is a danger they might be steamed off and reused. It also helps to know what the word for "stamp" looks like in the local language, as few counters are labelled in English and staff generally speak little English.

Poste restante

You've got a few options to receive mail. Most convenient is to use the poste restante service available at post offices in most Asian cities: you just turn up with your passport for ID, and collect it.

The actual system varies enormously across the continent. In some places you get to look through the entire batch of mail that has arrived for any foreigner over the last two years; in others you ask for a particular letter of the alphabet to trawl through. Sometimes you give your name to the clerk who hunts through the mail for you, and some post offices even keep a record of all mail logged in a book or on a computer. In most countries the service is free, although there is sometimes a small charge (in China, for example). Generally the post offices in the more popular tourist destinations are the most reliable and organized – Bangkok, Singapore, Kathmandu and Kuta (Bali) are some of the better places to receive mail; on the other hand, poste restante services are currently most restricted in Cambodia (Phnom Penh only) and Laos (Vientiane and Louang Phabang only).

You should be able to get the precise address of the post office you want to use from a good guidebook; otherwise mail bearing your name followed by "Poste Restante, General Post Office" and the name of the city should get to the main post office. Anyone who writes to you should print your surname in capital letters and underline it. Most places file mail alphabetically by surname, but it pays to check through under your first name as well, or any other name, title or pet name that your nearest and dearest may have used.

Generally post offices only keep mail for a month or so before either returning it or junking it. This means you have to tread a fairly careful line between getting there too early or too late for your letters. The best plan is to get mail sent to a few key places on your itinerary which have reasonably fixed dates rather than try anything too complicated. Some post offices operate a forwarding system for mail that arrives after you've left. You must go in person and register for this service, but it's generally not very reliable.

An alternative to GPO services is to use American Express offices – they accept and hold mail on behalf of their clients and also accept faxes. The branch offices in your home country have a worldwide list of offices and representatives detailing the services they offer. You qualify if you have an Amex card or carry Amex traveller's cheques; you could consider taking an Amex traveller's cheque or two if you want to use the service but are carrying the bulk of your money using another brand of traveller's cheque.

Getting mail addressed to you at hotels is generally the last resort. It'll be coming through the post office in any case, so it's just as easy and probably safer to collect it from there. You can't rely on hotels to have an efficient system and your letters could easily end up in someone's desk drawer, the waste-paper basket or winging their way back home to the sender.

Receiving parcels

It'll save some grief if you remember that parcels and packages are generally less reliably received by travellers than straightforward letters. So many parcels go missing en route that it's better to tell people at home not to send them.

If you really must get stuff sent out to you, it's better to use courier companies. These specialize in getting stuff moved around the world reliably and quickly, but at a price; they charge by both the weight and size of the package. Because they operate door to door, they will not deliver to poste restante addresses – your best bet is to arrange to collect it in their local office. Packages should take between four and seven working days to arrive from the US, UK or Australia. While it's handy to know it can be done, it probably isn't something you'd want to do very often.

Sending letters

Sending letters and postcards from Asia isn't difficult. Address them clearly, writing the destination country in the local language and script, if you can, to speed up processing. Label as airmail, get them weighed at the counter, stick on the stamps or franked label (some post offices use a franking machine) and drop them in the appropriate box. Usually an express service and a registered service are available at extra cost. A few correspondence tips:

● Warn those at home that mail can take three weeks or so in each direction. Nepal is notoriously slow and airmail to the West from Vietnam varies between four days and four weeks (however, post from Singapore is among the fastest in Asia).
● If there has been a big disaster in your area, then, as well as a letter, a quick phone call home will set minds at rest.
● Don't make rash promises to write to people that you are then going to break. If you tell your parents you'll write daily/weekly or whatever, then you really should stick to it or they'll panic about your safety. If you're an irregular and unenthusiastic letter writer, then don't forget that just a signed postcard is enough to stop people worrying. Faxes can be useful – cheaper than phoning but more immediate than letters.
● If your personal stereo has a record button, then as well as or instead of letters, you can send tapes of yourself describing your experiences.

- Don't write to close friends and family in the midst of a bout of dysentery or the day before a bungy-jump and then not contact them again for a few weeks.
- Ask whoever is your most regular correspondent to keep your letters – they make vivid reading when you get back. Some travellers don't write a diary but keep copies of the letters they write as a record of the trip (take carbon paper with you or buy it en route).
- If you send a huge number of postcards the cost can add up, so include it in your budget. The postage rate for cards is often equivalent to that for an aerogramme, which can carry much more news. For example, in China it costs the equivalent of around 20 cents to send a postcard or aerogramme, but around 30–70 cents/20–45p for a letter, whilst from Vietnam you'll pay 50 cents/35p for a postcard and just under $1/65p for a letter to the West.
- Number the letters to people you are writing to regularly so they know if any have gone missing. Get them to do the same if they are writing to you.
- Take some stamps from your home country with you – you may well meet other travellers from home at the end of their trip who'll be happy to drop a few letters in the box for you when they land.

Shipping stuff home

Sending parcels home is rather more time-consuming than sending off letters. You should probably set aside at least half a day to get the formalities completed, but this is definitely preferable to carrying a Sri Lankan mask or Indian rug with you on the rest of your six-month trip.

Basically, your choices are to send them airmail (the most expensive option) or surface mail, or via cargo agents. Charges for parcels sent through the postal system, whether airmail or surface, are calculated by weight. Many post offices in tourist areas sell boxes and tape for packing your goods; others, such as Hong Kong, even have a packing service. In Vietnam it is obligatory that the parcel is wrapped for you. The Indian system involves a time-consuming process whereby the customs desk at the post office first needs to examine the goods you are sending. You are then required to have them stitched into white linen parcels (the stitchers operate outside all post offices) before they are accepted for mailing.

Most cargo agents, on the other hand, ship by volume, with one cubic metre the minimum amount they'll handle. This is the best

Suits you, sir

The tailors in Khao San Road, Bangkok, said they could make me a suit in two days for the equivalent of £30. Despite my ten-month backpacking itinerary still stretching ahead of me, I decided that a made-to-measure silk suit was something I must have. In fact, I ordered two.

The process itself was fascinating: after just two fitting sessions the assortment of pieces of fabric that had been tacked inside out, draped around my body and marked up deftly with chalk lines were transformed into two superb suits – a pale cream one and a rich, deep brown one.

I packaged them up at the main post office, labelling them merely as clothes being returned home – two pairs of trousers and two jackets. In hindsight, parcels like this containing clothes from Bangkok are probably viewed fairly suspiciously, or else I was just unlucky.

The box was opened when it arrived several months later at Liverpool docks, and duty of £60 was imposed on these imported items. Despite costing me twice as much as I had expected, my suits were still bargains.

Jonathan Tucker

option if you have something very heavy to send. Delivery times will be much faster if you're sending from port cities than from inland towns where the goods will have to be transported to the coast first.

Whichever method you opt for, it makes sense to send fewer larger amounts rather than many small ones. Always make sure that, *including* the packaging, what you're sending is just under the maximum of the weight/volume band rather than just over into the next band, which might be considerably more expensive. Bear in mind that whatever you send home is subject to examination by customs in your own country. They are not only looking for illegal substances, but are entitled to charge import duty/taxes on new goods that you are bringing into the country. For example, for parcels sent back to the UK, you have to pay duty once the value of goods in a parcel exceeds £18, although you can send as many parcels as you like.

Finally, classier souvenir stores the world over will always offer to arrange shipping for you. You'll be paying them extra for the service, and there are always some rip-off merchants who take your money and send nothing, so try to go by personal recommendation if you can.

Photographs

One thing worth thinking about is what to do with your photographs on a long trip. Quite apart from the hassle of keeping exposed film with you for months on the road (it deteriorates fast after exposure, and heat and humidity are particularly bad for it), prints weigh a lot and you don't really want to keep negatives and prints together just in case your stuff gets stolen. One option is to send the undeveloped film back home for processing. There are intermittent scares about the theft of exposed film in the post – it is supposedly repackaged and sold as new film – but by sending them one at a time, packing them carefully and registering the package, you'll cut down the danger. Alternatively, send the prints and keep the negatives, or vice versa.

Sending your pictures home is a good way of keeping friends and family informed. A list of pictures with each film sounds extremely anal, but if you are trying to remember which Thai temple, Malaysian island or Tokyo skyscraper your shots are of after another six months' travelling, it'll prove invaluable and give your folks regular up-to-date information about what you're seeing and doing.

Some clued-up cybercafés (see p.322) can even scan your holiday snaps, adding suitable captions ("Look Mum, this is me in the jungle"), and send them along with an email. It's a pretty neat personalized postcard. A few of the more advanced Asian cybercafés can also download images from digital cameras straight into computers but the technology isn't widespread yet.

Phoning home

You'll be able to call home from pretty much any city or large town in Asia and the wide availability of direct dialling means you don't have to cope with an operator in a foreign language. Don't forget the time difference when you phone, though. You'll probably get a better reception from your loved ones if you don't wake them at 3am.

You'll find public telephones throughout the continent, both coin- and phonecard-operated, and some countries (Thailand and Singapore, for example) have phones that accept credit cards. However, with public phones, don't count on having instructions

in English. In most cases, if you're calling home, it's easier to phone from post offices or telephone offices rather than phones on the street, if only to avoid the noise. Avoid making international calls from hotels as they not only charge higher rates for the call, but often slap a service charge on top too.

When calling from a post office or telephone office you'll be directed to a booth, in some cases having paid a deposit, and you can then dial your call directly. The length of the call is logged and the price calculated automatically; you pay the balance or get change from your deposit when it's all over. It's worth checking whether there is a cheaper discounted time to call (typically at weekends and in the middle of the night), if calls are charged by the minute (in which case you'll be charged for the full minute even if you just use ten seconds of it) or by the second, and whether there is a minimum call time (typically 3min).

Reverse-charge calls, charge cards and phone cards

Many telephone offices allow you to make reverse-charge calls or have a Home Country Direct facility, but you may pay a nominal charge for these. With a reverse-charge call, the person you are calling is contacted and asked to accept the charges for that call before you are put through. Home Country Direct is a system that allows you to call the operator in your home country and then use a credit card to pay for the call or arrange a reverse-charge call through them.

You can use telephone charge cards issued in your home country in many Asian countries. These cards enable you to bill the cost of the call to your home number or put the cost onto a previously authorized credit card account. There are also an increasing number of companies issuing prepaid telephone cards that you can use across Asia. In general you apply for the card, add money to it with your credit card and then use an access number once you are overseas to get into the system and make your calls, typically at a discount when compared with the cost of paying for a call locally.

The advantage of telephone charge cards is that they save you using up your cash when you're travelling. When applying for any of these cards you need to check they are usable in the countries you intend to visit. As it can be difficult to get hold of the right local number to access the system when you're on the road, get a list of these from your issuing company for every country you intend to visit, and make sure you carry it with you.

Shall I take the mobile?

Taking your mobile phone from home on your Asian travels isn't as daft as it sounds. Mobile telephone systems in many Asian countries are highly sophisticated – when you land and switch on your phone, your network searches for the local partner, you confirm that you want to use them and off you go. One potential difficulty is that you'll need to recharge your phone as usual, so you may need to carry an adaptor to cope with the local electricity supply. You'll also need to investigate carefully the precise costs involved in calls that you make, and that are made to you, while you are overseas – or you could easily end up bankrupting yourself while you are away. The advantages of not needing to mess with local phone systems are clear and it may well put family minds at rest to know that you are fairly accessible – although whether you want that is another matter entirely and it may simply make everyone frantic if you switch off and don't let them know.

Fax

Facilities for faxing are widely available across Asia, but take a bit more hunting out than phones. Try post offices, telephone offices and the business centres of international-class hotels (the most expensive option). You'll be charged by the page or minute (find out which before you send the message) and you will also pay a charge if you receive faxes. Charges for faxes are usually in line with the telephone charges of the country.

Email

Access to the Internet is pretty much global these days and public facilities are increasingly available. There are already scores of cyber-cafés on Bali and in major tourist centres in Thailand, a brilliant Internet centre in the departure lounge at Changi Airport in Singapore, public email services in major post offices across Indonesia

and cybercafés in at least four Cambodian cities; even in remote Kathmandu you'll find private companies offering email access. However, don't expect too much outside the major population and tourist centres; check out ⓦ*www.cybercafe.com* or ⓦ*www.cybercaptive.com* for an idea of just where to find cybercafés across Asia.

The way cybercafés charge varies enormously; some do it by the minute, others in 10- or 25-minute units, but generally costs do work out a lot cheaper than sending a fax or making a phone call. If you're going to be passing through cyber-friendly towns and tourist centres on a fairly regular basis, email can make a good alternative to poste restante – even if you're not on the Internet at home. There are three different ways of doing this.

Using your existing account

One option is to use your existing, home-based email account accessed via the Web site of your Internet Service Provider; check before you leave home whether or not this is possible and make sure you know your username and password. Even if you have an existing account, consider subscribing to a free email account for the duration of your trip and getting all your friends to copy their mail to the new account in case your home account is difficult to access.

Setting up a free email account

Even if you don't already have Internet access at home, you can set up a free Web-based account either before you leave home (using someone else's system or a cybercafé) or in a cybercafé somewhere in Asia; staff at the cybercafé can help you do this. Several companies offer free, private and personal accounts, such as ⓦ*www.yahoo.com* and ⓦ*www.mailcity.com*, but by far the most popular is Hotmail ⓦ*www.hotmail.com* – any cybercafé will have Hotmail bookmarked for easy access. All you need to do to set up an account is access the Web site of the free account provider and follow the instructions.

Give friends and family your new address and they can send you messages any time – it will stack up in a nice pile in your inbox, ready for you to access whenever you can. You can of course use your new account to send out email as well.

Using cybercafés as poste restantes

The third option is to use local cybercafé addresses as email poste restantes. This involves getting a particular cybercafé's email address (see ⓦ *www.cybercafe.com* or ⓦ *www.cybercaptive.com*) and giving it to the people who'll be emailing you, so it's only really viable if you're staying in one place for a while. It isn't really an ideal option, though, as places do vary quite a lot in efficiency. Many cybercafés print out the day's emails and keep them in a file for a few weeks, much as a post office would with letters; others just let you scroll through their inbox, which means anybody could open your stuff and so it could easily get deleted by accident. The important thing to remember when using cybercafés' addresses is that your correspondent should write your name in the subject box. These cafés let you use their accounts to send email as well, so it doesn't matter that you haven't got your own.

The media

You won't have to rely solely on contact with your friends and family for news from home. Newspapers from Europe, Australia and North America are often available a few days late in Asian capital cities and tourist centres. However, the supply is sometimes unreliable and the price high. Most Asian countries also publish good-quality English-language newspapers of their own for English-speaking local people, tourists and expatriates. Several of the magazines mentioned in Chapter Five, such as the *Far Eastern Economic Review* and *Asiaweek*, as well as the Asian editions of *Time* and *Newsweek*, are published locally – airports and the bookshops in luxury hotels are usually a good source if you have any difficulty finding them. Alternatively log on to the electronic versions from a cybercafé.

Television

Satellite and cable television have reached some very remote corners of Asia, and you'll find league soccer from England and Italy is a great favourite throughout Indonesia and Malaysia. Most mid- to top-range hotels offer CNN or BBC World, and Asian satellite networks such as Star or MTV, while some restaurants use them to lure in customers.

Radio

Worldwide radio networks, including the BBC, Voice of America and the Australian Broadcasting Corporation, broadcast across the globe 24 hours a day, while many countries have an indigenous English-language radio station or schedule. A radio is a great way of getting up-to-the-minute news in the more remote areas and it's well worth considering travelling with one. A pair of earphones will mean you can listen when people around you, on buses, in dorms, etc, are sleeping.

Buy a radio with the greatest number of short-wave bands you can afford, as most stations change their frequency during the day and you'll want to be able to follow them through the changes. Get hold of a copy of the programming schedule for your country's international network before you leave home – it'll tell you which frequencies to pick them up on at which times across Asia. Major international broadcasters, such as the BBC World Service ⓦ*www.bbc.co.uk/worldservice*, the Voice of America ⓦ*www.voa.gov* and Radio Australia ⓦ*www.abc.net.au/ra/*, publish schedules and frequencies on their Web sites.

13

Crime, safety and sleaze

While it is news of tragic accidents, violent weather conditions, kidnappings and fatalities that reaches the world's media, most people who run into trouble in Asia are the victims of far more ordinary petty theft, robbery and con tricks. However, having your stuff stolen is no joke, getting taken for a ride leaves a nasty taste in the mouth, and losing your passport, traveller's cheques and credit cards can land you with major inconvenience and possibly ruin your trip. The information in this chapter should help to steer you away from the pitfalls that await the unwary in Asia, and help you to cope if disaster strikes.

The underlying rule is to travel with the instincts you use to keep you safe at home. If it's your first time in Asia it can be difficult to establish the norm; it's easy to overreact and get spooked without real reason. However, it's better that way than blithely marching into danger with eyes fixed wonderingly on the blue horizon, white-sand beach and glittering sunshine. Just because you're on holiday, the crooks aren't.

We've said it before, but nobody should set foot in Asia without adequate insurance; see p.150 for more information.

Read up, find out, calm down

Supplement your guidebook reading with up-to-the-minute information from newspapers and magazines. Even the most dramatic civil war isn't going to find its way into a guidebook for several months at the least, but it'll be splashed across the world's media in a couple of hours. Travellers' newsgroups and bulletin boards on the Internet are also an excellent resource (see p.368 for a list of some of the best).

All Western governments are concerned about keeping their citizens safe abroad. They each have a department at home to advise on safety issues overseas (see p.365) – contact them to find out the current situation in the places you are intending to visit. In the event of an emergency while you're travelling, contact your embassy or consulate abroad (see p.336 for advice on how they can help you); a list is available from the relevant government departments at home.

Get it into perspective

Asia has its own specific hazards, aside from the ones that travellers will find anywhere in the world. These include landmines in Cambodia, Vietnam, Laos and along the Cambodian–Thai border; terrorist groups in the southern Philippines; civil unrest in parts of Indonesia; the violence that usually precedes elections in India; active volcanoes right across the continent; riptides on many Indian Ocean beaches; and drug-resistant malaria on the Thai–Cambodian and Thai–Burmese borders.

However, you should always put the information you receive into perspective. If you read about rioting in Xinjiang province in China and you're heading for Shanghai, it's a good idea to stay alert, but with the distance between the two at almost 4000km, chances are you'll be out of the line of fire. If, on the other hand, one of the larger Indonesian volcanoes erupts fairly exuberantly on a small island just 20km across a stretch of ocean from where you were planning a fortnight by the sea, it may be an idea to think again. You might also want to take a look at *The World's Most Dangerous Places* by Pelton, Aral and Dulles (Fielding Worldwide), which, despite its decidedly gung-ho title, is a detailed and fascinating account of wars, political upheaval and crime across the world, putting some of the dangers to travellers into the global political context.

Theft

Most crime against tourists is opportunistic theft of one sort or other. A few guidelines will help you cut down on the chances of it being you that gets robbed:

- Carry money and vital documents in a concealed money belt kept on you at all times, unless they're in short-time storage in security boxes or safes at a hotel.
- Never leave your valuables on the beach while you swim – most travel shops sell waterproof money belts or plastic canisters that you can wear round your neck.
- Never leave your passport, traveller's cheques and credit cards in a guesthouse safe "for safekeeping" while you go off trekking. Many a visitor has returned a week or so later to find everything intact, only to realize, when their credit card bill comes in, that the card has been used right up to its credit limit while they've been slogging through the jungle.
- Keep photocopies of important documents (e.g. passport, traveller's cheque numbers, airline tickets, insurance policy) in a separate place, plus a small stash of cash in case of robbery.
- Don't flaunt what you've got. Avoid wearing a lot of jewellery, use a cheap watch and carry your camera in your daypack.
- Use padlocks to lock your pack and attach it to immovable fittings on long-distance journeys. This also protects against unwanted items, such as drugs, being stored in your pack.
- Use your own padlock to supplement or replace the one on your guesthouse door.
- Never carry important stuff in rucksack pockets on your back; they are especially vulnerable to theft. You can always carry a small pack on your front where you can keep an eye on it.
- Beware of accepting food or drink from fellow passengers on journeys. Some rogues ply the unwary with drugged food and drink and, while they are sleeping off the effects, steal everything they

own. This is an alarmingly common occurrence in Thailand, among other places.

- Don't automatically trust other Westerners, and be just as careful in dormitories as you are in other situations – a small percentage of travellers fund their own journeys by thieving from others.

The natural world

Asia is full of volcanoes that erupt, winds that transform themselves into typhoons, snakes that bite, rivers that flood, land that slips, and earth that moves and cracks asunder at regular intervals. Or so it appears if you have a disaster mentality and don't manage to temper what you read with reality. If you're the sort of person who likes to have a plan for every eventuality, take a look at *The Worst Case Scenario Survival Handbook* by Joshua Piven and David Borgenicht (Chronicle Books) which details how to escape killer bees or a mountain lion, and how to wrestle free from an alligator, along with a host of other unlikely scenarios.

Volcanoes and earthquakes

Being at the confluence of several of the world's largest tectonic plates, which are constantly shifting, Asia has a much higher level of volcanic and earthquake activity than many travellers are used to. Seismologists are notoriously unable to predict when and where the next big event will take place, but realistically the chances of being caught in a severe earthquake or a volcanic eruption are extremely slim.

If you are unfortunate enough to be involved in a strong quake, you should stay indoors if possible (corrugated-iron sheets flying off roofs are a common cause of fatalities). Stay away from windows to avoid splintering glass; shelter in a doorway if the building looks in danger of collapse (the lintel that supports the wall above the door is the strongest part of the structure). Although phone lines will be damaged after a major quake, try to get in touch with friends and relatives at home as soon as possible, to let them know you're safe.

Typhoons

If you know that a typhoon is expected in your town, the best advice is to get yourself established in a guesthouse or hotel that feels safely and solidly built (don't be stingy about paying up and moving to a better place for the night), and to stay indoors. Ideally you should sleep in a room that is not on the ground floor as it could get submerged. Keep all windows closed and move your bed away from them if possible – flying debris might smash the glass. Expect to be stranded in your room for up to 24 hours after the typhoon hits, while you wait for the flood waters to subside, so get yourself enough drinking water, some food and a good book before you tuck yourself away.

Dangerous animals

The chances of coming face to face with poisonous snakes and savage animals are obviously higher in the jungles of Kalimantan than most places back home, but you should be fine if you listen to local advice and take sensible precautions:

- Don't antagonize any snake, anywhere. They usually avoid human contact, but will strike if threatened.
- Trek with local guides who know the terrain and the hazards.
- Keep fires or lanterns burning at night if you are camping in the jungle.
- Never walk without shoes – you're giving snakes and biting insects a better chance of getting bare skin when they attack.

" Typhoon Linda

I arrived in Chumphon, South Thailand, to find preparations in full swing. Typhoon Linda was on her way, due in around 1am, and was expected to cause more damage than her predecessor who'd hit the town two months earlier. What happened then, I asked. "The water came up to here," said the guy in the restaurant, indicating a tidemark on his wall that was 1.5m above the floor, "and we all had to stay indoors for 48 hours because you couldn't get down the street without swimming." At the house next door, a lady was dragging her best teak furniture up to the first floor – she didn't want a repeat performance of the last time, she explained, showing off her own tidemarks, also 1.5m high. Her husband, meanwhile, was storing his motorbike in a neighbour's upstairs loft.

Every downstairs room in the town seemed to have a tidemark. And Linda was set to be even more vicious. A crowd stood outside the TV shop, where all the sets were tuned to the weather station, and a loudspeaker van was circulating through the town, issuing official sounding instructions.

Faced with the prospect of spending two soggy days confined to my hardboard cell of a guesthouse, I decided to relocate, choosing a hotel room on the third floor, where the outside walls didn't seem likely to crumble in a Force 10. I stocked up on 48 hours' worth of food and water, battened down the window shutters, got my torch out in case the power lines went down, and fell asleep wondering how things would look in the morning.

Not very different, as it turned out. A few puddles, but no obvious devastation. The guesthouse manager looked happy: Linda had diverted at the last minute, and had struck Prachuap instead, 170km up the coast. And so it was that the newspaper pictures of razed houses and submerged town centres, and the scenes of distraught families that filled the TV screens that evening, were of a town that I'd left the day before, and not of Chumphon after all. **"**

Lucy Ridout

- Shake out your shoes each morning; scorpions love to sleep inside and won't take kindly to a bare foot disturbing their rest.
- If you get bitten by a snake, immobilize the limb and avoid all movement. The aim is to reduce your heart rate and the speed with which any toxin spreads through your body. Send someone for medical help.

Transport

Anyone who has spent even a few minutes on a bus hurtling along the Trans-Sumatran or West Bengal highways (or, in fact, almost any main road in Asia) has a very clear idea of the dangers of road travel on the continent. Driving is fast, furious and often heedless, with overtaking on blind corners the norm and horns rather than brakes the response to any surprise event or potential hazard. Vehicles are poorly maintained, road conditions horrendous and driving schedules very pressurized, so drivers are often exhausted.

The trouble is that the other options are often no better. Ferries in Asia are regularly overloaded and lack even the most basic safety equipment, and many of the small domestic aircraft companies have dubious safety standards. For this reason, many travellers feel much safer on trains and, in countries where there is a rail network, it is often the least hazardous way to travel. Make safety rather than economy your main consideration, and if it means surrendering your ticket rather than boarding what seems like a certain death trap or simply getting off a bus halfway to your destination, then do it.

Wars, unrest and bandits

Gruesome as it seems, there is a new type of tourism prevailing today, known as "terror tourism". Some people, reading of civil unrest, war, conflict or other examples of the worst that human beings can do to each other, book their plane ticket and head off to the danger zone to view the proceedings at close quarters. For the rest of us, this type of news is an indicator to reroute ourselves, and fast.

The sad fact is that armed conflicts are more frequent around the world than we'd like to think in our snug little armchairs at home. The big ones, new ones and ones that are particularly relevant to our economy hit the media big time; the others smoulder away, largely ignored by the rest of the world. Some of the most significant for travellers to Asia are those in:

- Irian Jaya, Aceh, Maluku and West Timor in Indonesia. Independence movements are in opposition to the Indonesian government in both Irian Jaya and Aceh. Problems also persist in Maluku where there has been religious violence between Christians and Muslims since January 1999, leaving hundreds dead and thousands injured and made homeless. Though East Timor has now won independence from Indonesia, the province of West Timor remains host to thousands of East Timorese refugees, and pro-Indonesian militias are still on the rampage here; travel in both is likely to be inadvisable for some time to come.

- There are a huge number of guns in Cambodia, and there have been incidents of armed robbery. That said, the security situation in Cambodia has improved significantly over the last few years; check the current situation before you go. Gun crime is a problem in Phnom Penh, and reaches a peak at festival times, most notably Khmer New Year. Taking a few simple precautions can reduce the risk; rather than walking, use a trustworthy moto-driver, preferably someone recommended by your hotel or guesthouse. If you are robbed, do not resist and do not run.

- Kashmir. Various militant separatist groups are fighting it out with government forces and Western hostages have been taken, never to be seen again.

- Sri Lanka. The Tamil Tiger guerrillas are fighting for an independent state, making the north and east of the country too dangerous for visitors. The rest of the island is also affected, with Colombo, the capital, the focus of an irregular bombing campaign.

- Mindanao (southern Philippines) and Eastern Sabah (Malaysia). Kidnapping has increased alarmingly on Mindanao recently, and this has spilled over into Malaysian territory. In April 2000, 21 hostages, including ten Western tourists, were kidnapped from the Malaysian diving resort of Sipadan Island and held for several months in the southern Philippines by the rebel Muslim Abu Sayyaf group. Check the situation in both areas before travelling.

However, bear in mind the earlier comments about getting things into perspective; many problems are very localized. Much of Indonesia, Malaysia and Sri Lanka continue to attract thousands of visitors who have trouble-free visits and return home safely. Things can change fast – be sure to keep abreast of Asian news, check the Web sites on p.365 at regular intervals while you're on the road and, most important of all, seek local advice if you are uncertain about any potential destination.

It's also worth bearing in mind that democracy in many parts of Asia is often a very different creature to the familiar form in the West, and in the run-up to elections there can be a very high level of tension and violence. Every election in India brings several deaths and hundreds of injuries through fighting between the supporters of different parties. In some cases, violence follows elections – particularly in the case of disputed results. Unless you are a political science student there for a purpose, it is best to give Asian elections a wide berth. If you do get caught up in trouble, obey any curfews imposed by the authorities. Similarly, strikes are very different events from those experienced in the West and often involve a high degree of local tension. Keep your ear to the ground for any that are planned and then just sit tight – everything will be shut down anyway.

Common scams

Many of the common scams perpetrated on hapless tourists in Asia are legendary. These scams change, evolve and become more sophisticated, but never really go away. They range from the ridiculous to potentially more serious ones, and the best source for up-to-date information on these is other travellers – they've been there, seen it, and probably been caught by it as well. Talk to people on the road and learn from their mistakes. Watch out for:

- various miscalculation tricks when you're changing money, especially prevalent when dealing with hundreds of thousands of Indonesian rupiahs. There are even rigged calculators in some places. Work out what you should have and count it carefully before you leave the counter.
- sleights of hand over the denomination of note you have given in

payment in a shop or post office. Tricksters hide the note and produce one of a much lower denomination, telling you that you haven't paid enough. Keep your wits about you and know what you are handing over.

- hotel touts and some taxi drivers, who will be desperate to get you to hotels where they either have an interest or will get a chunk of commission (it'll go on your bill, never fear). So beware if they tell you the hotel you want is full or perhaps even burned down. If they claim that the place has no beds, go and ask at reception yourself; they sometimes have stooges on the steps outside, looking official and repeating the misinformation.

- certain taxi drivers who tell you major sights are closed and that you're much better taking a tour with them as your driver for the day – or going to visit their brother's shop instead of the Taj Mahal. Again, go and check for yourself.

- the classic scam in Thailand – persuading gullible, and greedy, tourists that they are being offered an incredibly good deal on cut diamonds or other gems. Travellers are attracted by the prospect of hundreds, if not thousands, of dollars' profit to be made in their own country by selling the diamonds at home. So, despite knowing nothing about precious stones, they spend $100 on a handful of sparklers and ten times out of ten

" Indian shoeshine

At 6am on my first day in India, I arrived by airport bus in the centre of New Delhi. Not wishing to appear more vulnerable than my bloodshot eyes and untanned skin made me look, I shouldered my pack and began to walk as confidently as I could.

After a few minutes my worst fears were realized when I felt a tap on my shoulder and turned round to face a very dark, scrawny man with a glint in his eye. He was frantically pointing at my feet. I looked down to discover a neat pile of dung – about the size of a molehill and as perfectly formed – resting on the top of my right shoe. My immediate reaction was amazement: how on earth had this pile of shit managed to tread on me?

As I stood awe-struck, my Indian friend knelt down, produced a rag from the cloth bag slung over his shoulder, and started to wipe my shoe clean. He performed this task with a full-bodied, jerking action, which caused the bag to slip from his shoulder. When I saw its contents, the penny dropped and the mystery was solved.

This man had crept up behind me, scooped a portion of dung from his bag and skilfully dolloped it on top of my shoe as I walked. Now, of course, he demanded his fee for cleaning my shoes, holding up his soiled rag as evidence of his hard work. "

Ross Velton

Room service

In a hotel in Danang, Vietnam, a woman walked straight into my room while I was lying there naked under my mosquito net. She didn't mess around: "Would you like sex, mouth, love, touch or massage with no clothes?" When I said a polite "No, thank you", she looked at me rather despondently and added, "Do you have any washing, then?"

Chris Humphrey

The only guest at the only hotel in town, I spent the evening on the veranda listening to tales of the days of the Raj. Charming and well educated, the manager was the perfect host, until he casually slipped into the conversation, "Do you need your own room tonight or would you prefer to share mine?" I acted suitably horrified and haughty, demanded my own room and barricaded the door, just in case. But the manager had already forgotten the incident.

Nicki McCormick

arrive home to learn their hands are full of pretty, but totally worthless, cut glass.

- rogue policemen at Delhi railway station, who insist that to remain in Delhi you have to register with them and, needless to say, pay to do so. The best way to tackle this is to offer to go to the police station and fill in the forms there.

Sexual harassment

Much of the Asian continent is awash with Western films, videos and magazines that portray the West as sexually rampant, with Western women taking an active part. When you graft onto that a population of Western female travellers who relate to men in ways unheard of in the Asian population, dress in ways local people may consider highly provocative and – perhaps the greatest difference of all – actually have the freedom to travel around the world unchaperoned, it isn't surprising that misunderstandings and misconceptions are rife. Generally, the local perception of Western female travellers is of sexual availability and promiscuity. This means that harassment, both verbal and physical, is unfortunately alive and flourishing across the continent. The following tips may help:

- Always carry enough cash on you in case you need to take a taxi to get back to your hotel.

- Make sure your hotel room is secure. Be especially careful to check door and window locks. You may want to use your own padlock and/or wooden door wedge.
- Observe how local women dress – if you cover up similar bits of flesh you may feel more comfortable and attract less unwelcome attention.
- Be aware of the different interpretations placed on some behaviour in other cultures. For example, smiling and making eye contact with a man in countries such as India, Pakistan and Indonesia is interpreted as a distinct come-on, as is a casual touch.
- Talk about the sister of the man hassling you; equate yourself with her and ask how he would want her treated in similar situations.
- Adopt a mythical husband: some women travellers wear a ring, carry his photograph and pictures of the mythical kids with which to bore potential pests.
- Try not to let any hassles get you down to the extent where you close yourself to all local contact and friendliness – it isn't personal.
- Join up with other solo women travellers for some of your trip if it suits you. Don't stay alone out of mistaken pride; there's no right and wrong way to travel.
- Don't automatically trust other Westerners because of familiarity and don't distrust local people because of their apparent strangeness.

Don't forget it can work both ways: some men feel extremely uncomfortable with the upfront approaches of many Asian prostitutes. Whilst many women cope with sexual harassment as a part of everyday life, for many men the experience comes as a rude, and often distressing, awakening.

Drugs

Asian governments appear somewhat schizophrenic about drugs: they openly condemn them but know they are sold to tourists in certain places and seem to turn a blind eye. However, the penalties for trafficking or possession are serious: Malaysia enforces the death penalty for drug smuggling, and in Thailand long prison sentences are the punishment for attempting to get drugs out of the country. Even buying drugs for your own immediate use isn't worth the risks; set-ups by dealers and the police are common.

The situation is made more complicated by the fact that in some areas of India, for example, drugs – typically marijuana and opium

– are sold openly in *bhang* shops, principally to help religious meditation, and are smoked in public without any retribution. Unless you are absolutely sure of the local situation, the best advice is still to steer clear. Unfortunately this doesn't always help – there have been worrying reports of travellers in Goa having drugs planted on them and then being blackmailed into parting with huge amounts of cash which often have to be forwarded from home, to escape prosecution.

If disaster strikes

Your embassy or consulate abroad can:

- issue emergency passports.
- contact friends and family and ask them to help with money or tickets.
- help you get in touch with local doctors, lawyers and interpreters.
- advise on local organizations which help trace missing persons.
- contact and visit their citizens in local prison.
- arrange for next-of-kin to be informed about serious illness or death.

However, your embassy or consulate cannot:

- give you money (though they may be able to cash a cheque or give you a loan under very strict criteria).
- pay your bills or pay to get you home, except in very exceptional circumstances.
- intervene in legal proceedings or give legal advice.
- get better treatement for you than other prisoners or hospital patients.
- get you out of prison.
- arrange employment, accommodation or work permits.

You may also need to:

- contact the police. If you are the victim of crime they'll need to take a statement from you.
- contact your insurance company. Carry your policy number and their emergency number with you and leave copies at home. There are claims procedures that you must take care to follow in the event of theft or your claim will be invalid. You will need

receipts for recently bought goods and for expenses you have incurred, and you'll need a police report to support your claim. Similarly, in the event of serious medical emergencies, the correct procedures must be followed; if you need hospitalization you will have to inform your insurers within certain time limits.

● cancel your credit cards if they're stolen; if traveller's cheques have been stolen, contact the issuing company to order your replacements (see p.178).

14

Coming home

Everyone expects to suffer from culture shock when they go away to distant places, but it can be an even greater shock when you arrive back home. People's lives have moved on, the dog has had puppies and Uncle Toby really doesn't want to hear in graphic detail about Delhi Belly or cosmic enlightenment on Mount Fuji. You may feel that your experiences have totally changed your life and the direction you see yourself moving, while those closest to you hope you've "got it out of your system" and are now ready to settle down. The following tips may help you cope:

- Before you go away, put some money aside as your arriving-home fund, and vow not to touch it while you are on your travels – coming home can be bad enough, never mind returning without a cent to your name.
- Make sure you have kept in touch with people at home and tried to paint a realistic picture about your experiences and thoughts. Then you can discuss these honestly when you get home, and people won't be too surprised by the way you've changed while you've been away.
- Get in touch with other travellers you've met on the road, who are probably going through similar experiences at the same time.
- Keep in touch with local people you've met on your travels rather than cutting yourself off from the experience – if you haven't yet sent them the photographs you promised, then do it as soon as you get home.

- While you're still travelling, make some plans, however rudimentary, for the immediate future after you get home. The worst possible homecoming is to come back to nothing. Even if it's only a plan to save up to travel some more, at least it's a plan of action.
- Compile an album or two of your best photos, with labels to remind you of place names, people and dates. Or edit down your slides into a really good show. Your beautifully presented photos and slides will give you pleasure for years to come and are a great way of sharing your experiences. They might even inspire you to return.

Getting involved

Whatever the delights of Asia, there is no doubt that some of the poorest people on the planet are inhabitants of the continent, their lives made harsher by autocratic political regimes, big-business interests, exploitation, poverty, ignorance and appalling health and educational opportunities. You may want to find out about these aspects of Asia before you set off on your trip or to get involved with these issues when you return; this is a positive way of using your experiences for the benefit of others and beginning to make sense of everything that you saw and did while you were away.

Below we list some major organizations campaigning about issues in

Half Westerner

I sat around the fire in a smoke-filled kitchen in the village of Buli, in the Keng region of Bhutan – one of the most isolated areas of one of the most isolated countries in the world. I'd been living and teaching in Bhutan for three years, learned enough of the language to make friends and crack jokes, and adored the rhythm of the rural, Buddhist lifestyle and the stunning countryside. I relished living with no electricity, telephone or running water, cooking my food over a wood fire and getting mail only every few weeks. Every way of thinking, every belief system, every way of being that I had ever known had been shaken and stirred. Yet I was planning to leave. I fumbled for the words to explain to my friends that I'd begun to lose who I was and where I came from. I was no longer a Londoner, no longer knew what that meant, but I wasn't and never could be Bhutanese either. One old lady, Ama Choden, nodded her head, "Wiji sem hab chillngpa wenta, hab Drukpa wenta." Your heart is half Westerner, half Bhutanese. As I write this I can see her fantastically lined face in the flickering firelight, taste again the local brew that we were drinking, feel the left-over burn from the fiery chillis in the curry we'd just eaten. I can see again the tears on her cheeks as she realized I was leaving and my own eyes fill again at the memory.

Letters are rare – most people can't write English or find money for stamps. Last month I heard a friend died almost two years ago. Even now, many years later, as I walk along the road I am suddenly transported and I can see again the first view of Buli on the trek over the pass, the deep-sided gorge of the valley or the fluttering white prayer flags under a brilliant blue sky. Some days I walk along the street practising the language so I don't forget. One day I may go back. Or I may never return. I became enough of a Buddhist while I was there to know that fate will decide. My soul is indeed half Westerner, half Bhutanese.

Lesley Reader

Asia. They can all offer a vital antidote to the tourist veneer you may have read. Though these are all big organizations, if you digest the information and follow the links in their Web sites, you'll end up learning about a lot of very important, small-scale campaigns:

- **Amnesty International** campaigns for human rights worldwide, publishing reports on the situation in countries across the globe. They are perhaps best known for their ongoing campaigns for individual Prisoners of Conscience, involving flooding various governments with letters and postcards on behalf of individuals they've unfairly imprisoned. Amnesty's Web site has a huge amount of information (much of it detailing stuff that governments would rather keep deeply buried) and a superb range of links to other human-rights related sites. **W** *www.amnesty.org*
- **The International Campaign to Ban Landmines** brings together over 1300 groups in 75 countries, all campaigning to ban landmines and increase the amount of the resources devoted to de-mining, the rehabilitation of victims, and increasing awareness of the problem of mines worldwide. This is highly relevant for Asian travellers; Cambodia and parts of Thailand, India, Pakistan, the Phillippines, Bangladesh, Laos and Vietnam are all affected. There's a long way to go; five hundred people are killed each week by landmines and for every mine removed, it is estimated that twenty more are planted. **W** *www.icbl.org*
- **One World** is just one of the organizations involved in the Drop The Debt campaign to try to combat the huge and often crippling debt that many developing countries still have outstanding to institutions in the developed nations. For every dollar in aid that the developed world currently sends to the less-developed nations, around $9 flows in the other direction in debt repayment, funds that the United Nations estimates could save the lives of more than seven million children each year if used for health and education instead. **W** *www.oneworld.org*
- Probably most famous for some of its well-publicized direct action protests, **Greenpeace** is a worldwide campaigning group concerned with all manner of environmental issues, including toxic waste disposal, climate change and forest conservation, several of which are directly relevant to Asia. **W** *www.greenpeace.org*
- The **World Society for the Protection of Animals** campaigns against animal cruelty and to relieve animal suffering throughout the world. Their campaigns include opposing bear-baiting in rural Pakistan and the deforestation and destruction of orang-utan habi-

tats in Indonesia, and improving the conditions of captive tigers in Taiwan. ⓦ *www.wspa.org.uk*

- Another campaigning organization concerned with animals, the **Environmental Investigation Agency**, probes, exposes and campaigns against the illegal trade in wildlife and the destruction of the natural environment. Current concerns include the trade in rhino horn, imported by Taiwan and China in particular; and the destruction of tigers in India, largely so their body parts can be illegally exported for use in traditional medicine. ⓦ *www.eia-international.org*

- Probably one of the most famous political campaigns, the **Free Tibet Campaign**, is working towards ending the occupation of Tibet by China and allowing the Tibetan people to decide their own future. They work through public campaigns (including letter-writing on behalf of individuals who have fallen foul of the Chinese regime in Tibet), direct action and raising awareness; their Web site has excellent links for anyone interested in Tibet. ⓦ *www.freetibet.org*

- We've not included Burma in this book because of global concern about the human-rights situation there and the suppression of democracy within the country; the pro-democracy leader Aung San Suu Kyi has called for outsiders to boycott the country because of this. The **Burma Campaign** has excellent briefing materials on the situation in Burma, and organizes letter-writing campaigns to support its work. ⓦ *www.burmacampaign.org.uk*

- The **End Child Prostitution in Asian Tourism Campaign (ECPAT)** is a global network of organizations and individuals working together to end the sexual exploitation of children for commercial purposes. It's estimated that a fifth of Vietnam's growing commercial sex industry, and around a third of the six thousand sex workers in Cambodia's capital Phnom Penh, are under 18 years of age. ECPAT's Web site has plenty of relevant news items on the issue. ⓦ *www.ecpat.net*

- Supporting tribal people throughout the world, **Survival International** campaigns against governments, companies, banks, extremist missionaries, guerrilla armies and anyone who violates tribal people's rights, and works closely with tribal people themselves to do this. They're currently campaigning on behalf of the Jummas, who live in Bangladesh's Chittagong Hill Tracts; the Jarawa people of the Andaman islands in India; the 250 tribes of Irian Jaya (West Papua) in Indonesia, and the Subanen people of the Philippines. ⓦ *www.survival-international.org*

Making your trip work for you

In the longer term you may be looking for work either at home or overseas. You'll be in a better position to sell yourself to future employers if you can not only describe your trip as a time of enormous pleasure but can also point to skills or experiences that you developed while travelling or once back home.

Don't forget your resolution to learn Hindi, Thai, Japanese, Mandarin or whatever language fascinated or defeated you while you were away. Local evening classes are the most sociable way of doing this, or if you've a university near you with foreign students, you may be able to arrange one-to-one tuition or exchange English lessons for the language you want to learn.

Putting up a Web site about your travels can be a satisfying way of crystallizing your experiences and feelings, as well as a great way of developing computer/Web-design skills in the process. True, the Net is already full of boringly self-important Web sites, but there are also plenty of quality personal sites too. The best travellers' sites are both entertaining and useful – see the online sections of Where To Go, pp.3–102, for some inspiration.

Working in the travel industry

In the longer term, your experiences in Asia can help prepare you for a job as a tour guide with a travel company. However, you'll need to qualify in first aid and convince the tour operator of your background knowledge, sense of responsibility and cool head in an emergency before they'll entrust a group of paying customers into your care. Look out in the travel press for job advertisements (in the UK, *Wanderlust* magazine carries these) before you go, so you've some idea of what they are after. Once you're on the road, keep your eyes and ears open, and you may encounter and have the chance to quiz some people already working in the industry; back home, travel fairs are a good place to talk to potential employers and people already working in the field.

Travel writing and photography

It may be possible to sell the story of your journey and/or photos when you get back, perhaps to student magazines or local newspapers. To sell your pictures, you'd be better off with slides rather than prints, and you should, in any case, have a good look at the type of travel articles favoured by different newspapers and magazines. Unless you have a track record or contacts, you're unlikely to elicit much interest before you go, but when you come back you can write your articles and submit them "on spec" to the publications you have chosen.

Travel writing and photography aren't easy areas to break into, but have a look at *Writing Travel Books and Articles* (Self-Counsel Press) by Richard Cropp, Barbara Braidwood and Susan Boyce; Guy Marks' *Travel Writing and Photography: All You Need to Know to Make it Pay* (Travellers Press); or Louise Purwin Zobel's *The Travel Writer's Handbook: How to Write and Sell Your Own Travel Experiences* (Marlowe) for some tips.

First-Time Asia

Basics

National tourist offices

Not all countries have a national tourist organization with overseas offices, but most at least have an official Web site. If there is no tourist office in your country, you could try contacting the embassy for information (see p.350 for embassy details), or check out the online directory of tourist offices worldwide, at Ⓦ*www.towd.com* There's plenty of useful information elsewhere online too: see p.367 for a list of recommended springboards.

Bangladesh

Ⓦ*www.bdonline.com/tourism*
No overseas tourist office.

Bhutan

Ⓦ*www.kingdomofbhutan.com*
Contact the Tourism Authority of Bhutan, P.O. Box 126, Thimphu, Bhutan ☏975-2-23251, ✆975-2-23695

Brunei

No overseas tourist office.

Cambodia

Ⓦ*www.cambodia-web.net*
No national tourist office.

China

Ⓦ*www.cnto.org*
Ⓦ*www.hkta.org*

UK and Ireland 4 Glentworth St, London NW1 ☏0891/600 188.

US 333 West Broadway #201, Glendale, CA 91204 ☏818/545-7507; 350 Fifth Ave, Suite 6413, New York, NY 10118 ☏212/760-8218.

Canada 480 University Ave #806, Toronto, Ontario M5G 1V2 ☏416/599-6636.

Australia China: 19th Floor, 44 Market St, Sydney, NSW 2000 ☏02/9299 4057; Hong Kong: Level 4, Hong Kong House, 80 Druitt St, Sydney, NSW 2000 ☏1-800/251 071.

New Zealand Contact the Sydney office or the embassy in Wellington.

India

Ⓦ*www.tourisminindia.com*

UK and Ireland 7 Cork St, London W1X 1PB ☏020/7437 3677.

US 1270 Ave of the Americas #1808, New York, NY 10020 ☏212/751-6840 or 582-3274; 3550 Wilshire Blvd, Suite 204, Los Angeles, CA 90010 ☏213/477-3824.

Canada 60 Bloor St W #1003, Toronto, Ontario M4W 3B8 ☏416/962-3787 or 416-962-3788.

Australia 46 Piccadilly Plaza, 210 Pitt St, Sydney, NSW 2000 ☏02/9264 4855.

New Zealand Contact the Sydney office or the embassy in Wellington.

Indonesia

Ⓦ*www.tourismindonesia.com*
Contact the information desk at the nearest embassy.

Japan

Ⓦ*www.jnto.go.jp*
UK and Ireland Heathcote House,

20 Savile Row, London W1
☎020/7734 9638.

US 360 Post St #601, San
Francisco, CA 94108 ☎415/989-
7140; 515 South Figueroa St, Suite
1470, Los Angeles, CA 90071
☎213/623-1952; One Rockefeller
Plaza #1250, New York, NY 10020
☎212/757-5640; 401 North
Michigan Ave, Suite 770, Chicago,
IL 60611 ☎312/222-0874.

Canada 165 University Ave,
Toronto, Ontario M5H 3B8
☎416/366-7140.

Australia Level 33, Chifley Tower, 2
Chifley Square, Sydney, NSW 2000
☎02/9232 4522.

New Zealand Contact the Sydney
office or the embassy in Wellington.

Laos

ⓦ *visit-laos.com*
No overseas tourist office.

Malaysia

ⓦ *www.visitmalaysia.com*
UK and Ireland 57 Trafalgar Square,
London WC2N 5DU ☎020/7930 7932.

US 818 West 7th St #804, Los
Angeles, CA 90017 ☎213/689-9702;
595 Madison Ave #1800, New York,
NY 10022 ☎212/754-1113.

Canada 830 Burrard St, Vancouver,
BC V6Z 2KA ☎604/689-8899.

Australia 65 York St, Sydney, NSW
2000 ☎02/9299 4441; 56 William St,
Perth, WA 6000 ☎09/481 0400.

New Zealand Contact the Sydney
office or the embassy in Wellington.

Nepal

ⓦ *www.welcomenepal.com*
No overseas tourist office.

Pakistan

ⓦ *www.tourism.gov.pk*
No overseas tourist office.

Philippines

ⓦ *www.tourism.gov.ph*
UK and Ireland 146 Cromwell Rd,
London SW7 ☎020/7835 1100.

US 30 North Michigan Ave #913,
Chicago, IL 60602 ☎312/782-2475;
556 Fifth Ave, New York, NY 10036
☎212/575-7915; 447 Sutter St,
Suite 507, San Francisco, CA 94108
☎415/956-4060.

Canada Contact offices in the US.

Australia Level 1, Philippine Centre,
27–33 Wentworth Ave, Sydney,
NSW, 2000 ☎02/9283 0711.

New Zealand Contact the Sydney
office or the consulate in Auckland.

Singapore

ⓦ *www.stb.com.sg*

UK and Ireland 1st floor, Carrington
House, 126–130 Regent St, London
W1 ☎020/7437 0033.

US 8484 Wilshire Blvd #510, Beverly
Hills, CA 90211 ☎323/852-1901;
260 Fifth Ave, 12th Floor, New York,
NY 10036 ☎212/302-4861.

Canada 2 Bloor St West, Suite 404,
Toronto, Ontario M4W 3E2
☎416/363-8898.

Australia Level 11, AWA Building,
47 York St, Sydney NSW 2000.
☎02/9290 2888; Unit 2, 226 James
Street, Perth, WA 6000 ☎08/9228
8166.

New Zealand 3rd Floor, 43 High St,
Auckland ☎09/358 1191.

South Korea

ⓦ *www.knto.or.kr*

UK and Ireland 8th floor, New Zealand House, Haymarket, London SW1 ☎020/7321 2535.

US One Executive Drive #100, Fort Lee, NJ 07024 ☎201/585-0909; 737 N. Michigan Ave, Suite 910, Chicago, IL 60611 ☎312-981-1717; 3435 Wilshire Blvd #1110, Los Angeles, CA 90010 ☎213/382-3435.

Canada 700 Bay Street, Suite 903, Toronto, Ontario M5G 1Z6 ☎416/348-9056.

Australia 17th Floor, Tower Building, Australia Square, 264 George St, Sydney, NSW 2000 ☎02/9252 4147 or 9251 1717.

New Zealand Contact the Sydney office.

Sri Lanka

ⓦ*www.lanka.net/ctb*

UK 22 Regent St, London SW1 ☎020/7930 2627.

Ireland 59, Ranelagh Rd, Dublin 6 ☎ 01/454 5640.

US One World Trade Center, Suite 4667, New York, NY 10048 ☎212-432-7156.

Australia c/o Atutil Pty Ltd, 39 Wintercorn Row, Werrington Downs, NSW 2747 ☎02/4730 3914.

New Zealand Contact the Australian office.

Taiwan

ⓦ*www.tbroc.gov.tw*

UK and Ireland c/o Taipei Representative, 50 Grosvenor Gardens, London SW1 ☎020/7396 9152.

US c/o Taipei Economic and Cultural Office, 405 Lexington Avenue, 37th Floor, New York, NY 10174 ☎212/867 1632; 555 Montgomery Street #505, San Francisco, CA 94111 ☎415/989 8677; The Wilshire Colonnade Building, 3731 Wilshire Boulevard #504, Los Angeles, CA 90010 ☎213/389 1158.

Australia c/o Taipei Economic and Cultural Office, Suite 1904, Level 19, MLC Center, Martin Place, Sydney, NSW 2000 ☎02/9231 6942.

New Zealand Contact the Australian office.

Thailand

ⓦ*www.tat.or.th*

UK and Ireland 49 Albemarle St, London W1 ☎020/7499 7679.

US 611 N Larchmont Blvd, 1st Floor, Los Angeles, CA 90004 ☎213/382-2353; 1 World Trade Center, Suite 3729, New York, NY 10048.

Canada c/o Mr Diderich, 116 Aldwych Ave, Toronto, Ontario M4J 1X6 ☎416/465-5620.

Australia Level 11, AWA Building, 47 York St, Sydney NSW 2000 ☎02/9290 2888; Unit 2, 226 James Street, Perth, WA 6000 ☎08/9228 8166.

New Zealand 3rd Floor, 43 High St, Auckland ☎09/358 1191.

Vietnam

ⓦ*www.vietnamtourism.com*

UK and Ireland 12 Victoria Rd, London W8 ☎020/7937 3174.

US and Canada No offices.

Australia and New Zealand No offices.

Embassies and consulates

Bangladesh

UK and Ireland 28 Queen's Gate, London SW7 ☎020/7584 0081.

US 2201 Wisconsin Ave NW, Washington, DC 20007 ☎202/244-0183, ✉www.banglaemb@aol.com Consulates in New York ☎212/599-6767 and Los Angeles ☎310/441-9399.

Canada 275 Bank St, Suite 302, Ottawa, Ontario K2P 2L6 ☎613/236-0138 or 236-0139.

Australia 35 Endeavour St, Red Hill, Canberra, ACT 2600 ☎02/6295 3328.

New Zealand Contact the embassy in Canberra.

Bhutan

For visa information, contact specialist travel agents or see ⓦwww.kingdomofbhutan.com

Brunei

ⓦwww.brunet.bn/homepage/gov/bruemb/govemb.htm

UK and Ireland 19/20 Belgrave Square, London SW1X 8PG ☎020/7581 0521.

US 3520 International Court NW, Washington DC 20008 ☎202/237-1838.

Canada 395 Laurier Avenue East, Ottawa, Ontario K1N 6R4 ☎613-234-5656.

Australia 16 Bulwarra Close, O'Mally ACT 2606, Canberra ☎02/6290 1801.

New Zealand Contact the embassy in Canberra.

Cambodia

UK and Ireland Contact the embassy in France: 11 Ave Charles Floquet, 75007 Paris ☎01/40 65 04 70.

US 4500 16th St, Washington DC 20011 ☎202/726 7742, ⓦwww.embassy.org/cambodia/ 53–69 Alderton St, Rego Park, New York 11374 ☎718/830 3770.

Canada Contact the embassy in Washington.

Australia 5 Canterbury Court, Deakin, ACT 2600 ☎02/6237 1259.

New Zealand Contact the embassy in Canberra.

China

UK 31 Portland Place, London W1 ☎0891/880808, ⓦwww.chinese-embassy.org.uk

Ireland 40 Ailesbury Rd, Dublin 4 ☎01/269 1707.

US 2300 Connecticut Ave NW, Washington, DC 20008 ☎202/328-2500; consulates in Chicago, Houston, Los Angeles, New York and San Francisco.

Canada 515 St Patrick's St, Ottawa, Ontario K1N 5H3 ☎613/789-9608; consulates in Toronto and Vancouver.

Australia 15 Coronation Drive, Yarralumla, ACT 2600 ☎02/6273 4783; 539 Elizabeth St, Surry Hills, Sydney ☎02/9698 7929; plus offices in Melbourne ☎03/9822 0607 and Perth ☎08/9321 8193.

New Zealand 588 Great South Rd, Greenland, Auckland 1 ☎09/525 1588.

India

UK India House, Aldwych, London WC2B 4NA ☎020/7836 8484, visa line ☎0900/188 0800, ⓦ*www.hcilondon.org*; consulates in Birmingham and Glasgow.

US 2536 Massachusetts Ave NW, Washington, DC 20008 ☎202/939-9839 or 939-9806; ⓦ*www.indianembassy.org*; consulates in Chicago, New York, San Francisco and Houston.

Canada 10 Springfield Rd, Ottawa, Ontario K1M 1C9 ☎ 613/744-3751, 744-3752 or 744-3753; ⓦ*www.docuweb.ca/India/*

Australia 3 Moonah Place, Yarralumla, Canberra, ACT 2600 ☎02/6273 3999; 25 Bligh St, Sydney, NSW 2000 ☎02/9223 9500; 15 Munro St, Coburg, Vic 3058 ☎03/9386 7399; India Centre, 49 Bennett St, East Perth, WA ☎08/9221 1485.

New Zealand FAI House, 180 Molesworth St, Wellington PO Box 4005 ☎04/473 6390.

Indonesia

UK and Ireland 38 Grosvenor Square, London W1X 9AD ☎0891/171210.

US 2020 Massachusetts Ave NW, Washington, DC 20036 ☎202/775-5200, ⓦ*www.kbri.org* Consulates in Chicago, Houston, Honolulu, Los Angeles, New York and San Francisco.

Canada 55 Parkdale Ave, Ottawa, Ontario, K1Y 1E5 ☎613/724-1100; consulates in Toronto and Vancouver.

Australia 8 Darwin Ave, Yarralumla, Canberra, ACT 2600 ☎02/6250 8600; 20 Harry Chan Ave, Darwin, NT 5784 ☎089/41 0048; 72 Queen Rd, Melbourne, VIC 3004 ☎03/9525 2755; 134 Adelaide Terrace, East Perth, WA 6004 ☎08/9221 5858; 236–238 Maroubra Rd, Maroubra, NSW 2035 ☎02/9344 9933.

New Zealand 70 Glen Rd, Kelburn, Wellington, PO Box 3543 ☎04/475 8697.

Japan

UK 101 Piccadilly, London W1V 9FN ☎020/7465 6500, ⓦ*www.embjapan.org.uk*; consulate in Edinburgh.

US 2520 Massachusetts Ave NW, Washington, DC 20008 ☎202/238-6700; consulates in Tamuning (Guam), Anchorage, Atlanta, Boston, Chicago, Denver, Detroit, Honolulu, Houston, Kansas City, Los Angeles, Miami, New Orleans, New York, Portland, San Francisco and Seattle.

Canada 255 Sussex Drive, Ottawa, Ontario K1N 9E6 ☎613/241-8541, ⓦ*www.embassyjapancanada.org*; consulates in Edmonton, Montreal, Toronto and Vancouver.

Australia 112 Empire Circuit, Yarralumla, Canberra, ACT 2600 ☎02/ 6273 3244; consulates in Melbourne, Sydney, Brisbane and Cairns.

New Zealand 7th Floor, Norwich Building, 3 Hunter St, Wellington ☎04/473 1540.

Laos

UK and Ireland Contact embassy in France: 74 Ave Raymond Poincaré, Paris ☎01/45 53 02 98.

USA 2222 S Street, NW,

Washington DC 20008 ☎202/332-6416, ⓦwww.laoembassy.com

Canada Contact embassy in Washington

Australia 1 Dalman Crescent, O'Malley, Canberra ☎02/6286 4005

New Zealand Contact embassy in Canberra.

Malaysia

UK and Ireland 45 Belgrave Square, London SW1X 8QT ☎020/7235 8033.

US 2401 Massachusetts Ave NW, Washington, DC 20008 ☎202/328-2700.

Canada 60 Boteler St, Ottawa, Ontario K1N 8Y7 ☎613/241-5182.

Australia 7 Perth Ave, Yarralumla, Canberra, ACT 2600 ☎02/6273 1543.

New Zealand 10 Washington Ave, Brooklyn, Wellington ☎04/385 2439.

Nepal

UK and Ireland 12a Kensington Palace Gardens, London W8 4QU ☎020/7229 1594.

US 2131 Leroy Place NW, Washington, DC 20008 ☎202/667-4550; consulate in New York ☎212/370-3988.

Canada 200 Bay St, Royal Bank Plaza, South Tower, Toronto, Ontario M5J 2J9 ☎416/865-0200.

Australia 203–233 New South Head Road, Edgecliff, NSW, ☎02/9328 7062; Level 7, 344 Queen Street, Brisbane ☎07/3220 2007.

New Zealand Contact the embassy in Sydney.

Pakistan

UK 36 Lowndes Square, London

SW1 ☎020/7664 9200.

US 2315 Massachusetts Ave NW, Washington, DC 20008 ☎202/939-6295, ⓦwww.pakistan-embassy.com Consulates in New York ☎212/879-5800 and Los Angeles ☎310/441-5114.

Canada Burnside Building, 151 Slater St, Suite 608, Ottawa Ontario K1P 5H3 ☎613/238-7881.

Australia 4 Timburra Crescent, O'Malley, Canberra, ACT 2606 ☎02/6290 1676.

New Zealand Contact the embassy in Canberra.

Philippines

UK and Ireland 9a Palace Green, London W8 ☎0891/171244, ⓦwww.philemb.demon.co.uk

US 1600 Massachusetts Ave NW, Washington, DC 20036 ☎202/467-9300; consulates in Chicago, Honolulu, Los Angeles, New York and San Francisco.

Canada 130 Albert St, Suite 606–608, Ottawa, Ontario K1P 5G4 ☎613/233-1121.

Australia 1 Moonah Place, Yarralumla, Canberra, ACT 2600 ☎02/6273 2535; Philippine Centre, Level 1 27–33 Wentworth Avenue, Sydney, NSW 2000 ☎02/ 9262 7377.

New Zealand 50 Hobson St, Thorndon, Wellington ☎04/472 9848; 8th Floor, 121 Beach Rd, Auckland 1 ☎09/303 2423.

Singapore

ⓦwww.gov.sg/mfa/consular/

UK and Ireland 9 Wilton Crescent, London SW1X 8SA ☎020/7245 0273.

US 3501 International Place NW, Washington, DC 20008 ☎202/537-3100; consulates in New York, Los Angeles and San Francisco.

Canada 999 West Hastings St, Suite 1305, Vancouver, BC V6C 2W2 ☎604/669-5115; consulate in Toronto.

Australia 17 Forster Crescent, Yarralumla, Canberra, ACT 2600 ☎02/6273 3944.

New Zealand 17 Kabul St, Khandallah, Wellington, PO Box 13-140 ☎04/479 2076.

South Korea

UK 60 Buckingham Gate, London W8 ☎020/7227 5500.

US 2320 Massachusetts Ave NW, Washington, DC 20008 ☎202/ 939-5660, 939-5661, 939-5662 or 939-5663, ⓦwww.mofat.go.kr/en_usa.htm Consulates in major US cities.

Canada 150 Boteler St, Ottawa, Ontario K1N 5A6 ☎613/244-5010; ⓦwww.emb-korea.ottawa.on.ca Consulates in Montreal, Toronto and Vancouver.

Australia 32 Martin Place, Sydney, NSW 2000 ☎02/9221 3866.

New Zealand 11th Floor, ASB Bank Tower, 2 Hunter Street, Wellington, ☎04/473 9037.

Sri Lanka

UK and Ireland 13 Hyde Park Gardens, London W2 2LU ☎020/7262 1841, ⓦourworld. compuserve.com/homepages/ lanka/

US 2148 Wyoming Ave NW, Washington, DC 20008 ☎202/483-

4025, 483-4026, 483-4027 or 483-4028; ⓦwww.erols.com/slembassy Consulates in New York ☎212/986-7040, Los Angeles, and New Orleans.

Canada 333 Laurier Ave W, Suite 1204, Ottawa, Ontario K1P 1C1 ☎613/233-8449; ⓦwww.magi.com/~lankacom

Australia 35 Empire Circuit, Forrest, Canberra, ACT 2603 ☎02/6239 7041; Level 11, 48 Hunter Street, Sydney NSW 2000 ☎02/9223 8729.

New Zealand Contact the embassy in Canberra.

Taiwan

ⓦwww.taipei.org

UK and Ireland 50 Grosvenor Gdns, London SW1 ☎020/7396 9152.

US Taipei Economic and Cultural Representative Office, 4201 Wisconsin Ave N.W., Washington, D.C. 20016-2137 ☎202/895-1800.

Canada Taipei Economic and Cultural Representative Office, 45 O'Conner Street Suite 1960, World Exchange Plaza, Ottawa, Ontario K1P 1A4 ☎613/231-5080

Australia Taipei Economic and Cultural Office, Unit 8, Tourism House, 40 Blackall Street, Barton, Canberra, ACT ☎02/6273 3344.

New Zealand Contact the Economic and Cultural Office in Canberra.

Thailand

UK and Ireland 30 Queen's Gate, London SW7 ☎0891/600150;

@www.thaiconsul-uk.com
Consulates in Birmingham, Cardiff, Glasgow, Hull and Liverpool.

US 1024 Wisconsin Ave NW, Suite 401, Washington DC 20007 ☎202/944-3600, @www.thaiembdc.org
Consulates in Chicago, Los Angeles and New York City.

Canada 180 Island Park Drive, Ottawa, Ontario K1Y 0A2 ☎613/722-4444.

Australia 111 Empire Circuit, Yarralumla, Canberra ACT 2600 ☎02/6273 1149; consulates in Adelaide, Brisbane, Melbourne, Perth and Sydney.

New Zealand 2 Cook St, PO Box 17–226, Karori,

Wellington ☎04/4768 618.

Vietnam

UK and Ireland 12 Victoria Rd, London W8 5RD ☎020/7937 1912.

US 1233 20th St NW, Suite 400, Washington DC 20037 ☎202/861-0737, @www.vietnamembassy-usa.org

Canada 226 MacLaren St, Ottawa, Ontario K2P 0L9 ☎613/236-0772.

Australia 6 Timburra Crescent, O'Malley, Canberra, ACT 2606 ☎02/6286 6059; 489 New South Head Rd, Double Bay, NSW 2025 ☎02/9327 1912.

New Zealand Contact the embassy in Canberra.

Discount flight agents

UK and Ireland

Apex Travel 59 Dame St, Dublin 2 ☎01/671 5933. Flights to Australia and the Far East.

Austravel 50 Conduit St, London W1 ☎020/7734 7755; 12 The Minories, Temple Court, Birmingham ☎0121/200 1116; 45 Coulston St, Bristol ☎0117/927 7425; 33 George St, Edinburgh ☎0131/226 1000; 16 County Arcade, Victoria Quarter, Leeds ☎0113/244 8880; 3 Barton Arcade, Deansgate, Manchester ☎0161/832 2445
@www.austravel.com Very good deals on flights to Australia and New Zealand via Indonesia, also on RTW tickets.

Bridge the World 47 Chalk Farm Rd, London NW1 ☎020/7911 0900,

@www.bridgetheworld.com
Specializes in RTW tickets, with good deals aimed at the backpacker market.

Cheap Flights @www.cheapflights.co.uk Online service that lists the day's cheapest flight deals available from subscribing UK flight agents.

Co-op Travel Care 35 Belmont Rd, Belfast 4 ☎028/9047 1717. Budget fares agent.

Destination Group 14 Greville Street, London EC1 ☎020/7400 7000, @www.destination-group.com Budget fares agent, especially good for Garuda flights.

Flightbookers 177–178 Tottenham Court Rd, London W1 ☎020/7757 2444; Gatwick Airport, South Terminal ☎01293/568300; 34 Argyle

Arcade, off Buchanan Street,
Glasgow ☎0141/204 1919
ⓦ*www.flightbookers.co.uk* I ꞏ ꞏꞏ
fares on an extensive offering of
scheduled flights.

Joe Walsh Tours 69 Upper
O'Connell St , Dublin 2 ☎01/872
2555; 8–11 Baggot St, Dublin 2
☎01/676 3053; 117 St Patrick St,
Cork ☎021/277959. Budget fares
agent.

The London Flight Centre 131 Earls
Court Rd, London SW5 ☎020/7244
6411; 47 Notting Hill Gate, London
W11 ☎020/7727 4290; Shop 33, The
Broadway Centre, Hammersmith
tube, London W6 ☎020/8748 6777.
Long-established agent dealing in
discount flights.

North South Travel, Moulsham Mill
Centre, Parkway, Chelmsford, Essex
☎01245/608 291. Travel agency that
supports projects in the developing
world, especially sustainable
tourism.

Quest Worldwide, 10 Richmond
Rd, Kingston, Surrey ☎020/8547
3322. Specialists in RTW and
Australasian discount fares.

STA Travel 86 Old Brompton Rd,
London SW7; 117 Euston Rd,
London NW1; 38 Store St, London
WC1; 11 Goodge St, London W1
☎020/7361 6262; 25 Queens Rd,
Bristol ☎0117/929 4399; 38 Sidney
St, Cambridge ☎01223/366966; 75
Deansgate, Manchester ☎0161/834
0668; 88 Vicar Lane, Leeds
☎0113/244 9212; 78 Bold St,
Liverpool ☎0151/707 1123; 9 St
Mary's Place, Newcastle ☎0191/233
2111; 36 George St, Oxford
☎01865/792 800; 27 Forrest Rd,
Edinburgh ☎0131/226 7747; 184

Byres Rd, Glasgow ☎0141/338
0000; 30 Upper Kirkgate, Aberdeen
☎0122/465 8222 and on many university campuses.
ⓦ*www.statravel.co.uk* Worldwide
specialists in low-cost flights for
students and under-26s, though
other customers welcome.
Also over two hundred offices
abroad.

Trailfinders 194 Kensington High
St, London W8 ☎020/7938 3939; 48
Earls Court Rd, London W8
☎020/7938 3366; 1 Threadneedle
St, London EC2 ☎020/7628 7628;
58 Deansgate, Manchester
☎0161/839 6969; 254–284
Sauchiehall St, Glasgow ☎0141/353
2224; 22–24 The Priory Queensway,
Birmingham ☎0121/236 1234; 48
Corn St, Bristol ☎0117/929 9000;
4–5 Dawson St, Dublin 2 ☎01/677
7888. ⓦ*www.trailfinders.co.uk* One
of the best-informed agents for
independent travellers.

Travel Bag 52 Regent St, London
W1 ☎020/7287 5558; 373–375 The
Strand, opposite the *Savoy Hotel*,
London WC2 ☎020/7497 0515; 12
High St, Alton, Hants ☎01420/
80828; ⓦ*www.travelbag.co.uk*
Discount flights, with good deals on
Qantas and BA flights.

The Travel Bug 125 Gloucester Rd,
London SW7 ☎020/7835 2000; 597
Cheetham Hill Rd, Manchester
☎0161/721 4000;
ⓦ*www.flynow.com* Large range of
discounted tickets.

Travel Cuts 295a Regent St,
London W1 ☎020/7255 2082;
ⓦ*www.travelcuts.co.uk* Specializes
in budget, student and youth travel
and RTW tickets.

usitCampus National call centre
☎0870/240 1010; 52 Grosvenor
Gardens, London SW1 ☎020/7730
8111; Fountain Centre, College St,
Belfast ☎028/9032 4073; 541 Bristol
Rd, Selly Oak, Birmingham
☎0121/414 1848; 61 Ditchling Rd,
Brighton ☎01273/570 226; 37–39
Queen's Rd, Clifton, Bristol
☎0117/929 2494; 5 Emmanuel St,
Cambridge ☎01223/324 283; 10–11
Market Parade, Patrick St, Cork
☎021/270 900; 19 Aston Quay,
Dublin 2 ☎01/602 1700; 53 Forest
Rd, Edinburgh ☎0131/225 6111;
122 George St, Glasgow ☎0141/553
1818; 166 Deansgate, Manchester
☎0161/ 273 1721; 105–106 St
Aldates, Oxford ☎01865/242 067;
⊕*www.usitcampus.co.uk*
Student/youth travel specialists, with
branches also in YHA shops and on
university campuses all over Britain.

Williames 18–20 Howard St, Belfast
☎028/9023 0714. Long-haul specialists.

USA and Canada

Air Brokers International 150 Post
St, Suite 620, San Francisco, CA
94108 ☎415/397-1383 or 1-
800/883-3273,
⊕*www.airbrokers.com* Consolidator
and specialist in RTW and Circle
Pacific tickets.

Council Travel 205 E 42nd St, New
York, NY 10017 ☎1-800/226-8624,
⊕*www.counciltravel.com* and
branches in many other US cities.
Student/budget travel agency.

Educational Travel Center 438 N
Frances St, Madison, WI 53703
☎1-800/747-5551 or 608/256-5551,
⊕*www.edtrav.com* Student/youth
and consolidator fares.

High Adventure Travel 442 Post St,
Suite 400, San Francisco, CA 94102
☎1-800/350-0612 or 415/912-5600,
⊕*www.airtreks.com* RTW and Circle
Pacific tickets. The extensive Web
site features an interactive database
called "Farebuilder" that lets you
build your own RTW itinerary.

Now Voyager 74 Varick St, Suite
307, New York, NY 10013
☎212/431-1616, ⊕*www.
nowvoyagertravel.com* Courier flight
broker and consolidator.

STA Travel 7810 Hardy Drive, Suite
109, Tempe, AZ 85284 ☎1-800/777-
0112 or 1-800/781-4040,
⊕*www.sta-travel.com* with branches
in most major US cities, including:
10 Downing St, New York, NY
10014 ☎212/627-3111; 7202
Melrose Ave, Los Angeles, CA
90046 ☎323/934-8722; 51 Grant
Ave, San Francisco, CA 94108
☎415/391-8407; 297 Newbury St,
Boston, MA 02115 ☎617/266-6014;
429 S Dearborn St, Chicago, IL
60605 ☎312/786-9050; 3701
Chesnut St, Philadelphia, PA 19104
☎215/382-2928; 317 14th Ave SE,
Minneapolis, MN 55414 ☎612/615-
1800. Worldwide discount travel firm
specializing in student/youth fares;
also student IDs, travel insurance,
car rental, rail passes, etc.

Travel Avenue 10 S Riverside Plaza,
Suite 1404, Chicago, IL 60606
☎1-800/333-3335 or 312/876-6866,
⊕*www.travelavenue.com* Full-ser-
vice travel agent that offers discounts in the form of rebates.

Travel CUTS 187 College St,
Toronto, ON M5T 1P7 ☎1-800/667-
2887 in Canada, or ☎416/979-2406,
⊕*www.travelcuts.com* and other

branches all over Canada.
Organization specializing in student
fares, IDs and other travel services.

UniTravel, 11737 Administration Dr,
Suite 100, St Louis, MO 63146 ☎1-
800/325-2222 or 314/569-2501,
Ⓦ*www.flightsforless.com*
Consolidator.

Worldtek Travel, 111 Water St, New
Haven, CT 06511 ☎1/800-243-1723,
Ⓦ*www.worldtek.com* Discount travel
agency for worldwide travel.

Australia and New Zealand

Anywhere Travel, 345 Anzac
Parade, Kingsford, Sydney
☎02/9663 0411, Ⓔ*anywhere@oze-
mail.com.au* Discount flight and holiday agent close to the airport.

Budget Travel 16 Fort St, Auckland,
plus branches around the city
☎09/366 0061 or 0800/808 040.
Discount flights and package holidays.

Destinations Unlimited Level 7 FAI
Building, 220 Queens St, Auckland
☎09/373 4033. Discount fares plus
a good selection of tours and holiday packages.

Flight Centres Australia: 82 Elizabeth
St, Sydney, plus branches nationwide
☎02/9235 3522, nearest branch ☎13
1600. New Zealand: 350 Queen St,
Auckland ☎09/358 4310, plus
branches nationwide. Ⓦ*www.
flightcentre.com.au* Competitive
discounts on air fares, and a wide
range of package holidays.

Northern Gateway 22 Cavenagh
St, Darwin ☎08/8941 1394,
Ⓔ*oztravel@norgate.com.au*
Specializes in discount fares and
packages to Southeast Asia.

STA Travel Australia: 855 George St,

Sydney; 256 Flinders St, Melbourne;
other offices in state capitals and
major universities (nearest branch
☎13/1776, fastfare telesales
☎1300/360 960). New Zealand: 10
High St, Auckland ☎09/309 0458,
fastfare telesales 366 6673, plus
branches in Wellington, Christchurch,
Dunedin, Palmerston North, Hamilton
and at major universities. Ⓦ*www.
statravel.com.au* Fare discount for students and those under 26, as well as
student cards, and travel insurance.

Student Uni Travel Level 8, 92 Pitt
St, Sydney ☎02/9232 8444; plus
branches in Brisbane, Cairns, Darwin,
Melbourne and Perth. Student/youth
discounts and travel advice.

Thomas Cook Australia: 175 Pitt St,
Sydney ☎02/9231 2877; 257 Collins
St, Melbourne; plus branches in other
state capitals (nearest branch
☎13/1771; telesales 1800/801 002;
New Zealand: 191 Queen St,
Auckland ☎09/379 3920.
Ⓦ*www.thomascook.com.au* Discounts
on flights,and holiday packages, plus
foreign exchange and traveller's
cheques and bus and rail passes.

Trailfinders 8 Spring St, Sydney
☎02/9247 7666; 91 Elizabeth St,
Brisbane ☎07/3229 0887; Shop 3,
Hides Corner, Lake St, Cairns
☎07/4041 1199. Specialize in low-
cost round-the-world air fares and
holiday packages.

Travel.com.au 76–80 Clarence St,
Sydney ☎02/9262 3555,
Ⓦ*www.travel.com.au*

usitBeyond cnr Shortland St and
Jean Batten Place, Auckland
☎09/379 4224 or 0800/788 336,
plus branches in Christchurch.
Student/youth travel specialists.

Courier flight agencies

UK and Ireland

Flight Masters 83 Mortimer St, London W1 ☎020/7462 0022.

Bridges Worldwide Old Mill Road House, West Drayton, Middlesex TW3 ☎01895/465 065.

International Association of Air Travel Couriers c/o International Features, 1 Kings Rd, Dorchester, Dorset DT1 ☎01305/264 564, ⓦ*www.aircourier.co.uk* Agents for lots of courier companies.

USA and Canada

Air Courier Association 15000 W 6th Ave, Suite 203, Golden, CO 80401 ☎303/279-3600 or 1-800/282-1202, ⓦ*www.aircourier.org*
Now Voyager, 74 Varick St, Suite 307, New York, NY 10013 ☎212/431-1616, ⓦ*www.nowvoyagertravel.com*
International Association of Air Travel Couriers 220 S Dixie Hwy, #3, PO Box 1349, Lake Worth, FL 33460 ☎561/582-8320, ⓦ*www.courier.org*

Specialist tour operators

UK

Asian Journeys 32 Semilong Rd, Northampton NN2 6BT ☎01604/234855; ⓦ*www.asianjourneys.com* Escorted small-group and tailor-made tours to most parts of Asia, with the emphasis on non-mainstream destinations.

Dragoman 14 Camp Green, Debenham, Stowmarket IP14 6LA ☎01728/861133; ⓦ*www.dragoman.co.uk* Extended overland journeys in purpose-built expedition vehicles.

Encounter Overland 267 Old Brompton Rd, London SW5 9JA ☎020/7370 6845, ⓦ*www.encounter-overland.com* Long-established organizer of overland expeditions.

Exodus 9 Weir Rd, London SW12 0LT ☎020/8675 5550, 24hr brochure requests 8673 0859; ⓦ*www. exodustravels.co.uk*. Adventure tour operators and overland expedition specialist (for travellers aged 18–45).

Explore Worldwide 1 Frederick St, Aldershot, Hampshire, GU11 1LQ ☎01252/760 000, brochure requests 760 100; ⓦ*www.explore.co.uk* Big range of small-group tours, treks, expeditions and safaris.

Imaginative Traveller 14 Barley Mow Passage, London W4 4PH ☎020/8742 8612, ⓦ*www.imaginative-traveller.com* Broad selection of tours to less-travelled parts of Asia, including walking, cycling, camping, cooking and snorkelling.

Royal Association for Disability and Rehabilitation (RADAR) 12 City Forum, 250 City Rd, London EC1V 8AF ☎020/7250 3222, minicom 7250 4119; ⓦ*www.radar.org.uk*

Produces a holiday guide to help disabled travellers plan long-haul trips.

Symbiosis 113 Bolingbroke Grove, London SW11 1DA ☎020/7924 5906, ⓦ*www.symbiosis-travel.co.uk* Environmentally aware outfit that offers specialist interest, cultural and cycling holidays in Southeast Asia.

World Expeditions 4 Northfields Prospect, Putney Bridge Rd, London SW18 1PE ☎020/8870 2600, ⓦ*www.worldexpeditions.co.uk* Adventure tours, including mountain and jungle trekking, and cycling.

US and Canada

Adventure Center ☎1-800/227-8747, ⓦ*www.adventurecenter.com* Economically priced Southeast Asian tours.

Backroads ☎1-800/462-2848, ⓦ*www.backroadsinternational.com* Specialist hiking and cycling adventures in Bali, Bhutan, China, Nepal, Thailand and Vietnam.

Geographic Expeditions ☎800/777-8183 or 415/922-0448; ⓦ*www.geoex.com* Specialists in "responsible tourism", with a range of customized tours and set packages.

Himalayan Travel ☎1-800/225-2380; ⓦ*www.gorp.com/himtravel.htm* Trekking and rafting expeditions to India, Nepal, Pakistan, Thailand and China.

Journeys ☎1-800/255-8735; ⓦ*www.journeys-intl.com* Adventure and culture tours to Nepal, China, India, Indonesia, Japan, Thailand and Vietnam.

Mir Corps ☎1-800/424 7289; ⓦ*www.mircorp.com* Trans-Siberian-Express trips.

Mobility International USA PO Box 10767, Eugene, OR 97440 (Voice and TDD ☎541/343-1284, ⓦ*www.miusa.org* Information and referral services for disabled travellers, plus tours and exchange programmes.

Overseas Adventure Travel ☎1-800/221-0814, ⓦ*www.oattravel.com* Walking tours of China, Nepal and Malaysia.

Worldwide Adventures ☎1-800/387-1483, ⓦ*www.worldwidequest.com* Trekking, rafting, wildlife and cycling adventures in India, Nepal, Pakistan, China, Thailand, Indonesia, Malaysia and Vietnam.

Australia and New Zealand

Abercrombie and Kent Australia: 90 Bridport Street, Albert Park, Melbourne ☎03/9699 9766 or 1800/331 429; plus branches in Brisbane and Sydney. New Zealand: 1/88 Rockfield Rd, Penrose, Auckland ☎09/579 3369. Up market rail tours of India, Thailand and Malaysia.

The Adventure Travel Company 164 Parnell Rd, Parnell, Auckland ☎09/379 9755. NZ's one-stop shop for adventure travel are agents for Intrepid, Perigrine, Guerba Expeditions, Encounter Overland and a host of others.

Adventure World 73 Walker St, North Sydney ☎02/9956 7766 or 1800/221 931, ⓦ*www.adventureworld.com.au* plus branches in Adelaide, Brisbane, Melbourne and Perth; 101 Great

South Rd, Remuera, Auckland
☎09/524 5118. Agents for a lot of
international adventure travel
companies.

Always Padi Travel 4/372 Eastern
Valley Way, Chatswood, Sydney
☎1800/259 297, ⓦwww.padi.com
All-inclusive dive package holidays to
prime dive sites in Indonesia, Malaysia,
Thailand and the Philippines.

Exodus Expeditions Agents in
Australia are Peregrine (see below);
New Zealand: Destinations Adventure,
4 Durham Street East, Auckland
☎09/309 0464, ⓔexodus@
destinations-adventure.co.nz
Extended overland trips through Asia.

Intrepid Adventure Travel 12 Spring
St, Fitzroy, Melbourne ☎1300/360
667, ⓦwww.intrepidtravel.com.au
Small-group tours to China and
Southeast Asia with the emphasis on
cross-cultural contact and low-
impact tourism.

Peregrine Adventures 258
Lonsdale St, Melbourne ☎03/9662

2700, ⓦwww.peregrine.net.au plus
offices in Brisbane, Sydney,
Adelaide and Perth. Small-group
adventure travel company offering a
range of graded trips.

San Michele Travel 83 York St,
Sydney ☎02/9299 1111 & 1800/222
244, ⓦwww.asiatravel.com.au plus a
branch in Melbourne. Customized rail
and adventure tours through Asia.

Sundowners Suite 15, 600
Lonsdale St, Melbourne ☎03/9600
1934 or 1-800/337 089;
ⓦwww.sundowners.com.au
Overland train travel, including
Trans-Siberian Express and the
Silk Route.

The Surf Travel Co. 2/25 Cronulla
Plaza, Cronulla Beach, Sydney
☎02/9527 4722 or 1800/687 873; 7
Danbury Drive, Torbay, Auckland
☎09/4738388,
ⓦwww.surftravel.com.au A well-
established surf travel company that
can arrange accommodation and
yacht charter in Indonesia.

Voluntary work and conservation projects

UK Organizations

**British Trust for Conservation
Volunteers (BTCV)** 36 St Mary's St,
Wallingford, Oxfordshire OX10 0EU
☎01491/839766; ⓦwww.btcv.org.uk
One of the largest environmental
charities in Britain, with a programme of international working
holidays (as a paying volunteer),
including restoring paddy fields in

Japan and turtle monitoring in
Thailand.

Coral Cay Conservation 154
Clapham Park Rd, London SW4 7DE
☎020/7498 6248; ⓦwww.coralcay.org
Two- to twelve-week reef and rainforest conservation projects, including
coral surveying in the Philippines and
Indonesia.

Earthwatch Institute 57 Woodstock

Rd, Oxford OX2 6HJ ☎01865/
318831; ⓦwww.earthwatch.org
Largest and longest-established
voluntary-holiday organization, with
lots of projects in Asia, including
one concerned with the snow
leopard in Ladakh and another
with the temple monkeys of Sri
Lanka.

Frontier 77 Leonard St, London
EC2A 4QS ☎020/7613 2422;
ⓦwww.frontierprojects.ac.uk
Tropical conservation and research
agency that aims to help volunteers
prepare for careers in conservation-
related areas. Projects last from ten
weeks to six months and include
rainforest surveys in Vietnam.

Greenforce 11 Betterton Street,
London WC2H 9BP ☎020/7470
8888; ⓦwww.greenforce.org
Environmental charity that runs sci-
entific surveys with the help of volunteers, including a project surveying the reefs off Sabah in East
Malaysia.

**Indian Volunteers for Community
Service (IVCS)** 12 Eastleigh Ave,
South Harrow, Middlesex HA2 0UF
☎020/8864 4740 evenings only;
ⓔendah@dircon.co.uk Three-week
visitors' programme at a rural development project in India.

i to i International Projects 1
Cottage Rd, Headingley, Leeds LS6
4DD ☎0870/333 2332; ⓦwww.i-to-
i.com Short-term voluntary English-
teaching and conservation work in
India and Sri Lanka.

World Service Enquiry Unit 233,
Bon Marché Centre, 241–251

Ferndale Road, London SW9 8BJ
☎020/7346 5956;
ⓦwww.wse.org.uk Umbrella organization which has contact details for
jobs and short-term placements
with overseas charities.

US Organizations

**Council on International
Educational Exchange** 633 3rd
Ave, Twentieth Floor, New York, NY
10017 ☎888-COUNCIL;
ⓦwww.councilexchanges.org Two-
to four-week volunteer projects.

Earthwatch 3 Clock Tower Place,
Suite 100, Box 75, Maynard, MA
01754 ☎800/ 776-0188 & 617/926-
8200; ☎www.earthwatch.org
Largest and longest-established
voluntary-holiday organization, with
several different projects in Asia.

Global Volunteers 375 E Little Canada
Rd, St Paul, MN 55117 ☎1-800/487-
1074; ⓦwww.globalvolunteers.org
Projects in Vietnam, Indonesia and
China.

Australian
Organizations

**Australian Volunteers
International** 71 Argyle St, Fitzroy,
Melbourne ☎03/9279 1788.
Postings for up to two years in
developing countries.

Earthwatch 126 Bank St, South
Melbourne, Vic 3205 ☎03/9682
6828; ⓦwww.earthwatch.org
Largest and longest-established
voluntary-holiday organization, with
sixteen different projects in Asia.

Accommodation booking agents

Hostelling International

UK 14 Southampton St, London WC2 7HY ☎020/7836 1036, ⓦ*www.iyhf.org*

US 733 15th St NW, Suite 840, PO Box 37613, Washington, DC 20013-7613 ☎202/783-6161, ⓦ*www.hiayh.org*

Canada Room 400, 205 Catherine St, Ottawa, Ontario K2P 1C3 ☎1-800/663-5777 or 613/237-7884.

Australia 422 Kent St, Sydney ☎02/9261 1111; 205 King St, Melbourne ☎03/9670 9611; 38 Stuart St, Adelaide ☎08/8231 5583; 154 Roma St, Brisbane ☎07/3236 1680; 236 William St, Perth ☎08/9227 5122; 69a Mitchell St, Darwin ☎08/8981 2560; 28 Criterion St, Hobart ☎03/6234 9617; ⓦ*www.yha.com.au*.

New Zealand 173 Gloucester St, Christchurch ☎03/379 9970; ⓦ*www.yha.co.nz*.

Homestays

American-International Homestays PO Box 1754, Nederland, CO 80466-1754, USA ☎1-800/876-2048, ⓦ*www.spectravel.com/homes* Stay with a local family in China, India or Nepal.

Experiment in International Living (EIL) In the UK: 287 Worcester Rd, Malvern WR14 1AB ☎01684/562577, ⓦ*www. experiment.org* In Australia: PO Box 355, Curtin 2605 ☎02/6282 5171, ⓦ*www.experimentaust.org.au*

Stays of one to four weeks with a family in India, Japan or South Korea.

Komestay ⓦ*www.komestay.com* Organization that arranges home-stays in South Korea for two or more nights.

Women Welcome Women World Wide UK ☎ & ☎ 01494/465441, ⓦ*www.womenwelcomewomen.org. uk* WWWWW (5W) is an organization of women living in all parts of the world who are happy to meet, show round and usually accommodate women travellers. There are members in nearly all parts of Asia, with a particularly large number in Japan. To join, you pay a minimal membership fee.

Online hotel finders

Asia Hotels ⓦ*www.asia-hotels.com/ aboutlg.asp* One of the best Asia-specific accommodation booking sites, with over 1300 hotels on their books, in 18 countries. Prices are discounted by up to sixty percent, with a few coming in at under $20/£14, but most from $35/£23 upwards.

Asia Hotels Network ⓦ*www.asiahotels.net* Reasonable selection of hotels in the major tourist destinations.

Asia Travel ⓦ*www.asiatravel.com* Recommended service with a good range of hotels across Asia and discounts of up to 75 percent. Reasonable number of options in the $20/£14 category.

Excite Travel ⓦ*www.excite.com/travel* Links to individual Asian countries, many of which have online hotel reservation sites.

Hotels Travel ⓦ*www.hotelstravel.com* Decent selection of hotels in the main spots, listed by country.

Health – Travel clinics, information lines and online resources

UK

British Airways Travel Clinic
Provides vaccinations, tailored up-to-the-minute advice and travel health-care products. There are 28 regional clinics in the UK; call ☎01276/685040 for the one nearest to you or consult ⓦ*www.britishairways.com* In London, visit 156 Regent St, London W1 ☎020/7439 9584, no appointment necessary, or call in advance for appointments at 101 Cheapside, London EC2 ☎020/7606 2977; and at the BA terminal in London's Victoria Station ☎020/7233 6661.

Hospital for Tropical Diseases Second floor, Mortimer Market Centre, off Copper St, London WC1E 6AU ☎020/7388 9600. Travel clinic and recorded message service ☎0839/337733 (50p per min) which lists appropriate immunizations.

Malaria Helpline 24hr recorded message ☎0891/600 350 (60p per minute).

Medical Advisory Service for Travellers Abroad (MASTA) London School of Hygiene and Tropical Medicine. Prerecorded 24hr

Travellers' Health Line ☎0906/822 4100 (60p per min), giving written information tailored to your journey by return of post. Or consult ⓦ*www.masta.org*

Nomad Pharmacy Tailored information and vaccinations at 40 Bernard St, London WC1 ☎020/7833 4114 for appointments; telephone helpline ☎0891/633 414 (60p a minute).

Trailfinders No-appointment-necessary immunization clinics at 194 Kensington High Street, London (Mon–Fri 9am–5pm, Thurs to 6pm, Sat 9.30am–4pm) ☎020/7938 3999.

Ireland

All of these places offer pre-trip advice.

Travel Medicine Services PO Box 254, 16 College St, Belfast 1 ☎028/9031 5220.

Tropical Medical Bureau Grafton St Medical Centre, 34 Grafton St, Dublin 2 ☎01/671 9200.

Tropical Medical Bureau Dun Laoghaire Medical Centre, 5 Northumberland Ave, Dun Laoghaire, Co. Dublin ☎01/280 4996, ⓦ*www.iol.ie/-tmb*

US and Canada

Canadian Society for International Health 1 Nicholas St, Suite 1105, Ottawa, ON K1N 7B7 ☎613/241-5785. Distributes a free pamphlet, "Health Information for Canadian Travellers", containing an extensive list of travel health centres in Canada.

Centers for Disease Control 1600 Clifton Rd NE, Atlanta, GA 30333 ☎404/639-3311, ⓦ*www.cdc.gov* Publishes outbreak warnings and suggested inoculations. International Travellers Hotline on ☎1/888-232-3228.

International Association for Medical Assistance to Travellers (IAMAT) 417 Center St, Lewiston, NY 14092 ☎716/754-4883, ⓦ*www.sentex.net/~iamat* and 40 Regal Rd, Guelph, ON N1K 1B5 ☎519/836-0102. Provides a list of local English-speaking doctors and leaflets on inoculations.

International SOS Assistance PO Box 11568, Philadelphia, PA 19116 ☎1-800/523-8930. Members receive pre-trip medical info, as well as overseas emergency services to complement travel insurance coverage.

Travel Medicine 369 Pleasant St, Suite 312, Northampton, MA 01060 ☎1-800/872-8633, ⓦ*www.travmed.com* Sells health-related travel products.

Travelers Medical Center 31 Washington Square West, New York, NY 10011 ☎212/982-1600. Consultation service on immunizations and treatment of diseases for travellers to developing countries.

Australia and New Zealand

Travellers' Medical and Vaccination Centre ⓦ*www.tmvc.com.au* Has vaccination centres throughout Australia, New Zealand and Southeast Asia, and provides general information on travel health. Branches include: in Australia, 7/428 George St, Sydney ☎02/9221 7133; 27–29 Gilbert Place, Adelaide ☎08/8212 7522; in New Zealand, 1/170 Queen St, Auckland ☎09/373 3531; Shop 15, Grand Arcade, Willis St, Wellington ☎04/473 0991.

Travellers' Immunization Service 303 Pacific Hwy, Sydney ☎02/9416 1348.

Travel-Bug Medical and Vaccination Centre 161 Ward St, North Adelaide ☎08/8267 3544.

Online-only resources

Yahoo! Health ⓦ*health.yahoo.com* Gives information about specific diseases and conditions, drugs and herbal remedies, as well as advice from health experts.

ⓦ*www.tripprep.com* One of the best sites dedicated to traveller's health – extremely comprehensive about all the tropical illnesses and risks.

ⓦ*www.24dr.com/reference/travel/* Offers plenty of straightforward health advice for travellers.

ⓦ*www.tmvc.com.au* This site is excellent on country-by-country information, and runs a lot of health news items of interest to travellers.

Official advice on international trouble spots

FCO Travel Advice Unit Consular Division, 1 Palace St, London SW1E 5HE ☎020/7238 4503, Ⓦ*www.fco.gov.uk*

US State Department Travel Advisory Service 2201 C St NW, Room 4811, Washington, DC 20520 ☎202/647-5225, Ⓦ*www.travel.state.gov*

Canadian Department of Foreign Affairs and International Trade 125 Sussex Drive, Ottawa, Ontario K1A OG2 ☎1-800/387-3124, Ⓦ*www.dfait-maeci.gc.ca*

Australian Department of Foreign Affairs and Trade The RG Casey Building, John McEwan Crescent, Barton, Canberra, ACT 2600 ☎02/6261-9111, Ⓦ*www.dfat.gov.au*

New Zealand Department of Foreign Affairs Stafford House, 40 The Terrace, Wellington, Private Bag 18 901 ☎04/494 8500.

Responsible tourism

UK and Ireland

Tourism Concern Stapleton House, 277 Holloway Rd, London N7 8HN ☎020/7753 3330, Ⓦ*www. tourismconcern.org.uk* British organization that campaigns for responsible tourism. Their Web site has plenty of useful links to politically and environmentally aware organizations across the world, and a particularly good section on the politics of tourism in Burma.

US and Canada

Partners in Responsible Tourism, PO Box 237, San Francisco, California 94-104-0237 ☎415/675-0420; Ⓦ*www.pirt.org* A network of individuals and tourism companies who work to promote responsible and sustainable tourism in Asia and elsewhere, particularly with indigenous peoples.

Australia and New Zealand

Responsible Tourism Network PO Box 34, Rundle Mall, Adelaide 5000 ☎08/8232 2727; Ⓦ*www.caa.org.au/travel/* A not-for-profit travel agency which sets up sustainable-tourism projects in India, Laos, Tibet and Vietnam, and runs small-group tours to visit them.

Online resources

About Ecotourism Ⓦ*www.ecotourism.about.com* Recommended umbrella site with a wide range of discussions, articles and links on varied aspects of the relationship between tourism and the environment, both in Asia and elsewhere. Also some links to eco-aware travel companies.

ronmentally aware travel companies around the world; search by country.

Travel book and map stores

UK and Ireland

Blackwell's Map and Travel Shop 53 Broad St, Oxford OX1 3BQ ⓣ01865/792792, ⓦ*bookshop. blackwell.co.uk*

Daunt Books 83 Marylebone High St, London W1M 3DE ⓣ020/7224 2295; 193 Haverstock Hill, London NW3 4QL ⓣ020/7794 4006.

Easons Bookshop 40 O'Connell St, Dublin 1 ⓣ01/873 3811.

National Map Centre 22–24 Caxton St, London SW1H 0QU ⓣ020/7222 2466; ⓦ*www.mapsworld.com*

Stanfords 12–14 Long Acre, London WC2E 9LP ⓣ020/7836 1321, ⓦ*www.stanfords.co.uk* Also at Campus Travel, 52 Grosvenor Gardens, London SW1W 0AG ⓣ020/7730 1314, within the British Airways offices at 156 Regent St, London W1R 5TA ⓣ020/7434 4744, and at 29 Corn St, Bristol BS1 1HT ⓣ0117/929 9966.

The Travel Bookshop 13–15 Blenheim Crescent, London W11 2EE ⓣ020/7229 5260, ⓦ*www.thetravelbookshop.co.uk*

US and Canada

Adventurous Traveler Bookstore 245 S Champlain St, PO Box 64769, Burlington, VT 05406-4769 ⓣ1-800/282-3963, ⓦ*www.adventuroustraveler.com*

Book Passage 51 Tamal Vista Blvd,

Corte Madera, CA 94925 ⓣ415/927-0960.

The Complete Traveler Bookstore 199 Madison Ave, New York, NY 10016 ⓣ212/685-9007.

International Travel Maps and Books (ITMB) 552 Seymour St, Vancouver, BC V6B 3J5 ⓣ604/687-3320, ⓦ*www.itmb.com*

Map Link 30 South La Petera Lane, Unit #5, Santa Barbara, CA 93117 ⓣ805/692-6777, ⓦ*www.maplink.com*

The Map Store Inc 1636 1st St, Washington, DC 20006 ⓣ202/628-2608.

Open Air Books and Maps 25 Toronto St, Toronto, Ontario M5R 2C1 ⓣ416/363-0719.

Phileas Fogg's Books & Maps #87 Stanford Shopping Center, Palo Alto, CA 94304 ⓣ1-800/533-FOGG; ⓦ*www.foggs.com*

Rand McNally 444 North Michigan Ave, Chicago, IL 60611 ⓣ312/321-1751; 150 East 52nd St, New York, NY 10022 ⓣ212/758-7488; 595 Market St, San Francisco, CA 94105 ⓣ415/777-3131; call ⓣ1-800/333-0136 ext 2111 for other locations; ⓦ*www.randmcnally.com*

Sierra Club Bookstore 6014 College Ave, Oakland, CA 94618 ⓣ510/658-7470

Travel Books & Language Center 4437 Wisconsin Ave NW,

Washington, DC 20016 ⓣ1-800/220-2665.

Traveler's Choice Bookstore 2 Wooster St, New York, NY 10013 ⓣ212/941-1535, ⓔ*tvlchoice@aol.com*

Ulysses Travel Bookshop 4176 St-Denis, Montreal ⓣ514/843-9447, ⓦ*www.ulyssesguides.com*

Australia and New Zealand

The Map Shop 16a Peel St, Adelaide ⓣ08/8231 2033.

Mapland 372 Little Bourke St, Melbourne ⓣ03/9670 4383.

Mapworld 173 Gloucester Street, Christchurch ⓣ03/374 5399, ⓦ*www.mapworld.co.nz.*

Perth Map Centre 891 Hay St, Perth ⓣ08/9322 5733.

Specialty Maps 58 Albert St, Auckland ⓣ09/307 2217.

Travel Bookshop Shop 3, 175 Liverpool St, Sydney ⓣ02/9261 8200.

Worldwide Maps and Guides 187 George St, Brisbane ⓣ07/3221 4330.

Online travel bookstores

Adventurous Traveler ⓦ*www.adventuroustraveler.com*

Amazon ⓦ*www.amazon.co.uk* and ⓦ*www.amazon.com*

Literate Traveler ⓦ*www.literate-traveller.com*

Online travel resources

For country-specific Web sites, see the individual country profiles on pp.3–102. Online accommodation booking services are listed on p.362, and Web sites for travel agents and tour operators are given in the section beginning on p.354.

Travel resources and links

Accommodating Asia ⓦ*www.accomasia.com* Heaps of good traveller-oriented stuff on nearly all parts of Asia, with especially interesting links to travellers' homepages, under "travellers notes".

Culture Connect ⓦ*cultureconnect.com* A good site with plenty of recent reports from travellers, as well as travel news and links to webcams across Asia.

Excite Travel ⓦ*www.excite.com/travel* Not a bad place to start, with links for individual Asian countries from Bangladesh to Vietnam, ranging from country information provided via the *CIA Factbook*, to hotel bookings, current weather forecast, and sightseeing.

Internet Travel Information Service ⓦ*www.itisnet.com* Specifically aimed at budget travellers, this is a really useful source of current info on many Asian countries, regularly updated by travellers and researchers. Up-to-the-minute info on air fares, border crossings, visa requirements and hotels.

Journeywoman

ⓦ*www.journeywoman.com* Highly recommended site aimed at women travellers, with all sorts of imaginative sections, including "What Should I Wear?" which features first-hand tips on acceptable dress in over 100 different countries. Also covers travellers' health, travelogues, advice for solo travellers and links.

1000 Travel Tips

ⓦ*www.1000traveltips.org* Useful site that gathers travellers' practical reports on fairly recent trips through Asia and elsewhere.

Online tourist information

ⓦ*www.efn.org/~rick/tour* Exhaustive online travel resource, with links for more than 150 countries. Links for the more developed destinations go to both tourist office and government Web sites and travellers' homepages.

Open Directory Project

ⓦ*www.dmoz.org/Recreation /Travel/Budget_Travel/Backpacking/* Scores of backpacker-oriented links, including a lot of Asia-specific ones, plus travelogues, Web rings and message boards.

Rec. Travel Library

ⓦ*www.travel-library.com* Highly recommended site, which has lively pieces on dozens of travel topics, from the budget travellers' guide to sleeping in airports to how to travel light. Good links too.

Utopia ⓦ*www.utopia-asia.com* Recommended Web site by and for gay and lesbian travellers, including details on the gay scene in most

Asian countries, plus plenty of useful links to gay meeting places and organizations.

Travellers' forums, newsgroups and bulletin boards

Boots 'n' All ⓦ*www.bootsnall.com* Has a travel forum and a constantly expanding list of experts on individual countries who are happy to respond to specific email queries.

Fielding's Adventure Forum

ⓦ*www.fieldingtravel.com/blackflag* Travellers' question-and-answer forum on adventurous and "dangerous" places to travel, created by the people who produce *Fielding's Guide to the World's Most Dangerous Places* and other guidebooks. Especially worth checking out for the less-travelled places such as Cambodia and Pakistan.

Lonely Planet Thorn Tree

ⓦ*thorntree.lonelyplanet.com* Very popular travellers' bulletin boards, divided into regions (eg islands of Southeast Asia). Ideal for exchanging information with other travellers and for starting a debate, though it does attract an annoying number of regular posters just itching for an argument.

rec.travel.asia

ⓦ*news://rec.travel.asia* This Usenet forum deals specifically with travel in Asia, and gets a lot of traffic.

Rough Guides

ⓦ*www.roughguides.com* Interactive site for independent travellers, with forums, bulletin boards, travel tips and features, plus online travel guides.

Online magazines

Asiaweek Ⓦ*www.asiaweek.com*
Good range of weekly articles,
accessible without subscription, a
user-friendly index, plus headline
snippets from the archives.

Far Eastern Economic Review
Ⓦ*www.feer.com* The week's articles
from this incisive political magazine.

No registration necessary, but you
can sign up for a free weekly email
newsletter.

New Internationalist
Ⓦ*www.oneworld.org/ni/* The online
version of this excellent campaigning magazine offers a selection of
the month's articles without subscription.

Travel equipment suppliers

UK

Cotswold Outdoor Ltd 42–46
Uxbridge Rd, London W12 8ND
Ⓣ020/8743 2976; Ⓦ*www.
cotswold-outdoor.co.uk* and branches
in Betws-y-Coed, Glasgow,
Harrogate, Manchester, Reading, St
Albans, South Cerney and
Southampton. Sells a huge range of
outdoor and adventure gear for pretty
much any activity and climate. Mail
order is available; to order a catalogue, call Ⓣ01285/643434.

Field and Trek 42 Maiden Lane,
Covent Garden, London WC2E 7LJ
Ⓣ020/7379 3793, and branches in
Ambleside, Brentwood, Bromley,
Canterbury, Chelmsford, Croydon,
Gloucester, Guildford and Slough;
Ⓦ*www.field-trek.co.uk* Stocks a
massive choice of gear by a variety
of manufacturers including their
own-brand items. Mail order is available, call Ⓣ01268/401444 for a catalogue.

**Nomad Pharmacy and Travellers'
Store** 3 Wellington Terrace, Turnpike
Lane, London N8 0PX Ⓣ020/8889
7014, and branches at STA, 40 Bernard

St, London WC1N 1LJ Ⓣ020/ 7833
4114 and 4 Potters Rd, New Barnet,
Herts EN5 5HW Ⓣ020/8441 7208,
Ⓦ*www.nomad-travstore.co.uk*
Specialist in travellers' medical
supplies and first-aid equipment,
but also stock general purpose
travel accessories.

YHA Adventure Shops 14
Southampton St, London WC2E
7HY Ⓣ020/7836 8541,
Ⓦ*www.yhaadventure.co.uk* and
branches in Ambleside,
Birmingham, Brighton, Bristol,
Cambridge, Cardiff, Leeds,
Liverpool, London, Manchester,
Nottingham, Oxford, Plymouth,
Reading, St Albans, Salisbury and
Southampton. A good range of gear
at competitive prices aimed at general outdoor activities. Call head
office Ⓣ01784/458625 for your
nearest branch.

US and Canada

Travel Medicine 369 Pleasant St,
Northampton, MA 01060 Ⓣ1-
800/872-8633, Ⓦ*www.travelmed.com*
Sells first-aid kits, mosquito netting,
water filters and other health-related

travel products.

Campmor PO Box 700, Saddle River, NJ 07458-0700 ☎1-800/226-7667 or 201/825-8300, ☎1-800/230-2153 or 201/825-0274; ⓦ*www.campmor.com* Clothing plus outdoor and camping gear.

The North Face Eight stores in the US and one in Canada selling camping equipment and clothing. For your nearest store, call ☎1-800/447-2333, ☎1-510/618-3529, ⓦ*www.thenorthface.com*

Recreational Equipment Inc PO Box 1700, Sumner, WA 98352-0001 ☎1-800/426-4840, ☎1-253/891-2523, ⓦ*www.rei.com* Sixty stores selling outdoor gear and clothing. Extensive mail-order catalogue.

Sierra Trading Post 5025 Campstool Rd, Cheyenne, WY 82007-1802 ☎1-800/713-4534, ☎1-800/ 378-8946, ⓦ*www.sierratradingpost.com* Clothes, shoes and small equipment.

Travel Smith 60 Leveroni Court #1, Novato, CA 94949 ☎1-800/950-1600, ☎1-800/950-1656, ⓦ*www.travelsmith.com*

Australia and New Zealand

A-Roving 112 Toorak Rd, Toorak, Vic 3142 ☎03/9824 1714. Suppliers of travel luggage and accessories, maps and travel guides.

Bivouac 5 Fort St, Auckland 1 ☎09/366 1966. Several stores in New Zealand stocking a full range of backpacking and camping gear.

Katmandu PO Box 1191, Collingwood, VIC 3066 ☎03/9417 2480 or 1-800/333 484. A mail-order company, with outlets in all major Australian and New Zealand cities, offering an extensive range of quality outdoor and climbing gear.

Mountain Designs 105 Albert St, Brisbane, QLD 4000 ☎07/3221 6756; branches also in Sydney, Melbourne, Perth, Adelaide, Canberra, Hobart and Auckland. Australian-designed, lightweight mountaineering and adventure equipment, specializing in sleeping bags, Gore-tex and fleeces.

Mtn Equipment Pty Ltd 491 Kent St, Sydney, NSW 2000 ☎02/9264 5888, and branches in Chatswood and Hornsby. This shop has a comprehensive range of lightweight, functional gear for outdoor and sporting activities. For mail order, call ☎02/9264 2645.

Paddy Pallin 507 Kent St, Sydney, NSW 2000 ☎02/9264 2685, and thirteen branches throughout Australia. One of the original designers and suppliers of hiking and camping gear specially designed for Australian conditions, but some may be of interest to people heading overseas. For mail order, call ☎02/9525 6829 or 1-800/805398, ⓦ*www.pallmail.com.au*

Final checklist

Documents

Full details on all the following items are given in Chapter Six.

- ❏ airline tickets
- ❏ credit card
- ❏ guidebooks
- ❏ insurance policy
- ❏ international drivers' licence
- ❏ International Student Card (ISIC)
- ❏ International Youth Hostel Card
- ❏ maps
- ❏ passport
- ❏ passport photos
- ❏ phrasebook
- ❏ phone card/phone home card
- ❏ photocopies of all your vital documents
- ❏ traveller's cheques

The bare essentials

- ❏ backpack/travel sack
- ❏ clothes
- ❏ daypack
- ❏ fleece jacket or sweatshirt
- ❏ money belt and/or neck pouch
- ❏ padlocks or backpack locks
- ❏ sarong
- ❏ shoes
- ❏ sun hat
- ❏ waterproof money-holder ("Surfsafe")

Basic odds and ends

- ❏ camera equipment and film
- ❏ contact lens stuff/glasses

- ❏ contraceptives and/or condoms
- ❏ first-aid kit
- ❏ flashlight (torch)
- ❏ mini-padlocks and a chain
- ❏ mosquito repellent
- ❏ sunglasses
- ❏ sunscreen
- ❏ tampons
- ❏ toilet paper
- ❏ toiletries
- ❏ towel

Optionals

- ❏ alarm clock/watch
- ❏ batteries
- ❏ books
- ❏ cigarette lighter
- ❏ compass
- ❏ earplugs
- ❏ games
- ❏ gluestick
- ❏ handkerchief
- ❏ mosquito net
- ❏ notebook or journal, and pens
- ❏ penknife
- ❏ personal stereo
- ❏ photos of home
- ❏ rain gear/umbrella
- ❏ sewing kit
- ❏ sink plug
- ❏ sheet sleeping bag
- ❏ short-wave radio
- ❏ stamps from your home country
- ❏ string
- ❏ wallet
- ❏ water bottle, water purifier or purification tablets

Index

Stay in touch with us!

ROUGHNEWS is Rough Guides' free newsletter. In three issues a year we give you news, travel issues, music reviews, readers' letters and the latest dispatches from authors on the road.

I would like to receive ROUGHNEWS: please put me on your free mailing list.

NAME . . . .

ADDRESS . . . .

Please clip or photocopy and send to: Rough Guides, 62–70 Shorts Gardens, London WC2H 9AH, England or Rough Guides, 375 Hudson Street, New York, NY 10014, USA.

IF KNOWLEDGE IS POWER, THIS ROUGH GUIDE IS A POCKET-SIZED BATTERING RAM

Written in plain English, with no hint of jargon, the Rough Guide to the Internet will make you an Internet guru in the shortest possible time. It cuts through the hype and makes all others look like nerdy textbooks

AT ALL BOOKSTORES • DISTRIBUTED BY PENGUIN

www.roughguides.com

Check out our Web site for unrivalled travel information on the Internet.
Plan ahead by accessing the full text of our major titles, make travel reservations and keep up to date with the latest news in the Traveller's Journal or by subscribing to our free newsletter ROUGH*NEWS* · packed with stories from Rough Guide writers.

ROUGH GUIDES: Travel

AVAILABLE AT ALL GOOD BOOKSHOPS

NO FLIES ON YOU!

**THE ROUGH GUIDE TO
TRAVEL HEALTH:
PLANNING YOUR TRIP
WORLDWIDE**
UK£5.00, US$7.95

DON'T GET BITTEN BY THE WRONG TRAVEL BUG

NORTH SOUTH TRAVEL

Great discounts

North South Travel is a small travel agent offering excellent personal service. Like other air ticket retailers, we offer discount fares worldwide. But unlike others, all available profits contribute to grassroots projects in the South through the NST Development Trust Registered Charity No. 1040656.

For **quotes** or queries, contact Brenda Skinner or Bridget Christopher, Tel/Fax 01245 608 291. Recent **donations** made from the NST Development Trust include support to Djoliba Trust, providing micro-credit to onion growers in the Dogon country in Mali; assistance to displaced people

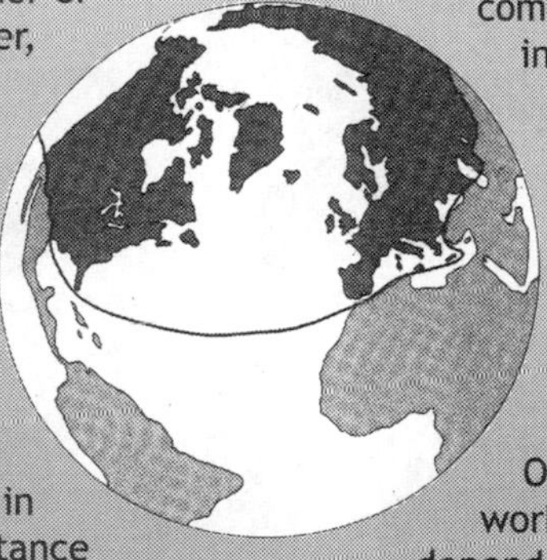

and rural communities in eastern Congo; a grant to Wells For India, which works for clean water in Rajasthan; support to the charity Children of the Andes, working for poverty relief in Colombia; and a grant to the Omari Project which works with drug-dependent young people in Watamu, Kenya.

Great difference

Email brenda@nstravel.demon.co.uk

Website www.nstravel.demon.co.uk

ATOL 75401

North South Travel, Moulsham Mill, Parkway, Chelmsford, Essex, CM2 7PX, UK

EXPERIENCE IS EVERYTHING

Discover the World

www.statravel.co.uk

National Telesales: 0870 160 6070

250 Branches Worldwide

Low Cost Travel for Students and Young People

STA Travel Ltd.   ATOL 3206   ABTA TRAVEL AGENT 99209

Book hostel accomodation in advance with Hostelling International's **International Booking Network (IBN).**

For a small fee you can secure a confirmed booking for up to 6 nights in each hostel, up to six months in advance

www.**iyhf**.org

usit CAMPUS

STUDENT & YOUTH TRAVEL

THE PLANET IN YOUR POCKET

- Low cost air, sea, rail fares & passes

- Adventure tours

- Worldwide budget accommodation

- Low cost travel insurance

- International identity cards

- Round the world flights

THIS IS WHAT WE DO

We make your travel dreams come true & we've been doing it, reliably, for years. We put a word of advice before the hard sell. We'll find the route & the deal that suits you best. Leave it to us.

USIT WORLD

Backing up all our services we have over 200 service points in 66 countries - handy if you need to change your flight route or date of travel, extend the validity of your ticket or cancel your journey. At our Gateway offices around the world you can check your emails, or book your local accommodation and tours.

NATIONAL CALL CENTRE
0870 240 1010

www.usitcampus.co.uk

MANCHESTER
0161 273 1721

EDINBURGH
0131 668 3303

Other branches in:
Aberdeen • Birmingham • Bradford • Brighton • Bristol • Cambridge • Cardiff • Coventry • Dundee • Glasgow • Leeds • Liverpool • London • Newcastle • Nottingham • Oxford • Plymouth • Preston • Reading • Sheffield • Southampton • Sunderland • Wolverhampton

ATOL 3839   **IATA**

see the world for
free

Discover what's really going on in the world with *Developments*, the free quarterly magazine that keeps you up to date with the fight against poverty in developing countries.

NEPAL

developments

INDIA

BANGLADESH

Produced by the Department for International Development

If you care about fair trade, the environment, human rights, debt and globalisation, subscribe FREE at our website

www.developments.org.uk
or call **01732 748661**

developments

It could change the way you see the world

Will you have enough stories to tell your grandchildren?

© 2000 Yahoo! Inc.

Yahoo! Travel

Do You YAHOO!?

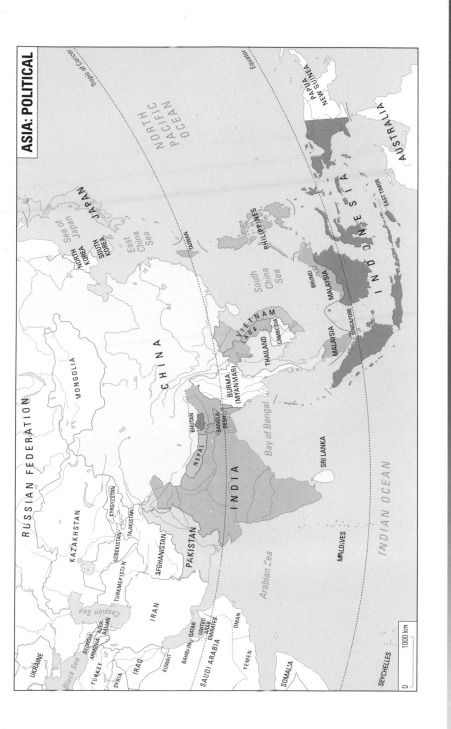

ASIA: POLITICAL

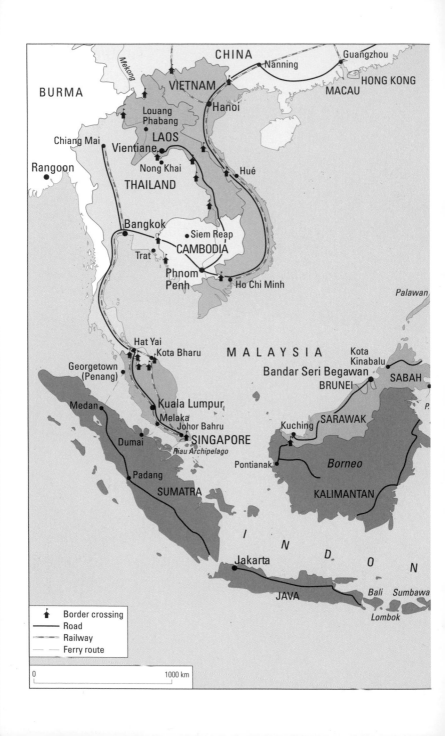

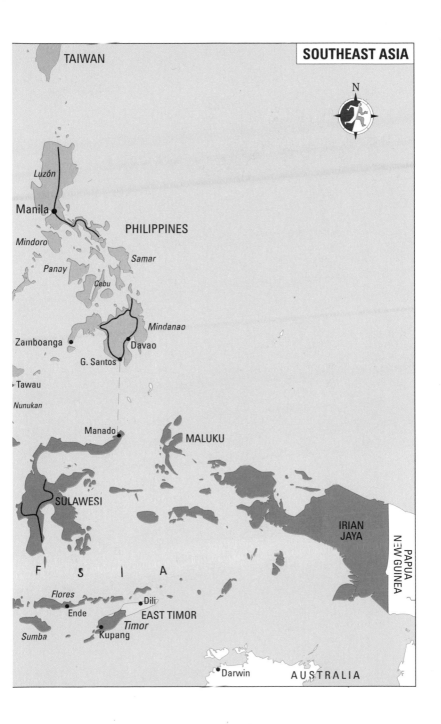

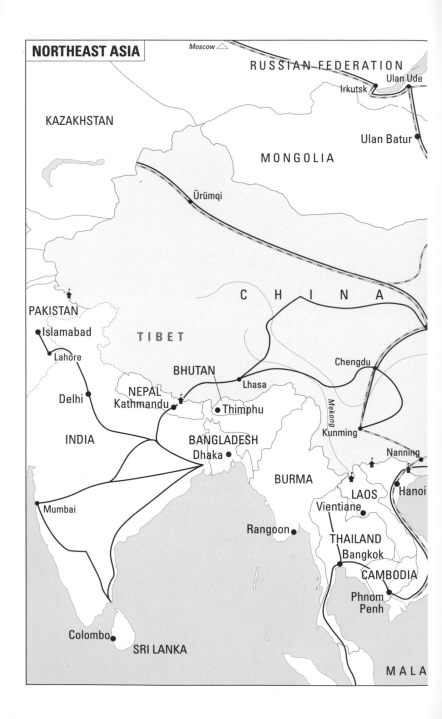

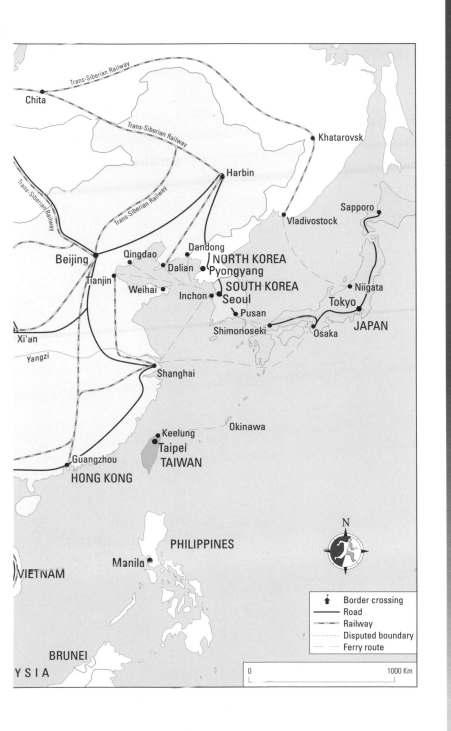

Trans-Siberian Railway
Chita
Trans-Siberian Railway
Khatarovsk
Harbin
Trans-Siberian Railway
Sapporo
Trans-Siberian Railway
Vladivostock
Dandong
Qingdao
NORTH KOREA
Beijing
Dalian
Pyongyang
Niigata
Tianjin
SOUTH KOREA
Weihai
Inchon
Seoul
Tokyo
Xi'an
Pusan
JAPAN
Yangzi
Shimonoseki
Osaka
Shanghai
Keelung
Okinawa
Taipei
TAIWAN
Guangzhou
HONG KONG

PHILIPPINES
Manila
VIETNAM

N

Border crossing
Road
Railway
Disputed boundary
Ferry route

BRUNEI
YSIA

0   1000 Km

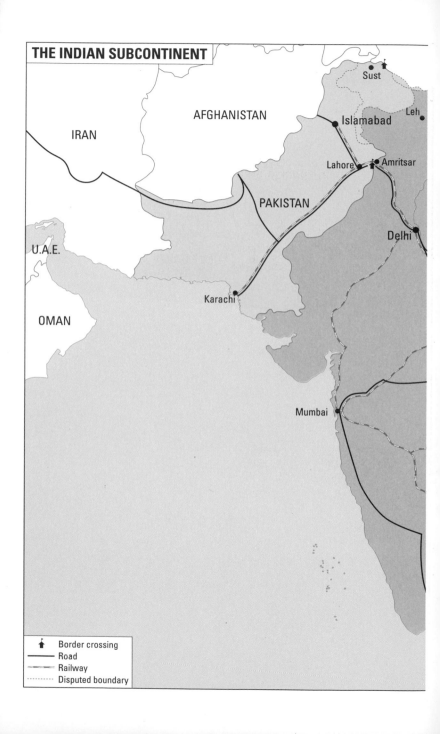

THE INDIAN SUBCONTINENT

IRAN

AFGHANISTAN

Sust

Islamabad

Leh

Lahore

Amritsar

PAKISTAN

Delhi

U.A.E.

OMAN

Karachi

Mumbai

⬆ Border crossing
— Road
═══ Railway
⋯⋯ Disputed boundary

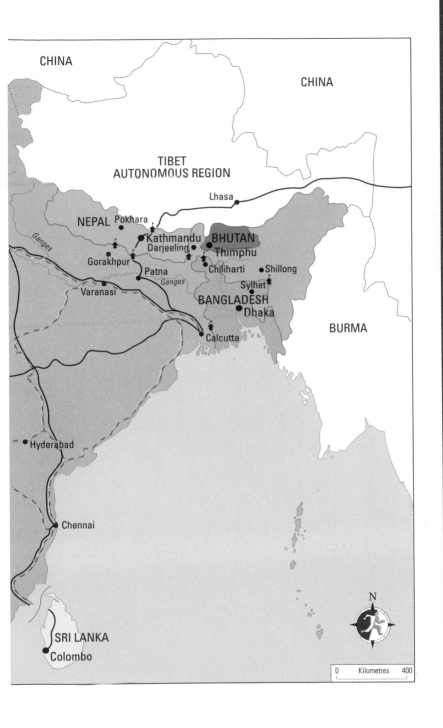

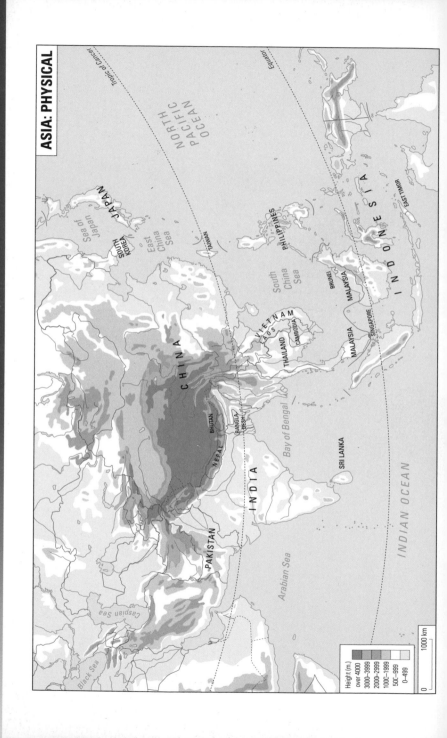

ASIA: PHYSICAL